Embedded Counselling

Embedded Counselling

Embedded Counselling

A practical guide for helping professionals

Julia McLeod
and John McLeod

Open University Press

Open University Press
McGraw Hill
Unit 4,
Foundation Park
Roxborough Way
Maidenhead
SL6 3UD

email: emea_uk_ireland@mheducation.com
world wide web: www.openup.co.uk

First edition published 2022

Copyright © Open International Publishing Limited, 2022

All rights reserved. Except for the quotation of short passages for the purposes of criticism and review, no part of this publication may be reproduced, stored in a retrieval system, or transmitted, in any form or by any means, electronic, mechanical, photocopying, recording or otherwise, without the prior written permission of the publisher or a licence from the Copyright Licensing Agency Limited. Details of such licences (for reprographic reproduction) may be obtained from the Copyright Licensing Agency Ltd of Saffron House, 6–10 Kirby Street, London EC1N 8TS.

A catalogue record of this book is available from the British Library

ISBN-13: 978-0-3352-5025-7
ISBN-10: 0335250254
eISBN: 978-0-3352-5026-4

Library of Congress Cataloging-in-Publication Data
CIP data applied for

Typeset by Transforma Pvt. Ltd., Chennai, India

Fictitious names of companies, products, people, characters and/or data that may be used herein (in case studies or in examples) are not intended to represent any real individual, company, product or event.

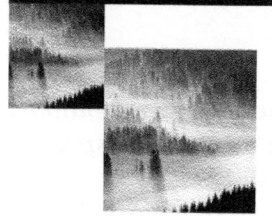

Praise for this book

"A beautifully crafted book that guides the reader through the theoretical, ethical, and practical ways of being and doing necessary when practicing embedded counselling within their existing professions. Additional to the strategy and skills, is the use of real-life experiences and reflective exercises within the text; highlighting how, incorporation of the pluralistic framework into existing practice, can be used in the service of the client. A must for all human beings who want to help other human beings."

Dr Patricia Joyce, Director, Grounded Learning Ltd.

"This is an excellent resource for anyone who requires an element of embedded counselling in a professional capacity. The text addresses many of the direct and indirect challenges that may be faced by different groups of professionals in relation to providing counsel to diverse groups of clients; particularly those professionals within the health and social care setting but also those within the broader professional services area. Developed over a number of years by experts in the field 'Embedded Counselling' represents an essential reference text for the bookshelf."

Dr William N. Scott, Lecturer in Biomedicine,
Atlantic Technological University, Ireland

"This is a superb book in every single respect: beautifully written, relevant, supportive and providing an accessible framework for all those in the helping professions to develop and enhance relationships with people. Additionally, it offers a vocabulary for different professions to think about their work in a truly trans-disciplinary way – a language and way of thinking for all. This book is a compelling resource for every professional in their work with others when supporting a process of change."

Professor Andrew Reeves, Professor in Counselling Professions
and Mental Health, University of Chester, UK

"This book should be read by everyone working in a helping profession. It exposes a cross-organisational web of pluralistic skills and defines how a public health approach to care and wellbeing can be consistently delivered across the helping professions in a way that reflects how people needing help actually interact with these services on a daily basis. It makes the reader recognise the windows of opportunity available to be a source of emotional support for someone in crisis. It promotes the *possibility of living, not just working, in a pluralistic way and enables the reader to use and develop these perishable skills in every aspect of their lives and in alignment with their core values and beliefs."*

Laura Burns, Training Lead for Hostage and Crisis Negotiation (2017-2020) and Inspector, Police Scotland, UK

"I have known of John and Julia's work for many years and experienced their compassionate and knowledgeable teaching and support. I am a qualified social worker and more recently a qualified counsellor and relationship therapist. Embedded counselling has featured greatly in my professional life and in particular since practicing in the field of children and then adult palliative care. It has enabled me to offer much needed empowering support as I walk with people impacted by loss and many of life's challenges. It has changed my professional approach profoundly. My believe in it has led me to facilitate members of the multi-disciplinary teams I lead to also become equipped with embedded counselling skills. I am delighted that this clear and accessible book will enable many more to learn this vital approach. Most importantly, I hope it enables those struggling with some of life's problems and dilemmas to believe in their own capacity to find solutions with a little support along the way."

Arlene Honeyman, Head of Supportive Care service, Ashgate Hospice Derbyshire, UK

"Aimed at people who have a background in helping, this is a useful and practical book that offers skills and ideas on how to offer emotional and social support to people. A must have for helping professionals, mental health trainees and therapists who are interested in evidence-based counselling research and how to put these skills into practice. The book focuses on embedding counselling methods and skills into supportive conversations, resourcing others to achieve their goals and working with difficulty issues."

Dr Helen Nicholas, independent private practitioner, author, and clinical supervisor

"Just like the companion texts recommended throughout, 'Embedded Counselling in the Helping Professions' provides a clear, accessible and engaging introduction to the topic. The framework of embedded counselling provided in the book will no doubt be extremely useful for those in helping professions such as teaching and social work, and the examples bring the tools suggested to life."

Dr Laura Anne Winter, Senior Lecturer in Counselling Psychology and HCPC Registered Practitioner Psychologist, University of Manchester, UK

"From the perspective of a healthcare professional, this book expertly defines the role we may find ourselves undertaking, often spontaneously, and sometimes unknowingly. By presenting a thorough contextualisation of the subject, this text provides a comprehensive overview of techniques and strategies available to professionals providing embedded counselling, while also understanding the challenges of incorporating this within the pressures of the work environment. In the pre-hospital emergency and urgent care environment there are times when communication moves towards a counselling process, in both patient care and interprofessional contact; this highly accessible text will enable recognition and an informed, knowledgeable response."

Kate Turnough, Lecturer, University of Brighton, UK,
Specialist Paramedic in Urgent Care, Southeast
Coast Ambulance Service NHS Foundation Trust

"'Embedded Counselling' is a dynamic modality for understanding therapeutic helping, suited to any professional with an interpersonal role. In my own profession, mental health nurses must establish meaningful relationships with their patients; affirming care and creating a therapeutic rapport around or within their task-orientated workloads, often in finite windows of time. This text offers applicable guidance for mental health nurses, supporting them to expertly create opportunities with patients which really matter."

Emily May Barlow, Lecturer in Mental Health Nursing,
University of Dundee, UK

"Julia McLeod and John McLeod provide a template for community and cultural transformation in their latest book. Their original concept of embedded counselling offers a way of being in relationship with other people; one that engenders and provides community based and focussed care and compassion. They offer a framework and approach for embedded counselling that accommodates the passion, paradox and trauma encountered by people in day to day living. Intentional and deliberate practice is exemplified through examples drawn from a diverse range of contexts. This book is important. It provides a timely call to action for people to consciously, conscientiously, compassionately, and collaboratively, offer those precious human communication skills embedded in counselling."

Lynne Gabriel, Professor of Counselling and Mental Health
and Director at York St John Communities Centre,
York St John University, UK

"This is an accessible, comprehensive and evidence-informed book that will undoubtedly empower teachers and other professionals with the *skills and confidence to provide effective emotional support. The McLeod's are attuned to the needs and priorities of frontline staff and have developed a practical and useful framework that supports practitioners through the counselling process. The practical exercises to facilitate reflection and learning are an invaluable resource for the personal and professional development of both individuals and teams. I am excited to share this book with my colleagues!"*

Steven Breckenridge, English teacher and Pluralistic counsellor, Fife, Scotland, UK

"What a wonderful addition to field! This book is an important and timely text for the mental health and supportive professionals. Outside of the psychotherapy realm, so many other supportive roles utilise counselling skills in their practice. This book is an excellent guide that will benefit social workers, doctors, addiction professionals, mental health nurses and, ultimately, anyone who works on the ground with people who are struggling. In a world that has been significantly stressed and distressed over the past few years, the need for effective listening and appropriate responding is vital, and out of necessity must transcend multiple professions. In this text, John and Julia McLeod offer practitioners a wonderful guide to embedded counselling that will be of enormous benefit to those on the front line."

Caitriona Kearns, Vice President, IICP College, Dublin, Ireland

For Kate, Emma and Hannah

For Kate, Shaun and Hannah

Contents

| *Preface* | xiii |
| *Acknowledgements* | xvii |

1	Where do people find support?	1
2	How counselling can help	19
3	Embedded counselling: a practice framework	39
4	Ethical principles for embedded counselling	67
5	Doing good work	89
6	Crisis	117
7	Emotions	130
8	Adversity and trauma	155
9	Transitions	175
10	Bereavement and loss	194
11	Making changes	214

| *References* | 241 |
| *Index* | 273 |

Preface

This is a book for practitioners who are involved in working with people in any kind of helping, managing or facilitative role - for example in teaching, social work, the health professions, clergy, advice work, training, human resources, housing and criminal justice. Anyone who does such a job is required to be skilled in many different types of interpersonal contact, such as influencing, guiding, instructing, communicating information, interviewing to gather information, and shared decision-making. The particular form of interpersonal contact that we explore in this book – embedded counselling – refers to interactions and conversations in which a service user is looking for emotional support to explore, understand or resolve a problematic or troubling personal issue or concern.

The following chapters provide a framework for making sense of episodes of counselling that are embedded in other activities and roles. It is a book about *counselling*, rather than about *being a counsellor*. It is intended for people who already possess professional knowledge and training in a field such as nursing or teaching, and who recognize the value of expanding their capacity to respond constructively and effectively to moments when the person with whom they are working needs to talk. This book explains what can be done at such moments and how to do it.

We also hope that what is in this book may turn out to be useful to specialist counsellors and psychotherapists, who deliver therapy on a stand-alone basis and have no other involvement with a client outside the counselling hour. For such readers, this book offers an opportunity to learn about the many creative and resourceful ways that colleagues in various frontline human service contexts respond to emotional and interpersonal issues presented by service users.

It is taken for granted in this book that it is possible for a useful counselling conversation to take place within about 10 to 15 minutes. This length of time represents a typical window of opportunity that a teacher, doctor or manager may have to allow someone to talk through something that is troubling them. Of course, there are many situations in which longer periods of time may be available, or where sequences of separate brief conversations may be linked together. But it is nevertheless important to recognize that a 10-minute talk can make a difference. Time pressure should not be used as an excuse for avoiding listening to a client's story.

Chapters 1–5 explore how embedded counselling functions as a key element in a broad array of potential sources of support that may be available to individuals. Specific chapters provide a practical framework for providing embedded counselling and emotional support, reflect on the moral and ethical dimension of

xiii

this kind of work, and review the organizational and training strategies that are necessary to ensure that embedded counselling is delivered in a safe and effective manner. Chapters 6–12 focus on how these general principles can be applied to specific service user concerns, such as overcoming fear and despair, coping with crisis, adversity and trauma, negotiating life transitions, coming to terms with loss, and behaviour change.

Topics are explored in terms of evidence and examples from a wide range of occupations and professions. Examples of embedded practice used in the book refer to the work of care home staff, clergy, community workers, complementary therapists, dentists, dieticians, doctors, nurses, occupational therapists, pharmacists, clergy, police officers, sexual health advisors, social workers, teachers and others. Although each of these professions has its own distinctive embedded counselling challenges and opportunities, an interdisciplinary approach makes it possible to draw on insights and innovation from a wide range of organizational settings and cultural contexts.

We believe that embedded counselling can make a valuable contribution to the humanization of care. We are also confident that attentiveness to client emotions and personal concerns has a positive impact on the quality and cost-effectiveness of treatments and interventions, by creating conditions in which clients and practitioners are able to work productively together to arrive at good outcomes.

This book has been written for practitioners of occupations and disciplines that have historically embraced evidence-based practice and the use of research to enhance accountability and the quality and accessibility of services. We have tried to provide sufficient references for research to enable readers to begin exploring the relevant research literature. There is a particular emphasis on qualitative research that describes and analyses the lived experience of the helping process and gives a voice to the points of view practitioners and clients.

At the end of each chapter can be found a series of learning activities that comprise opportunities for reflection on how specific topics covered in the chapter might connect with one's own personal experience and work situation. For anyone using the book as part of their professional training, we suggest it can be helpful to keep a reflective learning journal that might allow deeper or extended exploration of key themes, and to meet with learning partners to share experience and develop a broader perspective.

We have many years of experience as counsellors, researchers and university teachers. Alongside our work as therapists, we have also regularly been involved in providing informal counselling and emotional support to our students, research participants and colleagues, and have been recipients of such support from doctors, nurses and other practitioners. However, we ourselves are not social workers, nurses, doctors, clergy, police officers or any of the other professions for whom this book is intended. We have done our best to learn from our own students, who have been members of these occupational groups, consulted widely on aspects of the book and have drawn extensively on relevant research evidence. Nevertheless, we accept that there are many places in this book where we may not fully appreciate the challenges, and also the opportunities, associated with offering embedded counselling in specific key frontline roles. We hope that readers will appreciate that such insights are balanced by the breadth of coverage made possible by an approach that explores embedded counselling from a broad, multi-disciplinary perspective.

Embedded counselling: a practical guide for helping professionals seeks to highlight key knowledge and skills that are useful for human service practitioners. There are many issues that are touched on in this book that we were not able to develop in detail because of word limits. Some of these topics are covered in a set of companion texts. Further detail on specific counselling skills, and how they can be developed, is available in McLeod and McLeod (2022) *Counselling Skills: Theory, Research and Practice.* An overview of counselling and psychotherapy theory and practice as a whole, can be found in McLeod (2019) *An Introduction to Counselling and Psychotherapy: Theory, Practice and Research.* Information about the role of research in counselling, and the rationale for different research approaches that have been used in this field, is provided in McLeod (2022) *Doing Research in Counselling and Psychotherapy.*

Acknowledgements

We would like to record our appreciation to the many friends and colleague whose ideas and conversations have helped us to develop our understanding of embedded counselling: Sophia Balamoutsou, Emily-May Barlow, Nicola Blunden, Art Bohart, Laura Burns, Mick Cooper, David Denborough, Marcella Finnerty, Lynne Gabriel, Arlene Honeymoon, Marc Johnson, Triona Kearns, Christine Kupfer, Sally Lumsdaine, Thomas Mackrill, Catherine Marriott, Dave Mearns, Marie-Claire Murphie, Hanne Oddli, Freya Payne, Andrew Reeves, Brian Rodgers, Alison Rouse, Alison Shoemark, Kate Smith, Bill Stiles, Fiona Stirling, Marcia Stoll, Rolf Sundet, Lynne Thomas, Mhairi Thurston, Dot Weaks, Sue Wheeler, Mark Widdowson and Simon Yeates. We are grateful to Beth Summers at the Open University Press, for her encouragement and advice, and to her colleagues for their efficient and timely practical assistance throughout the process of production. We would also like to record out appreciation for all that we have learned from our students on the MSc Counselling and Certificate in Counselling Skills programmes at the University of Abertay Dundee (with a special mention and warm thanks to the students from Rachel House), and the MSc in Pluralistic Counselling and Psychotherapy at the Institute for Integrative Counselling and Psychotherapy, Dublin.

CHAPTER 1

Where do people find support?

Introduction	1
The concept of problems in living	3
Sources of emotional support	4
Emotional support provided by frontline practitioners: key perspectives	7
Humanizing care	8
Windows of opportunity	9
Task sharing	11
Situated counselling	12
Using interpersonal skills	13
An embedded counselling perspective	14
Conclusions	17
Learning activities	17

Introduction

This book is primarily aimed at people who work in, or are training to work in, occupations where the main task is to support and care for other people. Health professionals, such as nurses, doctors, physiotherapists, occupational therapists, pharmacists, dieticians and many more, who look after people who are sick. Social workers and care workers who respond to the needs of people who are vulnerable. Teachers who help people to acquire skills and learning. Police officers who keep people safe. Clergy who function as a source of meaning, faith and community. Those who work in such professions can be seen as representatives of society as a whole, in terms of making a special contribution to the fulfilment of a collective commitment to human rights, compassion and dignity. Such practitioners often see themselves as privileged to be able to serve others and to be following a vocation that offers a great deal of meaning and satisfaction.

Contemporary life is characterized by high levels of social and technological change, and political ideologies, that can be dehumanizing and generate fear, uncertainty and lack of connection. In response, a wide array of sources of emotional support have evolved, ranging from conversations with family and friends, through to long-term psychotherapy and residential places of sanctuary. Seeking support from human service/helping profession practitioners plays a central role within this spectrum of options. For most people, a nurse, social worker or teacher is someone they have already met and have decided is competent and trustworthy. The practitioner may already be familiar with aspects of their problem, and is bound by professional standards and ethics. Many practitioners in such occupations engage in brief, effective conversations with their clients and service users that can be understood as comprising a form of counselling that is embedded or incorporated into wider professional responsibilities and tasks.

Human services and caring/helping profession workers, such as nurses, doctors, social workers, teachers, police officers and clergy, play a unique role because they are widely respected, accessible and are most likely to be the first to be consulted at times of trouble.

Typically, human services workers tend to be very busy. Most of their time is tied up in carrying out core work tasks and roles, such as delivering treatment or teaching students. Increasingly, human service work is regulated by protocols, guidelines and monitoring systems, by practitioners who constantly need to have one eye on the clock or a screen. In such situations, the human contact and emotional support element of these jobs can be all too readily sidelined, with the result that service users have a sense of not being heard, or met, and feel themselves to be a number or 'case' within a labyrinthine, fragmented bureaucratic system. Those who work in service professions are generally well aware that this is happening and do their best to operate within the system in ways that enable them to maintain a caring, emotional connection with clients.

Counselling can be understood as a process that takes place when one person has a need or wish to talk about, and arrive at some degree of resolution in relation to, a personal concern or life difficulty. Counselling occurs when there is someone to listen and assist the other to talk things through within a private space. Although practitioners such as nurses, teachers and police officers do not claim to be *counsellors*, providing *counselling* is something that they are called upon to do on a regular basis. The premise of this book is that it is useful to view such activities as part of, or embedded within, the overall work role or job description of being a nurse, teacher, social worker, doctor or other human services practitioner.

The idea of *emotional* support is not intended to imply that problems in living necessarily take the form of emotions that are out of control or unbearable, for example being constantly terrified or in a rage. Although such difficulties do occur, the things that people want to talk about typically encompass a very wide range of issues, including relationship conflict, difficulty making a decision, intrusive images and memories, dealing with loss, being stressed, and lifestyle change. The reason that it makes sense to describe the process of working through these challenges as 'emotional support' is that they usually include some kind of emotional aspect. For example, a person who is unable to make a decision may feel annoyed with themselves or sad. Or there may be a lack of emotion: 'I know that this is a crucial life decision that I need to make, but I just feel dead inside when I think about it – I don't have any feelings one way or the other'. When a person seeks help, the expression of emotion (or non-emotion in a situation where feelings would be expected) is a signal that the individual is troubled. In addition, helpful counselling-type support tends to make a person feel better – there can be a positive emotional effect associated with being able to get a troubling issue out in the open and beginning to tackle it with the help of another person.

When using the term 'emotional support', it is important to keep in mind that any form of help that involves a counselling approach also operates as a form of *social* support, through the sense of solidarity, connectedness and reduced isolation that comes from one person listening in an empathic and caring way to another. It may, as well, sometimes encompass practical support (e.g. providing information or taking action on the person's behalf).

The present chapter looks at two key questions. First, how does the kind of frontline, grassroots counselling provided by practitioners in education, health, social care (and other helping, caring and human service professions) sit alongside other types of emotional support and intervention? Second, how can such activities be understood in terms of concepts and practical initiatives that have been developed?

The concept of problems in living

It is not accurate or sufficient to view the emotional support provided by human service practitioners in terms of treatment or intervention for mental health problems. The personal concerns that a person might want to explore with a nurse, teacher or other practitioner rarely comprise diagnosable mental health conditions. Rather, they are more appropriately understood as comprising 'problems in living'. A problem in living refers to any kind of interpersonal, emotional or behavioural issue that stands in the way of a person pursuing a satisfying and productive life. Some of the main types of problem in living that trouble people are discussed in later chapters of this book: crisis, fearfulness, lack of hope, coping with the impact of adverse life events, and struggling to manage or change self-destructive habits. Although such challenges and difficulties are inevitable within any family or community, they are exacerbated by the stress of living in modern societies that are characterized by high levels of insecurity, inequality and injustice. For example, the sociologist Richard Sennett (1998) has studied the ways that changing patterns of employment, brought about by the global economy, have resulted in the loss of a secure identity as a worker. As people shift from one temporary job to another, are allocated to ever-changing teams within an organization, or work from home, it becomes harder to develop deep relationships with colleagues. Zygmunt Bauman (2004) argued that the global capitalist economy and depletion of planetary resources has been responsible for a vast number of what he calls 'wasted lives' – people such as immigrants, refugees, the unemployed, the disabled, and war veterans, who are surplus to the requirements of the economic system and who therefore cease to matter. Many writers and political activists have drawn attention to the extent to which centuries of colonialism, racism and unearned privilege have undermined and corroded relationships between people from different backgrounds and distorted the inner lives of most of us. Violence against women is a routine aspect of everyday life. A theme that runs through these sociological accounts of modern life is the extent to which many people feel excluded, silenced and isolated and look to relationships with professional carers and helpers to enable them both to connect at a deep level with another human being and get a handle on a life that is confusing and out of control. Further discussion of how social adversity generates problems in living that call for emotional and interpersonal support can be found in McLeod (2019, Chapters 22–26).

Sources of emotional support

When introduced to the idea of embedded counselling, some human services practitioners with whom we have worked tell us that allowing their clients and service users to open up about their concerns and problems in living is too great a responsibility to accept. They worry that they have enough to think about just being a teacher, nurse or social worker and feel that they are not able to do justice to anything further, particularly given the immense pressure of time and external scrutiny under which they operate. They worry that an ill-considered attempt to help might merely exacerbate their client's problem and that the best option is to leave these issues to specialists such as counsellors, psychologists, mental health nurses and psychiatrists. While it is important to acknowledge that offering emotional support can be demanding for the helper, it is also essential to keep in mind that the support provided by a teacher, nurse or social worker does not take place in a vacuum – most service users have potential access to a wide range of other people to whom they can turn. One of the key functions of counselling provided by human service and care practitioners is that – alongside whatever helpful processes they are able to facilitate themselves – they function as an information source and access point to other forms of help and support that are available.

Informal social support represents a massively important source of help and guidance around problems in living (Barker and Pistrang 2002). Most of the time, people who are troubled by a problem in living talk to other people whom they know and trust – family members, friends and work colleagues. For example, Brownlie (2014) carried out in-depth interviews with people about sources of emotional support in their everyday lives and found many examples of everyday kindness and a capacity to 'be there' for each other. A study by Depow et al. (2021) found that people reported an average of 10 opportunities each day to empathically respond to another person and six occasions when they felt that another person could have responded empathically to them. The sociologist Ramon Oldenburg (Oldenburg and Brissett 1982) suggested the term 'third places' to describe locations outside the home and workplace, such as pubs, hairdressers and libraries, where people could meet and talk on an informal basis to give and receive empathic emotional support. Studies of such environments have found that many individuals use them to talk about their problems in living, and receive support and advice (Cowen 1982; Cowen et al. 1979; Milne and Mullin 1987). Hart (1996) and McLellan (1991) investigated the experiences of university students who reported themselves as having experiencing emotional and interpersonal difficulties. Some of them had consulted counsellors, while others had spoken to their friends or informal helpers about their difficulties. When asked about the quality of their relationship with their professional counsellor or informal helper, there was no difference between the two groups in terms of amount of time they received, helper/counsellor availability, or the extent to which they felt understood or accepted.

Snyder (1971) used the phrase 'well-trodden pathways in the community' to refer to the way that family doctors, nurses, clergy, social workers and lawyers functioned as the first line of support for people who felt suicidal. A large-scale health survey conducted in South London by Brown et al. (2014) found that individuals with even quite severe problems in living made use of informal sources of support (friends and family) more frequently than they consulted professional helpers. Milne et al. (2004) identified multiple non-professional support networks in one English county that provided a mix of informal and organized/formal support. Topor et al. (2006) analysed the ways in which family and friends complemented professional inputs in the process of recovery from a life crisis. Influential figures within health care have characterized informal support networks as recovery resources (Priebe et al. 2014) or recovery capital (Tew 2013). In schools, teachers function as an early warning system for students with mental health problems (Dimitropoulos et al. 2021; Stoll and McLeod 2020). 'Interviews and surveys of members of the public have found that the majority of people are well aware of informal and non-medicalized support resources that are available to them (Mount et al., 2020; Jorm et al. 2000).'

A further significant type of informal support can arise through participation in activities that are not overtly organized around problems in living, such as walking a dog, being a member of a choir, knitting, or membership of a political organization. Any of these activities (and many more) can be viewed as *cultural resources* (Cooper and McLeod 2010) – options with the culture within which a person lives their life. These activities can be helpful in relation to problems in living in a variety of ways: meeting other people; health and well-being benefits associated with exercise and being in nature; a sense of meaning, purpose and achievement; and distraction from everyday worries. Some cultural resources can be categorized as work. For example, compared to being unemployed, having a job is generally more conducive to positive well-being; for older people, being a grandparent can be a source of great meaning and satisfaction. Other cultural resources can be regarded as forms of 'serious leisure' (Axelsen 2009; Denovan and Macaskill 2017; Dieser et al. 2015).

In addition to informal support and cultural resources, there are many focused and organized strategies for addressing problems in living that do not involve contact with a professional helper, such as self-help books and websites, apps, peer support groups and peer-run helplines.

In terms of formal professionally-operated counselling, psychotherapy and psychiatric interventions for dealing with problems in living, there exists a massive array of possibilities, including: medication; individual, couple, family and group therapy; face-to-face, online and telephone therapy; specialist therapy services (e.g. for eating disorders or personality disorders). Beyond community-based counselling, psychotherapy and psychiatric treatment, there are also a variety of residential or in-patient centres and programmes.

Box 1.1 Social connection as a means of promoting health and well-being

A distinctive aspect of contemporary society, compared to life at earlier points of history, is the extent to which individuals feel lonely (Holt-Lunstad et al. 2017). Social mobility, smaller family sizes and the replacement of active sources of social capital (e.g. living in a neighbourhood where you regularly see the same people in local shops and attend the same church) with anonymous modes of interaction (shopping at a huge supermarket, watching TV) have resulted in a growing proportion of the population who have few meaningful or supportive contacts with other people. Lack of social connection has been shown to contribute to a wide range of physical and psychological health problems (Holt-Lunstad 2021a, b). For some people, an interaction with a health or social care practitioner may represent a highly significant point of contact with the outside world. An important aspect of emotional support from human service practitioners involves recognizing the underlying loneliness of a patient or service user and doing as much as possible to make sure that such meetings offer an experience of an affirming personal interaction. In some situations, a practitioner may also be able to facilitate access to additional social networks, for example by showing an interest, offering encouragement, providing information or brokering opportunities to meet new people or re-establish lost connections.

Box 1.2 Being willing to be an important person in someone else's life

There are few more troubling circumstances for any parent than falling into a pattern of conflict and disconnection with one's children. In research carried out by Neander and Skott (2006, 2008), parents who had successfully come through this kind of episode were interviewed about the people who had exerted a decisive positive influence on the child and the family during that period. These key figures included nurses, social workers, teachers, a youth leader and a school principal. What were the characteristics of these important persons? Their specific professional role and training did not seem to matter. What made a difference was the development of mutual trust, genuine feelings of warmth and acceptance, a sense of being treated as worthwhile and 'special', a clear focus on what was best for the child, making progress through a series of small everyday events and developing a new and more positive story about the child. At the heart of this process was a perception that these helpers were able to create new situations in which the children and parents could feel comfortable and do well. Similar themes have emerged in studies of cancer patients who have made exceptional recoveries (Engebretson et al. 2014) and young people who had been helped by a school nurse to find their way through difficult periods or stressful situations (Langaard and Toverud 2009, 2010).

All of the sources of social and emotional support outlined above operate within specific cultural contexts. For example, different support options are available in large urban centres than in rural communities, indigenous/traditional communities, different faith communities and different sub-cultures.

Emotional support provided by frontline practitioners: key perspectives

The evidence and examples considered in this chapter so far have attempted to provide an overview of how the stressfulness of modern life has created a huge need for emotional support, and that in response to this situation a very wide range of sources of support have evolved – and continue to emerge. It has also been suggested that practitioners in caring and human professions such as health, social work, education, the clergy and criminal justice (and other occupations) play a vital, pivotal role as readily-accessible, skilful, resourceful, known and reliable individuals who can be turned to in relation to the challenge of dealing with personal concerns and problems in living. Within the present book, this aspect of professional work is discussed in terms of the concept of embedded counselling. However, it is also important to be able to draw on other ways of conceptualizing this type of activity. The following paragraphs summarize the contribution of a range of influential perspectives, each of which is associated with its own research literature, training programmes and professional contexts: humanizing care; the windows of opportunity/empathic opportunities model; task sharing; situated counselling; using interpersonal skills.

Humanizing care

Historically, the functions undertaken in contemporary society by doctors, nurses, social workers and teachers would have been fulfilled by family members and members of the community who had developed particular skills. It has only been quite recently that these practices have been professionalized in the sense of requiring formal training and accreditation and centralized bureaucratic regulation by the state. This has led, in turn, to requirements to adhere to pre-determined evidence-based procedures that can often involve the use of different forms of technology (computerized records, surveillance of both clients and carers, pharmacological interventions, robot carers, collecting data to demonstrate that targets have been achieved, etc.). At the same time, the complexity and costs of such services, along with the demands of an ageing population and political resistance to raising taxes to pay for education and care, has meant that practitioners are under increasing pressure. Within the health and social care professions, and in society as a whole, these trends have resulted in a widespread sense that these types of work have become de-humanized and care-less. They have also resulted in a growing literature that seeks to promote the humanization of care and societal recognition of the importance of care (Galvin and Todres 2013; Lynch et al. 2016; 2021). A central focus of this approach has been around emphasizing that while most practitioners do their best to respond to service users in a humane, compassionate and caring way, this dimension of their work is not sufficiently supported at an institutional level and that it is necessary to use research, theory and practical initiatives to develop a clearer understanding of what a humanized way of responding means in terms of routine practice and how it can be maintained on a day-to-day basis. Todres et al. (2009) developed an overarching values framework for humanized healthcare, incorporating attentiveness to the unique lived experience and personal journey of the service user, their active involvement in sense-making and decision-making, and the significance of specific places. By contrast, in their view, much of the care being provided for people had the effect of treating them as passive objects and isolating them from relationships and places that were meaningful to them.

These ideas have been associated with a wide range of initiatives around promoting more humanized forms of practice in different professional contexts, including (but not restricted to) aphasia clinics (Pound and Jensen 2018), dermatology

Box 1.3 Uncaring professional relationships

Many studies have documented the damage caused to people by an absence of humanity and care in the practitioners who are looking after them. Berglund et al. (2012) described how, for hospital patients, a sense of being powerless in relationships with doctors and nurses and being exposed to a fragmented and objectified approach to treatment resulted in long-term suffering. Brüggemann and Swahnberg (2013) analysed patient stories of the use of domination techniques by staff. Pratt-Eriksson et al. (2014) found that women who had experienced domestic violence reported that many of the practitioners to whom they turned for support responded with a lack of care and empathy. Young people whose parents had alcohol addiction problems felt abandoned by practitioners who were involved in supporting their families (Werner and Malterud 2016). Kenny (2004) interviewed patients whose treatment for chronic pain had not been successful; analysis of the transcripts revealed a fundamental breakdown in relationships between these people and their doctors. Key themes included the need for the doctor to be in control, doctors who did not listen and an inability or unwillingness to engage with what patients were feeling and experiencing. These are just some of the many studies that have shown that poor relationships between practitioners and service users do not have a neutral effect. It is not that empathic care is an added bonus – its absence significantly undermines recovery and diminishes well-being.

out-patient clinics and stroke rehabilitation units (Ellis-Hill et al. 2021; Galvin et al. 2020). A good example of how this approach is implemented is the 'caring conversations' model implemented by Dewar and MacBride (2017) in care homes for elderly people, based on the intention of ensuring that, in their interactions with residents, care workers should seek to be curious and courageous, connect emotionally, collaborate in ways that take account of a range of perspectives and allow for compromise, and make space for authentic celebration.

Windows of opportunity

Whereas the starting point of a humanizing perspective is a philosophical, ethical and political stance, the concept of 'window of opportunity' refers to a much more pragmatic perspective on emotional support. For practitioners in professional roles such as a health worker or teacher, it can be difficult to know whether a client or service user is actually looking for a chance to talk about a personal issue or whether they are happy enough for the conversation to remain focused on a primary task associated with nursing care or learning. In recent years, particularly in the area of doctor–patient interaction, there has emerged a valuable perspective in relation to making sense of whether the use of a counselling intervention might be timely and appropriate. By analysing radio and video recordings of real-life doctor–patient interactions, researchers discovered that, in a consultation, a patient may present their doctor with occasional 'empathic opportunities'. Most of what patients talk about in consultations mainly consists of reporting relevant medical information, usually in response to questions asked by the physician. From time to time, however, the patient may signal an area of personal concern or worry. The question then is whether the doctor acknowledges this empathic opportunity and whether (and how) they are able to follow it up.

For example, in a study carried out by Branch and Malik (1993), video recordings were made of 20 doctor–patient consultations conducted by experienced and highly regarded physicians. The length of these consultations ranged from 12 to 20 minutes. Within this series of doctor-patient clinical interviews, the researchers were able to identify five episodes in which patients discussed their concerns about personal, emotional and family issues. These 'windows of opportunity' lasted for between three and seven minutes each. Typically, the doctor would begin the interview by addressing current medical issues. After a few minutes, in response to a felt sense that the patient was worried or concerned in some way, the practitioner would ask an open question, such as 'anything more going on?' or 'what else?'. The patient's response to this question would be accompanied by what the researchers described as a 'change of pace' on the part of the doctor – they would listen, speak more slowly and softly, be silent and lean forward. These physicians were also skilled in ending these counselling episodes, which they did by expressing understanding, empathically summarizing key themes and making suggestions for further action (for example, making a referral to a specialist counsellor). Although these doctors did not use a counselling approach throughout their interviews with patients, they were able to do so within the context of specific, focused micro-episodes. Branch and Malik (1993) concluded that the patients they observed in these consultations seemed satisfied that they had adequately expressed themselves because their physicians had been able to employ brief but intense windows of opportunity to deal with their concerns. This study provided compelling evidence for the potential value of brief counselling conversations that take place within routine consultations. It also illustrates the relative infrequency of such encounters – even in this group of expert physicians, such episodes only took place in 25 per cent of consultations, despite psychosocial issues being brought up by patients in the majority of these meetings.

A substantial body of research has confirmed and extended the work of Branch and Malik (1993) – see, for example, Arborelius and Österberg (1995), Bylund and Makoul (2002), Eide et al. (2004). Studies have explored such topics as to how doctors detect patient concerns (Giroldi et al. 2020), how patients express concerns (Pecanac et al. 2021), how doctors follow through on patient concerns that have been identified (Poulsen et al. 2020) and the impact of such episodes on patient recovery from illness (Rakel et al. 2011). Key themes and lines of inquiry in this overall programme of research have been the nature and functioning of empathy in healthcare interactions, the capacity of health (and other) professionals to be responsive to patient emotion (Finset 2012; O'Connor 2020) and strategies for training practitioners to become competent in these areas (Dean and Street 2014; Derksen et al. 2021; Henderson and Johnson 2002).

There have been many informative studies into specific aspects of how practitioners respond to empathic opportunities. Adams et al. (2012) identified three distinct patterns of physician responses to patient expressions of negative emotion: 'away', 'toward' and 'neutral'. 'Toward' and 'neutral' responses were associated with patient exploration of personal concerns, with 'toward' responses also linked to positive patient ratings of the doctor–patient relationship and higher rates of agreement around eventual treatment plans. In a programme of research on counselling with perpetrators of domestic violence, Lómo et al. (2018) found that the most effective counsellors were those who were able to be guided by subtle client statements that represented invitations or gateways into their concerns. Further evidence around that kind of process emerged in research into physician empathic sensitivity in palliative care contexts. Back and Arnold (2013; 2014) analysed the ways that doctors responded to patient statements such as 'isn't there anything more you can do?' and, in particular, how replies along the lines of 'I can see this isn't what you were hoping for' had the effect of both acknowledging the personal and emotional content of the patient's question, while allowing the patient to keep the conversation on the territory of treatment options if that is what they preferred.

While theory and research on empathic opportunities in practitioner–service user interactions has primarily focused on finding and disseminating examples of good (or poor) practice that can be used to inform training, it is important to recognize that attentiveness to client concerns and emotions, and use of empathy, are also part of a broader humanizing agenda. In particular, Halpern (2001, 2014) has argued that there exists a continuum that extends from (at one end) a kind of detached, clinical responsiveness to appreciation of the profound existential meaning of the suffering and life choices of the client or patient.

Task sharing

The concept of 'task sharing' or 'task shifting' represents an organization-level policy perspective on the issue of practitioner engagement with problems in living expressed by clients and service users. A task sharing approach is based on the assumption that in an ideal world, everyone with a problem in living or mental health condition would have access to a trained specialist counsellor, psychotherapist, psychologist or psychiatrist. The reality of insufficient funding and resources in most healthcare systems means that such an ideal can rarely be achieved. What is possible, instead, is to share the task of psychological and emotional support between a small group of specialist practitioners and a much wider network of other health and social care practitioners (e.g. general community health workers, care assistants and even lay people) who have received limited training in a relevant psychotherapeutic intervention (Winiarski et al. 2019). Evidence relating to the impact of task sharing initiatives has been reviewed by Lange (2021) and Verhey et al. (2020) and the experience of helpers trained to use such approaches by Shahmalak et al. (2019).

The area of emotional support for women experiencing depression and other difficulties represents a domain of practice in which several different types of task sharing provision have been developed. There is considerable evidence that ongoing psychotherapy can be helpful for women troubled by anxiety, depression and stress during pregnancy. However, specialist therapy may not be available because of cost factors or may be viewed by women as daunting or impossible to fit into an already busy life. Laurenzi et al. (2021) and Nyatsanza et al. (2016) have described the development and implementation of task sharing perinatal counselling intervention for women in South Africa delivered by generic community health workers. These studies provide valuable insights into the experiences of both clients and care providers. Another form of emotional support task shifting in relation to women during and after pregnancy has been the practice of 'listening visits' by health visitors trained in basic counselling skills (Brock et al. 2017; Segre et al. 2010; Shakespeare et al. 2006; Turner et al. 2010). A further approach has been the use of birth *doulas*, who accompany a pregnant woman through the whole birth process and provide emotional, practical and informational support as required (Attanasio et al. 2021; Gilliland 2011; Gruber et al. 2013).

In practice, task sharing draws on skills and strategies – such as knowing when and how to take advantage of empathic windows of opportunity (see previous section) – that occur in any form of emotional support that is provided by a human services practitioner. The distinctive feature of task sharing is that it arises from the appreciation within a service-delivery organization that there is a gap in its capacity to meet the needs of its clients. The task sharing schemes highlighted in this section reflect a snapshot of the types of initiative that have been developed in a particular area of practice and have been researched and written up. In reality, there are many task sharing projects that have evolved at local levels, in different practice areas, that are not widely publicized. One of the themes of the present book, explored in later chapters, is the idea that while it is valuable as a practitioner to be able to provide emotional support as an individual, in some situations it can also be necessary to think in terms of how colleagues in an organization or area of practice can work together to fill the gaps.

Situated counselling

Some advocates of making organized and professionally-delivered emotional support readily accessible to individuals with problems in living have experimented with forms of practice based on finding and creating spaces outside of professional settings that offer clients or service users opportunities to participate in flexible and informal counselling-type conversations (Smith 2021). Bank and Nissen (2018) have characterized such settings as comprising a 'neutral ground' and Hanser (2020) as 'in-between zones' and 'informal locations for connectivity'. Perhaps the best-known example of this approach is the 'friendship bench', originally developed by psychiatrist Dixon Chibanda in Zimbabwe, to address the limited availability of mental health care in that country. A friendship bench is a wooden bench in a secluded outdoor location where anyone can turn up and talk to an older person ('grandmother') who has received training in a problem-solving approach to counselling. The effectiveness of this approach, particularly with younger clients, has been demonstrated through an extensive programme of research (Broström et al. 2021; Chibanda et al. 2011; Ouansafi et al. 2021; Wallén et al. 2021). Originally conceived as a task-sharing initiative in a country with inadequate mental health provision, the friendship bench concept has been implemented and adapted on a worldwide basis. For instance, Hanser (2020) has pioneered the use of a mobile shepherd's hut that can be positioned in different places within a community. The hut provides a private and 'special' place that allows for both individual and small group meetings and the use of expressive arts activities. In addition to benches and huts, similar initiatives have used pop-up venues, tents and walk-and-talk. Many practitioners, in occupations such as teaching, social work, community nursing and criminal justice, have developed their own list of situations conducive to supportive private conversation that are not within their office or building.

Using interpersonal skills

The provision of training in interpersonal skills comprises an important strand within both primary and post-qualifying educational programmes in professions in which practitioners may be called upon to provide emotional support for clients. This kind of training is described using a range of terms – interpersonal skills, human relationship skills, communication skills, helping skills. Typically, such skills are intended to enable the practitioner to be more helpful in relation to core professional tasks, as well as in situations in which clients are emotionally troubled. For example, good listening skills will enable a doctor to be better able to arrive at the right diagnosis through more comprehensive understanding of a patient's symptoms and health behaviour, as well as enabling them to be empathically sensitive to that patient's sense of being worthless as a result of the way their medical condition has affected their relationships with other family members. Many interpersonal/counselling skills texts are available, including for doctors (Moulton 2016), social workers (Seden 2005), nurses, midwives and health visitors (Freshwater 2005) and faith workers (Ross 2003).

An embedded counselling perspective

The various ways of conceptualizing practitioner responsiveness to the emotional support needs of clients – humanizing care; the windows of opportunity/empathic opportunities model; task sharing; situated counselling; and interpersonal skills – have each made a valuable contribution to training, research and practice and are well established within the professional literature. The present book is organized around a concept of 'embedded counselling' that brings together all of these existing ideas into an overarching framework that has the added value of allowing practitioners to draw on skills and ideas from the field of counselling and psychotherapy. Counselling can be defined as making a space for a person to talk through an area of fearfulness or 'stuckness' (a concern or problem in living) in a way that then allows them to move on in their life. Embedded counselling refers to an ability to facilitate such conversations alongside the fulfilment of other professional tasks. Key aspects of this perspective include an emphasis on the emotional support purpose or goal of using interpersonal skills, flexibility in being able to respond to different client needs and concerns and attention to how this kind of activity can fit alongside other professional activities and organizational demands.

Compared to both formal counselling or psychotherapy, and also informal emotional support, there are several ways in which embedded counselling provided by a teacher or social worker is particularly attractive for clients. One important factor is that, for someone who is troubled, a qualified practitioner would be expected to have more (or different) knowledge and experience, compared to talking to a friend, family member or peer helper. Compared to the process of making an appointment with a specialist counsellor, psychotherapist or psychologist, the person seeking help is in a position to make an informed decision about who they want as a counsellor. For example, a school student may know several teachers fairly well and from among this list may be able to choose the one who seems most trustworthy or sympathetic. What this means is that the client does not need to spend time during counselling in a process of testing out their counsellor and making up their mind whether they think that their counsellor is someone they might trust or who has the potential to be helpful. It is also likely that an embedded counsellor, such as a teacher, will already know something about the client and so does not need to go through a process of collecting basic information. Beyond this, it is probably the case that people talk to (or try to talk to) trusted professionals who are within their immediate orbit, before they take the step of making an appointment to see a counsellor, and then waiting until they receive an appointment time.

In addition to the advantage that the recipient is able to make a choice around speaking to someone they have already assessed as potentially suitable, other ways in which embedded counselling makes a unique contribution to emotional support include:

- resolving pressing worries and concerns may enhance the capacity of a client or service user to make best use of the primary service (e.g. education, health care, social care) being provided
- the support being offered is not conditional on psychiatric diagnosis or to a requirement to commit to an ongoing series of sessions
- part of the function of the practitioner is to function as a 'care broker' who can advise on other sources of assistance that may be of value.

Taken together, what all this means is that practitioners of embedded counselling are likely to hear about problems earlier, at a point where they are perhaps more readily dealt with. The flexible, grass-roots nature of embedded counselling means that there is little opportunity for the counsellor to seek to inculcate the client into a therapy theory or methodology that is alien or harmful to them – the counsellor needs to stick pretty closely to what fits with the client's common sense. Finally, the fact that – a lot of the time – embedded counselling is oriented toward activating the client's strengths and resources means that there is a good chance that whatever the client learns in the counselling session will have the effect of empowering them in their everyday life.

It is important to recognize that embedded *counselling* (a practitioner such as a nurse, social worker or teacher facilitating a brief, focused counselling process with a service user) is different from the use of embedded *counsellors* (a specialist counsellor or psychologist relocating in order to be more accessible to clients). For example, some large universities have found that the uptake of

Box 1.4 The effectiveness of counselling provided by practitioners with limited therapy training

Several research studies have compared the effectiveness of practitioners who possess counselling skills and relevant life experience, such as embedded counsellors, paraprofessional and volunteer counsellors and practitioners in task-sharing initiatives, with the client outcomes observed for fully-trained professional counsellors, psychotherapists and psychologists working with comparable clients. Such studies have consistently found that similar outcomes are attained by both minimally-trained helpers and those who have received several years of specialist training (Atkins and Christensen 2001; Stein and Lambert 1984; Tandon et al. 2021). An international review of how societies responded to mental health issues in the early part of the Covid-19 pandemic, found that emotional support in low-income countries, provided by minimally-trained helpers, was more effective than the services offered by specialist counsellors, psychologists and mental health practitioners in more prosperous parts of the world (Kola et al. 2021).

counselling is increased when student counsellors are moved out of offices in a main health centre or administrative block, into offices in academic departments, closer to (and more visible to) students and faculty (Adams 2017; Beks et al. 2018; Schreier et al. 2021). Similar initiatives have been undertaken in areas such as schools counselling (Harrison 2019), cancer care (Buchhold et al. 2018; Singer et al. 2009) and liaison psychiatry. In principle, embedded counsellors have the potential to support the efforts of colleagues providing embedded counselling, through joint working, cross-referral and providing consultation, support and advice. However, while this type of inter-professional collaboration undoubtedly occurs at a local level in many organizations and services, it is rarely highlighted in the professional or research literature. A crucial difference between embedded *counselling* and embedded *counsellors* is that in the former situation the counselling process is heavily adapted to and shaped by the specific situation in which it occurs, whereas in the latter the client is offered a standard therapy intervention or package.

Conclusions

To be able to offer effective emotional support, it is essential to be able to keep in mind what this type of process looks like from the point of view of a client or service user. Very few patients or students regard their nurse or teacher as their sole, or most significant, source of support. Virtually everyone has other people they talk to or other sources of advice and guidance on how to deal with life difficulties. Even individuals who are socially isolated and lonely have potential contacts to whom they can reach out. At the same time, engaging in ongoing counselling or psychotherapy is not viewed as an option by the majority of people, even if they acknowledge that they are struggling to cope. For those who do see therapeutic treatment (pharmacological or psychological) as valuable, there are often barriers to accessing it, such as waiting lists, costs, knowing which one to choose and fitting it into a crowded life. From the point of view of a troubled individual, embedded counselling sits somewhere in the middle of all this. While it shares many of the characteristics of informal support – being listened to and heard, someone who will be there for me and small acts of kindness and connection – it has the possibility of added value through being provided by someone who is independent of one's personal circle and who has potentially relevant knowledge, skills and experience. A professional person also symbolizes the wider community, in affirming that I do matter and that my concerns are worth taking seriously.

Although it can represent a highly satisfying and meaningful element of professional work, embedded counselling can also be challenging. Hard decisions need to be made in the moment about whether to respond to an empathic window of opportunity and how to offer something that is helpful with what is typically a limited period of time. Chapter 3 describes a model of embedded counselling practice that is intended to make such a process manageable for the practitioner, helpful for the client and ethically safe. Although counselling and psychotherapy skills and knowledge represent a resource that can usefully inform this type of work, it also comprises a vast literature that is daunting and can be somewhat contradictory in terms of what it offers.

Learning activities

The following activities may be explored individually and/or with a group of learning partners.

Exercise 1.1 Your own experience of emotional support
Take a few minutes to reflect, and make notes, on your own personal experience of receiving emotional support from a practitioner with whom you were in contact, such as a doctor, nurse, social worker or teacher. What did they do that was helpful? What did they do that was unhelpful? What are

the implications of what you have learned from this reflective exercise, in terms of your own practice?

Exercise 1.2 The support available to your clients
In relation to the clients with whom you work, how aware are you of the emotional support that that might be available to them? If you are concerned about a client who seems socially isolated and lacking in support, what are the options that are available to you (both in terms of what you can offer yourself and other places and services that you might be able to refer them to)?

Exercise 1.3 Being an important person for someone else
Reflect on an occasion in which you became an important and significant person for one of your clients, in the sense of having been able to make a decisive difference to the course of their life? What was it that enabled you to have such a major impact? What effect did that experience have on your own well-being and work satisfaction? What have you learned about yourself, and your professional role, from that episode?

Exercise 1.4 The values that underpin your commitment to your work
To what extent, and in what ways, did the ideas about humanization of practice, and an ethics of care, that were briefly outlined in the present chapter resonate with you? How have you developed, elaborated and added to these ideas in respect of the particular context within which you work? How do you express these principles in your actual practice? In what ways would you ideally wish to be able to articulate them more powerfully or consistently?

CHAPTER 2

How counselling can help

Introduction	**20**
The fragmented landscape of therapy	**20**
The difference between counselling and psychotherapy	22
The common ground of therapy	**23**
Making a space to talk it through	23
Affirming and caring connection	25
Listening	26
Safety, trust and affirmation	27
Working together in ways that activate the person's own strengths and resources	29
Developing new skills and perspectives	30
Enabling the person to see how current difficulties fit into their life as a whole	31
Supporting the person to move forward in their life	33
Potentially unhelpful aspects of counselling and psychotherapy	**34**
Over-individualized and psychologized perspective on problems	34
Over-reach and over-confidence	34
Not sufficiently collaborative	35
Troubled relationship with research	35
Conclusions	**37**
Learning activities	**37**

Introduction

The origins of counselling and psychotherapy can be traced back to converging strands of development within psychiatry, social work, education and religion (McLeod 2019). From around the middle of the twentieth century, counselling and psychotherapy became established as freestanding professions with their own knowledge base, training and societal niche. There now exists wide appreciation of the value of psychological therapies within modern industrial societies. In any given year, five to ten per cent of the adult population make use of some form of talking therapy (Forslund et al. 2020; Olfson and Marcus 2010; Page et al. 2021). Alongside actual participation in therapy, knowledge of psychotherapeutic ideas and practices is disseminated through self-help books and websites, movies and other popular media and articles in newspapers and magazines. In a large-scale survey conducted in the UK, more than 30 per cent of individuals expressed a positive attitude to therapy as a potential source of help around personal issues (Anderson and Brownlie 2011; Anderson et al. 2009). Professional training in medicine, nursing, social work, teaching and other occupations generally includes some coverage of psychotherapeutic skills and concepts. Taken as a whole, these factors mean that both informal emotional support and support provided by human service practitioners are inevitably heavily influenced by therapeutic ideas.

The counselling and psychotherapy literature encompasses an array of competing therapy theories and procedures (McLeod 2019) and is to a large extent dominated by schools of therapy such as psychoanalysis, client-centred/person-centred therapy and cognitive behavioural therapy (CBT).

The present chapter stands back from debates between competing therapy approaches. Rather, the aim is to convey the spirit of counselling in the form of key psychotherapeutic ideas and principles that are relevant to the everyday work of human service practitioners and to signpost how and where to learn more about them. This chapter also considers aspects of counselling/psychotherapy theory and practice that may be unhelpful in human services contexts.

The fragmented landscape of therapy

Although their origins can be traced back to the end of the nineteenth century, counselling and psychotherapy only became widely available from the 1950s. In earlier times, emotional support, and guidance on life decisions and relationship conflict, were available to individuals through membership of a family group and community or by consulting a priest. Historically, such issues were often handled on a collective basis, through various types of communal rituals. Over the course of the nineteenth century, European and North American society changed in fundamental ways in response to urbanization, more time-disciplined work regimes (e.g. in factories), reduction of contact with nature and the rhythms of life, and the gradual replacement of religious beliefs with a more secular, science-informed worldview. Each of these factors contributed to the emergence of counselling and psychotherapy as individualized and professionalized vehicles for emotional support. A detailed account of the history of counselling and psychotherapy can be found in McLeod (2019).

Anyone trying to gain an overview of what is happening in the world of therapy today will find a broad, and sometimes confusing, array of ideas about how therapy can help people. The diversity and fragmentation of therapy theory and practice can be understood as arising from three main sources:

- *contrasting values positions*. Within contemporary society there exist different ideas about what a 'good life' consists of. For example: being a member of a tight-knit family or community (collectivism) vs. fulfilling one's potential as an individual (individualism); rational scientific knowledge as the basis for making life decisions vs. openness to aesthetic or spiritual ways of knowing. These underlying values are reflected in models of therapy. For example, cognitive behavioural therapy (CBT) can be viewed as a rational, scientific-rational technique for being successful at work and coping with stress, whereas humanistic therapy is a more intuitive, feeling oriented, embodied technique for facilitating personal growth.
- *competitive political ideologies*. Since the 1980s, ways of thinking in many spheres of life have been strongly influenced by Reagan and Thatcher neoliberal economic and political theory, which argues that the best solutions to social problems arise from competition within a marketplace. This approach – and in particular its implementation in universities and healthcare systems – created an environment in which new and innovative ideas about therapy were almost always developed as competing separate stand-alone products or approaches, rather than becoming part of a shared or unified professional knowledge base.
- *multiculturalism*. Therapy originated within white, middle-class Judeo-Christian culture and the ideas and techniques generated by the (mainly male) early pioneers can be seen as reflecting various aspects of that worldview. However, global travel and communication, and information about how people live in indigenous cultures, has increasingly meant that ideas and practices from other cultures are widely available. Many important new ideas in therapy, which have become widely disseminated in recent years, have come from non-Western cultures (e.g. mindfulness, yoga, therapeutic use of music-making and art-making, outdoor rituals and open dialogue).

The effect of these factors, and the interplay between them, has been to produce a kaleidoscopic and ever-changing combination of elements of therapy that can be hard to navigate for both potential users of therapy and those who are interested in developing psychotherapeutic skills.

The framework for embedded counselling that forms the core of the present book represents the common ground of counselling and psychotherapy – ideas and strategies that come up over and over again in the therapy literature, that have been shown to be useful in many different contexts. These basic principles are introduced in the following sections and then the following chapter looks at how they can be applied, in the form of embedded counselling, by human service practitioners in their various professional settings.

The difference between counselling and psychotherapy

Although they emerged from different historical starting points, counselling and psychotherapy (as well as other forms of practice such as life coaching and careers guidance) are essentially similar in the kind of change processes that are involved, the theoretical models and research evidence that are used to inform practice, and the skills and knowledge of the practitioners. The term 'counselling' is more likely to refer to support around specific social and life-course issues, such as student counselling, bereavement counselling and workplace counselling, whereas psychotherapy is more likely to refer to the use of a particular model of therapy for a specific psychiatric condition (e.g. CBT for depression or

---

Box 2.1 The underlying structure of psychological healing

In the 1960s, the psychiatrist and psychotherapy researcher Jerome Frank conducted wide-reaching research of approaches to healing in different cultures, published in the form of book titled *Persuasion and Healing*. Wherever he looked, Frank found a similar process for supporting individuals through problems in living. On the whole, people dealt with everyday concerns and difficulties through the resources and strategies that were immediately available to them, such as talking to friends and family members. In some situations, however, these approaches were not sufficient to address the problem and the person became demoralized and turned to some kind of socially-sanctioned healer (a priest, shaman, witch, elder or doctor) for guidance. The healer was a trusted individual who was recognized as having special powers, who might live on the edge of the community. They provided the person with an explanation for what was troubling them and encouraged them to engage in a set of healing rituals or procedures that generally involved expression of painful emotions and initiatives designed to repair relationships. An important feature of all stages of the healing process was the instillation of hope. Taken together, these activities resulted in the remoralization of the person and allowed them to resume functioning as a valued member of the community.

psychodynamic therapy for borderline personality disorder). However, there are many exceptions to these distinctions.

Throughout the present book, the term 'counsellor' is not intended to imply 'professionally qualified and accredited as a stand-alone counsellor'. Rather, it refers to someone engaged in offering an episode of counselling *at that moment* – someone who is fulfilling the function of counsellor for another person who needs to talk through a matter that is concerning them (and will switch back to functioning as a nurse or teacher after that episode has been closed).

The common ground of therapy

Underneath the complex jargon, debates and jockeying for position that dominate the world of contemporary counselling and psychotherapy, it is possible to identify a set of key principles or simple truths that capture what good therapists are able to do and make it possible to understand how and why so many people find therapy useful. Therapy operates by:

- making a space to talk it through
- offering a connection with another person that is affirming and caring
- working together in ways that activate the person's own strengths and resources
- developing new skills and perspectives
- enabling the person to see how current difficulties fit into their life as a whole
- supporting the person to move forward in their life.

These ideas are elaborated below. In relation to how each topic is introduced and discussed, the aim has been to use the kind of straightforward everyday language that might be deployed when responding to a client or service user who asks questions such as: 'What is the point of talking about how I feel? How can that help me?'

Making a space to talk it through

At the heart of any form of counselling is 'making a space to talk it through'. This phrase functions throughout the present book as a touchstone and reminder of how counselling operates. The phrase 'making a space to talk it through' carries a great deal of meaning:

Making a space… The idea of *making* implies that counselling is an intentional, purposeful activity. It is not something that just *happens* – it has to be *made*. This *making* is an activity that is carried out by both participants, working together. The person cannot make a counselling space in the absence of the willingness and involvement of the counsellor, and vice versa. The notion of making a space also invites consideration of similar concepts, such as creating, building and constructing, all of which are valuable in terms of understanding this process – counselling can be understood as an activity that is co-constructed. The use of these terms in turn introduces the question: what are the materials that are being used in this making or building process? There are several personal powers or abilities that are brought into service in the making of a counselling space: attention, physical posture and proximity, language, the arrangement of seating, control of time and so on. What can be made will depend on the materials that are available in any specific situation.

Making *a space* to talk.... What is meant by *a space* in the context of counselling? What kind of space is this? It is a space that exists both in the life of the person who wishes to talk about a problem, and in the relationship between that person and their counsellor. One of the main themes of this book is that it is important to understand people as living their lives within a personal niche that they have made for themselves within their society and culture. This niche, or personal world, can at times be hard to live in – things go wrong. Counselling is a space outside of the person's everyday life, in which they can stand back from their routine and reflect on how they might wish to change things to make them better. A counselling space is like a bubble, haven or place of emotional safety into which the person can step for a period of time, and to which they can return when necessary. A counselling space is also a space in the relationship between the person and the counsellor. There are many aspects to the relationship between a person and someone who takes the role of counsellor to them: making arrangements to meet ('Next week at the same time?'); gender/age/ethnic similarity or difference; shared experiences outside of the counselling room (bumping into each other in the supermarket). However, if counselling is to happen, there needs to be a time when these other facets of the relationship fade into the background, to allow a different kind of conversation to develop. The idea of a space implies boundary – there is an edge to a space. A space is surrounded by other things, but within the space there is nothing – it is a *space*. In counselling, while various structures may be brought in from outside ('Let's use this problem-solving format to work through the difficulty you are having in making a decision on your career options....'), the basic premise of counselling is that it starts with an empty space, where the person is offered the possibility of talking about (or not talking about) anything they like. The notion of space invites reflection on the nature of other spaces in which meaningful personal and emotional learning can occur. There are ways in which a counselling space is similar to, as well as different from, the space that a person enters when they read a good novel, the space created on the stage of a theatre or the space experienced when walking in the hills.

A space *to talk* it through... Counselling is essentially about talking. Putting something into words, or bringing it into language, can be a very powerful healing experience. Language incorporates an infinite number of ways of making meaning. Words, phrases and discourses reflect the meaning-making activity of multiple generations of people. There is always another way to talk about something and each way of talking is associated with a different position in relation to the topic and a different set of things that might be done. Finding the words to say it, naming, differentiating – these accomplishments of talk bring an issue or concern into a space where it can be examined by talker and listener together. It also makes it possible for the talker to hear themselves – talking opens up possibilities for reflection. The talker can observe the impact of their words on the hearer. The shift from monologue (this problem has be rattling around in my head) to dialogue dissolves isolation and social exclusion and introduces the possibility of sharing and support. Talking invites laughter. Joining together all the separate bits of things that might be said about something, to arrive at the whole story, provides a sense of coherence.

To talk *it* through… The significance of *it* lies in the fact that the issue or concern that a person wishes to talk about is rarely clearly-defined. Usually, there is a vague sense of something being wrong – a painful feeling, a need to talk. The task of counselling typically involves activities that can be described as 'mapping', 'exploring' or 'naming' the issue, or 'getting a handle on it'. The act of finding the right words to capture the sense of *it* can lead to a sense of relief ('*that's* what it's about'). Mapping the shape and contours of *it* opens up possibilities for what can be done about *it*. This process can also be understood in terms of finding a *focus* for a counselling conversation.

To talk it *through*… To talk something through implies that a conversation aims to be comprehensive and thorough, encompassing all relevant aspects of an issue. It also implies the possibility of resolution, of talk that reaches a point where nothing more needs to be said. When a person is talking about a significant personal issue, there is a sense of a story unfolding. The person has the experience of being on a 'track', with an awareness of 'nextness' in their talk – there is something else to be said. This something else is rarely pre-planned on the part of the person, but instead arises from being in a situation of being given permission to talk. Talking it through also invokes a sense of movement through a landscape, to arrive at another place.

The idea of making a space to talk it through defines the central purpose of counselling – this is what counselling is essentially about. It represents an understanding of counselling that places an emphasis on the existence of a relationship within which such a space can be created, and the role of language, storytelling and conversation as the medium through which two people can work together to make a difference.

Affirming and caring connection

Effective counselling depends on the establishment of a bond or alliance that is strong enough for the person to be able to tolerate talking about issues that are emotionally painful, embarrassing and shameful, out of control or confusing. This requires the person to trust the counsellor and to feel safe with them. The counsellor is someone who is supportive and accepting, while at the same time being independent of and external to the web of everyday relationships within which the person lives their life. This degree of separation from other relationships give the person the confidence to talk candidly about things that they would not want a friend, family member or work colleague to hear. A counselling relationship is bounded in relation to both purpose and confidentiality. Any limits to confidentiality need to be clearly explained and mutually understood.

Sometimes, a person who is seeking help and the practitioner who is in the role of counsellor to that person may just hit it off from the start and be able to understand, appreciate and trust each other without difficulty. More usually, however, a relationship needs to be *built* – a person seeking help may need to test out the relationship before they can come to rely on it. Good counsellors pay attention not only to the problems and dilemmas presented by the person seeking help, but also continually monitor the quality of the relationship or contact they have with the person and look for ways to strengthen it.

In terms of the healing potential of a counselling relationship, the key underlying process centres on the experience of *connection*. In the counselling and psychotherapy literature, terms such as 'therapeutic relationship' and 'therapeutic alliance' are used to refer to ongoing interaction between client and therapist, typically comprising several hours of being in each other's presence. By contrast, brief episodes of embedded counselling may occur within a short period of time – say 20 minutes – with no certainty of further contact. In any type of long-term counselling or helping relationship, it will be necessary to take account of exigencies such as relationship ruptures, the challenges associated with being a reliable ally and the possibility that each participant may re-enact familiar and habitual dysfunctional relationship patterns within their interaction. These processes do occur in embedded counselling situations – for example, some teachers, social workers and health practitioners may be involved with a client or service user over a period of several years. However, they are counterbalanced by the need to work together on practical issues regarding the provision of learning and care. From the perspective of a person seeking emotional support, the most significant helpful or healing aspect of the relationship with a practitioner is the sense of being received as a person rather than being treated as a 'case'.

Listening
A major feature of meaningful connection within any counselling relationship is that a counsellor *listens*. There are many other situations in life where a person can tell someone else about a problem that they have been struggling with. However, rarely does the person on the receiving end really listen. For example, telling a friend about a problem will usually elicit reciprocal disclosure from the friend – they will move into describing a similar problem that they have encountered themselves. This is a useful response, within a friendship, because it demonstrates solidarity and sharing and may lead to learning something about the coping and problem and problem-solving strategies that are used by the other person. Telling a professional person, such as a doctor, nurse or social worker about a problem, is not likely to lead to reciprocal problem-sharing on the part of

the practitioner or to deeply attentive listening. More usually, a practitioner will offer an advice-giving or information-gathering response. This is because the professional helper may not have time to listen, they believe that it is their job to sort out the problem by offering a concrete, immediate solution, they assume that they need to conduct an assessment or diagnosis that would allow them to refer the person to a specialist service. Most people understand and accept that it is inevitable that such responses represent the default mode of most practitioners with whom they are involved. This means that a more empathic or emotionally engaged practitioner response is likely to have a greater impact.

In counselling, listening is understood as an *active* process. Listening is not a matter of being a passive recipient or recorder of information. In listening, a counsellor is expressing curiosity and interest. It is a form of listening that comes from a position of wanting to know more. There are two senses of wanting to know more. One sense reflects a desire to learn about what happened next or about the context within which an event took place. The other sense of knowing more is a curiosity about gaps, pauses and significant moments within the person's telling of their story. A counsellor wants to know more about what is being held back in these moments, what is not being said, what is perhaps difficult to say. It involves curiosity or sensitivity around the *edge* of the person's awareness of what they are talking about. This curiosity, sensitivity and interest marks out the kind of listening that a counsellor is not merely listening for information (who did what, what their names were, when it happened), but listening for *meaning*. A counsellor is listening for clues about what makes this set of events significant for a person and why they wish to talk about it *now*.

Safety, trust and affirmation

Another critical characteristic of a counselling relationship is that it is *safe*. A counsellor is someone who is unequivocally on the side of the person, whose aim and purpose is to be helpful. By contrast, a counsellor is not someone who has any intention of using, abusing, harming or exploiting the person who comes to them for help. The counsellor has no axe to grind, no stake in whether the person decides to do one thing or the opposite. The counsellor is a person who can be *trusted*.

One of the main things that a person is looking for when they seek counselling is for their experience to be *authenticated* and *affirmed* by another person. Authentication can only take place when the listener responds in a human and personal manner, which conveys fellow-feeling. If a counsellor comes across as too detached, impersonal and 'professional' or as perpetually nice and agreeable, the person seeking counselling is always left wondering whether they are getting a 'real' response, or whether the counsellor's apparent empathy and concern is all just an act. By contrast, the more that a counsellor is willing to state his or her true position on things, to disagree or challenge, to acknowledge uncertainty and confusion, express feelings and set limits on what they are able to give or do, the more confidence the person will have that the counsellor has a genuine interest in them.

A further essential quality of a helpful counselling relationship is emotional honesty. When someone is emotionally honest, they tend to be experienced as being transparent, at not hiding anything. If, on the other hand, a counsellor is experienced at being emotionally elusive or false, then the relationship tends to be undermined because the person is thrown into a state of doubt through beginning to wonder about what may be being left unsaid by the counsellor.

In deciding to enter a counselling relationship, a person is looking for someone who will *care* about them. The concept of care has been largely ignored or devalued within the counselling literature, probably because it might be taken to imply a lack of professional expertise and detachment. This is a pity, because, as the philosopher Heidegger has pointed out, caring represents a fundamental aspect of involvement in the world – the experience of caring discloses what is important and has meaning for us.

In a counselling relationship, caring can be expressed by:

- paying attention to the person
- being there
- anticipating the other person's needs
- small acts of kindness
- remembering information about the person's life
- thinking about the person when they are not there
- proceeding gently and slowly, and with patience – checking things out
- putting one's own needs aside, in the interest of the other
- genuine curiosity about the experience and views of the person
- celebrating the person's achievements.

A further sense of the importance of care in counselling situations can be reinforced by considering that, in seeking counselling, a person is allowing themselves to be someone who is fragile, vulnerable, in pain, lost, needy or confused. In doing so, they are opening up parts of themselves that may have been hidden from others for fear of rejection, ridicule or misunderstanding.

In conclusion, it is possible to see that the creation of a counselling space does not only function to allow the person to reflect on, and take stock of, what is happening in their everyday life. It is also a space within which it is possible to have an affirming experience of emotional and personal connection with another person and a sense of being important enough as an individual to be worth caring about. Although the significance of this kind of interpersonal connection runs like a thread through all of therapy literature, it is described and explained most powerfully within the relational cultural model of therapy (Jordan 2000; 2008) and in the approach known as functional analytic psychotherapy (Tsai et al. 2012; 2013; 2014). Introductory accounts of these therapy perspectives are available in McLeod (2019).

Box 2.2 The importance of small things

Interviews with therapy clients have consistently found that, from a client perspective, it is often the small things that make a difference. For example, when they asked clients about events in therapy that cemented their relationship with their therapist, Bedi et al. (2005) found that they mentioned incidents such as their therapist greeting them at the beginning of each session with a warm smile; walking them to the door at the end of the session, opening it for them and walking out together; and serving tea and snacks at the beginning of each session. In another study, an adolescent client reported that it meant a lot to them that their therapist picked them up after school and drove around for an hour (Bòe et al. 2019). What seemed to be happening in these situations that the authenticity of the therapist's actions conveyed a sense of being human together (Skatvedt 2017; Skatvedt and Schou 2008, 2010) that created a heightened sense of closeness that the client experienced as a micro-affirmation of their worthiness as a human being (Stiver et al. 2008; Topor et al. 2018). Such moments of connection create the conditions for the client to trust their therapist and to go on to make more effective use of the support and guidance that they can provide.

Working together in ways that activate the person's own strengths and resources

In most counselling situations, there is a need to find a balance between problems and capabilities. For the majority of people, it is not an easy step to seek help. It can be hard enough to ask for emotional support from a friend or family member and in many cases even harder to open up to someone in a professional role, such as a teacher or nurse. The moment of seeking help inevitably involves admitting that one is unhappy and troubled in some way. As a result, what is presented to the listener or counsellor is a description of an aspect of their life that the person has – so far – not been able to handle in a satisfactory way. Effective emotional support requires being open to the person's unhappiness and suffering – 'cheer up' or 'pull yourself together' tend not to be helpful ways of responding. A crucial aspect of being supportive is to be willing to engage with the other person's problems and take them seriously. There can be risk, in this process, of adopting a perspective of seeing the person only in terms of their difficulties and losing sight of the fact that at the same time they possess many strengths, capabilities and resources. In addition, they almost certainly have developed their own way of making sense of the problems that beset them, have used a number of strategies for addressing or at least containing the problem and have ideas about further strategies that might be relevant. One of the most significant ways in which counselling and psychotherapy has evolved over the last century has been a shift away from a position that predominantly defines the person seeking help in terms of pathology, to an approach that recognizes their strengths and resources. An important task in counselling is to work with the person to identify capabilities or possibilities in themselves, or within their life, that they may have taken for granted or have neglected.

Developing new skills and perspectives

In seeking help from another person, an individual who is struggling with a problem in living is hoping that something will emerge from the conversation or interaction that will make a difference to them. All types of emotional support can be understood as comprising bundles of difference-making possibilities. Sometimes, these difference-making activities are heavily signalled, for instance in the form of a 12-step programme for overcoming addiction, a cognitive-behavioural intervention for panic disorder, or participation in a mindfulness class. However, most difference-making aspects of counselling operate on a more subtle level, such as:

- the decision to talk about a problem to someone else, and admit that one has a problem or describe an experience that may never have been talked about before
- the experience of being listened to or to have one's worries and concerns taken seriously
- being invited to think about what one wants from a counselling session or what would be helpful
- the counsellor saying something or using an idea, concept or image, that allows you to make sense of your actions in a new way
- carrying the counsellor's voice, or their presence, in your mind
- listening to yourself as you talk to a counsellor, observing how they respond to you and getting a sense of how you come across to another person
- being invited by the counsellor to pay attention to things that you may have rarely attended to in the past, such as how you feel or thoughts/situations that trigger your emotions
- what happens when you talk to a person who listens without judgement
- starting to remember or reclaim your own capabilities
- a helper or counsellor offering an opportunity to come back and talk again at a particular date in the future.

The key point here is that the creation of a space to talk things through and the experience of connection with someone who cares and is independent of your everyday situation provide a new context that in itself has the potential to make a difference. Even therapy approaches that are organized around explicit techniques depend on the operation of these context-dependent processes – it is just that they harness them in a particular way for a specific purpose. In addition to new skills and perspectives that might be generated by interaction with a counsellor, the person is almost certainly continuing their own personal search for ways of making a difference, such as accessing self-help books and websites or trying out complementary therapies. An important part of the counselling process can involve inviting the person to talk about the pros and cons of these personal initiatives.

A useful way to think about the development of new skills and perspectives can be to recognize that life is never static. Everything is in a process of change. There are always differences, openings and possibilities. One of the ways that counselling helps people is to provide opportunities to notice these differences and build on them.

Enabling the person to see how current difficulties fit into their life as a whole

Effective counselling operates as an open space that allows the person seeking support to talk about whatever seems relevant to them. Many research studies have shown that the occasions when counselling goes wrong tend to be associated with therapist-imposed restrictions on what can be discussed – for instance if a counsellor is uncomfortable with the client talking about a topic such as race, sex or religion/spirituality or is unwilling to accept that the client is not satisfied with the direction being taken in a session. A crucial dimension of relevance relates to how the problem or concern highlighted by the person seeking help fits into their life as a whole. In order to address the problem in living that is bothering them, the individual may need or want to consider how it relates to:

- what has happened at earlier points in their life
- what is happening right now (today, this week, this moment)
- other domains of life (e.g. family difficulties arising from work stress)
- the kind of future that the person wants to have or has assumed they would have.

Counselling that imposes a focus on only one of these dimensions of life (e.g. assuming that all problems have their origins in adverse childhood experience or in dysfunctional here-and-now thought patterns) runs the risk, for many clients, of not allowing them to explore areas that they know, or believe, to be significant for them. In addition, counsellor curiosity about all facets of the person's life can lead to valuable steps forward. For instance, a person who is depressed may be preoccupied with past events in their life where they see themselves as having failed in some way. Being invited to talk about how they would ideally like their future to be may lead into conversations around how to make such things happen.

Similarly, someone who is anxious in work situations may discover that, in the part of their lives where they pursue leisure activities, there exists some potentially transferable anxiety-management skills.

> **Box 2.3 A single session of therapy can be helpful**
>
> A significant area of misunderstanding in relation to counselling and psychotherapy is that these forms of help require a heavy investment of time. While it is certainly the case that some therapists and clients may work together for months or years, there is also a substantial amount of evidence that psychotherapy can have a significant impact in a single session. There exists a substantial literature on single-session, one-at-a-time, drop-in, crisis and brief therapy consultation (Dryden 2020a, b; Young and Dryden 2019). An international survey by Flückiger et al. (2020) found a huge variation in number of sessions used by clients, with an overall average of 12 sessions and several centres reporting that the majority of their clients typically attended for three to six sessions. Analysis of attendance rates in a group of therapy services in Italy found that 26 per cent of clients attended for only a single session (Cannistrà et al. 2020). A further study by the same research team reported that, in clients who had specifically opted for a single-session consultation, 52% felt that the one session they had received had been sufficient to resolve their problem. A review of research into counselling in Aotearoa/New Zealand found that, across several studies, the average number of sessions per client was less than five, with around half of all clients receiving a single session (Manthei 2021). The widespread prevalence of single-session therapy has been accompanied by the development of guidelines and training programmes for undertaking this kind of work (see, for example, Dryden 2020b). A key principle is to enter the therapeutic episode with the assumption that this will be the only time you meet and to make every effort to identify what the client wants from your time together, keep close to that goal and finish by reviewing the take-home learning, implications and future action arising from what has been discussed. Taken as a whole, research and practice around single-session therapy suggests that there may be a substantial overlap between the therapeutic processes facilitated by specialist stand-alone counsellors and psychotherapists and the emotional support offered by practitioners of embedded counselling. In both contexts, while there are many clients and service users who are looking for, and need, some kind of ongoing support, there also exist a substantial proportion of clients who benefit from a one-off, focused, therapeutic conversation.

Supporting the person to move forward in their life

A fundamental aspect of being a person is to be able to imagine a future. Human beings exist in time, with a sense of directionality (Cooper 2019) that is informed by cultural images and beliefs around what a 'good life' might look like (Taylor 1989). This idea has some important implications for counselling. One of these is that it is helpful to explore, and agree, what the person wants from counselling. The person's sense of what they want from counselling will be linked to, but not the same as, their sense of what they want from their life as a whole. For example, a person may see the ultimate purpose of their life as achieving spiritual enlightenment or being a good partner and parent. But what they hope to achieve in counselling will almost certainly be more modest, such as overcoming crippling self-doubt that is preventing them from gaining a degree qualification, which would allow them to get a job that would enable enough financial security to allow bigger life goals to be accomplished. An understanding of what the person wants is also relevant to what is helpful (or otherwise) in a particular counselling session. For instance, a client wanting to overcome crippling self-doubt may want to use one session to look at how their self-belief was undermined by bullying at school and another session to practise more constructive self-beliefs.

Another potentially important implication of client directionality for counselling is that a client may evaluate the helpfulness of counselling in terms of progress toward a goal, rather than its complete accomplishment. A person may seek help for a problem because they have run out of ideas about how to deal with that issue and feel utterly helpless and demoralized. In such a situation, breaking the log-jam – beginning to take a few steps in the desired direction – may be hugely significant, particularly if the person has gained an appreciation of what it is they need to continue to do to make a long-term difference. Within the therapy literature, this issue is sometimes discussed in terms of a distinction between *cure* and *recovery* (Dell et al. 2021). From a medical perspective, a patient is cured when their disease or disorder has been eliminated. Translated into a psychotherapy context, this would mean that a good outcome of therapy would be defined in terms of reduction in symptoms (e.g. frequency or intensity of anxiety) to the level that would be observed in a healthy person. By contrast, a recovery perspective refers to the idea that people usually engage in multiple activities in order to overcome a problem in living, none of which are decisive in the sense of producing a cure, but each of which will make an appreciable difference. The distinction between cure and recovery is crucial for human service practitioners offering embedded counselling to service users who are looking for emotional support for problems in living. It is not realistic for such a practitioner to look at what they are offering as curative. What is more appropriate is to assess the effectiveness of the support they provide in terms of the extent to which it supports (probably alongside other sources of help) a process of recovery.

Potentially unhelpful aspects of counselling and psychotherapy

The present chapter explores how counselling and psychotherapy can be helpful for people who are experiencing problems in living. The aim has been to demonstrate to health and social care (and other) practitioners who have not undergone training in counselling or psychotherapy, but who nevertheless are frequently faced by service users who are emotionally troubled, that psychotherapeutic skills and ideas may have something to offer. Incorporating such skills and ideas in everyday practice is likely to involve contact with the world of therapy, in the form of reading books and articles, attending training courses and seminars and talking with therapists. In relation to entering that world, it is important to be aware that, alongside many gifts and much that is of value, there are also ways in which it can be unhelpful.

Over-individualized and psychologized perspective on problems

There are significant strands of therapy theory and practice that are based on an appreciation of the social, cultural and political context of people's lives. However, most mainstream therapy approaches tend to view clients as autonomous and bounded entities whose difficulties can be resolved through attention to psychological processes and immediate interpersonal functioning. This kind of primarily individualized focus of most therapy has meant – despite massive efforts in recent years to come to terms with this issue – that it has struggled to meet the needs of people with collectivist ways of living (i.e. people who think about life more in terms of 'we' than 'I') or with entrenched patterns of inequality arising from colonialism and racism.

Over-reach and over-confidence

Despite a degree of movement in the direction of integrative and pluralistic forms of practice, it is still the case that most training, practice and research in psychotherapy is dominated by major schools or approaches, such as psychodynamic, humanistic and cognitive-behavioural, that are grounded in the work of founding figures such as Freud and Rogers. Therapists who identify with these main schools have generally undergone years of study of that approach, including receiving their own personal therapy. As result, they may find it hard to envisage that any other way of working with clients could be of any value. A key element of established approaches to therapy is that they are based on an assumption that therapeutic success is due to the effective implementation of the theory and that cases where the client does not benefit from therapy are due to the inadequacy of the client (not ready to change, resistant, in denial), the therapist (lacking in skill, has not had enough personal therapy, deviated from the protocol) or the clinic (not enough sessions were available).

Not sufficiently collaborative

The concept of collaboration refers to the idea that in most situations, to achieve anything worthwhile it is necessary for people to work together in ways that pool their experience, knowledge and skills. In helping and human service contexts, such as education, social care and health care, collaboration occurs between practitioners (e.g. members of a team, or across professional and occupational boundaries) and between practitioners and service users (e.g. shared decision-making, co-production and co-design of services). Although it exists, collaboration is not well established or widely prevalent in counselling and psychotherapy. The need to be able to offer the client a confidential relationship makes most therapists reluctant and uncomfortable about talking about cases to anyone other than their own clinical supervisor. Shared decision-making between client and therapist tends to be limited in scope because most therapists are only ever going to offer the client one thing (the therapy approach within which they have been trained) and because a lot of the time the focus of therapy is around (or is perceived by the therapist to be around) the client's difficulties in making decisions. Alongside these practical barriers to collaboration, there is also the fact that therapists operate on the edge of society, as recipients of, and witnesses to, what is not talked about – what is hidden, secrets. Schools, universities, hospitals, churches, temples, police stations and courts are major, visible, public institutions. By contrast, counselling and psychotherapy offices and clinics tend to be discretely positioned and often unmarked.

Troubled relationship with research

One of the distinctive features of contemporary counselling and psychotherapy is the extent to which it has been shaped by findings from research into the outcomes and effectiveness of therapy. The psychotherapy research literature has hugely expanded over the last 30 years to incorporate evidence from qualitative, quantitative studies, mixed method studies and systematic analysis of single cases. All of this has greatly contributed to accountability and to the ability of practitioners to use research – for instance, studies that explore the client's view of what is helpful or unhelpful – to inform their practice. However, in a crowded mental health marketplace in which there are many different types of therapy on offer, including pharmacological treatments, there has been a strong emphasis on research that aims to establish which type of therapy is most effective for which condition or client group. Such studies are of particular interest to governments and health insurance companies who are commissioning and paying for therapy provision. Unfortunately, the type of outcome research that has been carried out, and the ways in which the findings of such studies have been interpreted, have resulted in policies that require therapists and clinics to deliver specific interventions that have been validated in randomized clinical trials for specific, diagnosable disorders. While this kind of administrative strategy may make logical sense at a managerial level, for instance in relation to ensuring value for money, it has had the effect of limiting the capacity of therapists to be responsive to client diversity and preferences. The question of how to reconcile scientific evidence from research into large samples of people, and the unique patterns of life exhibited by particular clients or patients in specific circumstances, has been challenging not only for psychotherapists, but also for doctors and other health professional (see, for example, Anjum et al. 2020; Gabbay and le May 2011). An important difference has been that while medical research has consistently been able to demonstrate that some interventions are more effective than others – and that the application of medical science has yielded cumulative, year-on-year improvements in survival rates and quality of life – research into the relative effectiveness of competing approaches to counselling and psychotherapy has never been able to generate such clear-cut insights.

The existence of these four problematic aspects of contemporary counselling and psychotherapy theory and practice – individualism, over-confidence, being expert-driven, and research orientation – do not detract from the underlying validity and helpfulness of conversations and interactions that are informed by psychotherapeutic skills and understanding.

The point of highlighting these unhelpful aspects of therapy in this chapter is to clarify why therapy is sometimes poorly understood. Therapists – even those who are routinely capable of helping people to turn their lives around – can often find it hard to explain what they do to both colleagues from other disciplines and the general public. Compared to similar professions, there is much less public discourse around counselling and psychotherapy. Anyone who watches TV and movies will readily acquire a detailed appreciation of what it is like to be a doctor, nurse, teacher, lawyer, police officer or even an archaeologist. By contrast, public knowledge of therapy tends to be based on first-hand personal experience or word of mouth recommendation (although, even here, many people who make use of therapy never tell anyone else about it, even close family members). There are only a small number of therapy writers who have found ways to communicate to a wider public, such as Irvin Yalom (1989, 2002, 2005, 2017) and more recently Matthew Elton (2021), Phillipa Perry (2019, 2020) and Jonathan Shedler (via his website and Twitter).

Conclusions

Counselling is an endlessly flexible and creative activity, that draws on awareness, skills and ideas that are part of everyday life (McLeod and McLeod 2022). Despite the complexity of current therapy and practice, it is possible to identify some basic strategies that represent the common ground of all forms of effective emotional support and healing. For the most part, these strategies have been developed and explored in the specific context of formal, contracted sessions – usually an hour long and continuing for at least a few weeks, with a practitioner whose sole purpose is to provide counselling or psychotherapy. Although the same skills, ideas and helpful processes can be integrated or embedded into the work of practitioners such as nurses, doctors, social workers, clergy and in many other occupational settings, they need to be adapted in order to operate appropriately in such arenas. The next chapter looks at how that can be accomplished.

Learning activities

The following activities may be explored individually, and/or with a group of learning partners.

Exercise 2.1 What do you know about counselling and psychotherapy?
To be an effective and resourceful practitioner of embedded counselling, it is necessary to have a working knowledge of counselling and psychotherapy theory, skills and practice. How would you describe your current knowledge base in relation to these topics? What are the therapy ideas, activities and approaches that might be helpful to know more about, in relation to your role as a practitioner?

Exercise 2.2 Opportunities to be known
What kinds of opportunities do you have in your own life to talk to someone else about issues that concern you? How satisfactory are these opportunities in enabling you to gain a sense that you have been fully able to 'talk through' the issue? What are the characteristics of these situations (for example, the attitude and qualities of the listener) that either help or hinder this process for you? What are the consequences for you of times in your life where you have *not* had access to such opportunities? How does your learning from this exercise translate into your work with clients in relation to such issues as whether a client wishes to be known by you and how sensitive you are to such wishes?

Exercise 2.3 The tension between cognitive change and emotional insight
One of the major differences of opinion within the counselling and psychotherapy communities is around whether it is more helpful to help clients to

change faulty ways of thinking (e.g. cognitive-behavioural and rational-emotive approaches to therapy) or to change destructive ways of relating to others (psychodynamic therapy). Each of these positions are convincingly articulated in the sources listed below, written by leading figures from each perspective. Read these papers, make up your own mind, and discuss your conclusions with learning partners. The position taken in the present book (explained in the next chapter) is that it is valuable to draw on each approach as necessary to meet client needs and preferences. How credible is that idea to you?

Dryden, W. (2020). Single-session one-at-a-time therapy: a personal approach. *Australian and New Zealand Journal of Family Therapy*, 41(3), 283-301 (open access article)

Shedler, J. (2006). That was then, this is now: Psychoanalytic psychotherapy for the rest of us. Available from http://jonathanshedler.com/writings/

CHAPTER 3

Embedded counselling: a practice framework

Introduction	**39**
A model of embedded counselling	**40**
Being ready	40
Facilitating a counselling episode	41
Using organizational resources	42
Skills and strategies for facilitating episodes of embedded counselling	**44**
What can you offer?	44
What does the client want?	47
A step at a time: tasks	52
Making a difference: methods	53
Being in alignment: deciding together on what to do	58
An example of goals, methods and tasks in action	**62**
Being on the alert for things going wrong	**64**
Conclusions	**65**
Learning activities	**66**

Introduction

Human services practitioners are busy people who carry high workloads, operate under considerable pressure of time and need to accommodate multiple tasks. They are usually part of a team of colleagues, each of whom may have different responsibilities but need to work together to collectively deliver a service. Practitioners tend to be employed within organizations that define roles and lines of managerial control, set standards and distribute rewards and sanctions. Both the organization and the individual practitioner need to adhere to standards and ethical codes defined by professional bodies and also, in some cases, the law. To provide embedded counselling and psychotherapeutic conversations within such settings, it is necessary to adapt and expand the theory, practice and training associated with stand-alone counselling and psychotherapy. The present chapter describes a model or framework designed to enable the effective delivery of embedded counselling episodes by practitioners in health, education, social care and other occupations. A summary of the model is presented, followed by more detailed exploration of the main skills and strategies that practitioners of embedded counselling need to be able to deploy.

A model of embedded counselling

Throughout this book, many examples are given of how embedded counselling is provided in different organizational contexts, to clients and service users with a wide range of concerns and difficulties. Most of these books, articles and research reports focus on particular aspects of the process of embedded counselling. The ideas summarized below present the picture that emerges when all of this information is brought together. While these areas will vary in significance, depending on the kind of embedded counselling that is called for, all of them are relevant. In broad terms, they add up to a model or framework that emphasizes three broad themes: being prepared and ready; skills for facilitating helpful and therapeutic conversations; and making best use of the possibilities arising from working within an organization and belonging to professional networks.

Being ready

- *Espousing a worldview and value position that emphasizes human resourcefulness and strengths and the importance of relationships.* People who seek help are viewed as actively and purposefully collaborating with others to find ways to resolve problems in living. In doing so, they draw on a range of ideas within their culture around how to make sense of problems and how best to address them. In general, people seek assistance from professional sources as a late, or last, resort and continue to make use of their personal or private coping strategies alongside any professional assistance that is offered.
- *Possessing a genuine interest in helping.* A practitioner who effectively engages in embedded counselling is someone whose life exhibits an ongoing curiosity and interest in making sense of their own life, a commitment to the importance of relationships, identification with life-affirming values and a caring approach to others.
- *Openness to the significance of emotions and embodied communication.* Awareness that people express their needs and values, and work together to solve problems, not only through rational and verbal modes of

communication, but also through the expression of emotion and nonverbal embodied communication.
- *Knowing what you can offer.* The counselling skills and methods used in embedded counselling arise from a combination of personal life experience and participation in relevant training and learning activities. An effective practitioner has reflected on these experiences so that they are aware of what they can offer to a client seeking emotional support and also of their own limits.
- *Taking account of organizational context.* The practice of embedded counselling is informed by a thorough, critical analysis of the organizational context within which the practitioner is employed and an appreciation of what is possible and appropriate within the particular organizational context in which the counselling occurs. Practitioners of embedded counselling actively seek to construct suitable arrangements for counselling within their workplaces.

Facilitating a counselling episode

- *Responding to empathic opportunities.* When engaged in routine educational or caring activities with a client or service user, the practitioner of embedded counselling is sensitive to the occurrence of windows of opportunity. These windows are understood as moments when the client expresses emotion, or in some other way refers to a problem in living that is troubling them, in a way that invites or evokes an empathic response from the listener.
- *Gaining consent for counselling.* The practitioner responds to such opportunities by reporting what he or she has observed and inquiring about whether the client would like to discuss what is happening in more detail.
- *Making a space.* If the client wishes to explore the matter further, the counsellor seeks to establish a counselling space, defined in terms of how much time is available, a suitable location and confidentiality boundaries.
- *Finding a focus.* Given that it is unlikely that there is, or could be, the possibility for ongoing, long-term counselling, the counsellor seeks to establish a focus for the conversation in terms of what the client wants to achieve in the time available (goals) and the immediate task or tasks that might be accomplished that could assist the client in making progress to that goal.
- *Flexible use of counselling methods and activities that make sense to the client.* Given that clients have different preferences around the type of activity that they regard as helpful, and that the practitioner does not have time to socialize the client into a pre-determined therapy approach, it is essential that the counsellor is capable of flexibly using their counselling skills to facilitate a range of methods of task completion.
- *Exploring the availability, relevance and utilization of the client's strengths and resources.* Developing an understanding of how the person has handled this problem (or similar problems and situations) in the past and successful

strategies and resources from other areas of their life (or previous points in their life) that might make a positive difference in relation to current concerns.
- *Exploring the availability, relevance and utilization of other sources of help.* What are the other agencies, services and support organizations that are being used by the person? Are there ways that the person might be able to use these resources more effectively? What are the additional agencies, services and support organizations, both within your own organization and that you can access, that might be helpful for the person to consider engaging with? In what ways might you be able to facilitate such engagement?
- *Collaboratively checking out that the counselling or emotional support process that you are facilitating is acceptable to the client at all stages.* The counsellor routinely and regularly invites the client to provide feedback on whether the approach that is being taken to their problem is helpful, whether it is aligned to their needs and preferences and if they have other ideas about what else might be helpful.
- *Monitoring the interaction in terms of risk.* The counsellor pays attention to anything that arises that indicates a risk of harm to the client or other people and, if necessary, invites the client to shift the focus of the conversation in the direction of how such risks might be managed. Successful resolution of the risk may require the involvement of other expertise in addition to, or other than, that of the practitioner.
- *Learning points and future action.* Toward the end of each counselling episode, summarize and review what has emerged from the conversation and how the person might use it (or has decided to use it) to make a difference to their concerns. If possible, document these learning points in the form of a note or email that the client can keep, and also for oneself as a bridge into any further sessions.
- *Closing the space.* The counsellor is aware of the time available and the undesirability of leaving the client in a state of increased vulnerability. The counsellor is responsible for managing time and exploring arrangements (if necessary) for further meetings or alternative sources of help.

Using organizational resources

- *Using supervision, consultation and self-care.* The organization promotes a culture of learning that encourages critical reflection on practice through such questions as: what have you learned from each counselling episode in which you have been involved? What did you do well? What might you have done better? What are the lessons for the future? How were you affected by your client, in terms of emotions and memories that were evoked or troubling images of their suffering? What channels are available to you to process such

reactions? An effective counsellor uses supervision or consultation to explore these questions and as a source of emotional support for themselves.
- *Developing a supportive community of practice.* Finding professional allies, both within your work setting and more widely, who do similar work, participating in formal and informal support and learning networks, and involvement in research (reading and participating in studies) provides opportunities for sharing information and learning about practice, and new ideas and approaches, on a global scale.
- *Building resources to support practice.* Learning and accumulating information about the types of emotional support issues that are most frequently presented by clients with whom you work. Devising ways of making this information available to clients (e.g. leaflets on a noticeboard, a website, a handout that you have prepared).
- *Contributing to the development of organizational initiatives.* What kind of training might be useful for you or for colleagues in your organization? How might organizational procedures be adjusted to enable emotional support to be provided more effectively (e.g. private spaces, use of time, rewriting user-facing information sources)? Are there collaborative projects and services that could be developed on an inter-organizational or inter-professional basis?

Box 3.1 Network-based help for women recovering from the experience of domestic violence

A valuable example of how embedded counselling may operate within a matrix of organizations and agencies can be found in the extensive literature around a network-oriented approach to supporting women who have left relationships in which they have been subjected to abuse and violence. Typically, women in such situations require not just emotional support, but also practical help around such issues as possible involvement with the criminal justice system, housing, childcare and employment. Practitioners with experience of working with such clients have identified a recovery process that starts by building emotional and practical safety and taking stock of relationships and life experience, and then gradually moves in the direction of engaging a widening circle of formal (e.g. health care, education and housing practitioners) and informal (e.g. friends and family) networks (Goodman, Banyard et al. 2016; Sullivan 2018). In some programmes, this approach has generated research-informed initiatives to bridge across different social groups and settings by developing new support roles within organizations, such as 'advocate' (Goodman, Fauci et al. 2016; Wood et al.2020) or 'social assistant' (Ogbe et al. 2021) and attention to cultural factors (Milani and Leschied 2020; Ogbe et al. 2021).

Skills and strategies for facilitating episodes of embedded counselling

For a practitioner who is faced with a client or service user who is upset or troubled, the primary aim is to find a way to work together to tackle the issue. Working together means combining the skills, knowledge and experience of the practitioner with the skills, knowledge and experience of the client. From a practitioner perspective, a capacity to work effectively together can be understood at two levels. At the level of moment-by-moment responsiveness to the person who is seeking help, it is necessary to possess sufficient sensitivity and competence around basic interpersonal skills or counselling skills such as listening, questioning, challenging, and self-disclosure. For example, if the practitioner is not really listening to what the client is trying to say, then their interaction is unlikely to have a positive outcome. The nature of basic counselling skills, and how to use them effectively, is discussed in detail in a companion text (McLeod and McLeod 2022). The general multi-cultural or global relevance of such skills is explored by Kohrt et al. (2015) and Pedersen et al. (2020). At a slightly broader level, working together can be understood in terms of a set of general principles, strategies or concepts. These broader ideas are explored in the following sections, in terms of questions that we have found useful for helping practitioners to reflect on what they are thinking about, and doing, when they are trying to work together with a client to support them in understanding and resolving a problem in living.

What can you offer?

An essential element of skilful counselling therefore involves finding (and then being able to implement) the right approach for each individual. There are substantial differences between individuals in terms of what they need or find helpful. For example, some people resolve issues by expressing their feelings and emotions, while others prefer a more rational approach. Some people look for a helper to take the lead, while for other people the sense of being in personal control may be of paramount importance within a counselling relationship.

A useful way of thinking about this issue is to use the concept of the counselling 'menu'. We are all familiar with restaurant menus, which list the various dishes and beverages that may be available. The items on the menu comprise the restauranteur's 'offering'. In many situations, it is possible to negotiate around the exact specification of menu items ('Can I have the salad without any dressing on it?') or even to ask for something that is not actually included on the published menu ('Could you do beans on toast for my grandson?').

When initiating a counselling episode, it is important to have some kind of pre-existing sense of how you are going to handle it. Some aspects of this sense of being prepared relate to practice issues such as how much time you have right now, what kind of future time commitment you might be able to make and how to create a private space where you can talk without being overheard. Other aspects refer to the use of specific counselling skills and interventions. For example, 'I am good at listening and helping someone tell their story and not too bad at challenging them if they seem to be putting their head in the sand...but I would have no idea what to do if they wanted to tell me about a dream.' These are all examples of potential items on a counselling menu.

Working together in counselling involves being open to the client's suggestions. Being clear about what you have to offer allows the client to know what options are available to them or how much room there might be to negotiate. Some of the ways in which a counselling menu may be applied in embedded counselling practice are illustrated in the following scenarios:

> Sandro is highly fearful of dental treatment. One of the nurses at the surgery has had some training in working with phobic patients, so arranges a consultation a few days before his scheduled treatment. She begins by asking him what he wants to achieve. He says he is not sure.
>
> 'Well,' she replies, 'some people who worry about going to the dentist believe that anxiety is something that is really big for them across their life as a whole. For example, they may be afraid of other similar situations, such as going to the doctor, and so they want to look at the whole issue of what is happening for them in these situations. Other people are just looking for a strategy that will help them to cope better with seeing their dentist.'
>
> Sandro indicated that he was just looking for a way of dealing with his fear of being in the dentist's chair. The nurse then asked whether he had any idea of what might help.
>
> 'Yes. I think I basically need to learn how to relax – I just get myself so wound up.'
>
> The nurse then outlined techniques that she could offer, which could be used to manage fear and anxiety, including relaxation techniques in an audio file, cognitive reframing training and a valium prescription. Together, they discussed what would be best for him.
>
> Agnes is a social worker who works in a centre that offers support to families. Inez is a single mother, with three young children, who has been struggling with a number of issues around controlling her children's behaviour, as well as ongoing financial problems. Inez comes to trust Agnes, and asks if they can have some time together on their own to talk about 'stuff I need to get off my chest'. When they meet and begin to talk, Inez breaks down and begins to talk in a confused way about her experience of being sexually abused as a child and how seeing her own children 'just brings it all back' and 'paralyses me'. As they talk, Agnes begins to sense that Inez is ready to face these memories and find ways of moving beyond them.
>
> She asks, 'I am wondering if what you are talking about– this stuff – has been around for a while, but now is something you want to really look at and put behind you.'

Inez agrees. 'I want to sort it all out and put my life on a different track.'

Agnes explains that she does not think that it would be a good idea for her to offer to do this with Inez. 'I haven't had the right kind of training to feel that I could give you what you need – also, as you know, with my caseload it would be very hard to guarantee that we could meet like this regularly enough.'

They explore the other resources that might be available to Inez in terms of long-term therapy, especially a specialist counselling service and a survivors of sexual abuse group offered by a women's co-operative. They then agreed on the 'bits that I might be able to help you with myself', such as support for making an appointment with one of these services, and 'looking at how the therapy might make a difference to the way you are with the kids'.

What is being described in these examples is not a formal system of assessment and contracting, but an approach to practice in which the counsellor is mindful of the fact that the person seeking help has their own ideas about what they need, is almost certainly aware that there are many possible ways of meeting these needs, and needs to know what is potentially on offer. It is important to recognize that, for anyone involved in offering counselling embedded with another role, such as that of teacher, doctor, social worker or nurse, what they have to offer may not necessarily be grounded in a high degree of training and theoretical knowledge, but can rely on their life experience and skills that they have acquired through their work role. In the example of Inez, for instance, the social worker had not received much training in counselling or psychotherapy, but was able to make use of her gut response to her client, which was along the lines of 'this would be too much for me to handle'. She was also able to recognize that, within the very broad life goal that Inez had identified ('put my life on a different track'), it was possible to isolate one sub-task ('looking at the effect on the kids') that was clearly within her competence to deliver. In the case of Sandro, by contrast, the nurse responding to his fear of dental treatment had received specific training in relation to this type of problem and was prepared to explore a sophisticated menu of possible techniques and interventions with her patient. The precise menu that is on offer in any particular counselling situation will depend on the counsellor and the organizational setting in which they are based.

Although the idea of a counselling menu refers to the repertoire of skills and ideas that a practitioner builds up through training and experience, it implies more than this. Menus exist to facilitate the interaction between a provider and recipient. The process of turning a list of skills into a menu requires developing a capacity to explain and communicate what is on offer in a manner that will make sense to the recipient and enable them to make informed choices.

What does the client want?

Many embedded counselling episodes start with the client conveying – verbally or nonverbally – that they are troubled or feel bad. The practitioner then responds by stating that they had noticed this and were wondering if the person wanted to talk about it. If the client or service user does want to talk about it, they will usually define or explain the problem in the form of a story and some kind of counselling/emotional support process is underway.

> Akira had frequently visited her GP for a wide range of minor ailments and issues around the health of her children and had been seen by several different doctors in the practice. On this occasion, the doctor who was seeing her had scanned through the notes and wondered if there might be some underlying psychological or emotional issue that was being missed. After a discussion of altering the dosage of asthma medication for Akira's son, the doctor tentatively said, 'I hope you don't mind me saying this, but you seem quite tense...is there anything else that is troubling you?'
>
> After an extended silence, Akira started to talk about her relationship with her husband and her mother-in-law, started to cry, and began to talk about a life that included regular domestic violence and abuse.
>
> At this point, mindful of the limited time that was available, the doctor gently interrupted with the statement 'Can I just ask... What would be helpful for us to do or to talk about today? I just want to know what would be most useful for you, given that we don't have a lot of time.' At that moment, the GP was able to imagine many possible things that her patient might want from their time together: antidepressant medication, a referral to couple counselling, a mediation service or social services, information about how to contact a women's refuge, advice on how to handle her husband's bullying. Or maybe just to talk. Each of these goals would have taken the conversation in a different direction. She was surprised by Akira's answer.
>
> 'I want *you* to know, I want it written down in my medical records, so that the next time I see you or one of the other doctors, they know to ask me about it. I need to know that there is someone I can trust to take me seriously if things get really bad.'
>
> They then spent the next 10 minutes talking about what could be written in the notes and the kinds of support that the practice could realistically offer if the time ever came for Akira to activate it. Akira left the session feeling a bit lighter and safer and pleased with herself that she had taken an important step toward a better life. Her doctor left the session with a note in her own diary to bring up the case at the next team meeting, to

make sure that all her colleagues were aware of the situation, and to review the options they were available to them around caring for women subjected to domestic violence.

The case of Akira illustrates the importance of establishing what the client wants, as early as possible in a counselling session. Similar to most busy practitioners, the default mode for a GP is to move as quickly as possible to a practical solution, such as medication or referral to a specialist service. In the event, for Akira such a course of action might have been irrelevant or even unhelpful. What she wanted was for her experience to be validated and witnessed and to prepare the ground for possible next steps if her situation deteriorated. Once these goals were mutually understood, it was not hard for her doctor to make an appropriate response.

A person seeking help always has an aim, or *goal*, in entering a counselling relationship. A counselling goal can be defined as a preferred state of affairs, or outcome, that the person seeking help and their counsellor have agreed to work together to achieve. There is always something that a person *wants* or desires, some area of discomfort with life that they wish to change, that brings a person into a counselling situation. When the person has resolved the issue, and achieved enough of their goals, then they know that they have had enough counselling and that it is time to stop.

The concept of 'goal' refers to those aspects of the life of a person that reflect their capacity to orient toward the future, to have intentions, plans, projects and wishes, to be able to draw on some kind of sense of direction. Although the word 'goal' is widely used in psychology, psychotherapy and professional discourse as a whole, there are many people for whom it evokes negative associations, for instance around sport or business jargon, or through not respecting the emergent and creative dimension of life. In exploring this area of experience with clients and service users, it is therefore important to find a way of talking about it (e.g. what you want, what you hope to get from counselling, where you would like to be) that is meaningful for both of you. Within the present book, 'goal' is used as a convenient shorthand term that has a broad set of meanings that can be expressed in many different ways. For example, in many cultural contexts, the question 'what matters most?' may be a more effective way of exploring what a client or service user wants to achieve through counselling (Mascayano et al. 2016; Yang et al. 2014).

As a counsellor, it can be useful to be aware of the complexity of personal goals. For instance, the concept of goal can be used to refer to aims and objectives that may be all-encompassing, or quite specific. Life goals are overarching issues or existential questions that give shape to a person's life. Examples of life goals are:

- can I move beyond the memory of the abuse I received in childhood, to the point where I can believe in my own value as a person?
- what do I need to do to prove that I am good enough to satisfy my mother or father?

- my Mum and Dad are Polish through and through, but I grew up in England – how do I define who I am as a person?

Life goals reflect personal issues that permeate all aspects of a person's life. For instance, 'moving beyond the memory of abuse' may be associated with difficulties and tensions in intimate and work relationships, in the capacity to be alone and in the capacity to make plans for the future. *Specific* counselling goals, by contrast, refer to more limited situations or scenarios. Examples of such goals might include:

- how can I feel less anxious in interviews?
- what can I do to convey to my doctor that I don't need to take this medication any longer?
- I am caught between wanting to retire and feeling that I should continue to bring home a salary – how can I make a decision?

For practitioners whose counselling function is embedded within other work roles and responsibilities, it is much easier to respond effectively to specific goals than to more existential life goals. The latter tend to be associated with a massive personal agenda of beliefs, dilemmas and concerns that may need to be explored – to tackle life issues in a satisfactory manner requires plenty of time. Psychotherapists and specialist counselling agencies are in a better position to work with life goals than are counsellors whose practice is embedded in other professional roles. On the other hand, specific or situational goals may be addressed very effectively within one or two brief conversations.

It is important to keep in mind that not everyone who seeks counselling wants to deal with issues at the 'life goal' level – a person who has identified a specific goal may prefer to focus on that one issue, rather than being expected to open out all aspects of their life, as might happen in psychotherapy. Nevertheless, when working with specific goals, it is important to keep in mind that, ultimately, they can always be understood as reflecting broader life goals and as nested within these wider goals. For example, a person who starts off by wanting to talk about 'telling my doctor that I don't want medication' may end up realizing that such a goal represented part of a broader personal agenda that they come to describe as 'moving beyond the memory of the abuse I received in childhood, to the point where I can believe in my own value as a person and stand up for what I want with people who I perceive as powerful and dominant'.

It is important to be clear about the difference between the concept of 'goal' on the one hand and the similar concept of 'problem'. A personal goal is always phrased in an *active* and *positive* way, whereas problem-language refers to states of being that are burdensome. A goal can be regarded as similar to a personal quest – a question that the person is trying to explore and answer. It can be useful, therefore, for a counsellor who is talking with a person about their goals to try to use active, positive language which reinforces the person's strengths so that counselling goals are not perceived as indicators of failure but as opportunities for development and connection. For instance, Sheila was a participant in a project that was designed to help women return to work after having been carers. She described herself as 'crippled by fear' at interviews and not able to tell those interviewing her about her relevant experience and qualities. In a consultation session with one of the project tutors, Sheila was asked what she would like to talk about. She replied that 'I have a problem with interviews. I am wracked with nerves. I am just so anxious all the time.'.

The tutor responded by saying, 'Is this something that we could look at more closely? From what you have told me before about this, I'm thinking that what you want to be able to do is to make sure that you can give these interviewers every chance to know about your experience and qualities and that the nervousness get in the way. Would that be a reasonable way to describe what we might aim to be able to work on together?'

If the tutor had accepted Sheila's initial formulation of the issue, as 'something that is wrong with me and needs to be fixed', he would have reinforced a way of describing the situation that portrayed Sheila as deficient and passive. By rephrasing the issue in active and positive language, Sheila's desired positive outcome is acknowledged ('letting the interviewers know about your good qualities') and the status of anxiety is diminished from a totalizing entity to being something that merely 'gets in the way'. This use of language on the part of the tutor immediately opened up a space for different kinds of things to happen within their conversation.

There are many ways of encouraging a conversation about goals. Some potentially useful counsellor statements include:

> 'I can hear from what you are saying that... However, in an ideal scenario, if everything was just as you wanted it to be, how would it be different? How do you want things to be?'
> 'Can you say what it is you would like to gain from talking to me about...?'
> 'What matters most for you, in terms of what we could look at that would make your life better?'
> 'You have described your problem... Are you able to tell me what would you hope to happen, if we can sort this problem out? What are you aiming for?'
> (At the end of a counselling session) 'I was wondering – have you got what you needed from our discussion? Is there anything else you need?'
> The questions 'why *now*?' and 'what would help *now*?' are potentially some of the most useful things for a counsellor to keep in mind (and ask a client about) as a person begins to talk about their troubles.

Much of the time, the specific goals that a person may have are implicit in the way that he or she talks about the problem for which they are seeking help. It is up to the counsellor to 'listen for goals', and then check out what he or she has heard, rather than paying attention only to problems. This strategy can be understood as a process of tentatively offering the person 'candidate goals' – your best guess or approximation of what it is that your client wants from counselling – in a manner that is open to correction from the client.

It is essential to acknowledge that people who seek counselling may have enormous difficulties in explicitly articulating what their goals are. They may *know*, at a feeling or gut level, what they want, but they may not readily be able to put this into words.

There are at least three reasons why a person may not be able to explain clearly what their goals are. First, the goal or purpose may be associated with a vague feeling – 'I'm just exhausted all the time and I don't know what it's about', or 'there's a big empty space inside me'. In these cases, it is as though the person's body has a sense of purpose and direction, in somehow using tiredness or the sense of an empty space to indicate that something is wrong. In these circumstances, all the person can do is to be willing to follow where their body is leading – the end-point is far from clear. A second difficulty that some people have in talking about what they want is that they know what their goal is, but they are afraid or ashamed to acknowledge it. For example, Danny knew full well that he needed help to talk about his sexuality and 'come out' as gay, but would not say this until he was fully convinced that his chosen 'counsellor' (for him, a youth worker based at the local community centre) would respond in a non-critical and sympathetic manner. It was only when he felt safe enough with his counsellor that Danny was able to articulate his goals. A third type of difficulty that some people have in expressing their goals for counselling is that they may never have had the opportunity to reflect on what they want, so they can only convey a confusing jumble of reasons. To return to an example used earlier in the chapter, Sunita had a sense that she had never been able to belong, or to have a sense of fitting in, but it was only when she attended a counselling skills evening class, and took part in personal development exercises, that this vague awareness crystallized into a desire to explore and define her cultural identity.

In situations where a person has difficulty being clear about their goals, it is important for a counsellor to be willing to work with the person around the best mutual understanding of their aims that is possible, rather than wait until a fully crystallized goal statement can be formulated. What is important is for the person seeking help, and the person offering counselling, to have a sufficient level of agreement over the goals they are working together to pursue, so that they are 'on the same wavelength'.

To summarize: the idea of 'goal' is important in counselling because it provides a way of structuring and organizing what happens in a counselling session. It is the ultimate reference point for whatever happens in counselling. A person seeking help will gauge whatever is being discussed in counselling against the touchstone of whether it is helping them to move closer to their goals. The concept of goal also provides a way of making a link between the immediate reason the person gives for seeking counselling ('I need to talk to someone about getting into fights with my dad', 'I feel sad a lot of the time') and the broader direction of the person's life ('can I accept myself as a person in my own terms?') – specific goals are always linked to broader existential questions of meaning, purpose and identity, even if these bigger questions tend to remain firmly in the background in the majority of microcounselling encounters. The notion of the person's goal acts as a reminder that the counselling space exists for a purpose – it is a kind of 'time out' to enable a person to repair their personal niche. It is also a reminder that the person seeking help is an active participant in life, a person who has purposes rather than (or as well as) problems and symptoms.

A step at a time: tasks

Although agreement over goals is essential as a way of ensuring that the person and counsellor are working toward the same ends, it is very difficult to do anything in counselling that will directly impact on a goal. What is necessary instead is to identify specific *tasks* whose completion can allow the person to take a step nearer their goal.

The model of counselling suggested in this book assumes a process through which a person who is troubled in some way by tensions within their relationships or life space, and has a sense of wanting to do something about it (goals), then seeks out a counsellor and negotiates the construction of a safe space within which they can talk through their problem. But what happens next? What does 'talking through' mean in practice? The process of counselling can be understood as being based on engagement in, and completion of, a set of distinctive counselling *tasks*. A counselling task can be defined as a sequence of actions carried out by a person, in collaboration with a counsellor, in order to be able to take a step in the direction of getting on with their life. A task is something that the person and the counsellor undertake together. For any specific counselling task, there are a potentially infinite number of different *methods* that can be used to complete it. The safest and most helpful practice occurs when the person and their counsellor *decide together* the task in which they are engaged and agree on the method that they will use to tackle the task.

The concepts of 'task' and 'method' are central to the framework for counselling practice that is used in this book. The following list of frequently-occurring counselling tasks provides a starting point for thinking about ways that goals can be broken down into smaller steps:

- talking though an issue in order to understand things better
- making sense of a puzzling or problematic personal reaction to a situation
- problem-solving, planning and decision-making
- changing behaviour
- dealing with difficult feelings and emotions

- finding, analysing and acting on information
- undoing self-criticism and enhancing self-care
- negotiating a life transition
- dealing with difficult or painful relationships.

The precise labels and definitions given to these tasks are inevitably fairly arbitrary. Experienced counsellors evolve their own ways of describing tasks. In practice, a counselling episode may focus on a single facet of one of these tasks (e.g. concentrating on understanding barriers to change, rather than working through a whole behaviour change sequence). Sometimes, an episode may encompass two or three interlocking tasks, which are pursued at the same time (e.g. *exploring* how I *feel* in relation to a *life transition*).

Breaking down the client's goals into step-by-step tasks is consistent with the idea that working together involves a process of selecting or adapting items on an imagined menu (or recognizing that none of the menu options are suitable and that some other way of moving forward needs to be devised). For example, with a client or service user who has experienced a bereavement and wants help to move on in their life (Chapter 10), any of the tasks in the above list may be relevant.

Being able to work with therapeutic tasks represent a set of basic competencies for anyone involved in offering counselling relationships. The tasks outlined above are firmly based in everyday, common-sense ability to cope with life. We are all able to hold meaningful conversations, make sense of puzzling reactions to situations, solve problems and so on. Being a good counsellor involves being willing to examine one's own individual strengths and weaknesses in relation to being able to carry out these tasks, developing flexibility and sensitivity in relation to engaging with other people around the tasks and being open to learning new methods and strategies for task resolution. A good counsellor is someone who knows the 'ins-and-outs' of the kinds of tasks that arise in their practice and are able to adapt or improvise methods of task completion that are appropriate to the individual with whom they are working.

Making a difference: methods

Any counselling task can be carried out using a number of different therapeutic activities or what can be described as 'methods'. People can learn, change or reconstruct their personal world in a variety of ways, depending on their upbringing, cultural background, temperament and on their awareness of change resources and techniques that are available within their social world. Theories of counselling, psychotherapy and psychology, spiritual/religious teachings and practices and self-help books, as well as everyday common knowledge, afford a vast repertoire of ways of dealing with problems in living. In any counselling situation, it is up to the person and the counsellor to decide together what they can do to complete a task.

Box 3.2 An example of a task model: counselling in dementia

New tests for the early diagnosis of dementia, and the availability of drug treatments that can slow down the development of Alzheimer's Disease, mean that there is an increasing number of people who have received a diagnosis of dementia yet may expect to live in their families, at a relatively good level of functioning, for many years. The diagnosis of dementia raises strong feelings, and evokes powerful negative images, not only in people with dementia but also within their surrounding family and community. In addition, it may be difficult to cope with the gradual memory loss that is associated with the disease. For these reasons, increasing attention is being given to the potential role of counselling at the time of diagnosis as a means of helping people with dementia, and their families, deal with this event. In some research carried out by Weaks et al. (2006), people with dementia and their families were interviewed regarding their experience of the diagnosis and the issues with which they had been confronted in the first six months following the diagnosis. Analysis of these interviews lead to the identification of a set of psychotherapeutic tasks that seemed particularly relevant to people in this situation:

- exploring the possibility of life as normal
- evaluating the usefulness of different sources of information
- understanding the changing roles within their families and wider social network
- understanding and dealing with the emotional process
- addressing deep philosophical questions, such as the possibility of loss of identity
- embracing and coping with social stigma
- creating a new and different identity
- telling and retelling their story
- finding a way through the health system.

Within each of these tasks there are many sub-tasks that operate at a more granular level. For instance, Weaks et al. (2015) found that, for many people with dementia and their families, telling other people about the diagnosis represented a specific and emotionally challenging yet necessary task that contributed to several broader tasks, such as developing a new identity. This programme of research found that the tasks associated with assimilating a diagnosis of dementia could be fulfilled using a variety of methods, including formal/specialist counselling or psychotherapy, embedded counselling from doctors, community nurses and clergy, participation in self-help groups, support from friends and family members and reading. The identification of these tasks led to a range of organizational initiatives around designing appropriate care systems, training and supervising practitioners and creating ways of informing people with dementia and their families so that they know what to expect.

Counselling methods can be defined as activities that a client and counsellor undertake together, that make a difference in terms of facilitating a shift or change in some kind of preferred direction. The range of task-resolution methods that can be employed is potentially limitless and continually being expanded as a result of human inventiveness and creativity. However, as a starting point, it makes sense to categorize the toolkit or menu of methods used in most counselling situations in terms of a set of very broadly defined types of activity:

- *conversation and dialogue* – the counsellor and the person seeking help talk about the issue or task and allow solutions and new understandings to emerge from their dialogue. This method relies on the vast richness of language and its potential for re-describing and re-conceptualizing events, sharing ideas and jointly developing new perspectives. Conversation, or 'just talking' is almost certainly the most frequently-used method (or 'default setting') in any counselling relationship: it can be seen as the 'default setting' for a counselling relationship.
- *using counselling skills* – there are many basic counselling skills – listening, empathic reflection, silence, counsellor self-disclosure, questions – that not only function as general enablers of a counselling process, but at specific points can make a substantial difference as change activities in their own right. For example, agreeing to allow as much silence as possible while the client tells the story of a traumatic event can represent a key element in a meaning-making task. Guided discovery questions can be used to facilitate the process of completing a decision-making task.
- *activities that expand awareness, understanding and capacity to learn from experience* – there are many counselling methods that make a difference by helping the client to develop new ways of experiencing themselves and the world. For example, mindfulness skills can be used in behaviour change tasks, such as mindful eating as a strategy for reducing binge eating. Various types of journal writing, diary keeping and video blogging can be used to document and reflect on emotions and relationship patterns. Learning new ways of making sense of experience, through psycho-education or reading, can allow a client to normalize experiences that they had previously interpreted as evidence of mental illness.

- *structured problem-focused activities* – either the counsellor or the person seeking help may suggest or devise activities or routines that can be applied to resolving the issue. Within the counselling world, cognitive behavioural therapy (CBT) in particular represents a rich resource of activities, such as relaxation training, homework assignments, initiating rewards for preferred behaviour, identifying and challenging irrational beliefs and much more. However, there are many situations in which a counsellor and client can devise their own change plan or programme, using their shared knowledge and experience.
- *arts-based creative activities* – there are many counselling tasks that can be resolved by drawing, painting, imaginative writing and enactment. For example, a person struggling to come to terms with difficult and painful emotions may find it very helpful to express their feelings in a picture or write a letter to someone with whom they feel angry.
- *cultural resources* – drawing on the everyday practices that are used within the person's cultural world to express feelings, maintain connectedness and maintain a sense of personal identity. For instance, many cultural resources that can potentially make a difference to someone who may be depressed and lacking in hope and purpose, including physical exercise such as jogging, voluntary work, talking to friends, walking in the countryside, spiritual practices such as meditation and prayer, listening to music, and attending the cinema or theatre. The role of the counsellor in relation to these methods is not to implement them within a counselling session, but to help the person to explore and find the cultural resources that are most personally meaningful, to provide support and guidance during the stage of starting to get involved and then, if necessary, to help the person to get maximum value out of the cultural activities they have undertaken in terms of making an impact on their initial problem in living.
- *the personal resources of the counsellor*. An important category of methods is the capacity of the counsellor to apply their experience of life, and personal accomplishments and learning, to address the needs of the person seeking help. Typical ways to do this are through the counsellor sharing stories from their own life or actively demonstrating how they deal with certain situations, for example, how they might use a breathing or grounding technique to manage anxiety and panic.

From a counsellor perspective, there are some key challenges associated with the effective use of change methods and therapeutic activities. It is important to be open to the suggestions of the client, in terms of both new ideas for change activities and how counsellor-initiated methods might need to be adapted to their situation. It can be hard for a counsellor to function collaboratively around this part of the counselling process because there is a tendency for the client to defer to what they see as the superior wisdom and experience of the counsellor, and because the client's own ideas might be conveyed in a diffident and tentative manner. Any indication that the client is resistant to what is being suggested by

Box 3.3 Counsellor self-disclosure: using examples from your own experience of life

An inevitable aspect of being in a helping role, and listening to a client talking about concerns and difficulties in their life, is that similar experiences from one's own life are triggered in one's own mind. It is not useful to immediately share these personal examples. While the kind of to-and-fro of 'you won't believe what just happened to me' and 'I know, I had a similar experience...' is a common (and valuable) part of everyday conversations between friends, it is generally not a good strategy in counselling. In counselling, where the aim is to focus on the client, reciprocal problem-sharing runs the risk of limiting the time that is devoted to the client's experience and possibly also shifting the balance of the encounter in the direction of the client feeling that they need to support the counsellor. On the other hand, it is also clear that in some situations it can be helpful for the counsellor to offer examples from their own life. For instance, sometimes a client may actively want to know certain bits of information about the counsellor that are relevant to their own issues, and ask questions such as 'do you have children?' or 'have you ever been depressed?'. There is also evidence from research studies that well-timed and sensitively formulated counsellor self-disclosure can be a useful method for facilitating client understanding and change, for example through conveying hope that an issue is resolvable, cementing the client-therapist bond or offering a model of how to cope with a difficult life situation. Useful summaries of relevant research, along with guidelines for the use of counsellor self-disclosure, can be found in Henretty and Levitt (2010) and in McLeod and McLeod (2022). From an embedded counselling perspective, one of the distinctive features of counsellor self-disclosure is that it is likely that the majority of clients will present broadly similar issues around a particular area of life (e.g. education, health, social care). By contrast, stand-alone counsellors and psychotherapists can be faced with client stories that relate to any and all aspects of life. What this means is that, rather than having to decide in the moment whether a personal experience might be useful for your client to hear (and then deciding at that same moment how to tell that story), practitioners of embedded counselling have the possibility of preparing and rehearsing potentially relevant personal life examples that they can bring forward as appropriate with their clients. A particularly insightful analysis and discussion of how some counsellors working with children and parents around educational issues purposefully used examples of their own educational experience, is available in a study by Mjelve et al. (2020). Similar practices have been described by practitioners working in fields such as mental health support (Mancini 2019) and eating disorder recovery (Wasil et al. 2019).

the counsellor should be treated as useful information because it implies that the client has some inkling of a better way forward. Another challenging aspect of devising and implementing change methods is to avoid inadvertently setting up opportunities for failure. For example, if a therapeutic activity is framed as a homework assignment, guidance, or a prescription, and the client is unwilling or unable to carry it out, they may end up feeling even more demoralized. It is better to talk about a change activity as a learning project, experiment or as akin to trying out a prototype. From such a perspective, if the activity or method does not have the wished-for effect, then the experience can be regarded as information that can feed in to an ongoing process of searching or building.

A further way in which using a therapy method can be challenging is that it can take the counsellor or client (or both at the same time) out of their comfort zones. On the whole, people live their lives in ways that avoid uncomfortable or threatening experiences and maximize positive and familiar experiences. This can have the result of perpetuating a self-limiting way of being in the world. For example, a person who is anxious in social situations may avoid social gatherings. Although this has the effect of maintaining a generally positive mood, it may reduce opportunities for social support or a sense of belonging. In counselling, such a person would almost certainly reach a point where accomplishing their goal of increasing their participating in social gatherings might involve such methods as cognitive rehearsal of how to handle such an event, or developing skills and strategies for managing anxiety or engaging in conversation with strangers and then applying them in real-life situations. These kinds of therapeutic activity would be likely to take them outside of their comfort zone and be experienced as scary or harrowing. The planning and designing of such activities therefore needs to involve attention to emotional safety. A lot of the time, the presence of the therapist, either in person or as an internalized image, is helpful in this respect. Another strategy is to proceed slowly, so that the client can try some new activity that is at or just beyond the edge of what they can tolerate. Or the client may be helped to develop self-soothing strategies, such as a relaxation technique or imagining being in their safe space.

Finally, when discussing methods in a counselling session, it can be useful to generate multiple options (e.g. 'you could talk about that time you had a panic attack and I will listen, or you could draw a picture of it, or I could interview you about it'). This has the effect of allowing the client to make a meaningful choice (rather than just take it or leave it) and also conveys the idea that there exist yet more possibilities that could be considered if none of the ones we have looked at so far seem useful. It is also a way of thinking that communicates a sense of hopefulness and confidence.

Being in alignment: deciding together on what to do

Having described the nature of goals, tasks and methods, and how they fit together in the process of embedded counselling, it may be worthwhile at this point to briefly review the basic assumptions about counselling and helping that underpin this approach. These are:

- the person who seeks help is already actively engaged in trying to resolve their problems.
- whatever the counsellor does, the person seeking help will modify and adapt what is offered to meet their needs – the person is far from being a passive recipient of 'expert help.'
- there is no one process or mechanism of learning and change that is right for everyone – there are a multiplicity of potentially helpful learning/change processes and each individual who seeks help will have their own preferences among them.
- there is not a counsellor alive who is competent to work with all the possible therapeutic methods and strategies that exist – each practitioner has their own knowledge base and strengths and weaknesses.

The reality of any counselling situation, therefore, is that there are multiple possibilities on both sides. There are many things that the person seeking help definitely wants, definitely does not want, and may be willing to try out. There are other things that the counsellor is either able or not able to offer. It is the job of the counsellor to be able to mediate between these two sets of possibilities. The idea of the counselling menu represents a way of arriving at a decision, within the shortest possible time, concerning what to do and where to start.

A key competence for any counsellor, therefore, is to be able to create opportunities for discussion about the range of choices that are on offer. At a broad level, this process is similar to principles of shared decision-making and co-production that are well-established and widely applied in fields such as healthcare and social care, where it is taken for granted that good practice involves making sure that clients have access to information about treatment options, have opportunities to ask questions and are given time and encouragement to arrive at a shared decision with their health or social care provider (see McLeod and McLeod, 2022, Chapter 8, and Chapter 11 of the present book). However, a counselling relationship is different in the sense that shared decision-making does not take place only at the start, but needs to permeate all stages or phases of the counselling process.

In counselling, competent and responsive shared decision-making is based on counsellor skill and self-awareness around values and use of language. The values dimension of negotiating around goals, tasks and methods is associated with the act of positioning the person as someone who is worthwhile, who knows what is best for them and whose views are worth knowing. Each opening that the counsellor makes to invite the person to say what they want is affirming these values and at the same time expressing the genuine interest, caring and curiosity that the counsellor holds towards that person. By contrast, every time that the counsellor pre-empts a decision about what is to happen in the counselling session, no matter how sensitively and 'nicely' this is done, it places the counsellor at an 'I know best' position, which negates these values.

Examples of language use that can contribute to shared decision-making are:

- *explaining how you work as a counsellor.* For example: 'I'd like to say a few words about the way I work as a counsellor. Would it be OK to do that now – I don't want to interrupt anything you might be going to say. The main thing for me is that we are on the same wavelength and that we agree on what you want to get from counselling and the best way to go about achieving what you want. Does that make sense? Sometimes what I need to do, therefore, is to just check in with you that we both understand what we are doing at that point. Would that be OK?'
- *explaining basic principles.* 'In my experience as a counsellor, I have found that different people need different things from me. Some people want me to listen, other people want me to give them feedback and so on. It's really important for me that this counselling is right for you. At any time, if you feel that what we're doing is not helping, then I would want you to let me know so we can change what we're doing and get things right for you.'
- *asking the person about how they perceive goals, tasks and methods.* For example: 'You have told me a bit about your problems. I'd like to ask you – what is it that you want to get from counselling? What's your aim or goal?'; 'I feel I have a pretty good idea of what you want to get from counselling. To get there, we need to take things step by step. At this point, do you have an idea of what you feel you need to do first?'; 'You've talked quite a lot about feeling angry. Would that be something we could spend a bit of time looking at now? I guess that there are different ways we could look at this. Do you want to shout, or hit that cushion, or something else – what do you feel would be the best way for us to approach this right now?'
- *checking out that the person's goal, task or method statement has been understood.* For example, 'Can I just check this out – what you are saying is that what you want to do now is....'
- *inviting the person to identify what has worked for them in the past.* "When you have felt stuck with an angry feeling before, is there anything that has helped you to deal with it? Is that something that is relevant for what we might do now?'
- *following the completion of a task, checking whether what happened was helpful.* 'We have spent a few minutes now talking through that issue about getting closer to people. We seem to have reached the end point of that, at least for the moment. Before we go on to look at some of the other issues you mentioned earlier, I'd just like to ask – was the way we approached that helpful? Is there anything that I could have done, or that you could have done, that would be more helpful?'

Box 3.4 Metacommunication: a crucial skill in relation to being able to work together in counselling

In counselling, it is essential for the helper and client to be in alignment with each other – to be thinking along the same lines, to be heading in the same direction, to have a shared understanding of the final destination and how to get there. A key skill for maintaining alignment is standing back from the immediate flow of conversation and interaction between the person and the counsellor and reflecting on what is happening. This activity can be understood as 'metacommunication' – communicating and reflecting on the process of communication and the state of the relationship. A capacity to engage in metacommunication is a crucial aspect of collaborative working. The nature of metacommunication can be illustrated by considering the usual shape and content of a conversation between a person and their counsellor. Most of the time in a counselling situation, both the person seeking help and the counsellor talk about the person's 'problem'. For example, a woman talking about her relationship with her teenage daughter might say, 'We just argue all the time. There doesn't seem to be anything we can do together that doesn't end up in a battle.'

The person offering counselling – who could be a teacher, nurse or social worker – might reply by saying, 'That sounds really frustrating... It's as though there is a real barrier between you...' And the person seeking help might then go on to say more about other aspects of this issue. In this example, the focus of the conversation is on the problem that has been identified by the person and the counsellor's response has the effect of continuing and possibly deepening the client's exploration of that issue. This is probably the kind of conversation that happens most frequently in counselling encounters – the counsellor acts as a kind of sounding board, and reflects back to the person the main threads of what he or she has been exploring, in a way that helps him or her to expand on the issue and gain some perspective on it. In addition to this kind of reflective response, it can be useful for a counsellor to build into their conversational repertoire the careful and consistent use of a slightly different way of responding to the person – using metacommunication to 'check out' whether the conversation is heading in the right direction or whether a change of direction might be necessary. So, in the case of the mother talking about difficulties with her teenage daughter, the counsellor might say, 'I can see that the situation with your daughter is important for you. But I'd just like to check whether that is the main priority for you in the time we have this morning, or if there may be other concerns that are also important for you or maybe even more urgent.' The process of checking out introduces important possibilities for conveying value and affirmation to the person and building the

> kind of relationship within which difficult issues can be explored safely. It can also have the effect of slowing down the interaction in a way that allows the person some opportunities to reflect on the feelings and thoughts that they are experiencing at that moment. Metacommunicative checking out basically involves pausing within the flow of the conversation to test out assumptions about what is happening or to inquire about the assumptions or the experience at that moment of the person who is seeking help. Rennie (1998) has described this activity as 'talking about the process of talking'. Further discussion of this skill can be found in McLeod and McLeod (2022).

The purpose of such statements is to punctuate the ongoing flow of the counselling conversation with brief opportunities where the person seeking help and their counsellor can re-orient themselves in relation to the person's goals and remain on track. The sentences and phrases used in the examples given above should not, of course, be regarded as a fixed 'script' to be followed by all counsellors – as with everything else in counselling, it is important for the practitioner to develop their own style that allows them to come across in a natural and genuine manner.

An example of goals, methods and tasks in action

Joey is a long-term prisoner nearing the end of a sentence for violent robbery. During his time in prison, Joey has experienced several episodes of what the medical officer has termed as 'depression' and has made several attempts to take his own life. In his current prison, there is a well-established peer counselling service, in which prisoners can be trained to provide emotional support to others. Joey has formed a good relationship with one of the peer helpers, who has spent many hours listening to Joey's story of a childhood lacking in love, care and consistency. It has been very important to Joey to learn that there could be someone who was able to accept him and like him, even when they knew about some of the things he had done. Although Joey and his peer counsellor had never explicitly agreed on the goals of their work, each of them knew that what Joey wanted was to know that he could be acceptable as a person, particularly in respect of his emotions and feelings. After many of these sessions, the helper observed that Joey seemed to talk in a way that was 'just full of pain'. There was an extended silence, broken eventually by Joey's admission that he felt an emotional pain all the time, but believed that it was not what 'a man' should do to admit this, or even worse to express it.

'I can't afford to lose control – look what can happen when I do,' Joey said.

The helper responded by saying, 'This is where we have got to – I'm wondering whether this pain is the next thing for us to look at.'

Over their next meetings, Joey and his helper worked together to find some ways that Joey could express his pain within their counselling sessions. Once they had made some progress with this, Joey announced that he could see that he needed to figure out how to let his wife know about his pain.

'She knows there is something wrong, but I never tell her what it is – its keeping us apart. When she visits, sometimes I just sit there in silence because I can't speak. Who knows what she thinks is going on?'

This triggered a new focus for the next counselling sessions – how Joey communicated with his wife and what he could do differently.

Having decided that 'the pain' was something that they would look at together, Joey and his helper talked about how to set about this difficult and demanding task. At first, Joey could not think of anything at all that he could do to express what he felt. His helper made a list of activities that he had personally tried himself and some that he had read about. These included: finding the part of the body where the feeling was located; making a drawing; writing a poem; working through a self-help book about emotions; keeping an emotion diary; and 'just talking about it'. Joey was worried about any activity that involved writing things down on paper, because he did not think he had the capacity to keep pieces of paper private. He was worried that any overt expression of emotion could lead to him being sent to the psychiatric unit. He said he would think about the suggestions between sessions. At the next meeting with his helper, he brought a piece of paper and a pencil and began, silently, to write from his pain – 'I am inside. I am crushed…' At the end of their meeting he carefully tore the piece of paper into very small pieces. At the next session, he talked about how he had allowed the pain to be in control during a workout in the prison gym. Some weeks later, he enrolled for an art class and made clay sculptures of pain. Gradually, he found his own way to do what he needed to do.

This example emphasizes the improvisational nature of counselling. Joey and his peer helper were not operating in an ideal environment, in terms of the level of privacy that was available to them. In addition, the peer helper was aware that he had relatively little training and experience in working with the type of issue that Joey was presenting. Nevertheless, between them they were able to talk about what they could do and find a way forward. The case therefore also exemplifies the basic resourcefulness of people. The counselling that Joey received was life-changing for him (and possibly also life-saving), in spite of the limited training and experience of his counsellor. He and the counsellor had a relationship that was strong enough to cope together until they could discover a method that would work for them.

This example illustrates two counselling tasks that frequently occur in counselling – *dealing with feelings and emotion* and *changing behaviour* – and describes a range of different methods that were used to achieve these tasks. Each of the tasks undertaken by Joey involved using the secure space provided by the relationship with a counsellor to deal with an issue arising from a difficulty within the person's social niche or life space. For instance, the world that

Joey lived in had silenced him in relation to a bundle of emotions that he came to describe as his 'pain'. And the way that he had learned to communicate with his wife no longer reflected the values that he wished to espouse in his family life. His discussions with his helper-counsellor allowed him an opportunity to reflect on what was happening in his life in relation to these issues and develop strategies for doing things differently in future.

Being on the alert for things going wrong

In an 'ideal' counselling conversation, which rarely happens, a person will explore an issue with the help of the counsellor, will arrive at a new understanding or plan of action, will learn something useful about him/herself and will leave happy. Alas, there are many things that can happen to disrupt this ideal script. For example, there can be a breakdown, rupture or falling-out in the counselling relationship, the person may become suicidal or a risk to others, the person may have a panic attack or other situations may arise that cut across any attempt to make progress around basic counselling tasks. An important competency in any counselling situation, therefore, involves routinely monitoring what is happening and knowing what to do if some kind of crisis occurs. At such moments, the counsellor may need to interrupt the ongoing flow of the counselling dialogue, for example to check on issues of client safety. An ongoing task of counselling, therefore, involves monitoring the interaction and conversation, in order to become aware of any possible threats to the integrity of the counselling space. If any such threats come to light, it is necessary for the person and the counsellor to review the situation together and decide what action might be needed to change, strengthen or repair the space or to look for sources of help outside of the counselling relationship that might be called upon. These issues are discussed in McLeod and McLeod (2022, Chapter 15).

Conclusions

The model of counselling goals, tasks and methods described in this chapter is equally appropriate for situations in which the helper and person may have a relatively short period of time in which to talk through a problem and for contexts in which it is possible to meet on a regular basis. If a practitioner is only able to offer 10 or 20 minutes to a person, it may still be perfectly possible to make substantial progress on a specific counselling task within that timescale. Also, if there can only be a relatively brief contact, it is much safer for a person to agree or contract to engage in a specific task ('let's look at what these feelings are telling you', 'would it be useful to try to get a sense of all the information that might be relevant to making a decision about this issue?') than to attempt to engage in a discussion around major life goals.

The process of identifying and agreeing goals, tasks and methods within a counselling session provides a series of opportunities for dialogue and joint decision-making between the counsellor and the person seeking help. It is definitely *not* the intention of this chapter to imply that the counsellor should adopt an expert stance in which he or she diagnoses and then prescribes the goals, tasks and methods that he or she deems appropriate to an individual client – not at all! As far as possible, there should be a rhythm of turn-taking in which both parties are involved in moving back and forward between leading and following. Key skills of any counsellor lie in being able to 'hit the pause button', to suspend the ongoing flow of what the client is saying, at the right moments, so that goals, tasks and methods can be discussed and agreed and in having a sufficiently wide repertoire of methods (and awareness of the how they can be applied to particular counselling tasks) to allow the maximum degree of client choice. It is essential to keep in mind, also, that all this takes place in the context of a relationship between the counsellor and the person with whom they are working. The counselling relationship, and the tasks of counselling, need to be viewed as two sides of the same coin. It is possible, it is possible to define the strength and quality of the relationship between the counsellor and the person in terms of the extent to which they are able to communicate effectively with each other around goals, tasks and methods, their capacity to arrive at a shared agreement over which goals, tasks and methods to pursue and their joint resourcefulness and creativity in imagining possible methods that might be helpful.

Further information on the approach to counselling outlined in this chapter can be found in McLeod (2018, 2019) and McLeod and McLeod (2020).

Learning activities

The following activities may be explored individually and/or with a group of learning partners.

Exercise 3.1 Finding the right way to talk about preferences and choices
In this chapter, the image or metaphor of the counselling 'menu' is used to characterize a situation in which a client has a capacity to choose and the person providing a service needs to be clear about what is on offer. There are other metaphors that might be employed equally well. The options for counselling could be described as 'on display in a shop window', or as a 'repertoire', 'toolkit' or 'palette'. The counsellor might talk in terms of using different 'modes of transport to take a journey'. Each metaphor that might be used introduces certain underlying or hidden assumptions. For example, a menu may imply nourishment, a shop window may imply payment and so on. Are there other images or metaphors that come to mind for you? Which images or metaphors feel right to you, in terms of conversations that you might conduct with clients? It can be instructive to carry out this exercise in a group – a greater number of images is likely to be generated, and you can try them out on each other by short interactions where one takes the role of client with another group members as client.

Exercise 3.2 Reflecting on your own experience of goals
Take a few minutes to reflect on occasions in your life where you have been a client in some kind of counselling. How clear were you about what you wanted from counselling and what your goals were? To what extent, and in what ways, did these goals shift over the course of counselling? What did your counsellor do to help you to clarify your goals and to check whether he/she understood what your goals were? What have you learned from this exercise that is relevant for your practice as a counsellor?

Exercise 3.3 Reviewing your competence as a counsellor
What's on your menu? What can you offer as a counsellor? Make a list of the counselling goals, tasks and methods that you are familiar with, and have had experience of, at this point in your career as a counsellor. This list can include goals, tasks and methods that you have used in a counselling role, as well as those that you have encountered when seeking help yourself. What are the 'special' items on your menu – with which goals, tasks and methods do you feel most comfortable? What are the gaps on your menu? What are the goals, tasks and methods that you would like to know more about?

CHAPTER 4
Ethical principles for embedded counselling

Introduction	67
Examples of ethical dilemmas in embedded counselling	69
Core ethical principles	70
Ethical practice in embedded counselling	72
Negotiating informed consent	73
Confidentiality	75
Being aware of the limits of your competence	76
Dual relationships	78
Sensitivity to cultural differences	80
Dealing with risk and self-harm	81
Using touch	83
Conclusions	85
Learning activities	86

Introduction

The ethical and moral basis of professional practice represents an area of enquiry and debate that is massively significant in health and social care, education and other professional contexts. In any of these settings, practitioners hold confidential information about clients and service users and have the power to make decisions or recommendations that can fundamentally change a person's life. At the same time, service user groups, sections of the legal profession, some politicians and other stakeholders, such as insurance companies, can be vigorous and unrelenting in pursuing the claims of clients who have been treated negligently or unfairly. Over and above the application of professional power and control, and client resistance to that power, there is the complexity of moral discourse in contemporary society. At times it appears as though there is hardly any agreed basis for making decisions about what is right or wrong – all moral judgement seems to be open to argument.

A counselling relationship can be viewed as an arena that calls for continuous vigilance around ethical issues. By definition, the client in a counselling conversation is speaking from a place of vulnerability. Implicit in the way that a client or service user describes their problem, or the counsellor formulates a potential solution to that problem, are multiple assumptions around values and about how the 'good life' is understood. On the whole, counselling theory, research and practice has been reticent about exploring ethical and moral issues. All counselling professional associations have produced their own ethical codes, which specify rules of conduct for counselling practitioners. Those who are teachers, nurses or social workers and whose counselling is embedded in such a primary role are similarly guided by their own professional codes. It is assumed that practitioner readers of this book will be familiar with such guidelines. The aim of the present chapter, therefore, is not to re-visit what is already known, in the sense of having been covered in initial practitioner training, or to provide information that can be readily accessed through relevant websites. Instead, it concentrates on the ethical dilemmas that arise in the course of applying counselling skills in what might be regarded as a border area between the territory of primary professions, such as nursing or social work, and the territory of specialist professional counselling.

Embedded counselling presents ethical issues that may be particularly challenging for human services practitioners. In professions such as nursing, medicine and social work, practitioners may be faced with highly sensitive ethical decisions, which may be linked to life or death issues such as taking a child into care or withholding treatment from a patient. However, in these contexts ethical dilemmas can usually be discussed within a team over a period of time. By contrast, ethical issues in counselling can often arise in the moment and in a situation in which other colleagues may not have access to the same amount of information about the client. Also, making the wrong call around an ethical issue can utterly undermine the counselling relationship.

Following a brief exploration of some examples of ethical dilemmas, this chapter provides an overview of ethical principles that inform practice in this area. A series of specific ethical issues are then highlighted.

An introduction to ethical decision-making skills and strategies for practitioners of embedded counselling can be found in the companion text on counselling skills (McLeod and McLeod 2022). A broader discussion of ethical issues encountered by counsellors and psychotherapists can be found in McLeod (2019). There are close links between ethical aspects of embedded counselling practice and the quality of organizational support and preparedness that is available to practitioners – topics that are explored in Chapter 5 of the present book.

Examples of ethical dilemmas in embedded counselling

Grania is a nurse who has been providing emotional support for some time, to James, a patient who has a long-term health condition and who has needed to talk about how the illness has affected his image of himself as someone who took care of others in his family. He brings in an expensive gift. He knows that the gift is something that Grania would like and he knows that she is aware that he would know this. In responding to her patient, Grania is open about her pleasure in being offered this gift and also her difficulty, as a practitioner bound by health service rules, in being able to accept the gift without consulting her line manager and supervisor. She encourages James to share his feelings around the gift-giving and her response. They agree that Grania will consult on the question of the gift and that they will discuss it further at their next meeting. Grania believes that the gift may be an expression of a strong wish on the part of James to be the caretaker and provider and reflects on how and when (and whether) it would be useful to explore that idea with him.

Ian is a community support worker who has been offering counselling support to a service user who has a serious medical condition and who needs help in relation to basic self-case tasks such as cooking and shopping. Ian has a similar medical problem himself. At the start of his contact with this person, he decided not to mention his own health problem to his client. However, he is now finding it extremely difficult to carry on with the counselling, because what his client is talking about reminds him of his own pain, despair and frustration associated with this medical condition and he keeps wanting to cry during sessions. Ian regrets not being open about his situation from the start, but imagines that it would be overwhelming for his client if he now began to share his own experience. As a means of coping with what is happening, Ian manufactures a rationale for handing the care of this person over to a colleague. The client is mystified about what has happened and feels rejected.

Sadiq is a social worker providing family support to a female client with mental health problems, mainly in relation to making sure that she was able to ensure that her children attended school regularly and that their everyday needs were catered for. At one point, this client was faced with a crisis in terms of the payment of her welfare benefits and needed someone to speak up for her at a tribunal. Although his manager decided that this task was not part of his role, Sadiq judged that any failure to put the case effectively to the tribunal, leading to reduction in the family's weekly income, would have a disastrous effect on his client's well-being and mental health. He accompanied his client to the meeting and 'just didn't tell anybody'.

Miranda is a youth worker attached to a secondary school. The school has a specialist counsellor and has a rule that any child under 16 needs to have parental permission to receive counselling. Miranda has just finished a group workshop on relationship skills for a class of 15-year-old children. At the end, one of the students, Kaya, comes up to her and launches into the story of her problems. When asked about whether she has considered using the specialist school counsellor, Kaya says that her parents had not given her permission to see the actual school counsellor, 'So I chose to speak to you instead.' Miranda acknowledges the difficult situation that Kaya finds herself in and talks for a few moments about the reason why parental approval is necessary. She asks Kaya if she would be willing to tell her what happened when she asked for her parents' approval and whether it would be helpful if Miranda perhaps met with her parents and Kaya together to review the situation.

These dilemmas illustrate the potential complexity of situations that may be ethically problematic in embedded counselling. In each case, the person seeking help was trying to get what they needed, but did so in a way that turned out to present their counsellor with an ethical dilemma. The task for these counsellors was to find a way to acknowledge and resolve the dilemma, while at the same time maintaining an ongoing counselling relationship with the person. In each case, the ethical dilemma and the counselling process were intertwined – there was no straightforward solution in either direction. These scenarios also illustrate the importance of being prepared. In the case of Ian, lack of foresight (either being open with the client or handing the client over to a colleague at the start) created a situation that just got harder to deal with the longer time went on.

Core ethical principles

The moral and ethical basis for the practice of any form of counselling can be expressed in different ways. At one level, the ethics of counselling is grounded in a common-sense appreciation of what is the 'right' thing to do, in terms of supporting another human being who is struggling or suffering. From a more reflective perspective, it is clear that counselling is informed by a set of core *values*, such as respect, appreciation of the irreplaceable uniqueness of each person and belief in a person's capacity to develop and learn. These values are reflected in an array of personal *virtues*, such as honesty and integrity, that characterize practitioners who aspire to the highest standards.

Counselling is also informed by 'ethical principles' that underpin the ethical codes found in all health and caring professions. Key ethical principles include:

- *autonomy*. People are understood as individuals who have the right to freedom of action and freedom of choice, in so far as the pursuit of these freedoms does not interfere with the freedoms of others.
- *beneficence*. The intention to promote human welfare. This principle also encompasses *non-maleficence* – the injunction to all helpers or healers that they must 'above all do no harm'.
- *social justice*. The fair and equitable distribution of, and access to, resources and services. Ensuring that human rights are respected; actively seeking to reduce exclusion and oppression.

Each of these principles can be seen as reflecting a commitment to act in good faith and as a model or exemplar of how people are expected to treat each other. Someone who is a member of a recognized profession can be viewed as being mandated by the wider society to carry out tasks that call for personal integrity. Entry into a professional role therefore implies willingness to fulfil a duty of care, in the sense of putting the client's needs before one's own.

A further set of ethical principles refer to the fact that counselling, and any type of emotional support and human solidarity, depends on the existence of a relationship. The ethical dimension of relationships is associated with qualities such as trust, caring, honesty and humility (Birrell and Bruns 2016; Gabriel and Casemore 2009; Jennings et al. 2005).

Important aspects of the work done by practitioners are subject to regulatory control in the form of legal statutes and ethical codes administered by professional bodies. Examples include laws regarding secure storage of personal data, sexual exploitation of children and vulnerable adults, and professional requirements regarding commitment to maintaining competence (e.g. regular attendance at CPD events, use of supervision).

These ethical values and principles need to be acted upon. Banks (2016) uses the term 'ethics work' to describe an ongoing process of ensuring that the delivery of care and other services is conducted in a moral, ethical, fair and just manner. She suggests that ethics work consists of a set of key features:

- framing work: identifying and focusing on the ethical aspects of situations
- role work: being an advocate, carer, critic and negotiating professional roles and relationships from an ethical perspective
- emotion work: being caring, compassionate and empathic and being willing and able to acknowledge and manage strong emotions associated with ethical dilemmas
- identity work: negotiating and maintaining an ethically-grounded professional identity

> **Box 4.1 The experience of moral distress**
>
> The concept of moral injury has emerged in recent years as a means of making sense of the effect on individuals of acting in ways that violate their moral beliefs or observing such actions in others (Litz et al. 2009). There is considerable evidence that moral injury can be experienced by human service practitioners who are expected to work: in situations in which they are not able to provide adequate care to patients and service users, for example because of low staffing levels due to financial constraints (Day et al. 2021). Such scenarios generate moral distress in the form of a range of emotional and physical symptoms (Morley et al. 2019a, 2019b, 2021).

- reasoning work: thinking-through (with others) ethically challenging scenarios, arriving at practical solutions and being able to explain and justify ethical decisions
- relationship work: engaging in dialogue with others around ethical issues
- performance work: being accountable, standing up for what one believes is right.

These various types of ethics work are expressed not only in relation to routine procedures, such as ensuring that client confidentiality is respected, but are also called upon when a practitioner finds themselves in a position of deciding to resist organizational rules and requirements that deny the humanity and needs of clients (Weinberg and Banks 2019) or engaging in 'moral entrepreneurship' around initiating change to organizational systems (Shdaimah and McGarry 2018).

Ethical practice in embedded counselling

Police officers are required to operate not only within the law, but within pre-determined procedures for handling particular situations. However, in relation to dealing with situations in which individuals with mental health problems are creating a disturbance, or have been the subject of complaints from neighbours or bystanders, officers can been seen as functioning in a 'grey zone' in which they need to strike a balance between administering justice and pragmatic emotional support and problem-solving that takes account of individual needs in a compassionate manner (Wood et al. 2017). There are occasions when a person may have committed an offence that could be prosecuted, but officers decide that a better course of action would be to assist them to access a relevant local service such as a mental health crisis centre. In such situations, it is possible to analyse the relevance of multiple ethical principles and work out what would be the best compromise. For instance, *justice* might imply that everyone should be treated equally in the eyes of the law, whereas, *caring* and *beneficence* might lead to the conclusion that an individual with longstanding mental health problems would only be made worse by being made to spend a night in a cell. But that is not how it works in practice – busy police officers do not have time to engage in detailed ethical reflection at an incident scene. What they need is to be guided by discussions that have already taken place, regarding what is acceptable within a particular police department, and agreement around how frontline officers can share information and decision-making with other professional stakeholders such as social workers and mental health colleagues.

The example of the kind of shared ethical understanding and pre-planning that is necessary for police who provide emotional support and interpersonal problem-solving was chosen because it is relatively clear-cut and is a situation with which most of us are broadly familiar, on account of watching police procedural crime dramas on television. However, similar anticipatory ethical conversations need to take place in any professional context where practitioners are intending to offer embedded counselling to clients.

A particularly useful resource, in relation to such negotiations, is the extensive and comprehensive literature on ethical issues arising in social work practice, a field that encompasses many different forms of intervention (see, for example, Banks 2020; Marson and McKinney Jr 2019). There is also much that can be learned from the analysis of ethical dilemmas associated with crisis support, available in Myer et al. (2021). By contrast – while also relevant – the literature on ethical issues in counselling and psychotherapy tends to focus more intensively on ethical issues associated with situations in which there is an exclusively therapeutic relationship (Corey et al. 2021; Jenkins 2017; Reeves and Bond 2021).

The following sections indicate some of the topics that might need to be addressed in conversations within organizations around ethics associated with how practitioners respond to emotional difficulties and problems in living expressed by clients.

Negotiating informed consent

When someone is seeking help, before the actual counselling commences it is the ethical responsibility of the counsellor to ensure that the person is sufficiently informed about what is on offer, what is involved and alternative types of help or care that might be available. In some situations, such as a patient receiving a surgical intervention or when an individual has been invited to take part in a research study, a formal consent process is employed that involves written information sheets and signing a consent record. Although it is not feasible to obtain documented consent in relation to all decisions made within busy routine practice, it is still important to do as much as possible to ensure that a client is fully appraised of what they are being offered, has sufficient opportunity to think about their response, is able to ask questions, and at the end of the day is free to say 'no'.

Examples of conversations around informed consent:

> Alicia, 15, attends a youth club and likes and trusts the community education worker who runs the club. One evening, when the club is quiet, she starts to talk about her problems at school. The youth worker says that she is very happy to talk about these issues, but that Alicia needs to know that she is only around one evening each week and so she cannot guarantee that they could talk every week. She checks out how Alicia feels about this and whether she might prefer it if the youth worker helped her to make an appointment at a local young person's counselling service.
>
> His GP suspects that Mike, an unemployed man who has visited regularly with a variety of physical ailments, is bottling up a lot of feelings about how his life has worked out but is afraid that other people might see how vulnerable he is. At one consultation, he suggests to Mike that it might be helpful if they took a bit more time to look at what was going on in his life that might be making him feel bad. He adds, 'Of course, there could be things that are upsetting to talk about. Maybe you would want to think about whether you want to go into these things right now. Sometimes it can be better to make an appointment at the end of my afternoon clinic, when the place is quiet and we can have more time. What do you think? It's up to you.'
>
> Elsa starts to tell her social worker about why she has taken her children out of the family home and moved in with her mother. Before Elsa gets into her stride, the social worker intervenes to say, 'I know you know this, but I'm just reminding you that if you tell me anything that's around harm to any of the children, I would have to do something. I don't have any choice about that. I'm really happy to talk all this through with you – we've got at least an hour if we need it – but any abuse or harm has to be reported. Is that OK?'

In these examples, the practitioner in an embedded counselling role is providing the person seeking help with the information that they need in order to make an autonomous decision about whether they want to proceed or not. In each instance, the counsellor was acting on the basis of an assumption that the person already possessed a reasonably good understanding of counselling and knew what they were looking for. There are some occasions where this would not be the case and a counsellor might need to take more time to tell a person what was involved in counselling, to the point where that person was capable of making a truly informed choice.

It is useful to see informed consent as a process. A client or service user may not fully appreciate what is involved in accepting an offer of help at the point when the offer is first made. It can be valuable to check out, at later points in the helping process, whether the person is still comfortable with what is happening.

Confidentiality

Confidentiality is a central aspect of counselling. The counselling process depends on the person feeling sufficiently safe to be able to talk openly and honestly about whatever it is that is bothering him or her. By contrast, if someone believes that what they say will end up as a topic for gossip, or will be used against them in some way, they are unlikely to engage in much meaningful self-disclosure. However, confidentiality can never be absolute. It is important for a counsellor to make use of supervision and consultation to maintain and ensure the effectiveness of the support they are providing for clients – this process necessarily involves conveying information to a third party (even though information that might allow the identity of the client to be known would usually be omitted). In addition, in exceptional circumstances, the legal system has the right to require any practitioner to pass on information that they have acquired within a professional relationship.

An almost obsessive concern about confidentiality is part of the training and professional socialization of counsellors and psychotherapists. Being a counsellor involves developing a capacity to store client information in separate 'boxes' in one's mind, and only to open each of these boxes when required to do so. This aspect of the role of counsellor is much more problematic in embedded counselling situations, where the practitioner will almost certainly be a member of a team that shares information and operates collectively. Their colleagues and organizational systems would usually operate on an expectation that all information about a client will be shared across a team or in a central file. The practice of embedded counselling therefore involves coming to a working agreement with colleagues and managers around what kinds of information need to be shared and kept on file and what can remain confidential to the counsellor. In some embedded counselling situations, it may make sense for colleagues to know that a client is using a particular worker as a person to talk to or even to know that certain issues are being talked about. But it may not be necessary for them to know the precise content of these talks. For instance, a client's notes may record that they are depressed, but not that this is due to the fact that they have been a victim of sexual violence. However, there is a lack of research evidence about how confidentiality around personal issues disclosed by clients is handled in different work settings.

It is a mistake to assume that a client will always want everything that they say to an embedded counsellor to be treated as confidential. There are many situations in which a client may assume that, by talking to one member of staff, they are in effect letting the whole team know about their situation. For example, a college student who uses their tutor to explore the impact of a bereavement may assume that other tutors on the course would be told about this issue and would as a result be sensitive to their emotional vulnerability at that time.

Part of the skill of being an embedded counsellor includes being able to choose the right moment to inform a client about confidentiality boundaries that

> **Box 4.2 Implications of informed consent for the effectiveness of counselling**
>
> There is a growing appreciation within the professional counselling and psychotherapy community that attention to informed consent has implications beyond the essential function of respecting the rights and autonomy of the client. Effective counselling requires the active involvement of the client, for example in relation to making suggestions about how the procedures being offered by the counsellor might be adjusted to their own needs and preferences. This is only possible if the client understands the counsellor's rationale for the therapeutic activities – even simple processes such as empathic listening – that they are using (Blease et al. 2018; Trachsel 2019). The more transparent the counsellor is about the way they work, and their reasons for exploring certain topics rather than others, the more the client will be able to invest their own energy and imagination in the change process (Blease et al. 2020).

may be relevant. From the point of view of respecting client autonomy, it is best to do this as early as possible in the conversation. However, if time is tight, or a client is upset, it can seem awkward and insensitive to deflect the client from talking about their troubles by initiating a discussion of confidentiality.

It can be useful in some embedded counselling situations (e.g. when an organization has set up a support group or listening service for a specific set of clients) to have written information about confidentiality, in a leaflet or on a website, to which the client can be directed. But even if such information is available, it is still necessary to ask the client if they have read and understood it and have any questions. Brief discussions around confidentiality can contribute to a strengthening of the counselling relationship and counsellor-client 'alliance' if they allow the client to gain an appreciation of the professionalism of the counsellor and a sense of being cared about. These discussions also have a preventative value – misunderstandings about confidentiality, or perceived breaches, that arise later in counselling can be very destructive. Many individuals who seek emotional support from a practitioner (such as a social worker, teacher or nurse) they have learned to trust, have personal histories characterized by relationships where they have been abused, manipulated, and lied to (Birrell et al. 2017). The experience of opening up to a professional helper, and then having one's privacy violated, can be experienced as a profound betrayal.

Being aware of the limits of your competence

The ethical injunctions to do good and avoid harm are closely linked to the question of counsellor competence. For example, there are many people who work in educational, health and social services jobs who get to know clients who have had experiences of sexual or emotional abuse in childhood. Sometimes, the practitioner may feel a strong urge to help the person by listening to their story and perhaps trying to help them to come to terms with what has happened. This is a very caring response, which may in many situations be appropriate, but there are also times when it may not represent the best possible course of action. If a person has been assaulted in childhood, the resulting sense of lack of trust, and perhaps self-hatred, may permeate many aspects of their life. Talking through all of that may take a long time, may involve strong emotions and requires a great deal of persistence and consistency on the part of the helper or counsellor. Any nurse or other practitioner faced with such a situation needs to consider whether they are capable, in terms of the time they can give, their confidence and competence as a counsellor and their capacity to access their own emotional support if they are personally affected by hearing the client's story. Starting a supportive relationship with a client and then pulling back clearly has the potential for hurt. At the same time, ignoring what the client has said about their abuse for fear of 'getting in over my head' also has the potential to be damaging for a client.

A further set of issues around counsellor competence arise from what might be described as 'temporary impairment'. For example, a counsellor who has recently experienced the loss of a close family member is unlikely to be much help to someone with a bereavement issue. A counsellor who is burnt out, stressed or tired is unlikely to be in a good position to offer ongoing emotional support to their clients.

Implementation of the ethical requirement to operate within the limits of one's competence is not a straightforward matter. For example, it can be difficult to know whether one is able to handle the emotional demands of supporting a person with a trauma background until some kind of initial conversation has unfolded. It can be difficult to know when a corner has been turned following a phase of personal emotional burnout and depletion and one is ready again to be responsive to client suffering. There are two key strategies that need to be in place. Being aware of one's limits as a counsellor is much easier when the practitioner uses regular supervision or consultancy support and there is someone who is close enough to the counsellor to challenge their attempt to be heroic rather than helpful. The other strategy is to build and maintain a network of potential referral possibilities (i.e. other individuals, groups and organizations who might be able to help a client) and to let the client know from the outset that these other services are available and might at some point be options to which it might be sensible to give close consideration. A crucial touchstone in all aspects of embedded counselling is to avoid 'either/or' assumptions (for instance: '*either* I support this patient *or* they are left handling this issue on their own'; '*either* I work with this student *or* I have to advise them to go to the medical centre'). It is better, instead, to operate from a 'both/and', 'as well as' or 'with' perspective that promotes the idea that problems are best solved by drawing on as many sources of support as possible.

Dual relationships

Much of the theory, literature and training that informs contemporary counselling practice takes it for granted that the counsellor and the person seeking help are or should be, strangers. Underpinning this view is the idea that the quality of the client-counsellor relationship, in terms of trust and confidentiality, is of paramount importance and that any contamination of that relationship with other kinds of ties should be avoided at all costs. This approach has the advantage of creating a pure kind of counsellor-client relationship, in which all that the counsellor knows about the person is what they say during their weekly session and the person can feel secure that whatever they say in counselling is safely and securely insulated from the rest of their life. Although this kind of formulation is neat and elegant, it flies in the face of several different types of 'dual relationship' situations in which counselling may occur:

- rural communities, where everyone knows everyone else
- self-contained sub-cultures within urban areas (e.g. lesbian, gay, bisexual and transgender communities, or groups of people who share a particular religious affiliation) where people choose to see counsellors who share their own values and lifestyle within a relatively restricted social network
- residential therapeutic communities where counsellors and clients may live and work together.

Although there exist many examples of counselling being delivered effectively within a dual role relationship, anyone with experience of providing counselling within such a setting knows that taking care around role boundaries is nevertheless absolutely essential. After all, there would be no one who would claim that counselling could reasonably take place between close family members, such as a husband and wife or parent and child. The crucial moral and ethical factor that represents the biggest challenge for any counselling dual relationship lies in the principle that counselling must be *in the interests of the person/client*. When the counsellor has some other kind of involvement with the person, it is necessary to be alert to any possibility that the counsellor might be responding on the basis of what would be right *for them* (i.e. the counsellor), rather than what would be right for the client. The recognition that it is feasible to carry out ethical and effective therapy in the context of a dual relationship has resulted in a reappraisal of this issue in recent years (see Zur 2021 for a comprehensive review of this literature). Moleski and Kiselica (2005) have introduced the useful concept of a 'continuum' of dual/complex client-counsellor relationships, ranging from the therapeutic to the destructive.

The issue of dual relationships is of particular importance in embedded counselling, because the helper is fulfilling different roles. For example, a probation officer may have the task of monitoring the behaviour of an offender living in the community, which could lead to re-imprisonment, and at the same time be trying to help the person to talk about his history of abuse or sexual identity issues. A nurse on a busy hospital ward may be under pressure to administer medication to 20 patients while knowing that one of these patients needs more of her time to talk about their fear of dying. A patient may become confused about where they stand in relation to their nurse – is this a time when I can talk about how I feel, or is it just another ward round? Who am I speaking to right now – the empathic listener or the task-driven health professional?

In embedded counselling, it is therefore essential to be as clear as possible about what is happening at different times as different roles are activated. The ethical principle of autonomy requires that clients should be informed at all times and able to make choices. The principle of avoidance of harm requires that shifting back and forward between roles does not frustrate or disappoint the client or result in breaches of confidentiality ('I thought that when I said these things, it was part of the counselling, and no one else would need to know…'). Addressing these issues effectively involves being open to discussing and reviewing them with clients on a regular basis, being willing to be flexible around the kind of boundaries and contracts that are appropriate in each case and making use of supervision and consultation.

When considering the issue of dual relationships in embedded counselling, it is obviously necessary to be mindful of potential risks. For even the most experienced practitioners of embedded counselling in educational or health and social care settings, there will always be some clients who need very clear-cut boundaries and as a consequence are better referred to a specialist counsellor, psychologist or psychotherapist. By contrast, there are other clients will see it as an advantage to be able to engage in counselling conversations with helpers who are close at hand and part of a care system with which they are already familiar.

For the most part, practitioners of embedded counselling are experienced professionals who are deeply socialized into codes of conduct that strongly emphasize the rights of clients or patients, and the establishment of clear professional boundaries. Similarly, most clients are well able to make a distinction between a counselling conversation and other types of interaction.

It is important to keep in mind that the caution about dual relationships that exists within the counselling and psychotherapy professional community has not arisen, to any great extent, from situations in which a counsellor wear two professional hats (e.g. being a patient's GP as well as their counsellor). Concerns about therapy dual relationships are almost entirely grounded, instead, in situations where the counsellor ends up wearing a professional hat and a non-professional one, such as developing a sexual relationship with a client or becoming their business partner.

There is no simple answer to the issue of dual relationships in embedded counselling. What is important is to be aware that difficulties may arise, to keep the situation under review and to routinely check with the client whether they are comfortable and satisfied with what is being offered to them or whether they would prefer greater clarity or separation between emotional support and other services being provided by the practitioner with whom they are in contact.

> **Box 4.3 The importance of collective responsibility**
>
> Some of the most shocking examples of breaches in ethical duty of care have occurred in cases where religious authority figures have sexually abused vulnerable young people who have turned to them for emotional support (Chowdhury at al. 2021; Raine and Kent 2019). Investigations of these incidents have found that, on almost all occasions, warning signs were apparent at an early stage, but that colleagues of the perpetrators were unwilling to intervene. The implication is that it is never sufficient to assume that careful selection and training of practitioners, or the existence of a strong moral and ethical code, are sufficient in themselves to prevent abuse. Instead, as Johnson et al. (2012) have suggested for all settings in which any kind of counselling or emotional support is offered, it is necessary for practitioners to operate as a community in which all members collectively share responsibility for maintaining competence and ethical standards, on a basis of openness to client and service user feedback.

Sensitivity to cultural differences

Ethical issues that arise in counselling situations usually reflect distinctive ideas about right and wrong that are based in cultural beliefs and attitudes. It is important, therefore, for practitioners to be sensitive to the ways that cultural difference can lead to ethical dilemmas. One of the most important dimensions of cultural difference, which can often have an impact on ethical practice, concerns the individualism-collectivism dimension. Western cultures, and in particular the more middle-class segments of such cultures, tend to view life from the perspective of the individual. The rightness of a decision or course of action, therefore, is based on whether the consequences are beneficial for the individual. By contrast, in most other cultures, people view the world from a more collectivist point of view that would assume that family members would be involved in decisions about care (Bhola and Chaturvedi 2017; Sinha et al. 2017). Further evidence of cultural differences in the ways in which ethical values are understood in different cultures comes from an analysis by Qian, et al. (2009) of the recent development of counselling in China. These authors point out, for example, that cultural norms in China mean that it would be unacceptable for counsellors not to accept gifts from their clients or to refuse to provide therapy to friends, close colleagues and family members. Another instance of how cultural differences have ethical implications is the way that in some cultures a mental health issue is viewed as highly stigmatizing to the extent that it might be hard to arrange a marriage for a young person who is known to have received psychiatric treatment.

Dealing with risk and self-harm

One of the most challenging situations for a counsellor is when a person seeking help talks or acts in a way that suggests that he or she may be at risk of harming themselves or harming another person. There are several different forms that risk may take in counselling. The person may:

- plan to take their own life
- be engaged in self-harming behaviour such as cutting, purging, starving, alcohol or drug abuse, unsafe sex, etc.
- be engaged in, or planning to, inflict harm on another person (which may include the counsellor) through physical, verbal or sexual violence, harassment or stalking, criminal activity or unprotected sex (for instance in cases of HIV/AIDS infection)
- report knowledge of harm being done to others (not necessarily by them), such as the safety or well-being of a child being compromised.

Situations in which a client or service talks about risk to self or others can be very difficult for a counsellor to deal with – there is a sense of a great pressure of responsibility, and typically there may be little or no opportunity to consult colleagues – the counsellor needs to respond, somehow, in the moment.

In any of the types of harm listed above, a counsellor needs to arrive at a position on whether it is helpful to proceed with counselling, or whether the situation requires some other kind of intervention. In order to make this kind of decision, a counsellor should be able to (a) listen out for indications from the person that some kind of harm may take place; (b) engage the person in conversation around their intentions and the meaning that the harm event holds for them; (c) estimate the level of risk; (d) implement strategies for avoiding harm.

Embedded counselling often takes place in organizational contexts (e.g. a school or GP practice) in which there already exist procedures and protocols around how to respond to risk. In such contexts, a practitioner offering embedded counselling is part of a system of collective responsibility. They need to be aware of the implications of organizational protocols for their response to a client and how to make use of these procedures in a way that respects the rights of the client and does not destroy the possibility of being able to offer emotional support on an ongoing basis.

The possibility of a client taking their own life is particularly troubling and problematic for many practitioners whose work involves offering emotional support. On many occasions where a person seeking help feels suicidal, they may be quite open and explicit about what is in their mind. At other times, however, the person may convey their intentions in a disguised, vague or metaphorical way of talking. There is some evidence that counsellors are not particularly sensitive at picking up subtle clues about harmful behaviour. In a study carried out by Reeves et al. (2004), a group of highly trained specialist counsellors were recorded in sessions with 'standardized clients', who had been instructed by the researcher to talk vaguely about suicidal intentions. Very few of the counsellors followed up the implicit cues the clients were expressing around suicidality within the sessions. This study needs to be understood in the light of evidence that individuals are generally reluctant to disclose suicidal intentions to any kind of practitioner, for fear of the possibility of forcible psychiatric in-patient referral that would deprive them of their freedom or result in lifelong stigmatization (Blanchard and Farber 2020; Love and Morgan 2021). In addition, even when a person admits to suicidal thinking and undergoes a risk assessment process by a health professional, there is a low probability that the practitioner will be able to accurately predict the likelihood of the client turning these ideas into action (Draper et al. 2008; Regehr et al. 2016).

There exists an extensive counselling and psychotherapy research and practice literature on how to respond constructively to a suicidal client. One important principle is to be transparent about organizational procedures that may need to be followed and the triggers for various courses of action – this information helps the client to understand what might be done, why and in what circumstances (Blanchard and Farber 2020). Another principle is to take a collaborative approach, based on developing a shared understanding of the meaning of suicide for the individual, and a co-created plan of action about how to keep them safe (Ellis 2004; Jobes 2016).

The extent to which a practitioner of embedded counselling might need to develop knowledge and skills around responding to risk will depend on the particular client group with whom they work.

Box 4.4 Moral responsibility around unreported criminal behaviour

Readiness to respond to risk includes being prepared to deal with a situation in which a client tells you about their past involvement in serious criminal activity (Daly-Lynn et al. 2016) or even that they have committed an unprosecuted murder (Walfish et al. 2010). Such disclosures are more likely to occur in communities characterized by high levels of violence, or when counselling is being provided in a prison or other criminal justice facility. However, Walfish et al. (2010) found that 13 per cent of therapists surveyed in typical practice contexts in the USA had experienced at least one client who admitted an unprosecuted murder. Such episodes place a high level of moral responsibility on a counsellor, in relation to finding a balance between their responsibility to the client and to wider society. Ort (2020) suggests that, even in counselling in prisons, where rules around disclosure of criminality are typically highly explicit (e.g. the therapist would be required to pass on the information), there can often be a lot of variability in how practitioners interpret their room for discretion.

Using touch

The use of touch represents a sensitive and problematic issue for many practitioners of embedded counselling. Several studies have shown that nurses and other health professionals routinely engage in physical contact with patients in ways that are perceived as valuable by patients (Kelly et al. 2018, 2020; Wearn et al. 2019). By contrast, teachers, social workers and other practitioners function in occupational environments characterized by fears where touch may be interpreted as sexual or disciplinary, particularly at moments when a client might be emotionally vulnerable. The ethical use of touch is further complicated by the fact that some people who seek counselling may crave touch and can feel rejected if their counsellor refuses to hold their hand or hug them. Other clients, who may have been exposed to exploitative or sexualized touching or torture during their lives, may be terrified at the possibility that their counsellor might move into their physical space. A further aspect of the role of touching in counselling concerns the attitude of the counsellor, who may have anxieties in this area.

In their comprehensive discussion of the use of touch in counselling situations, Hunter and Struve (1998) recommend that touch may be appropriate and helpful when:

- the client wants to touch or be touched
- the purpose of touch is clear
- the touch is clearly intended for the client's benefit
- the therapist has a solid knowledge base about the clinical impact of using touch
- the boundaries governing the use of touch are clearly understood by both client and therapist
- enough time remains in the therapy session to process the touch interaction
- the therapist–client relationship has developed sufficiently
- touch can be offered to all types of clients
- consultation/supervision is available and used
- the therapist is comfortable with the touch.

It is risky and *not* advisable to use touch when:

- the focus of therapy involves sexual content prior to touch
- a risk of violence exists
- the touch occurs in secret
- the therapist doubts the client's ability to say no
- the therapist has been manipulated or coerced into the touch
- the use of touch is clinically inappropriate

- the touch is used to replace verbal therapy
- the client does not want to touch or be touched
- the therapist is not comfortable using touch.

An underlying concern that is present for many counselling supervisors, trainers and managers, is the fear that touch may be taking place to fulfil the needs of the counsellor, rather than those of the client. A further worry is that in the (rare) cases where a counsellor engages in sexual exploitation of their clients, the early steps of the seduction always involve secretive touching. As a result, there has been a tendency in recent years for the counselling profession to err on the side of safety and to seek at all costs to avoid counsellor–client physical contact. This is unfortunate and unhelpful, because appropriate touch has a demonstrable healing potential. When considering the use of touch in an embedded counselling session, it is important to take account of cultural and organizational norms around touch, check out with the client whether touch would be welcome (and if so, what type of touch – sitting side by side, holding hands, stroking, hugging, etc.) and then check out after the event whether what happened was helpful for the client.

Box 4.5 Ethical issues in online counselling

Although online and telephone counselling have been in existence for many years, the use of such approaches expanded hugely during the Covid-19 pandemic, to the extent that online therapy is likely to remain a major sector of practice for the foreseeable future. There are distinctive additional ethical considerations that need to be taken into account when using such methods. These include: ensuring that the client is in a place where they are safe to talk (e.g. not being overheard by a violent spouse, etc.), risk assessment when it is not possible to physically see a client and lack of ability to implement risk management procedures when the client is in a different city or even country (McVeigh and Heward-Belle 2020; Stoll et al. 2020). There are also equity issues around lack of access to counselling for clients who do not have suitable technology.

Conclusions

In counselling, ethical issues are not separate from practice – they are part of practice. A counsellor who feels morally secure in what they are doing tends to be more relaxed, and conveys a sense of confidence to the client. Similarly, a client who has a fundamental trust in the integrity of their counsellor is more likely to talk about important stuff. Each of the ethical domains that have been discussed in this chapter can also be regarded as an aspect of the counselling process. For example, talking about the limits of confidentiality is a necessary step in ethical good practice *and* a means of strengthening the counsellor–client relationship. Asking a troubled client if they wish to proceed with counselling is similarly an element of ethical practice *and* a means of positioning them as a person with strengths and a capacity to decide what is best. While it is important for anyone in a counselling role to be as prepared as they can be to deal with ethical dilemmas, through reading, discussion and role-play, the key strategy that needs to be employed in all ethical scenarios is a willingness to proceed on a collaborative basis. Resolving ethical dilemmas is not a matter of applying an algorithm or set of rules in one's head, but instead consists of engaging in a process of consultation and collaborative decision-making with the client, with colleagues, and (if available) with one's supervisor.

The issues in this chapter are interconnected. Each of them represents a different way of thinking about the importance of *caring* (Lynch et al. 2016, 2021). The vast majority of practitioners in health and social work (and other occupations) operate from a position of love, care, kindness and solidarity in their relationships with colleagues and service users. Ethical issues arise when faced with decisions about caring in a responsible way (is it really a caring or kind act for me to try to give emotional support to this person, when what they need is ongoing, good quality specialist psychotherapy?) or different calls on the capacity to care are in conflict (if I commit myself to supporting this service user over the next few months, it is possible that I might burn myself out and struggle to care for my own children and other family members?). The various ethical tasks highlighted in this chapter (informed consent, confidentiality, competence, cultural sensitivity, etc.) can be viewed as ways of being careful and taking care. By contrast, we live in a culture that is all too often dominated by the pursuit of competitive self-interest and the imposition of a market economy ideology on public services – practices that lead to carelessness around relationships. In addition, there exists a gendered assumption that caring is women's work and considered to be less valuable than the kinds of technical, managerial and interventionist roles that are more likely to be undertaken by men. Caring also involves a commitment to epistemic justice – giving people a voice so that their needs and interests can be heard (Fricker 2007).

Learning activities

The following activities may be explored individually and/or with a group of learning partners.

Exercise 4.1 Legal considerations within your embedded counselling practice
What are the legal considerations or specific professional or organizational codes that are most relevant for your own counselling practice? To what extent, and in what ways, do you need to address these considerations in your everyday work with clients (for example by explaining to them that if they talk about certain issues you would be required to take certain types of action)? In what ways does the organization provide you with support around these issues, for example in the form of supervision, consultation and training?

Exercise 4.2 Setting the scene for informed consent
What might you say to a client who wishes to enter into a counselling relationship with you, about what is involved in counselling? When do you say it? Is this information backed up by written materials? How adequate is this information as a basis for the client to consent to what will follow? If you have been a client yourself, what kind of consent procedure was conducted? As a result of the information you were given, did you have a sense of actively giving consent for counselling to take place?

Exercise 4.3 Negotiating confidentiality
What is the confidentiality framework that you operate within in your own workplace? How do you inform people who look to you for counselling about the limits of confidentiality? How satisfactory are the confidentiality structures within which your counselling takes place? How might they be enhanced or clarified?

Exercise 4.4 The limits of your competence
What are the types of client, or presenting issue, that you regard as being beyond your competence at the present time? What do you do, or might you do, if you came across such a client or issue in your current counselling practice? How do you take care of (a) your needs and (b) the client's needs in this kind of situation? What kind of supervisory or consultative support is available to you in relation to dealing with these events?

Exercise 4.5 Responding to the challenge of dual relationships
Within the setting where you practise embedded counselling, what are the different types of dual relationship that can occur? How are these dual relationships negotiated and handled by other colleagues and by you?

What are the warning signs or risk factors that suggest to you that it may not be wise to offer a counselling relationship to a particular client (or group of clients)?

Exercise 4.6 Your experience of touch in a counselling situation

Take a few moments to reflect on your personal experience as a recipient of counselling – either formal counselling/psychotherapy or informal/embedded counselling. To what extent, and in what ways, was physical contact involved in this relationship (or in each relationship)? (Include all forms of touch, from a welcoming handshake to a full hug.) What was the impact on you of the touch that took place (or the *absence* of touch)? What are the implications of these experiences for your own work as a practitioner of embedded counselling?

Exercise 4.7 Encompassing a diversity of ethical viewpoints in counselling

What are some of the different ethical and moral values expressed by clients in the counselling setting in which you work? Identify two cases where you have had a sense that your client's ideas of what is 'right' or 'wrong' did not correspond to your own values. How did you respond to these situations? What strategies or policies has your agency or organization developed in order to respect cultural differences in values and ethical principles? How helpful or effective are these strategies and policies?

Exercise 4.8 Boundary awareness

It is essential for anyone involved in offering counselling relationships to have a clear understanding of the *boundaries* that are appropriate to the work that they are doing. In any counselling situation, there are usually boundaries in operation around:

- time – when does counselling happen? How long does it go on for? How are the start and finish points signalled?
- space – where does counselling take place? How private is this space (is there anyone else there?)? How are the edges of the space marked off?
- information – who gets to hear about what has been said in the counselling session (confidentiality)? How is information recorded? What information is held?
- intimacy – how close is the relationship? How willing is the counsellor to be known? Is touch permissible?
- access – what kind of contact is possible between counselling sessions? What happens if the person feels a need to talk with their counsellor between sessions?

- safety – the safety of the person and/or the counsellor both within and outside of formal meetings, for example, what happens if the person becomes violent, or threatens suicide?

In relation to how each of these boundary dimensions operate within your practice as an embedded counsellor, make notes on: (a) what the boundary is; (b) who decides on the boundary, and how it is decided or negotiated; (c) how the person seeking help learns about the existence of the boundary or is invited to negotiate it; and (d) what happens if the boundary is violated. Share and discuss your answers with learning partners.

CHAPTER 5

Doing good work

Introduction	90
Organizational context	90
Creating a support network	92
Developing community resources	93
The influence of the emotional life of an organization	93
Finding and making physical spaces in which counselling can take place	96
Developing an organization-wide strategy	99
Supervision, consultation and support	100
The process of supervision	102
Supervision in action	103
Alternative ways of organizing supervision and consultation	106
Assembling a toolbox of therapy resources	106
Self-care	107
Personal therapy	109
Training	109
Making use of research and enquiry	111
Being part of a community of practice	111
Conclusions	113
Learning activities	113

Introduction

This chapter explores different activities that contribute to the development and maintenance of good practice in embedded counselling. A range of factors are explored, including creating an organizational context that supports this kind of work, and the contribution of supervision and consultation, training and research.

Organizational context

It is important to emphasize that counselling and psychotherapy are *always* influenced by the organizational context in which they take place. Many practitioners have an image of private practice therapy, or a therapist working in an NHS clinic, as operating in an environment in which some kind of 'pure' therapy can unfold. This is far from being the case. For example, private practice therapy is powerfully influenced by money – there may be a tendency for the therapist to recommend long-term therapy as a means of income maintenance. The experiences of clients receiving counselling or psychotherapy in the NHS or other healthcare systems is typically shaped by such factors as waiting lists and limits on the number of therapy sessions that can be offered (Carney et al. 2021). These are just some of the organizational factors that operate in specialist counselling settings. The most comprehensive review conducted so far, by Falkenström et al. (2018), identified organizational culture as a key source of influence on the effectiveness of therapy delivered in clinics and services. Other studies have suggested that organizational leadership is a key factor (Clark 2018). From a client perspective, the degree to which a service is welcoming and responsive can make a big difference to whether they engage in therapy (Cooke et al. 2020; Kehoe et al. 2016; Sandage et al. 2017).

Whenever counselling is to be offered to clients, there are a number of organizational or environmental issues that need to be sorted out in advance to enable a safe and productive counselling relationship to be possible. These include:

- time – how much time is available for counselling and how often might counselling take place?
- space – can a suitable, comfortable private space be found?
- confidentiality – who will know about what the person talks about? What are the limits of confidentiality?
- scope and freedom to express emotion without shame or unwanted attention – what happens if the person starts to cry or shouts out loud in an angry voice?
- voluntariness – to what extent is the person an informed user of counselling? Do they know what they are being offered? How do they learn this? Do they feel free to refuse an offer of counselling?

- attitudes to counselling – what do service users, colleagues and managers think and feel about counselling? Do they understand or approve of it or is counselling a furtive activity?

Each of these factors can have a major impact on the ability to offer a counselling relationship. In addition, there are also organizational factors that relate to the capacity of the counsellor to be effective in their work on a sustained basis:

- the level of support that is available to the counsellor – are arrangements for supervision, consultation and peer support in place? How acceptable is it to seek out a colleague for support following a demanding counselling session?
- procedures for referring people in need to other practitioners and services. What happens if it emerges during a counselling conversation that the person would be better served by a specialist service or an agency that could offer a greater amount of time or support? Are referral networks in place and information available for clients (such as leaflets) about alternative sources of help? What happens if a person mentions suicidal intent during a counselling session?

This list of organizational factors indicates the extent to which careful planning is necessary before offering counselling within other helping roles.

Where counselling is embedded in other practice roles, it is necessary to develop mechanisms for both conveying to clients and service users that practitioners are open to talking about problems in living and feelings while at the same time informing them that in some instances the practitioner may recommend specialist sources of psychological or other help. There are many ways that this can be done, including written materials such as leaflets, posters and websites, face-to-face contact and using other service users (e.g. peer support groups) as intermediaries. The ideal is for the person seeking counselling to be an informed consumer of this kind of service – to know what they want and how to get it.

> Alison was a nurse who had always had an interest in counselling and had completed a substantial amount of counsellor training. She was appointed to a post of senior nurse within a haemodialysis unit for patients who had experienced kidney failure. Knowing that living with renal disease presented individuals with significant problems and stress, she anticipated that she would be able to give expression to her counselling skills in her new job. Over her first few months in post, Alison developed a counselling relationship with several patients and felt satisfaction at being able to help some of them work through difficult life issues. Gradually, other staff on the unit recognized Alison's skills and directed any patients with emotional and interpersonal difficulties in her direction. She began to feel overloaded. When she made a request for protected time for this area of her work, and funding to pay for access to a counselling

supervisor, she was accused of being 'elitist' and 'promising patients a service that we can't deliver'. She felt increasingly isolated in the unit and began to look for another job.

Henry was one of the patients who was helped by Alison. His illness had resulted in loss of his job, bodily changes that made him feel physically unattractive and lethargic, and, in time, a deteriorating relationship with his wife, who was increasingly required to take on a role as carer. Henry felt that Alison understood what was happening to him and helped him to talk through his problems in a non-judgemental manner, to the point where he was beginning to be able to develop a more hopeful and constructive attitude toward his situation. He was 'devastated' when Alison said that she would not be able to continue with their occasional half-hour 'chats'. Temporarily encouraged by the suggestion that he might be able to see a clinical psychologist, he described himself as 'shattered' by the news that there was a nine-month waiting list to see a psychologist.

This nursing example illustrates some of the issues that can emerge when practitioners begin to respond to the counselling needs of service users, without engaging in sufficient planning and organizational groundwork. In this medical unit, there existed a well-organized system which prioritized physical care, while giving limited time to the emotional and psychological needs of patients. The introduction of counselling (more attention to emotional and personal issues) unbalanced the system. Colleagues felt both appreciative and envious of the counselling that was taking place. Patients' expectations began to shift, which placed demands on the staff group as a whole. Either the system had to change (to accommodate counselling as an integral part of the nursing service) or the 'experiment' needed to come to an end, to allow the system as a whole to resume its previous state of balance.

Creating a support network

A key aspect of the kind of organizational planning that is necessary in order to ensure that embedded counselling is sustainable and effective is to create a support network for practitioners. The support network that is required for embedded counselling to take place includes three main elements:

- managerial – an understanding on the part of management of the role of counselling, the resources (time, money, space) that are required to be able to offer high-quality counselling help and the nature of confidentiality (e.g, not expecting the details of every counselling conversation to be recorded in case notes)
- collegial – acceptance by co-workers of how counselling operates and what it can achieve, potential demands on time and space and the limitations of

what can be provided (not expecting 'the counsellor' to be able to deal with everything)
- external – suitable arrangements for access to supervision and consultation and avenues for referral of people who require more specialized services.

It can require a substantial investment of time and resourcefulness in order to build a personal and professional support network. Rather than attempting to achieve such a network through individual effort alone, it is more effective to find a group of colleagues who share an interest in the development of counselling within an organizational setting and then work together towards these goals.

Developing community resources

Ethical practice in embedded counselling (as in any other area of professional activity) means being aware of the limitations of one's competence. In a situation where a practitioner in a field such as social work, nursing or education may only be able to offer limited or intermittent parcels of time to people seeking counselling or has received only limited training in responding to problems in living, it is essential to be prepared to refer people seeking help to specialized services whenever this is necessary. To be able to do this effectively requires assembling information about the services that are available locally, what they offer and how to access them. In addition, some people who may benefit from engaging in embedded counselling with their nurse or teacher may also benefit from additional concurrent help that runs alongside this counselling relationship. There is a wide variety of activities that are potentially therapeutic for people, in relation to resolving problems in living; self-help groups and websites, reading, faith community groups, community action groups, environmental groups, involvement in learning and education, voluntary work, sport and outdoor activities and so on. It is important to keep in mind that effective counselling does not mean that the person's problem can only be resolved through a conversation or relationship with a counsellor – in many instances, effective counselling can involve supporting the person to find other resources within their community or personal niche that may be of assistance. Good counsellors (whether practitioners in embedded counselling roles or stand-alone counsellors) are informed about the resources that are available for the client group with whom they work and, where appropriate, will act as a gateway to these resources.

The influence of the emotional life of an organization

There are two perspectives from contemporary organizational theory that are valuable for counsellors who are endeavouring to make sense of the impact of organizational factors on the process of counselling. Ideas about organizational *structure* refer to the way that an organization is arranged, in terms of hierarchies of authority and access to knowledge. Ideas about organizational *climate* or *culture* address questions around the 'feel' of an organization – what is it like to work there or to be a user of its services?

Most large public-sector organizations, such as education and social service departments, health trusts and police forces, operate in terms of a formal hierarchical management structure, with clearly defined lines of responsibility. Typically, the work done by employees who actually interact with clients, or with the public, is defined in terms of protocols, manuals and guidelines, which are intended to ensure that everyone engages in best practice. Also, the activities of frontline workers may be closely monitored in respect of use of time and audited in respect of adherence to quality standards. These aspects of organizational structure may mitigate against the provision of counselling if counselling has not been defined at a higher management level as a sufficiently important activity to be incorporated into protocols or time allocation systems. On the other hand, when the need for counselling has been acknowledged by senior management, then these same structures can be used to ensure that training and supervisory support is in place and that time for counselling is factored into workload planning. The implications of organizational structure, for the provision of embedded counselling, are therefore complex. It is inevitable that most state-funded health, education and social care will be delivered within large organizational units that require military-style discipline and accountability in order to function properly. In such environments, local or grassroots counselling initiatives may be hard to set up and sustain. A lot will depend on the extent to which senior managers and policy-makers are aware of the potential value of counselling. A further consideration is that not all education and health/healthcare is provided by large bureaucratic organizations. A certain proportion of this work is done by smaller organizations in the commercial sector or third (voluntary) sector, which may operate with more of a flat hierarchy, where it may be easier to be innovative.

The idea of organizational 'culture' encompasses a wide range of processes. Culture is a holistic concept, which includes the history of a group, the way that people relate to each other, beliefs and myths, language, values, attitudes to leadership, what people wear, norms for expressing emotions, use of physical space and 'territory' and much else (Schein 2004). In relation to the role of counselling in an organizational setting, one of the most significant aspects of organizational culture is concerned with the expression of emotion. In many organizations, the expression of emotions is not encouraged. For example, staff are not supposed to acknowledge the feelings and emotions that are stirred up for them through their interaction with clients and service users and are not meant to discuss these experiences with their colleagues. In some organizations, the only acceptable emotion is *anger*. For example, anger can be channelled in a positive sense in the form of feedback to colleagues who have made mistakes. Less positively, anger can be expressed through bullying and domination by managers towards employees or at a colleague-to-colleague level. Neither emotion-denying organizations nor 'blame culture' organizations are fertile territory for counselling to thrive because counselling involves creating spaces in which people have permission to feel whatever emotions are around for them at that moment. Many organizations seek to develop a 'rational culture', in which every decision is informed by statistical information, research evidence and logical decision-making. Within such environments, counselling may take root as a 'counter-culture', through which some staff seek to create enclaves of more 'humanizing' forms of interaction.

A useful way of thinking about the difference between organizational structure and culture is that the former is based on a rational analysis of how authority and information flow through an organization, while the latter is concerned with a much less tangible set of unwritten rules that are driven by emotional needs rather than rational planning. A great deal of what can be considered as 'cultural' factors in organizations occur at an unconscious level and seem to operate in much the same manner as unconscious processes in individuals. The analysis of organizational life in terms of unconscious processes was originally developed by the psychoanalyst and organizational consultant Isabel Menzies Lyth and her colleagues at the Tavistock Institute (Menzies 1959; Menzies Lyth 1988, 1989; Obholzer and Roberts 1994). One of the key ideas that was developed by this group was the concept of 'institutional defence mechanisms'. The notion of 'individual defence mechanisms' refers to the process through which a person protects himself or herself against painful and threatening memories and emotions by keeping these contents out of conscious awareness through mechanisms such as *projection, splitting, denial* and *repression*. Menzies Lyth and her co-workers observed that similar processes also occurred at an organizational level. For example, in an organizational setting such as a hospital, where staff deal with pain, loss and death, it can be unbearable for a nurse or a doctor to allow himself or herself to be emotionally affected by what was going on – to do so would make it hard to continue with their work. In a hospital, however, there is usually an institution-wide defence against emotion, in the form of *splitting* – the nurses and doctors are rational and distanced at all times, with the result that emotions are separated off and are expressed somewhere else, such as in the presence of the hospital chaplain or when the patient's family comes to visit. This can create problems for nurses or other healthcare staff who wish to adopt a counselling approach because their actions threaten and challenge the existing system of cultural defences. One of the ways that the validity of counselling approaches is diminished in such organizational settings is to describe them in derogatory terms such as 'touchy-feely'. There may also be anger and resentment directed towards colleagues who try to use counselling methods – they may be seen as wasting time and resources. Counselling practitioners can perpetuate this kind of splitting when they view themselves as the 'caring' ones and management as 'unfeeling, insensitive bureaucrats'.

Another aspect of the unconscious dynamics of organizational culture is captured in the concept of 'parallel process' (McNeill and Worthen 1989). The idea of parallel process refers to a process through which a pattern of feeling and relating that exists in one situation is unconsciously reproduced by the person in a different situation. This concept was originally developed as a means of understanding some of the things that can happen in supervision, for example when the counsellor, in a session with his or her supervisor, acts out some of the behaviour and emotions that were earlier expressed to them by their client. Another type of parallel process is when the counsellor behaves to the client in a similar way that their supervisor behaved toward them. Crandall and Allen (1981) suggest that there can often be significant parallels between counselling issues and organizational issues, and that parallel processes occur at an organizational level. In other words, what happens between counsellor and client is influenced by what happens between the counsellor and the organization. For example, a social worker might be under pressure to prioritize risk assessment in her work with clients to avoid any possibility that a crisis might occur that would be reported in the media. When the social worker and client then agree to take a whole hour to explore the meaning of a personal issue that is bothering the client, the social worker may be subtly responding to her client in ways that serve to 'keep the lid on' any emotions. A teacher may work in a school where there the staff operate on the basis of two categories of students: 'hard workers' who deserve help and 'troublemakers' who need to be controlled. When a teacher develops a counselling relationship with one of his students who is known as a 'troublemaker', he may project this image on to the young person and create a barrier between them. It is important to realize that the theory of parallel process does not suggest that these attitudes are consciously held by social workers or teachers – it is more that aspects of the underlying emotional ethos of the organization permeate their way of being with clients and subvert their counselling skills and values.

Finding and making physical spaces in which counselling can take place

A counselling conversation is different from other types of conversational interaction. What makes a counselling relationship helpful is that it allows the person to step back from the action of everyday life for the purpose of reflecting on that action and possibly deciding to do things differently. In the theatre, sometimes the main character will step to the side of the stage, away from the 'scene', and speak reflectively, honestly and personally to the audience. The main scene is in darkness and the character may be lit by just one spotlight. A good counselling session has some of this quality. It takes place in a bubble or special space, out of the action. Within that space, the person may well talk and act differently from the way they perform elsewhere.

A counselling space requires two key features:

- a boundary – it must be clear when the space has been entered, who can enter it and when it is exited
- rules for what can happen inside the space.

In specialist counselling and psychotherapy centres, a great deal of work is done to set the scene, in terms of boundaries and rules, well in advance of a client arriving. The client may receive a leaflet explaining how the agency operates, what to expect from a counselling session, and the nature of confidentiality. They will be given appointment information that makes it explicit that the counselling session will begin and end at certain times. When a counselling relationship occurs in a different kind of organizational setting, such as a hospital ward or in the person's own home, boundaries and rules need to be negotiated in such a way as to create the best possible space given the circumstances that prevail. To return to the theatre analogy, there are similarities here to street theatre companies, who are able to stage compelling dramas in all kinds of situations. However, even in a formal counselling or psychotherapy agency or clinic, the counsellor can never take it for granted that, at the outset, the client or patient will fully understand the counselling 'contract' – it is always good practice to give the client an opportunity to ask questions, or to revisit key points, particularly if the person has never received counselling before.

A counselling space can be regarded as a place where a person goes in order to look back on, and reflect on, what has been happening in their everyday life. In counselling relationships that take place outside of specialist counselling agencies, a key task for the counsellor or helper is to set the scene – to assemble a space within which a meaningful counselling conversation can take place. Part of this task involves verbally agreeing and checking out that both participants are agreed that they have now moved away from whatever other tasks they have been involved in and are now focusing on exploring the problem in living that the person has brought up. Another aspect of the task is to attend to the physical space within which the conversation is being conducted, for example, can other people overhear? A third part of the task of making a space is to do whatever is necessary to construct a boundary by agreeing the limits of confidentiality, the length of the session, the possibility of further meetings and the role of the helper. Competence in making a space also involves knowing how to close the space at the end of the conversation.

Once there is agreement with a client that they wish to talk, it is helpful to provide some indication of the length of the space that is available. This may involve a statement such as 'we could talk about this for few minutes now, if you like' or 'I have about 15 minutes until my next appointment – would that be enough time to begin to look at what's happening for you?'. In some circumstances, it may be necessary to ask the person about how much time is available to him or her – 'Would it be possible to keep going for a few minutes so I could hear more about the situation you are in?' What is essential is to avoid a situation where the person in the role of counsellor begins to get distracted by the fact that they are running way behind schedule or they abruptly bring the conversation to an end because they have run out of time. Another useful way of signalling time boundaries is to indicate that 'we only have a couple of minutes left', or to use a phrase such as 'we need to finish soon for today' and then offer a brief summary of what has been said or the action that has been agreed. An enormous amount can be covered in a few minutes if the person talking knows that the space is there for them. People know that professional helpers such as doctors, nurses, teachers and social workers are operating under time pressures and will usually accept the realities of what can be offered in terms of time.

Another practical consideration in relation to establishing a workable space for counselling is to be mindful of the physical space. Seating arrangements, proximity, ensuring that the sound of voices does not travel to others and the availability of drinking water and tissues all make an important contribution to creating the right kind of space. Counsellors and psychotherapists in private practice go beyond these basic material considerations and give a great deal of thought to developing the right kind of emotional ambience, using lighting, soft

---

Box 5.1 The healing fields

It is a mistake to think that a nicely decorated room with two armchairs is the only, or even necessarily the best, environment for conducting a counselling session. In a profoundly moving and informative book, Linden and Grut (2002) described the psychotherapeutic work carried out in London under the auspices of the Medical Foundation for the Care of Victims of Torture. This group worked with families who had been exiled from their home countries and had been subjected to unbelievable cruelties. For the majority of these people, sitting in a room and being asked to talk about their experiences to a therapist from a different culture would have been a difficult experience. Instead, the Medical Foundation secured the use of a set of garden allotments. In these spaces, people who had been exiled worked with their families to clear ground and cultivate plants, some of which came from their home country and some from England. Together, the participants created a remembrance garden for all of their friends, colleagues and family members who had not been able to escape. As they worked in their plots, counsellors would work with them and find moments to begin conversations about their old life that had been destroyed and their new one that was gradually growing. The experience of gardening made possible moments of peace and reflection, as well as a wealth of shared metaphors, associated with activities such as clearing the ground, planting seed, keeping fences in good order, seasons, light and darkness, putting down roots, death and much else. This work shows how spaces for counselling can be built into another activity in a way that deepens the possibilities for relationship, connection and meaning-making. There are many other examples of counselling in garden settings, including O'Brien (2018) and Parr (2007). Examples of therapy carried out in a wider range of outdoor settings, such as walk-and-talk therapy and wilderness therapy are discussed in McLeod (2019).

Box 5.2 Creating stillpoints

There is an understandable tendency, when operating in the role of counsellor, to seek to arrive at a resolution or answer to the problem being presented by the person. However, it may be helpful at times for the person to have access to a space in which there is no pressure to do or achieve anything at all. Jevne (1987, 1998) describes such moments as 'stillpoints', and has written about their importance in her experience of working with people who have cancer, pain and long-term health problems. She describes one of her aims as a counsellor as being that of enabling the person to experience a sense of calm and strength in the midst of threat, where they may find their own strength to handle whatever is necessary. An important implication of the idea of a stillpoint is that it suggests that one of the criteria for choosing a location for a counselling session is that it should be suitable for allowing such moments to emerge.

furnishing and art. This kind of environmental control is seldom possible in situations where the counsellor is also performing another role, such as that of teacher or nurse. Nevertheless, part of the preparation for being willing to offer a counselling relationship needs to involve identifying the best spaces, within a school or clinic, where private, emotional conversations can safely take place. An issue that confronts many practitioners of embedded counselling is that of seeing a client in their home, and finding some way to make an appropriate space in a household where the TV is on. Other people are around and there may be a budgie flying about in the room. In such a situation, it may well be necessary to explain to the person why it is essential to create a space in which there is some privacy and quiet. Similarly, in an organizational setting such as a school, it may be hard to find a quiet private place to meet.

Developing an organization-wide strategy

It is difficult to sustain the delivery of good quality counselling to clients within the context of a busy organization in which practitioners are required to juggle multiple roles and pressures. Stein, Frankel and Krupat (2005) describe the development of a programme within Kaiser Permanente, one of the biggest health providers in the United States, which was devised to ensure that doctors engaged empathically, effectively and in a culturally-sensitive manner with the emotional and clinical needs of patients. The programme evolved over a 17-year period and included training workshops designed to be accessible to doctors and relevant to their needs, the use of patient satisfaction surveys to collect data on the use of communication skills by practitioners and the creation of a group of 'communication consultants' – physicians or psychologists selected on the basis of their outstanding interpersonal skills who provided a supervisory and coaching role with colleagues. A particularly innovative feature of the programme was the adoption of a memorable phrase that captured the key elements of the Kaiser Permanente approach – 'the four habits model'. Practitioners were trained in interpersonal competencies related to good practice with regard to four main areas of interaction with patients: invest in the beginning; elicit the patient's perspective; demonstrate empathy; and invest in the end (Stein et al. 2010). Taken together, these four 'habits' encapsulated the dimensions of counselling skills that were considered to be most relevant to the role of a primary care physician within that specific organizational setting. The habits model provided a readily-understood language that all the doctors across the organization were able to use to discuss and reflect on their practice and explained what was needed in practical terms that helped to address the criticism of many physicians that such issues were merely 'time-consuming' irrelevancies. Stein et al (2005) provide a detailed account of the strategies that were used by the champions of this approach within Kaiser Permanente to maximize its chances of being taken seriously, such as building on success, enlisting the support of senior managers, using research evidence to convince tough-minded clinicians that interpersonal skills made a difference to health outcomes and linking salary increases to ratings of patient satisfaction. This process was supported by a programme of research studies evaluating the effectiveness of training (Krupat et al. 2006) and four habits training materials have been translated into Brazilian Portuguese, French, German and Norwegian (Bellier et al. 2020). Similar strategic initiatives have also been developed on the basis of several other communication and helping skills models (see, for example, Black et al. 2014; Dewar and MacBride 2017).

Supervision, consultation and support

One of the distinctive accomplishments of the counselling and psychotherapy profession has been its insistence on the key principle that anyone who is involved in a counselling role must receive regular supervision from an experienced colleague who is not their line manager. This principle reflects an appreciation that the task of engaging on a one-to-one basis with the life difficulties of another person presents a set of challenges that cannot be effectively resolved alone. There is a lot happening in a counselling session and it is invaluable to know that there is someone else available to act as a sounding board for questions such as 'have I missed anything?', 'is there anything else I can be doing to help?' and 'how can I make sense of the complex and confusing story I am hearing?'. Supervision is also a place where the personal impact of the work can be explored and the counsellor can receive support and develop strategies for self-care. Inevitably, the stories of some people seeking counselling will trigger memories and emotions in the counsellor, linked to similar types of experience in the counsellor's own life. In addition, the emotional and relationship needs and patterns of some people who come for counselling can invite unconscious reciprocal responses on the part of the counsellor, which may not be helpful. For example, a client who copes with their difficulties by getting into arguments with other people may talk about their problems in living in a way that subtly irritates the counsellor and leaves a strong residue of emotion at the end of the counselling session. Supervision provides a place for exploring this – 'What is happening that makes me feel angry every time that Ernie tells me about his problems?'.

The separation of supervision and line management is important because the focus of line management supervision is usually on the performance of the individual in relation to organizational goals, whereas the focus of counselling supervision is more exploratory, supportive and personal. Effective counselling supervision requires that the counsellor should feel free to admit possible mistakes and disclose personal vulnerabilities – it is harder to do this with someone who may be responsible for continuing your contract or recommending you for promotion. There is obviously an overlap between management supervision and counselling supervision – for example, a counselling supervisor needs to be able to communicate their concerns and have them acted on if they believe that a supervisee is not working effectively – but on the whole, it has proved most useful to keep these roles separate. In organizational units where people work in teams and managers adopt a more collaborative style, it may be possible to include a manager in supervision arrangements. But even in these circumstances, it is valuable for a practitioner to have the option of consulting someone who is not part of their line of management.

There are a number of different ways that supervision can be organized. Many people who work in counselling roles arrange to meet their supervisor for a single 60 or 90-minute session each month, with the option of telephone or email consultations in emergencies. Some counsellors meet as a group with a supervisor, typically for a longer period or on more occasions, each month to ensure that each member receives sufficient individual time. Other counsellors meet in peer supervision groups, while some belong to networks where they can call on other members as required for consultative support. Accredited counsellors operate within professional codes of conduct that specify the amount of supervision that is required and the level of qualifications and experience of supervisors. At the present time, such guidelines do not exist for practitioners who provide counselling within the context of other work roles. This situation can lead to difficulties for such counsellors in terms of getting their managers to agree to the allocation of dedicated supervision time or to reimburse supervisors.

When arranging supervision, it is important to recognize that different counsellors have different supervision needs. Just as people have different learning styles and coping strategies, they have different ways of engaging with supervision. The supervision style or needs of a counsellor may shift through their career, for example as they become more experienced or are faced with different client groups.

The process of supervision

Just as a counsellor creates a space within which the person seeking help can explore and resolve a wide range of different types of problems in living, a supervisor provides a similar kind of space for a counsellor. There are many aspects of the work of a counsellor that may usefully be addressed in supervision. Hawkins and McMahon (2020) have devised a model of supervision that has been widely adopted within the profession. They suggest that supervision can have three broad functions: education, support and management. The *educative* dimension of supervision relates to such aims as understanding the client better and exploring methods of working with the client's problems. The *supportive* dimension refers to the task of becoming aware of how the emotions and needs of the person seeking help have had an impact on the helper and avoiding burnout. The *management* dimension is concerned with ensuring that the highest standards of care and service are maintained. Hawkins and McMahon (2020) have observed that these functions can be explored by reflecting on, as necessary, seven distinct areas:

1 The content of what the person seeking help was talking about
2 The strategies, interventions and methods used by the counsellor
3 The relationship between the counsellor and the person seeking help
4 The counsellor's personal reactions to the person seeking help
5 The relationship between the counsellor and the supervisor
6 The supervisor's personal reactions to the counsellor
7 The organizational and social context of the counselling.

The relevance, in supervision, of areas 5 and 6 (what is happening during the supervision session) lies in the significance of a phenomenon known as 'parallel process'– the re-enactment in the supervision relationship of issues being played out in the counselling relationship. An example of parallel process might be if a person seeking help found it hard to talk about their problem and then in turn their counsellor was vague or hesitant in describing the case within the supervision session. Most supervision is carried out through talk – discussing the work that the counsellor is doing. However, as in counselling, supervision can be facilitated using a number of different methods. For instance, Lahad (2000) describes the use of expressive arts techniques within individual and group supervision contexts.

Underpinning all effective supervision is the establishment of a good working relationship between supervisor and supervisee. The evidence from research on supervision is mixed. There are some counsellors who find supervisors with whom they are able to form a strong, productive and supportive partnership and from whom they never wish to part. There are other supervisor–supervisee relationships that seem almost to enter a downward spiral, in which the counsellor becomes reluctant to share any evidence of difficulty or vulnerability with their supervisor and the supervisor becomes more and more critical of the counsellor. This kind of experience can be highly damaging for counsellors because it can take some time to decide to withdraw from such a relationship, given the authority of the more experienced supervisor, and the tendency to accept that their criticism might be soundly based. Lawton and Feltham (2000) includes a useful analysis of the factors involved in abusive or unhelpful supervision. Although the majority of experienced counselling practitioners are able to offer satisfactory supervision or consultation to colleagues, there also exist a range of supervision training courses that are invaluable in enabling would-be supervisors to become aware of the complexities of the supervisor role and the issues involved in constructing appropriate supervision contracts.

When constructing a supervision or consultation system, it is helpful to build in diversity and choice. Ideally, over a period of time, any person in a counselling role should be able to work with different supervisors and gain experience of different modes of supervision and support (e.g. individual, group-based, face-to-face, online). Supervision and consultative support also need to be viewed in a broader context of continuing professional development and learning, in which practitioners view themselves as 'reflective practitioners'. Reflecting on practice is an activity that should be integral to practice, in the form of thinking through different courses of action, keeping a personal learning journal, writing notes and attending training events. Formal supervision probably works best when it leads to self-supervision – the best supervisor is the one with whom one can carry out a conversation in one's head and arrive at a productive answer to an immediate dilemma. It is also important to recognize that there can often be significant organizational barriers to the development of an effective supervision network. Particularly within a busy organization such as a health centre, in which counselling does not play a central role within the service that is provided for clients but is embedded within other practitioner activities, it can be all too easy to argue that there is 'no time' for supervision, or that supervision is a 'luxury we can't afford here'. In other organizational settings, there may be a blame culture or an over-bureaucratic approach that makes it hard to achieve authentic supervision relationships. Leading supervision texts such as Carroll (2014) and Hawkins and McMahon (2020) include detailed discussion of organizational barriers to supervision and suggest ways in which supervision can contribute to the creation of a learning organization.

Supervision in action

The cyclical model of supervision, developed by Page and Wosket (2014), pays particular attention to the creation of a 'reflective space' in which the supervisee can explore dilemmas arising from his or her work and to the crucial task of applying supervision insights in practice. Page and Wosket (2001) suggest that the work of supervision can be divided into five stages:

Stage 1: *Establishing a contract.* The counsellor and supervisor negotiate such matters as ground rules, boundaries, accountability, mutual expectations and the nature of their relationship.

Stage 2: *Agreeing a focus.* An issue is identified for exploration and the counsellor's objectives and priorities in relation to the issue are specified.

Stage 3: *Making a space.* Entering into a process of reflection, exploration, understanding and insight around the focal issue.

Stage 4: *The 'bridge' – making the link between supervision and practice.* Consolidation, goal setting and action planning in order to decide how what is to be learned can be taken back into the counselling arena.

Stage 5: *Review and evaluation.* Supervisor and counsellor assess the usefulness of the work they have done, and enter a phase of re-contracting.

Page and Wosket (2020) emphasize that this series of stages is cyclical, with each completion of the cycle leading to a strengthening of the counsellor–supervisor relationship, and concluding with the negotiation of a new contract. The case example below illustrates how these stages can unfold in practice.

> Helen is a social worker in a drug and alcohol service, and provides counselling to clients referred by the court system. Dave is her supervisor. The client she is taking to supervision is Anna, who is 32 years of age, single and has a well-paid, highly-skilled job in the laboratory of a commercial manufacturing company. Anna has difficulties in forming relationships and feels anxious in social situations. She drinks too much and has had two suicide attempts (three years ago) that ended in A&E visits. Throughout her childhood, her mother was an alcoholic and her father was frequently away from home on business trips. She has been coming to counselling for three months.

Establishing a contract. Helen asks to devote most of the supervision session to her work with Anna. She says that she feels stuck and doesn't know where the counselling is going. Dave (her supervisor) agrees, but says that he wants to make sure there is some time to get updates on Helen's other cases.

Agreeing a focus. Dave asks Helen what she would specifically like to look at, in terms of her work with Anna. Helen says that the first priority is to make sense of why it's so hard for Anna to talk in sessions and to find ways of handling that issue more effectively.

Reflection on the content of the counselling session. Dave asks Helen to describe what is happening in counselling sessions, specifically the most recent sessions. Helen outlines a pattern where Anna sends her emails almost every day about how bad she feels, but then sits in the session and won't speak and ends up sitting in silence for long periods.

Exploration of the techniques and strategies used by the counsellor.

Dave: 'What do you do when she doesn't talk? What do you do to encourage her to talk?'

Helen: 'Initially, I would let the silence develop, but that is too uncomfortable.'
Dave: 'Who is it uncomfortable for?'
Helen: 'Me. Anna seems OK with it. What I have started to do is to remind her of what we have talked about before, and ask for more information. This doesn't have much impact, though. What else can I do?'

>   They briefly brainstorm other strategies that might be more effective in enabling Anna to open up, such as Helen gently feeding back to Anna that it seems hard to talk and asking what that is like for her and whether there is anything Helen could do differently that might make it easier for her to talk. They also take a few minutes to think about the room in which Helen meets Anna and whether there might be anything about where the room is located, or how it is laid out, that might be problematic for Anna.

Exploration of the therapeutic relationship. Helen describes the relationship as 'close but inconsistent'. She says that Anna often tells her how important the counselling is and how helpful she has been. Helen says that she really cares about Anna. Dave asks Helen about how *empathic* she is with Anna.

   'I think I am being empathic, but it is hard to tell. I don't know how much I'm getting inside her world. I think that I am maybe asking her too many questions, rather than really connecting with her in an empathic way.'

The feelings of the counsellor towards the client. Dave asks Helen to say a bit more about how she feels toward Anna – whether she is able to *accept* Anna the way she is and how *congruent* she is in respect of how she is feeling. Helen replies that she feels frustrated with Anna – it is hard to accept the part of Anna that holds things back and wants to go slowly.

Counter-transference of the supervisor. Dave talks about how the issue that Helen has presented has triggered his own recollection of the first time that he was a client in his own therapy and how hard it was for him to tell his counsellor how he was feeling. This helps Helen to gain a different perspective on what might be happening with Anna.

What is happening here and now between supervisor and supervisee. Both Dave and Helen agree that their discussion about the case of Anna seems different from the other supervision sessions they have had. There seems to be a parallel process occurring in the session, where Helen seems reluctant to talk and keeps expecting Dave to come up with the answers and guide her in what to do. They discuss the similarities between what is happening between them and what happens when Helen works with Anna. This discussion adds a further layer of understanding.

The 'bridge' – making the link between supervision and practice. Having discussed these issues, Helen acknowledges that she is better able to understand where her own frustration and stuckness with Anna is coming from, in terms of her own style of dealing with things. This then enables the two of them to explore creatively the options open to Helen in relation to taking a different approach to Anna's silences. They agree that it might be a useful strategy for

Helen to work more with the here-and-now process of what is happening in Anna, or in the relationship and connection between them, at the moments when it is hard for Anna to talk.

Review and evaluation. In wrapping up the session, they agree that it would be helpful to review the work with Anna, at their next supervision meeting.

Alternative ways of organizing supervision and consultation

The discussion of supervision within this section has focused on the use of an experienced or senior colleague who provides supervision of the counselling work undertaken by a practitioner or group of practitioners. However, other models are possible. Some practitioners arrange to meet regularly, or on an ad hoc basis, to give each other peer supervision (Golia and McGovern 2015). When practitioners work in close proximity to each other, in a building or corridor, it may be possible to engage in regular brief consults and conversations around troubling cases, for instance by catching a colleague between clients/patients or during coffee and lunch breaks (Gabbay and Le May 2010). Some practitioners seek informal supervision from colleagues, fellow trainees or even friends and family members (Coren and Farber 2019). Each of these approaches has its own distinctive advantages and limitations. For example, as documented by Coren and Farber (2019), informal supervision is limited by the requirement to be highly cautious around the confidentiality of client information. On the other hand, it is experienced by those who make use of it as more playful and creative than formal supervision and a more effective context in which to explore personal reactions to clients.

Assembling a toolbox of therapy resources

The importance of counselling *methods* (practical activities that can be used to accomplish tasks and achieve goals) is highlighted throughout this book. Probably, when beginning to offer counselling to people who are seeking help, any practitioner will rely on a limited set of methods – some acquired during training and others based on personal experience of life. Over the course of a career, one of the enjoyable aspects of continuing professional development can be that of acquiring awareness and competence in new methods. Perhaps one of the key messages of this book is that there are many, many things that a counsellor can do to be helpful. There are methods that have been devised by psychologists and psychotherapists, methods that are drawn from the arts, business, education, sport and many other fields. It may be valuable to accumulate a collection of 'counselling objects' – buttons, stones, driftwood, toys – that can assist the depiction of emotions and life situations. It can be useful to collect metaphors, images and stories that seem relevant to the client group with whom one is working. Information about other sources of help and referral/access pathways into these services may also be valuable items in a counsellor's toolbox. Examples of the kinds of things that experienced counsellors have accumulated in their therapy toolbox can be found in Carrell (2001) and Yalom (2002).

Self-care

The practice of counselling is stressful and it is essential for anyone doing this kind of work to make sure that adequate emotional support and self-care is available to them. There are several sources of stress that need to be taken into consideration:

- typically, counsellors work in settings where the potential need (i.e. number of people seeking help) is greater than the resource that is available to meet that need and so there is a pressure to work long hours or find space to see another person
- quite a lot of the time, counselling either appears to make little positive difference to the person seeking help or the benefit that does result is hidden from the counsellor (for example, following a helpful counselling session, a person may decide that they do not need to return to see the counsellor again, with the consequence that the counsellor never learns about their good news)
- some people who engage in counselling have very harrowing and tragic stories to tell, or live in states of terrible emotional pain – being exposed to these realities inevitably has a powerful impact on a counsellor
- most counselling is carried out on a one-to-one basis under conditions of confidentiality – this can lead to counsellor isolation and lack of social support and a sense of being exposed ('I am responsible for what happens to this person') in comparison with other occupations where teamwork is possible.

The intensity and relative importance of each of these sources of stress will depend on the setting in which counselling is being carried out. For example, workers in agencies dealing with women who have been abused are regularly exposed to high levels of emotional pain, but can usually depend on strong collective support from colleagues. By contrast, a nurse in a busy hospital ward may be less likely to encounter stories of abuse but will probably experience a high workload, time pressure and more limited emotional support from colleagues.

There are two main patterns of stress that appear to be prevalent in people who do counselling work. The first of these can be described as 'burnout'. The theory of burnout was developed by the psychologist Christina Maslach (2000) to account for the effect on people of working in the human service and helping professions. People enter these professions with a passion to help others. Over time, the emotional consequence of always 'giving' to others results in the passion to help becoming 'burned out'. It is as though the energy and motivation of the person has become used up. The main symptoms of burnout are: a sense of emotional exhaustion; a tendency to treat clients in a detached way, as objects or 'cases' rather than as people; and a deep disillusionment or lack of personal accomplishment ('it's all a waste of time… I have been doing this job for 10 years and nothing has changed…'). A counsellor who is 'burned out' is therefore merely going through the motions and not really engaging with the people with whom they are working. This state also has serious negative implications for the private life of the person and their capacity to sustain close relationships. Burnout is a type of stress that gradually accumulates day-by-day and week-by-week when people care for others without taking care of themselves.

A second form of stress that can occur in those involved in offering counselling relationships has been described as 'secondary traumatization'. This type of reaction takes place when counsellors work with people who have themselves been traumatized (Morrissette 2004). When a person has been through an awful event, such as torture, natural disaster, war and the like, a range of psychological consequences can occur. Often, the sensory images of the event are so frightening that they cannot readily be assimilated into the person's memory. Images of the event continue to be intrusively re-experienced and then locked away or avoided as the person's cognitive processing struggles to integrate what has happened into their pre-existing understanding of the world. What this means, for a counsellor, is that when the person does begin to talk about these awful events in a counselling session, the images and re-experiencing and levels of fear are so strong that is almost as though the counsellor is some kind of witness to the original event. A counsellor may find that he or she cannot get the client's story, or images from it, out of their mind. Another process that can take place arises from what Janoff-Bulman (2010) has called 'shattered assumptions'. When a person has experienced events that should 'never happen', then their basic assumption of trust in the world as a safe place, and people as good, is shattered. A counsellor working with such a person may find that the person's story has, in turn, shattered or threatened their own belief in a safe and good world. One of the hazards of counselling, therefore, is the danger of developing secondary traumatization, which can be expressed in a lack of trust in people, recurring images of cruelty and destruction, and general hyper-alertness to any source of potential threat.

The term 'compassion fatigue' is sometimes used to describe the combination of burnout and traumatization. These effects may also incorporate a dimension of moral injury, in relation to being affected by events that are unfair or unethical (see Chapter 4). The development of compassion fatigue in counsellors is often subtle and hidden. People who develop an interest in counselling and readily offer counselling relationships to others generally view themselves as possessing a good level of self-awareness and capacity to deal with stress. Probably this is true, much of the time, and results in effective self-care in the majority of counsellors. But it may also lead to an unwillingness to acknowledge difficulty and vulnerability in the interest of maintaining a facade of competence – counsellors can be good at keeping their burnout hidden from others and from themselves.

Spending time with a burned out counsellor is unlikely to be satisfying. A very tired nurse in a casualty department can probably record blood pressure and administer injections at an acceptable level of reliability. A very tired counsellor, by contrast, is only minimally open to a relationship. Ultimately, the main resource in counselling is the self of the counsellor and their capacity to be there in the moment for a client.

It is important to retain a sense of perspective around counsellor stress. Many counsellors experience great satisfaction and sense of privilege from the work they do and report that their involvement in even the most demanding clients and therapy processes has made a positive contribution to their learning and growth, allowing them to be more resilient both as therapists and as people – see, for example, the accounts of counsellors working with refugees (Puvimanasinghe et al. 2015) and child victims of sexual abuse (Wheeler and McElvaney 2017).

There is an extensive literature on self-care for counsellors. Widely-used self-care strategies include: maintaining work–life boundaries and balance; supportive colleagues; regular engagement in activities that are completely separate from the world of work, such as time in nature or involvement in art; spirituality and meditation; personal therapy; and healthy diet. Key texts on counsellor self-care are Rothschild (2006) and Skovholt and Trotter-Mathison (2016).

Personal therapy

Over the course of their career, almost all specialist professional counsellors and psychotherapists undergo one or more episodes of therapy. For therapy practitioners, the experience of being in the client's chair is usually referred to as 'personal therapy'. The main reasons that counsellors or psychotherapists enter therapy is because they wish to deal with a problem in living that is troubling them. A further reason for being in therapy is to stay well – regular therapy sessions are a good way of maintaining one's emotional availability for one's own clients. There can also be an additional goal of learning about counselling. Being a client is one of the best ways to understand how the counselling process works (and doesn't work). In the client's chair, it is possible to watch what one's counsellor is doing. It is also possible to monitor one's own reactions to what the counsellor has said and done, both in the session itself and in the days or weeks following a session. Further information on personal therapy can be found in Geller et al. (2005) and McLeod (2019).

Training

The skills that are of use in counselling are ultimately based on our life experience, on many thousands of interactions where we have either offered emotional support to someone, been recipients of support ourselves or observed others engaging in such activities. However, it is also essential to use training to fill in gaps in our skills repertoire, learn and adapt skills for new situations and generally review, renew and refresh our competence. The field of counselling skills training has generated several evidence-based training approaches. The 'microskills' perspective is based on demonstration and explanation of a specific skill (e.g. questioning, summarizing meaning) and then practising it with other learners and getting feedback. In 'interpersonal process recall' (IPR), the trainee makes an audio or video recording of them working with a client (or learning partner in the role of client), then listens/watches it, pausing the recording at points where they wish to reflect on or discuss what was happening during the session. The 'deliberate practice' approach to skill development has emerged from an extensive programme of research which showed that expert performers in any occupation are those who pay close attention to negative feedback (i.e. when things went wrong), identify the underlying deficit in their skills and knowledge, formulate a strategy for remedying this deficit, engage in practising these new skills in a safe environment outside of the frontline work situation and monitor improvement in their effectiveness in real-life work settings. Finally, the concept of 'self-practice' refers to learning activities in which practitioners develop therapeutic skills by applying them to issues in their own life. More detailed information about these approaches, and how they are implemented in practice, can be found in McLeod and McLeod (2022).

Some organizations, particularly in the healthcare sector, have assembled elements of these training models into hybrid programmes that are designed to meet the needs of employees in their own specific service delivery context and can be delivered in-house (see, for example, Hollis et al. 2021; Stein et al. 2010; Wolderslund et al. 2021). Counselling skills training is available in many degree-level initial professional qualifying programmes in occupations such as medicine, nursing, teaching and social work – often labelled as communication skills training, clinical skills or interpersonal skills. In some places, counselling skills training is also provided through stand-alone post-qualifying courses. For example, in Scotland, the main professional body for counselling (COSCA) validates a long-established 120-hour part-time Certificate in Counselling Skills programme that has been completed by thousands of human services practitioners.

A common element in all counselling skills training is the opportunity for live practice, in which a student or trainee will act as client (usually talking about a genuine personal issue), in a situation in which the trainee has the freedom to try different skills and responses, make mistakes and learn from constructive feedback.

In many human service organizations, there are likely to be practitioners who possess professional qualifications in counselling or psychotherapy, but who continue to work as nurses, teachers, or in some other non-therapist role. Because being a counsellor or psychotherapist is a particularly demanding and intense way to make a living, a significant proportion of therapists choose to combine it with other paid work. Others may be planning to retire early from their primary profession and become therapists in the closing segment of their career. In many of these cases, what this means is that there may be practitioners who are already employed in an organization who are able to advise on counselling skills training and the design, delivery and supervision of embedded counselling provision.

Making use of research and enquiry

In modern industrial societies, characterized by high levels of social and technological change, there are few occupations that rely solely on the application over a lifetime of knowledge and skills acquired during a period of apprenticeship. Instead, there is an expectation, in most contemporary professions, that new knowledge and information will constantly be generated by research and that competent practitioners will continue to update their approach by being research-informed. The domain of practice-based research can be viewed as a continuum. On one end are large, theory-driven or policy-driven studies carried out by full-time researchers based in universities. There are also many smaller scale studies that are carried out by practitioners. At this end of the continuum, which is concerned with knowledge generation, research is an activity in which a person is actively involved, a form of complex problem-solving. At the other end of the continuum, research is a product that is consumed. Detailed research reports can be read in research journals. Less detailed reports can be found in professional journals. Digested research knowledge finds its way into textbooks.

There exists a range of different research approaches that can be employed in looking at the process and outcome of the use of embedded counselling skills. Making use of research and enquiry is a valuable way to stand back from practice and engage in constructive and critical reflection. It is also a good means of learning about the ideas and methods developed by colleagues in other places – it makes it possible to keep abreast of best practice. An overview of research on the ways that different types of research can contribute to competence in embedded counselling is available in McLeod and McLeod (2015). Many other relevant studies are cited throughout the present book. An introduction to different methodologies used in counselling and psychotherapy research can be found in McLeod (2022).

Being part of a community of practice

All occupational groups operate within networks of colleagues who share stories about good and bad practice, how to deal with things that go wrong and similar issues. Members of such networks are on hand to offer each other support and to share skills. Lave and Wenger (1991) used the term 'community of practice' to describe this form of learning. An influential study of how GPs use conversations with colleagues as a means of participating in a community of practice was conducted by Gabbay and le May (2011). The concept of a community of practice refers to everyday learning, outside of classrooms, colleges and universities, through which people in a particular line of work share their experience in order to develop a broader understanding of issues and strategies related to their job. A community of practice includes more experienced members, who are widely regarded as being expert practitioners, and 'peripheral' members who are at the point of entering the profession or occupation – as well as participants at various levels of experience between these poles.

There are many different types of community of practice that can be relevant for the development and maintenance of competence in embedded counselling. Colleagues in a particular organization, such as a hospital, social work department or school district, may create a structure such as a Facebook page, or regular seminars and workshops, where they get together to exchange ideas and support each other around an area of shared interest such as how to respond to the increasing use of video counselling or how to offer emotional support to people from minority backgrounds. There are also larger, national or regionally-based networks that have been established around areas of practice such as bereavement and loss, eating disorders and suicide prevention. Involvement in research can also provide networking opportunities, for instance through participation in a practice research network (see McLeod 2022) or a reading group. Studies of professional knowledge can represent a useful way to document and disseminate practice-based learning to a wide audience. For example, studies of embedded counselling by clergy and faith workers, based on interviews with practitioners, have been invaluable in terms of creating greater awareness of the challenges and possibilities associated with that line of work (Leavey et al 2007; O'Kane and Millar 2002; Zust et al. 2017).

Conclusions

This chapter has discussed a wide range of topics that need to be considered in relation to the aim of being a competent practitioner of embedded counselling. There are some key themes that weave through these topics. The first is that the *organizational context* of any time of counselling exerts a huge influence on the quality of the counsellor–client relationship and the types of therapeutic conversation that are possible. A further theme reflects the significance of the notion of *craftsmanship*. A good counsellor, no matter whether the context they operate in is high-end private practice or the corner of a busy inner-city health clinic, functions as a craft worker. The satisfaction of the job comes from making the best of the materials that are available, and in producing something that is valued by customers and fellow workers. The essence of craftsmanship is attention to the task in hand, the gradual deepening of skill over time and pride in a job well done. Another key theme is *resourcefulness*. Throughout this book, the idea has been highlighted that people encounter problems in living because they lack the resources to resolve difficulties that arise in their lives. People seek help because their resources are not sufficient to cope adequately with the situation within which they find themselves. The same analysis can be applied to the role of the counsellor. Virtually anyone can be an effective counsellor to a limited set of people – those people whose problems and assumptions about change most closely match the helping resources of that practitioner. But in the longer term, anyone who hopes to offer counselling to a wide range of people needs to expand their repertoire of helping resources.

Learning activities

The following activities may be explored individually and/or with a group of learning partners.

Exercise 5.1 The possibilities for counselling in your place of work
Take a few moments to think about the counselling that you do, or would like to do, in your organizational setting. Make notes about the ways in which organizational factors impact on the following issues:

- the amount of time that you can spend with clients
- access to private spaces where you can talk without being overheard
- access to spaces that are comfortable and nicely decorated
- how acceptable it is to be cry or express anger
- how acceptable it is to talk to a colleague about how upset you feel after speaking with a client
- the limits of confidentiality

- support for you to engage in counselling training
- support for you to get counselling supervision
- recognition and praise when you do good counselling work.

Finally, look through this list again and note down any possibilities that come to mind around how you can exert influence within different levels and areas of the organization to enhance the counselling that you do.

Exercise 5.2 Referral pathways and alternative sources of support for clients

One of the things that inhibits many practitioners from responding to empathic opportunities presented by their clients is the worry that they will get 'in over their heads' – they will be overwhelmed by the severity and/or complexity of their client's difficulties and perhaps even make things worse by doing the wrong thing. These are real fears. In embedded counselling scenarios, to work ethically within one's zone of competence involves developing practical knowledge about alternative sources of help that are available to your clients and how these resources can be accessed. Take a few moments to (a) make a list of referral pathways and alternative sources of support in your area that might be relevant to your clients and (b) a list of people you can consult for advice and guidance if you feel that your client might need more than you can offer them. Reflect on the adequacy of these lists – is there more that you need to do to strengthen your embedded counselling 'back-up' system?

Exercise 5.3 Reflecting on your own personal and professional knowledges

What are the areas of personal and professional knowledge that you possess, that could be of potential value in your counselling? What do you do to integrate these knowledges into your counselling role with clients? Do you feel that you make sufficient use of these sources of knowledge? What might you do to acknowledge these sources more consistently? Suggested further reading on how professional training can submerge and marginalize personal and cultural knowledge can be found in White and Hales (1997).

Exercise 5.4 A narrative perspective on organizational culture

From a narrative perspective, the culture of an organization is transmitted through the stories that are told around key events in organizational life. Take a few moments to think about recent events in your own organization that represented genuine 'water-cooler' moments – things that happened where everyone gathered round the water cooler (or equivalent) to hear the latest news. To what extent did the events described in these stories exemplify counselling values? Did the protagonists of these dramatic stories exhibit high levels of congruence, acceptance and empathy toward each other? If not, then what values were expressed through their actions? Finally – what do these stories suggest to you about the place of counselling within your organization?

Exercise 5.5 Your use of supervision and consultation
What opportunities do you have to talk about your counselling work, either with a formally contracted supervisor or through consultation with colleagues? How satisfactory are these arrangements? In terms of the ideas about supervision outlined in the present chapter, what are the positive aspects of the supervision that you receive and where are the gaps? What can you do to improve this situation?

Exercise 5.6 Creating a suitable space for counselling
How satisfactory is the physical setting in which you work, in terms of providing spaces for counselling relationships to occur? What improvements would you like to make to the physical environment in which you see people?

Exercise 5.7 What's in your toolbox?
What are the ideas and methods that are currently in your counselling 'toolbox'? Which items would you like to add to your range of tools over the next two years?

Exercise 5.8 Reflecting on your use of personal therapy
Take a few minutes to reflect on what being a client in therapy for yourself has meant for you and what you have learned from it. What contribution has personal therapy made to your ability to offer an effective counselling relationship to clients? If you have *not* had experience of personal therapy for yourself, relevant reflective questions might include: what other activities have you engaged in that have served a similar function for you? What is stopping you from trying therapy? It can be particularly useful to carry out this exercise in a group, and share experiences.

Exercise 5.9 Mapping your support system
Take a large sheet of paper and on it draw a map of the support system that allows you to be at your best in the embedded counselling that you offer to your clients. In the middle of the paper draw a symbol or picture of yourself. Then around this picture or symbol draw pictures, symbols, diagrams or words to represent all things and people that support you in learning, being creative and being resilient in your work. These may be the walk to work, books you read, colleagues, meetings, friends, etc. Represent the nature of your connection to these supports. Are they near or far away? Is the link strong and regular, tenuous or distant? Are they supporting you from below like foundations or are they balloons that lift you up?

When you are satisfied with your initial map, take a completely different colour and draw on the picture symbols that represent those things that *block you* from fully using these supports. It may be blocks within you, or within the support or in the organizational setting. Draw whatever you feel stops you getting the support you need.

When you have completed your support map, share it with one or more learning partners. The ensuing discussion might touch on the following questions:

- is this the kind of support you want?
- is it enough? What sort of support is missing? How could you go about getting such support?
- what support is really positive for you to the extent that you must ensure that you nurture and maintain it?
- which blocks could you do something about reducing? How might you achieve this?

Your learning partner should encourage you to develop some specific *action plans* as to how you might improve your support system. An action plan should include what you are going to do; how you are going to do it; when and where you are going to do it; and who might be involved.

CHAPTER 6

Crisis

Introduction	117
Making sense of crisis	118
Counselling skills for responding to persons in crisis	119
Organizational strategies	122
Helplines and single-session therapy	122
Working with colleagues from other occupational groups	124
Mobilizing those who care about the person in crisis: open dialogue	124
Training in mental health first aid	127
Culturally sensitive practice	127
Supervision and support	127
Conclusions	129
Learning activities	129

Introduction

A client or service user may seek support during an episode of crisis in their life. Although there are many types of crisis, such situations can be understood as events during which a person experiences themselves as being confronted by a situation that is threatening, overwhelming and out of control. Being able to respond to a person in crisis is an important aspect of embedded counselling. Formal counselling and psychotherapy tend to be organized around a process during which the person contacts a therapist, then waits to see them, then returns for weekly sessions. In this kind of helping scenario, there is almost always a gap between any initial triggering crisis and actually meeting with a therapist. As a consequence, even though a client may wish to use therapy to explore the meaning of a crisis, they are unlikely to still be *in* crisis at the point of seeing their therapist. In formal therapy, although real-time crises may occur later in therapy, by that point the therapist and client would have established a relationship and way of working together that supported them in dealing with whatever had come up. By contrast, in embedded counselling, it is much more likely that the first contact with a client – or at least, the first counselling-type contact – will occur at a moment of crisis.

The aim of this chapter is to provide an introduction to how to make sense of how people react to crisis, the skills and strategies that can be used to provide emotional and psychological care in such situations and the resources and procedures developed by organizations that regularly encounter this kind of issue. Although there are some common features associated with all forms of crisis event, it is important to be able to appreciate how the meaning of a crisis is shaped by the context in which it occurs, such as bereavement, trauma or in response to a severe political or climate event. Individuals whose life opportunities are limited by poverty, racism or other types of adversity are more likely to be vulnerable to crisis, whereas those who are more socially privileged tend – on the whole – to be more insulated from such experiences.

Making sense of crisis

The focus of the present chapter is on individual experiences of crisis. Although the concept of crisis is also used to refer to threatening and out-of-control events within society as a whole, such as the financial collapse of 2008 or the Covid-19 pandemic, the relevance of counselling and other types of therapeutic conversation in such situations is limited to supporting individuals to come to terms with specific personal consequences of these bigger social crises, such as having one's home repossessed or losing a family member to Covid-19. There are some events, such as disasters, that can be understood as comprising collective crises because they affect everyone in an area in the same way at the same time, such as Hurricane Katrina, which devastated the city of New Orleans in 2005 (Rosen et al. 2010).

A state of personal crisis can be defined as an experience of being faced by an event that appears to be a fundamental and insurmountable obstacle to the person's capacity to carry on their life as before. Whatever it is that has happened, the person believes that their usual strategies are not sufficient to allow them to cope. As a result, the person does not know what to do or which direction to turn. It is if their life and sense of identity and existence has been suddenly swept away (van Deurzen 2021). This can produce different types of psychological and bodily response: immobilization, dissociation, being frozen, irrationality, fear, panic, shock, grief, anger, or hyper-activity. The person may oscillate between these states. At some point, the physical and emotional demands of this way of being may mean that the person reverts to 'survival mode' (i.e. passively doing only what is necessary to get through the day). A crisis episode may be brief (a few hours or days) – if it continues beyond a few weeks it becomes the person's 'new normal' and is no longer a crisis. A core element of the experience

> **Box 6.1 Responding to high pressure crisis events**
>
> Imagine you are a police negotiator, trained to deal with events in which a person is threatening to take their own life or to harm another person. You work with a colleague and the two of you may be on call for days at a time. Calls often come at night. On this occasion, you are alerted to attend an incident on the bridge over the local river. A young woman has been observed through CCTV cameras, apparently preparing to jump into the river below. As you approach her, you can see that she is agitated. You know that the bridge has been closed. There is already a considerable back-up of traffic. There is an ambulance parked out of sight close by. You know that there is a rescue boat below. But, right now, it all hangs on your ability to make a connection with this desperate young woman. She is about the same age as your own daughter. You move close enough for her to hear you.
>
> "I'm Jane. I can see that you are really upset. What happened? Can we talk about it?"
>
> Although you are a police officer, this incident is unlikely to end up in a visit to the custody suite at the local station. Instead, you are, at that moment, the single point of contact between that person and a whole structure of care that is there to help her. Although police officers are not generally considered as practitioners of embedded counselling, their experience and skills in being able to resolve this kind of scenario represent an invaluable learning resource for anyone engaged in crisis work (Grubb et al. 2021; Royce 2005; Sikveland et al. 2022).

of crisis is that the person is faced with choices in a situation in which it is far from clear which course of action is for the best. A consequence of this choice-making is that a crisis can have long-lasting effects. For example, if a person chooses to battle through a crisis by suppressing their emotions, it is likely that these feelings will re-emerge at a later date.

There are many different types of events that can trigger the experience of crisis – disasters, accidents, being a victim of violence, relationship breakdown, mental health breakdown. The complex nature of crisis, and the ways in which crisis is shaped by situational and cultural factors, are examined in detail in crisis intervention textbooks such as Duffey and Haberstroh (2020), James and Gilliland (2020) and Kanel (2014).

Counselling skills for responding to persons in crisis

Providing emotional and psychological support for a person who is in a state of crisis, in a manner that helps them both to cope with their present situations as well as make the best decisions about how to move forward in their life, requires both personal qualities on the part of the helper and effective counselling skills. At a personal level, the helper needs to be able to handle the intensity of the client's needs, time pressures and relationships with other colleagues who may also be involved with the same client. In addition, a range of counselling skills needs to be implemented in what may be a short space of time with little scope for developing an ongoing therapeutic relationship in which mistakes can be corrected.

Traditionally, most crisis intervention models suggest that it is helpful to follow a sequence of stages in which different aspects of the client's difficulties are addressed in turn (James and Gilliland 2020; Kanel 2014; Roberts and Ottens 2005). For example, the widely-used model developed by James and Gilliland (2020) identifies six stages:

1. Exploring and clarifying the problem from the client's perspective
2. Ensuring the safety of the client, in terms of self-harm, suicidality, medical needs, food and shelter
3. Offering support – making it clear that you are on the person's side, and will do whatever you can to help
4. Exploring alternative actions, coping strategies and sources of further help that might contribute to dealing with the person's distress and the situation that threatens them
5. Making plans – deciding on which strategies will be pursued and how/when/by whom
6. Reviewing what has been agreed in terms of whether the person is willing and able to commit to them.

James and Gilliland (2020) suggest that it can be valuable to view these stages as following a path from listening to action. They also point out that helpers need to be able to work effectively with clients who vary hugely in their capacity to approach these issues in a collaborative manner. Some clients may be passive, defeated and exhausted, others may have very clear ideas about what they need, while others still are able to engage in shared decision-making and dialogue with the helper.

Myer et al. (2013) caution against assuming that stages of crisis intervention will necessarily occur in the same order with all clients. In their experience, there are three tasks to which a crisis helper needs to attend all the way through a helping episode: assessment, safety and support. There are also specific tasks that can be accomplished on a one-off basis in a relatively fixed sequence: contact, re-establishing control, problem-solving and follow-up.

Because the client may be preoccupied with their own inner experience, low in hope and energy, or have been passed around from one helper to the next, the task of establishing contact, rapport or connection represents a key aspect of the process of crisis counselling (Sikveland et al. 2022). As far as possible, the immediate physical environment should be arranged to enable face-to-face

Box 6.2 Responding to crises arising from domestic violence

An important aspect of responding to a person in crisis is the capacity to access and activate their pre-existing support network. Violence and emotional abuse within intimate relationships was discussed in Chapter 3 as an example of using social networks in embedded counselling practice. It also provides an illustration of how effective crisis counselling makes use of social support. Although violence can occur in same-sex relationships or be inflicted by women on their male partners, the majority of cases of domestic violence reflect situations in which women are attacked by men. Professional involvement in addressing domestic violence takes many forms, many of which (e.g. family therapy, living in a women's refuge or shelter) extend over months or years. However, a distinctive feature of this type of problem in living is the occurrence of a crisis event, such as a sudden escalation of violence, involvement of the police, or reaching a point of having no option other than moving out of the family home (often with children and with no immediate source of income). In terms of embedded counselling, there may be a period of time when a social worker, minister or shelter worker may represent an essential source of emotional and practical support. However, in the longer term, support from family, friends, co-workers and other women who have had similar experiences is a crucial factor in eventual recovery from intimate partner violence (Larance and Porter 2004; Lewis et al. 2015; Stylianou et al. 2021). Practitioners who work in this area develop many strategies for enabling clients to build, rebuild and utilize social support (Goodman and Smyth 2011; Goodman et al. 2016). For example, a woman's partner may have controlled her life to the extent that earlier friendships and family bonds have been severed or convinced her that she is worthless and unlovable. In such circumstances, an important aspect of any kind of therapeutic conversation may be to develop an understanding of how this has happened, 'find herself' again and look at how such losses might be repaired. In respect of making new relationships, there may be uncertainty over who can be trusted to be a good person in one's life. The study by Goodman et al. (2016), based on interviews with counsellors and other support workers about how they approach such tasks, provides an invaluable source of ideas about relevant skills and strategies for mobilizing support networks, not just in the area of domestic violence, but also in other situations in which a person may be in a state of crisis.

communication, privacy and the possibility of touch. It may be helpful to ensure that the person is not left alone or that any moments of being left alone are explained. The key counselling skills in such a situation include listening, checking out that the helper has an accurate empathic understanding of what the person is trying to convey, affirming the client's reality and being non-judgemental. Using a soft, soothing voice, speaking slowly and being sensitive to the person's body posture and breathing can be useful ways to facilitate empathic connection with a person in crisis.

How to assess need, risk and resilience represents an important challenge for any practitioner faced by a client or service user who is in a state of crisis. For some clients, it may be sufficient to engage in a supportive interaction that encourages them to get further help from individuals or organizations who are part of their pre-existing network. However, other clients may be too depleted to make use of such resources, or such resources may not exist or may not be able to be activated at that moment. The following sections of this chapter highlight some of the ways that helpers may need, in some situations, to draw on wider networks of care within the community. In order to be able to do this effectively, it is necessary to be able to evaluate risk (checklists are available in textbooks such as James and Gilliland 2020 and Kanel 2014) and to be prepared at least to the extent of knowing who to call for information about what kinds of further support might be available in the local area.

Organizational strategies

The experience of crisis, and seeking professional help to manage a personal or community crisis, are widespread features of contemporary society. As a consequence, there exist many different types of organizational initiatives and services that have been created to address this area of need.

Helplines and single-session therapy

In terms of being a practitioner who might be called on to respond to clients who are in a state of crisis, it can be helpful to know about crisis helplines and single-session therapy. These services provide organized and focused emotional and psychological support for individuals in crisis. From an embedded counselling perspective, they not only offer valuable referral possibilities, but also represent potentially valuable learning resources in terms of models of brief supportive interventions and training in such approaches.

The original crisis helplines, such as Samaritans in the UK, provided telephone counselling for individuals who were suicidal. Over the years, this type of service has expanded into crisis helplines for a wide range of specific life difficulties, such as domestic violence, child abuse and medical conditions such as cancer. Some helplines also make use of synchronous online support, in some instances alongside other online resources such as a community discussion forum and self-help materials (see, for example, Kooth, a UK-based helpline for young people: www.kooth.com).

It is not easy to evaluate the effectiveness of crisis helplines, because callers are offered complete confidentiality (typically, names are not recorded), are unlikely to be in a state where they can readily complete a questionnaire or be interviewed and are hard to follow up. Despite these challenges, there exists considerable evidence that such services are valued by users and make a difference to the course of their lives (Coveney et al. 2012; Hoffberg et al. 2020; Mazzer et al. 2020; Middleton et al. 2016).

In effect, crisis helplines offer single-session counselling. A parallel development has been the provision of single-session therapy (sometimes also described as one-at-a-time or walk-in therapy) by counselling and psychotherapy practitioners and agencies in the context of more conventional ongoing therapy provision. The single-session therapy literature comprises an invaluable source of ideas around skills and strategies for offering meaningful and helpful therapy within the constraints of a one or two-hour single meeting. In general, therapists who offer single-session approaches tend to draw on a set of general principles, such as finding out what the client wants and needs and agreeing a goal for the session, activating the client's personal strengths, resources and coping strategies, keeping the session focused and encouraging the client to rehearse and practise possible solutions during the closing stage of the meeting. These general principles are combined with specific techniques and ideas associated with the theoretical model in which the therapist has been trained. As a result, each therapist develops their own personal version of single-session practice, shaped by the circumstances within which they work and their own knowledge base. A good example of this kind of synthesis can be found in an article by Windy Dryden (2020a) in which he illustrates how he combines general single-session principles and ideas from rational emotive behaviour therapy.

The collaborative pluralistic model of practice advocated by the present book is designed to be appropriate and applicable to both long-term counselling support and single-session encounters. There is a growing body of evidence to support the effectiveness of single-session therapy, including with younger clients (see, for example Cait et al. 2017; McLeod 2019, Chapter 31). The possibilities of single-session therapy are being increasingly acknowledged by service providers worldwide (Dryden 2019, 2020b; Hoyt et al. 2021; Young and Dryden 2019).

For frontline practitioners of embedded counselling, it is important to understand that crisis helplines and single-session therapy cater for more than just clients who are in a state of crisis at the point when they talk to a counsellor or helper. For example, there are many individuals whose personal preferences or life situation might lead them to want to make use of counselling one session at a time, rather than committing to an ongoing therapy contract. In addition, both crisis centres and single-session therapy users include people who may be looking for support to prevent a crisis from occurring or reoccurring.

Working with colleagues from other occupational groups

An important feature of crisis intervention work has been the use of multidisciplinary teams. Clearly, responding to a major disaster such as a climate event, like a fire or flood, or an accident or terrorist attack, calls for involvement of people able to provide a wide range of specialist skills and knowledge (Rosen et al. 2010). At a more local and everyday level, there are many examples of practitioners working together, both informally on the basis of personal contact and through formal structures, to respond effectively to the needs of individuals in crisis. For example, in cases of domestic violence, frontline healthcare staff such as GPs and community nurses may make use of contacts in social services, shelters, accommodation and housing services and police with whom they have collaborated before. Within a school, college or university, there are usually policies and procedures to facilitate the collective involvement of a caring network of teachers, counsellors, nurses, faith representatives and administrative staff in situations where a student or students have committed suicide or been involved in a fatal accident (Hannon et al. 2019; Rodgers and Hassan 2021).

A well-developed example of collaborative responding to individuals in crisis is the joint approach taken by police officers and mental health workers (social workers, psychologists, mental health nurses, etc.) in relation to incidents where a person creates a public order disturbance or commits a crime as a result of a mental health crisis. These initiatives have been described as a crisis intervention team (CIT) approach, as 'street triage' or implementation of a 'co-responder' model (Horspool et al. 2016; Puntis et al. 2018; Rodgers et al. 2019). In such situations, police are typically the first to arrive at the scene, and are able to ensure the safety and security of those who have been involved in the incident. The mental health worker is then able to make use of their own skills in relation to assessing the person in crisis, then de-escalating their distress and facilitating access to appropriate services such as mental health, accident and emergency or accommodation. The process of working together in this way, and receiving training in a collaborative approach, can produce valuable learning for both sets of practitioners. It can also reduce demands on police and criminal justice time and resources by avoiding the necessity (in some instances) of charging the individual with an offence and bringing forward a prosecution. The complex and challenging reality of this kind of 'gray zone' work has been vividly documented by Wood et al. (2017), who were able to accompany police officers in Chicago over the course of typical shifts in community settings, and in interviews by Horspool et al (2016) with police officers and crisis workers in the UK.

Mobilizing those who care about the person in crisis: open dialogue

Quite often when a person is in crisis, there may be both practical and time limits to the amount of support that a practitioner can offer. An obvious strategy in such circumstances is to look to those closest to the person, such as family and friends, to provide ongoing support. An example of the possibilities associated with this kind of response are illustrated by the use of open dialogue meetings to support individuals who are undergoing a psychotic episode. Psychosis is an extreme form of psychological crisis, in which a person appears to lose touch with what would generally be assumed to be objective reality. The individual may feel threatened by hostile internal voices or external forces and talk in a garbled and confusing way. Particularly at the first time it occurs, such an experience can be terrifying and overwhelming for both the individual concerned and those close to them. The first onset of psychosis is most likely to take place in young adulthood. Although there may be complex individual, family and biological factors that contribute to such events, the first priority is to make sure that the person is safe. There are major cultural differences in the way that psychotic episodes are understood. Most indigenous cultures regard such processes as meaningful and highly valued expression of a capacity to express fundamental truths and insights about the world. By contrast, the trend in western industrial societies has been to view psychosis as a medical condition triggered by biochemical imbalances and to treat it with medication and hospitalization.

In an attempt to avoid medicalizing this condition, from the 1970s, psychiatrists and psychologists in North Finland began to develop strategies for creating flexible care packages for individuals experiencing first episode psychosis that drew on community resources. This approach made use of an early meeting with the family of the unwell person, and other people who knew them, to look at available options and agree a treatment plan. What they came to realize was that such meetings had a therapeutic effect in themselves. As a result, these practitioners added more meetings and became more skilled in how to facilitate them. By the 1990s, this had evolved into what became known as 'open dialogue therapy' (Seikkula and Olson 2003). The open dialogue model requires a meeting to be convened within 24 hours of the start of the psychotic crisis, usually around 90 minutes in duration and held in the person's home. Sessions are facilitated by two mental health practitioners and include the person, immediate family members and any others who may have something to offer, such as friends, college tutors or employers. The key principle is that everyone is invited to talk and everyone must listen. Meetings continue, if necessary, on a daily basis until consensus is reached about arrangements for long-term support of the person in crisis. Several research studies, in Finland and elsewhere, have found that this approach leads to minimal use of medication and hospitalization and produces long-term recovery.

Subsequent research has looked into what makes it possible for such a simple intervention, largely delivered by untrained lay people, to be so effective in helping a person to move on from such a profound personal crisis. Important aspects of the process include the ability of the practitioners facilitating group meetings to support participants to generate a wide range of perspectives in a respectful manner that allows for tolerance of uncertainty. When this happens, viable solutions gradually begin to take shape. At the same time, the presence and ongoing commitment of those who attend allows the person in crisis and those close to them to feel loved and cared about and to become less fearful (Seikkula and Trimble 2005). Further information about recent developments in open dialogue, and evidence of its effectiveness, can be found in Bergström et al. (2019), Gidugu et al. (2021), Ong and Buus (2021) and Putman and Martindale (2012).

Although psychotic breakdown is – thankfully – a relatively rare event, the principles and strategies used in open dialogue include many ideas that can be adapted for use in other crisis situations in which family and community support is potentially at hand. A valuable by-product of the adoption of open dialogue in a community is that, over time, there grows a significant proportion of the population who have had some level of involvement in such practices and are equipped to respond constructively to any crisis situations they might encounter in future.

Box 6.3 Crisis as an opportunity for change

If appropriate support is available and can be accessed, a crisis episode in a person's life has the potential to become a significant positive turning point. An example of this phenomenon can be found in crisis care for individuals diagnosed with borderline personality disorder. This term is a psychiatric label that is generally used to categorize individuals (often women) who have undergone prolonged abusive relationships in childhood and as a result have entered adult life with a very low sense of self-worth and value and a tendency to distrust other people and expect close relationships to be likely to end in disappointment. Within psychiatric and psychotherapy services, clients classified as borderline are regarded as hard to help and prone to suicide attempts at times when their sense of hopelessness and the stress of living becomes overwhelming (Warrender et al. 2021). A project in Geneva, Switzerland was set up building on earlier observations that such suicide attempts generally occurred following an experience of an intimate relationship coming to an end. In this initiative, such clients were immediately offered the opportunity to receive 'abandonment therapy', delivered by a trained nurse, starting during their time in hospital recovering from their suicidal injuries (Andreoli et al. 2016, 2021). The majority of these clients participated fully in therapy, were largely recovered from being borderline as a result of this help and remained well at three-year follow up. This programme also produced cost-savings by reducing future hospital admissions. While abandonment therapy is not a service that is widely available at the present time, it demonstrates how the radical personal disruption associated with a crisis can – if channelled effectively – make it possible for an individual to be open to new learning to which they might be much more resistant in 'normal' times.

Training in mental health first aid

A further organizational-level strategy for supporting individuals in crisis is to make sure that any person with a duty of care in relation to them (e.g. a nurse, social worker or teacher) possesses skills and awareness in psychological 'first aid'. Several different training programmes have been developed, usually comprising one or two-day attendance, in mental health first aid (Booth et al. 2017; Scantlebury et al. 2018) and suicide first aid such as the applied suicide intervention skills training (ASIST) or SafeTalk packages (Holmes et al. 2021). Modified versions of programmes have been developed for different occupational and cultural groups (see, for example, Jorm et al. 2018; Lu et al. 2020). First aid guidelines usually cover how to recognize that there is a problem, how to approach a person, what to say and do and where to find specialist help. A useful summary of the kinds of topics addressed in different first aid packages is available in Jorm and Ross (2018). Guidelines are usually compiled on the basis of expert judgement along with evidence from persons with experience (Nicholas et al., 2020).

The organizational and societal-level crisis approaches discussed above – helplines, single-session therapy, collaborative working, open dialogue and mental health first aid training – represent crucial sources of learning and support for any practitioner faced with a person in a state of crisis. Each of these approaches have generated training courses, online videos and reading material that feed in to ongoing learning and professional development. Most of them have had a global impact, with the result that there may be colleagues and agencies close by who can offer advice or to whom clients can be referred.

Culturally sensitive practice

Cultural awareness and sensitivity are extremely important when offering emotional support to individuals experiencing crisis. All of the skills perspectives and organizationally-based service discussed in this chapter place a strong emphasis on this factor. Although a person in crisis may exhibit a range of emotional and bodily patterns and reactions that reflect fundamental, universal responses to threat, the way they express these reactions, and what they mean to them, are shaped by the person's language and culture. In a situation in which it may be hard for the person to talk, and time is limited, there is a great risk that cultural insensitivity and missteps can be highly damaging. In addition, the ongoing support that is available to the person will almost certainly be influenced by specific types of family and community rights and responsibilities.

Supervision and support

Crisis counselling is an area of practice that has the potential to be highly stressful (Taylor et al. 2019). Clients are likely to be highly distressed, there are likely to be many issues to consider in a short period of time and, in many instances, the helper may never learn whether their inputs were ultimately beneficial or otherwise. It is important to create opportunities to make use of supervision and consultation from experienced colleagues and peer support (Richardson et al. 2020). As well as the emotional intensity of this kind of work, the experience of interacting with someone whose life has fallen apart, or been ripped apart, can trigger the helper's own fears and uncertainties around their own personal sense of security. This helper's personal vulnerability is heightened if they, and the client, belong to a community that has been collectively subjected to a catastrophic event such as a fire or flood or a violent incident. Organizations that routinely deal with individuals in crisis typically provide follow-up support for the staff who have been involved in such an episode in the form of group-based critical incident stress debriefing, individual psychological first aid or the option of referral to a counsellor (Feuer 2021; Mitchell and Everly 2006; Twigg 2020). Research into these forms of post-crisis support has tended to show that they are valued by staff, so long as they are delivered in a way that is consistent with organizational culture and practical realities (e.g. time demand) and do not undermine everyday forms of informal emotional support (e.g. by asking participants to share their feelings before they are ready to do so).

Conclusions

A person who is experiencing crisis is undergoing a process in which they feel as though their usual way of life has been taken away from them. A practitioner or helper who is called on to try to support such an individual – even if only for a short period of time – is in a position of being a representative of society as a whole. The implicit message is that there are people who care and that it is possible to move on and re-establish a meaningful life. The tasks of crisis counselling encompass practical as well as emotional support and generally need to be carried out under time pressure and in improvised counselling spaces. Ultimately, the capacity to be helpful in such scenarios depends on personal depth of compassion and ability not to overwhelm oneself. The aim of the present chapter has been to provide some ideas, informed by the experience of crisis workers in high-intensity situations, that may be adapted for use within a range of embedded counselling roles.

Learning activities

The following activities may be explored individually and/or with a group of learning partners.

Exercise 6.1 Reflecting on your own personal experience of crisis

Identify an episode in your own life that you experienced at the time as a crisis. What was helpful for you in terms of dealing with your immediate sense of being overwhelmed and enabling you to move on? What was missing or might have been more helpful? It may be useful, if you have time, to also consider different crisis episodes in your life or crises in close friends and family members. What are the implications of these events for your approach to working with a client or service user who is in a personal state of crisis, in terms of skills and strategies that you either already possess or might need to develop?

Exercise 6.2 Reflecting on your own learning

Looking at your capacity as a whole to provide a supportive and facilitative counselling relationship to a person in a state of crisis, what are the skills or areas of theoretical knowledge that you feel that you need to strengthen? What options are available to you in respect of taking forward this learning agenda?

Exercise 6.3 How your organization responds to personal crises

How does the organization in which you currently work respond to clients and service users who are in a state of personal crisis? In what ways might your organization respond more effectively to the needs of such clients?

CHAPTER 7

Emotions

Introduction	**131**
Examples of emotion tasks in embedded counselling	**131**
Making sense of anxiety and depression	**134**
The meaning of anxiety	134
The meaning of depression	136
Intersections of anxiety and depression	137
How counselling can help	**139**
Respectful and affirmative listening	140
Curiosity about how the person has coped with difficult emotions in the past	140
Be kind	140
Find out what the person wants	141
Agree step-by-step tasks	142
Agree on how each task might be accomplished	143
Work on tasks and review progress	144
Using therapy theories and approaches	145
Responding at an organizational level	**148**
Developing resources	148
Supporting practitioners whose work involves high levels of emotional intensity	149
Climate anxiety and grief	**152**
Conclusions	**153**
Learning activities	**153**

Introduction

A client or service user conveys that they are troubled in respect of some aspect of their life or may respond positively to an invitation to talk from a practitioner who has picked up a sense that there is something wrong. These moments can be understood as offering empathic opportunities – gateways into a client's personal life and concerns. The nature of what is troubling the client then begins to emerge as they talk. The previous chapter looked at what can be done when a client describes troubles that reflect a sense of being in crisis. The present chapter explores how practitioners support clients in understanding and dealing with life situations characterized by disruptive and painful emotional states.

The chapter focuses particularly on anxiety and depression – emotional states that are experienced as problematic by a substantial proportion of the population. Key characteristics of patterns of feeling and emotion associated with anxiety and depression are outlined, followed by a discussion of skills and strategies that can be utilized within individual therapeutic conversations to support clients to manage and overcome these emotions and finally, an exploration of organizational initiatives. It is important to recognize that anxiety and depression frequently co-exist with other problems in living. Themes and issues discussed in this chapter have links with topics covered elsewhere in this book, such as crisis, trauma, behaviour change and bereavement and loss. Anxiety and depression may co-occur and reciprocally interact with each other in ways that may heighten and intensify a person's life difficulties. A mix of anxiety and depression – sometimes described by client and service users as a general state of 'feeling bad' or as emotional and physical pain – can often be the trigger for seeking professional help.

Examples of emotion tasks in embedded counselling

The following examples describe three broad categories of emotion-focused counselling tasks that may be relevant when a client is troubled by anxiety and/or depression.

Awareness: exploring feelings that are elusive, vague or hidden. The marker for this task arises when the person may have a vague sense of how they feel about an issue, but be unable to put this into words or to be able to stay with the feeling long enough to really know what it is about. Sometimes, a person may claim that they do not feel anything at all. The counselling task here is to bring what is felt sufficiently into awareness for it to become a source of meaning and information that can be useful to the person. For example, Gina, a supervisor in a medical laboratory, consulted her human resources (HR) manager about how best to handle one of the technicians who was persistently late in arriving for work.

Following Gina's account of the issue, the HR manager said, 'I can see that the facts here are fairly straightforward. But there seems to be something else around too. Maybe this isn't relevant, but as you were talking, I found myself wondering how you felt about this person.'

This question threw Gina off balance. She replied that she was not aware of having any particular feelings about this colleague. The HR manager asked her whether she would be willing to just pause for a second or two and reflect on any feelings that she might be aware of at that moment. After a brief silence, Gina laughed and said that, yes, she realized that she was very fond of this technician.

'She reminds me of my own daughter. She is very warm and affectionate. She is the one all the others will turn to if they need to talk about something.'

In discussing the situation further, Gina became able to recognize the ways that she had felt anxious and worried about openly admitting her liking for her colleague, for fear of being seen to be behaving in an 'unprofessional' manner. These worries had resulted in her taking too formal and rigid an approach to the lateness problem, which in turn prevented her from holding the type of 'friendly' conversation with her that might have resolved the problem in a creative fashion. For Gina, becoming more aware of how she felt was the vital clue to the solution of her difficulty.

Releasing: articulating emotions that have been held back. If a strong emotion is stimulated by an event, it seems that there is a basic human need to give outward expression to that emotion in some way. If the emotion is not expressed or released, the person may have a sense of incompleteness, or 'unfinished business', which can interfere with normal functioning. The idea that emotions demand expression and that it can be psychologically and physically damaging to hold back emotion, can be traced to the ancient Greek theory of 'catharsis'. The marker for this kind of task may simply be that the person recognizes for themselves that there are emotions near the surface – 'I just need a good cry' or 'I feel so angry inside but I just can't do anything with it'. The counselling task involves creating the conditions for, and facilitating, the safe release of the emotion.

Ali was a refugee who had fled with his family from an oppressive regime. Safe in Britain, and waiting for his work permit to be finalized, Ali began to visit his GP every two weeks with a series of ailments – back pain, stomach spasms, headaches. On one of these visits, the GP asked Ali if he thought that it might be helpful to book a longer consultation to give them more time to talk about Ali's situation in greater detail and whether these different illnesses might be linked in some way. Ali readily agreed and on his way out of the room joked that 'you'd better watch out, Doctor. Have some tissues ready for our next meeting. Once I start to talk, I have five years of tears waiting to come out'. At the beginning of their next consultation, the GP started by saying that he had wondered if Ali was depressed, adding that this would be perfectly understandable given his current situation. Ali responded by saying that yes, he felt powerless in the face of bureaucratic delays, but that the main problem was the despair he felt about what had happened to his family and himself. He then went on to tell the whole story of what had happened to him in leaving his country and travelling to Britain. Within a few moments, Ali was in tears, as he described scenes of fear, torture and loss. The doctor moved his chair alongside Ali and placed his hand over Ali's hand. He encouraged Ali to keep talking, to continue with his story, and occasionally reassured him that 'you are alright now. You are safe here'. At a follow-up consultation one week later, Ali reported that 'it was the first time I have felt well in years. I have been busy with voluntary work and looking after the children and haven't been thinking about headaches and backaches at all.'

Limiting or managing the expression of emotions that are experienced as being out of control. The emotion-focused tasks that have been described above share an aim of learning how to bring buried or suppressed feelings into awareness and accepting what they may contribute to a person's participation in life. By contrast, another type of emotion-centred task in counselling can comprise the effort to control the experience, expression and enactment of emotions that are regarded by the person as being unwelcome or out of proportion to the situations in which they find themselves.

Alistair was a policeman who had worked on a motorway patrol for several years, witnessing on a routine basis a large number of fatal road traffic accidents. His colleagues and his wife had noticed that he seemed to be 'on a hair trigger' and likely to become verbally, and occasionally even physically, angry at the slightest provocation. She also thought that he was becoming depressed about 'letting everyone down'. Persuaded to consult the force occupational health nurse, Alistair could not be convinced to accept a referral to a counsellor or psychologist – 'I'm not mental, I just need to sort this out'. The nurse decided to invite Alistair to return for a longer consultation to explore the issue further. At this meeting, she asked Alistair if he was aware of a pattern to his anger episodes. Alistair described three episodes in which he had 'lost his head' and acknowledged that he had felt so 'hyper' at points in these incidents that he was close to having a full-scale panic attack. He said, 'There are times when I need to take command of people and speak in a clear, loud voice to give them directions for their own safety, but I can see now that I am going much too far…and it's starting to spill over into my family life.' The remainder of the session was spent discussing how a referral to a clinical psychologist might be helpful and what it would involve.

These examples demonstrate how emotion work can be the main focus of embedded counselling in some instances, or may be subsidiary to other tasks. For example, in the cases of Gina and Ali, a relatively brief conversation made it possible for them to acknowledge (Gina) and express (Ali) feelings and emotions in a way that was sufficient to allow them to see what they needed to do in order to move on in their lives. In the case of Alistair, although being able to recognize the emotional process that connected his work life and his family life was a valuable step, it was also clear that it opened up other issues around his work role, his way of regulating emotion and possibly also his assumptions about how men should think and act in different situations.

Making sense of anxiety and depression

It is essential to be able to meet the clients at the level of their everyday lived experience and concerns. Anxiety and depression are broad categories that refer to a complex array of experiences and processes. Because these are terms that are widely used in everyday discourse, many clients and services users talk about what is troubling them as 'anxiety' or 'depression'. However, to get to a point of being able to facilitate productive change, it is important to be able to arrive at a shared understanding of what a client actually means when they use these concepts.

The meaning of anxiety

Anxiety consists of a set of experiences, feelings, cognitive processes and action tendencies that are all ultimately grounded in fear and fearfulness. Fear is a basic human emotion that evolved as a means of ensuring personal safety in situations of danger. When confronted by a predator such as a bear, lion or snake, there was considerable survival value for early humans in possessing a powerful, immediate and automatic biologically wired-in activation of a fear response that took the form of fight-or-flight reaction and which for a brief period would take priority over all other behaviours.

Even though that kind of fear-based alarm and energizing mechanism still exists in the human nervous system, the way it operates in contemporary society is bound up with many other factors such as learned patterns of behaviour, cognitive processes and cultural norms. Most of the time, in present-day conditions, it is necessary to be able to suppress fearfulness rather than act on it. Key aspects of the experience of fearfulness include:

- bodily state that may include such features as rapid breathing, racing pulse and heart rate, muscle tension, restlessness and churning gut
- strong wish or intention to escape
- constriction of attention and cognitive capacity – in a state of fearfulness, the person struggles to think about anything other than this one thing – they are largely restricted to a polarizing (awful/terrified vs. wonderful/free) way of thinking rather than being able to engage in flexible problem-solving
- rumination – thinking about the fear event before it happens and then afterwards, imagining what might happen (catastrophizing) and replaying what did happen
- avoidance – actively organizing one's life around not being required to revisit the fear-inducing situation – this can expand into wider and wider circles of avoidance, possibly including obsessive and compulsive rituals
- concealing an underlying fear that is hard or shaming to own up to by channelling that emotional energy into feeling states that one is more comfortable with, such as annoyance, tiredness or sickness

- disrupted and problematic relationships – fearfulness tends to be exacerbated when the person's social network is not experienced by them as offering sufficient emotional safety to support them in facing up to difficult situations. In addition, the strategies used to handle fearfulness – such as avoidance or excessive rumination – can have the effect of undermining relationships and intimacy.

Taken together, these manifestations of the experience of being afraid are often described by clients or service users and organizations as 'anxiety'. Medicalized or pharmaceutical treatment may employ medication that aims to have an effect on many of these aspects of anxiety at the same time. A counselling perspective, however, usually involves breaking anxiety down into specific fearfulness processes and experiences such as bodily states, rumination, avoidance and relationship effects, which can be separately addressed step-by-step.

In many instances, the fears that may be expressed by a client or service user are connected to a specific situation or context. For example, a person may be afraid of being out of doors, being in a closed space, attending work or school or performing particular tasks at work or school such as speaking in front of a group or being examined/assessed. In healthcare contexts, a patient may be afraid of receiving an injection, receiving dental treatment or undergoing an internal examination or fearful that their symptoms may signal a serious or fatal illness. There are many, many different situationally-grounded patterns of fearfulness or anxiety. From a counselling perspective, these forms of anxiety are relatively straightforward to deal with. First, it is possible to focus in detail on what happens in that particular context, in terms of specific triggers, what the person is saying to themselves in their head, their actions and sources of support that might be available. This kind of exploration will usually lead to the identification of various points in the fearfulness cycle when the person might be able to learn how to respond in a different way. The second way that situational fears and anxiety are amenable to a counselling approach is that it is likely that a person who is troubled by a specific situation (e.g. talking in public) will be confident in other situations that require them to demonstrate skills that may be transferable or applicable to the feared situation. Helping people to overcome specific situational fears is one of the success stories of present-day counselling and psychotherapy, particularly cognitive behavioural therapy (CBT) (see McLeod 2019).

In addition to people who are troubled by specific fears, there are individuals for whom fearfulness is all-pervasive. This pattern is sometimes described as generalized anxiety disorder (GAD). It tends to be harder to help people to overcome this form of fearfulness, because it is not readily addressed through a focus on specific situations, and the client may find it hard to identify occasions when they are free from anxiety (i.e. situations that might serve as sources of personal anxiety management strategies). There are also people who try to control their fears by strategies such as obsessive rituals and perfectionism. For others, deeply suppressed fears (usually in respect of abusive relationships or unliveable life situations) may become overwhelming and lead to an overall breakdown in their capacity to cope (sometimes this is categorized as psychosis).

Persistent fearfulness and sense of being under threat contributes to stress, which for some people may be expressed through vulnerability to physical illness.

A further pattern of fearfulness can occur when a person uses food, alcohol or drugs to produce emotional states that have the effect of masking their fears. For example, someone might take a drink to give them courage before meeting new people or to help them to suppress fearful rumination that is preventing them from sleeping at night. A similar anxiety control process may be associated with behaviour that is generally considered to be healthy, such as taking exercise.

There are important cultural meanings associated with fearfulness, such as the idea that men should be brave and strong (i.e. not admit to being afraid). There is also evidence that for many people, an underlying fear of death (their own, or of someone close to them) is a significant aspect of the psychological problems that they are experiencing (Menzies et al. 2019). Although death anxiety is a universal aspect of existence, the fact that death is largely denied and made invisible in contemporary western society means that few people have the opportunity to develop a realistic appreciation of death or to talk to others about this issue. Finally, at a cultural level, the medicalization of fearfulness through the widespread use of psychiatric categories such as anxiety disorder and panic disorder and the use of anti-anxiety medication conveys a sense of fearfulness as being solely a problem that needs to be eliminated. However, fear and anxiety can also be understood as markers of positive development. For example, although a child may worry about going to school for the first time, and may exhibit separation anxiety and other symptoms, the process of learning that they can cope and thrive in this new environment and that their parents and teacher can be trusted to take care of them and support them through this experience represent significant steps forward in the life journey.

Taken as a whole, fearfulness and anxiety can be seen as concerns that touch the lives of a large proportion of the population. Fearfulness manifests itself in many different ways, and co-exists alongside concerns such as bereavement, depression, trauma and other problems in living.

The meaning of depression

Depression is a complex and multi-faceted phenomenon that is experienced, described and reported by different people in different ways. Although depression is similar to, and overlaps with, feelings of sadness and loss, the latter terms more usually refer to relatively short-term states of feeling arising from a specific event – 'I am sad because my daughter has emigrated to Australia and she will not be part of my life in the same way she has been for the last 20 years'. Depression is a persisting condition characterized by despair, powerlessness, hopelessness and helplessness. In terms of relationships and social contact, the person may isolate themselves from others, believe that they do not matter to anyone else, do not belong anywhere or see themselves as unworthy of being loved or cared about. The person may have a sense of being stuck in their life with a restricted or non-existent sense of the future or a future that can only be imagined as bleak. The person's time orientation may be predominantly focused on negative experiences and actions from the past. Often, there are harshly self-critical thoughts and internal voices and dialogues. Many people who are depressed report physical effects, such as difficulty in sleeping, deep lethargy and tiredness and pain. Depression can be ongoing and continuous or cyclical. Although many people who commit suicide do not appear to have been depressed in the months leading up to their death, some people who are depressed experience their lives as so unbearable that death may be viewed as a welcome escape. Depression may arise from the experience of adversity, such as a long-term debilitating health condition such as multiple sclerosis, the experience of being a refugee or through the kind of loneliness and social isolation that are common in urban societies.

Unlike anxiety, which is associated with cognitive distortions such as catastrophizing and selective attention to negative experiences, depression is often considered to represent a distinctively clear-eyed way of seeing the world (i.e. people who are not depressed may have a tendency to view the world through rose-tinted spectacles).

Intersections of anxiety and depression

There are similarities between anxiety and depression in terms of how they function and are understood in contemporary society. In recent years, as a result of developments in neuroscience, there has been a growth in the extent to which both professional helpers and lay people understand these emotional states as being fundamentally caused by biological imbalances and manageable through pharmacological intervention (Whitaker and Cosgrove 2015). This trend has been helpful for some people, in respect of the availability of medication, such as antidepressant pills, that they find useful. On the other hand, there is a risk that medical model approaches may make some people disregard psychological and interpersonal forms of help and long-established healing rituals that may be equally (or in many cases, more) effective. Such medications are also associated with side-effects and the possibility of dependency and withdrawal effects. The means of production of modern medicines can also harm the natural environment.

Another point of connection between anxiety and depression is that they are both significantly shaped by cultural belief and traditions. Cross-cultural psychology and psychiatry, and studies carried out by social anthropologists, have also repeatedly shown that anxiety and depression take somewhat different forms in different countries.

There are also historical shifts within specific regions. For example, although reliable and standardized figures are not always available, the incidence of these problems appeared to markedly increase in Europe and North America in the period from around 1950, probably due to the fact that social mobility, the pace of modern life and the adoption of a more individualized, competitive and consumerist way of life eroded long-established forms of mutual support and solidarity. Anxiety and depression are also more commonly found in women rather than men.

Anxiety and depression also overlap in the sense that both of them can be regarded as ways of not being angry. Analysis of adverse experiences that are associated with eventually becoming an anxious or depressed person suggests that many such individuals would have been exposed to a great deal of cumulative stress, unfairness, personal setbacks and disappointments, losses and other

---

Box 7.1 Most people already possess their own ways of dealing with anxiety and depression

The fact that so many people struggle with fearfulness, despair and low mood has meant that there has developed an extensive reservoir of everyday strategies and folk wisdom around how to cope with these conditions. In many studies conducted in different countries, individuals have readily identified how they manage anxiety and depression (Jorm et al. 2000; Kinnier et al. 2009; Smith et al. 2015), including such activities as finding support from others, reading about the problem, physical exercise, music, spending time with animals, changing diet, spiritual practice, life-planning, accepting that what they are feeling is a normal response to a difficult situation, developing a broader perspective, recognizing one's own strengths and potential, living in the moment and many more. Individuals troubled by anxiety and depression routinely manage their problems by using a wide range of self-healing activities that they have decided are most relevant for them. Professional assistance tends to be sought as a supplement to ongoing coping strategies, at a time of high stress or when existing strategies for some reason are no longer available (e.g. a close and supportive family member has died or loss of income makes dietary choice or exercise options unaffordable). The existence of everyday ways of coping with anxiety and depression opens up a potentially valuable line of exploration within brief embedded counselling. It can often be helpful to ask a client if it might be useful to look at how they have dealt with their concern (e.g. fearfulness or despair in relation to some aspect of their life) in the past, and whether there might be strategies that are familiar to them that could be used to better effect, or modified, to address current difficulties more effectively. Even highly trained psychotherapists are unlikely to be able to suggest techniques and interventions that are radically different from the client's everyday knowledge. What a good therapist or practitioner of embedded counselling can offer is support in applying these techniques in a focused, resolute and persistent manner.

types of negative events over the course of their lives. It seems likely that people who are effective in addressing and overcoming such adversities (and even growing or thriving as a result of them) are those who are assertive and are able to channel their anger into action (rather than withdrawing) – in other words, have a capacity for self-protective anger. By contrast, those who have grown up in oppressive and controlling families and communities in which the expression of self-protective anger is not considered acceptable, or may even be punished, are more likely to learn to suppress and disavow their anger and fighting spirit, eventually leading to anxiety and/or depression.

A common aspect of anxiety and depression is that people who exhibit these patterns can be hard to be around. For example, a fear-based or depression-driven tendency to avoid emotionally problematic experiences and activities can undermine friendships and work relationships. Anxious or depressed young people, at school or college or in their first jobs, may inhabit a relatively fluid social landscape in which they can move on and re-invent themselves afresh. By contrast, older people whose anxiety or depression has been around for a long time may be difficult to help – they may have already tried many ways of dealing with their difficulties to the point of being sceptical about whether anything will ever make a difference.

How counselling can help

For a practitioner in a frontline caring or human service role, such as a social worker, teacher, nurse or doctor, there are several ways that a client, service user, student or patient may convey fear-based concerns. The person may say that they are afraid or worried about some aspect of the care or service that they are receiving, or about something that is happening in their wider life. They may sound or look afraid. It may be apparent that they are avoiding doing something that is necessary for their well-being or success in life or are engaging in self-destructive behaviour as a means of suppressing their worries. Any of these scenarios can be taken as a potential empathic opportunity and followed up by an open question about whether the person might find it useful to say a bit more about what concerns them. If the person is willing to go down this route, it is then valuable to agree the length of time that would be available and (if possible) what the person would want to get from the conversation.

The following skills, strategies and principles outline some ways to ensure that such a session is helpful and facilitative. Because fearfulness is a frequently-occurring area of concern that co-exists alongside almost all difficulties that trouble clients, the process of supporting a person to address their fears is explored in detail. Discussion of strategies that can be utilised by embedded counselling practitioners to support clients to overcome low mood and depression can be found in Levine (2007), McLeod (2016) and McLeod and McLeod (2022). An understanding of how people handle depression in their everyday lives is available in Hänninen and Valkonen (2019) and Wilson and Giddings (2010).

Respectful and affirmative listening

It is crucial to allow and assist the person to tell their story. It is quite possible that they may never have shared their worries with anyone before. They may be ashamed or embarrassed about what they have to say and scrutinize your every reaction for signs of disapproval or rejection. For example, a client may say that they have not been to the dentist for 10 years because the very thought of registering with a dental practice makes them shake and feel sick. It is not helpful to jump in with reassuring statements such as 'you'll be fine', 'we all feel like that – it's never as bad as you think it's going to be', 'it's all over in half an hour' or 'once you get there, you'll be alright'. Any responses along these lines are likely to lead the person to close down because they perceive you as basically telling them to 'get over it' or 'pull yourself together'. By contrast, summarizing the main themes in what the person has said allows them to see that you have understood their experience. Open questions and invitations to say more convey genuine curiosity and empathy, encourage the person to explore the issue at a deeper level and create a decision space in which client and helper can work together to find the best way forward.

Curiosity about how the person has coped with difficult emotions in the past

Typically, a person in a counselling/helping role will have lots of useful and well-intentioned ideas and suggestions about how the speaker might be able to deal with their fear and anxiety. Such information may be extremely valuable for the client, but needs to be shared at the right time. Making suggestions too soon risks positioning the client as a passive recipient of counsellor wisdom and knowledge. A better approach is to view the client as the expert on their own life. In all likelihood, they may have lived with fear and anxiety for a considerable length of time before speaking to you about it and have done their best to understand and handle this concern. Almost certainly, some of the strategies they have used in the past will have been effective to at least some extent. Anchoring counselling in the client's personal knowledge, understanding, strengths, insights and resources has the effect of creating a platform for adding new strategies, reviving or adapting strategies that were previously helpful and suspending strategies that have been ineffective or even counterproductive.

Be kind

An important aspect of fearfulness for some people is that it is can be hard for them to tolerate the physical and embodied feeling of being afraid. In the therapy literature, this phenomenon is often described as difficulty in 'self-regulation' or 'self-management' of emotions. When faced with a threatening situation, there are people who are able to suppress their feelings of fear, for example by resolutely attending only to the task in hand, and are able to accept that their fearfulness is a normal response. By contrast, there are others who may have been socialized into believing that being afraid is wrong or weak, or have never had the experience of being comforted and held at a young age when something has scared them. What can then happen, later in life, is that it can become extremely difficult to acknowledge one's own fearfulness – even small steps in that direction may trigger harsh self-criticism. These processes have important implications for anyone counselling a person who exhibits fearfulness and anxiety. Any response that conveys a message that fearfulness and anxiety are somehow wrong, stupid, or trivial is unlikely to be helpful. The harsh self-critic or perfectionist part of the person may be happy enough to join in such a conversation, but at the expense of exploring the underlying problem of how to tolerate feelings of fear and be able to use them as a source of information. Whatever techniques or methods are eventually deployed (see below), it is important to continue to listen and attend to the vulnerable and fearful part of the person.

Find out what the person wants

In a professional role, when a client, student or service user comes across as afraid and anxious or describes themselves as being troubled or concerned about such emotions, there can be a tendency to assume that your job is to make the fear go away. In counselling terms, such a response reflects an assumption that the client's goal is to acquire solutions. In some instances such an assumption may be correct, but at other times it may be quite wrong. For example, a client who has recently been diagnosed with Alzheimer's disease may tell their social worker, community mental health nurse or GP that they worry a lot about what is going to happen to them in the future, sometimes to the extent of having terrifying nightmares that wake them up at night. In the context of what may be quite a brief conversation, it is important to make sure that the time that is available is spent talking about what is most significant for the client at that moment. For example, in relation to telling you about their fears, the client might hope to achieve one (or more) of the following goals:

- just talking – having an opportunity to explore what these fears might mean, by speaking about them to another person rather than just running through them over and over again in their own head
- letting *you* know – it may be important for the client that you realize and appreciate that this is something that is happening for them, for instance so that you are able to ask them at future meetings whether it is still a concern
- making sense and understanding – why is this happening now? Is it normal? Why does it come out as nightmares? Does it mean I have a mental illness?

- looking at how other people react to these fears – 'My daughter who cares for me just won't talk about anything to do with what the future might bring.'
- wanting to make use of your contacts and network, such as referral to specialist help such as counselling or a memory clinic, or information about patient self-help groups in the local area
- exploring solutions and coping strategies that might be helpful
- implementing a solution as soon as possible.

It may not be that the client will have a clear and explicit idea at the start of what they want to achieve by talking about their concerns. What is more likely is that they will have a vague sense of what they need to talk about, which may become more concrete and specific as the conversation develops.

Agree step-by-step tasks

It can be helpful to think about counselling as a process of 'making'. From this kind of perspective, the client's goal or goals can be viewed as creating or building something that will fill a gap in their life or will be used for a specific purpose. For example, a person may be troubled by panic attacks triggered by performance situations such as talking in public or taking an exam. There is no simple solution to such a problem. Instead, what is necessary is to piece together ways of making sense, relationships with others and practical skills that together make up an alternative way of approaching such high-pressure situations. As with the act of making anything at all in any area of life (making a meal, turning a piece of land into a productive garden, making a flower arrangement), arriving at the final end-point requires successfully accomplishing a series of constituent tasks. In relation to overcoming panic attacks, these tasks may include:

- creating a detailed moment-by-moment description of an occasion when a panic attack occurred
- identifying performance situations that did not evoke panic and considering whether there were aspects of these events that could usefully be applied in other challenging situations
- identifying thought processes that occurred at each stage of a panic episode, including thoughts that heightened the level of fear and those that reduced it
- identifying breathing patterns that occurred at each stage of a panic episode, including patterns that heightened the level of fear and those that reduced it
- learning a model of the panic process (e.g. a CBT spiral model) and how it might be applicable to your experience
- considering possibilities around potential emotional and practical support from other people

- practising ways of thinking, breathing, behaving and relating that might reduce panic
- using an app (Sucala et al. 2017) to reinforce application of new strategies in everyday situations.

Not all of these tasks will necessarily be relevant in every case, and there may be additional tasks that need to be added. Thinking about counselling as a process of making something in this kind of step-by-step manner has a number of advantages. It establishes a way of working together, through agreeing on tasks and pursuing them together. It also makes it possible to prioritize if time is limited (e.g. decide on one task to focus on that would make the most difference in the short term) and to divide up the work (e.g. a client might need direct help to practise different breathing and relaxation techniques, but be happy to read about models of panic in their own time).

Agree on how each task might be accomplished

Being able to work together to identify step-by-step tasks that have the potential to help the client move in the direction of their goal represents a key element of the counselling process. People who are troubled do not lightly ask for help. There can be a certain degree of shame in admitting to someone else that you are not able to cope. Seeking help from a practitioner is an indication of being stuck, not able to see a way forward. Being able to begin to identify some kind of destination, and map out how to get there, can be energizing and hope-inducing. In the previous section, some possible therapeutic tasks were identified that might be relevant to the goal of dealing with panic attacks. Susannah was 15 years old and had stopped going to school because she had started to have panic attacks in situations where she felt she was being evaluated by teachers and even her friends. The panic attacks had led to anticipatory anxiety about the very idea of going to school and then to depression, despair and harsh self-criticism about 'being a failure'. At the point of admitting this to a social worker, both Susannah and her mother were struggling to know what to do. They were reassured by the social worker's caring, empathic and respectful way of listening to Susannah tell her story and were happy to go along with his suggestion that they might begin to build an action plan together. Quite quickly they were able to agree on some initial tasks: (i) understanding what was happening during a panic attack and how to prevent such attacks taking place or closing them down if they seemed to be starting; (ii) meeting with class teachers and her friends, outside of the school day, to explain how they could help Susannah and enlist their own suggestions and support; and (iii) with the support of her mother, change Susannah's diet to reduce sugar intake and binge eating, with the aim of enabling her to feel more alert and confident. As they explored these tasks, it was clear that each of them could be accomplished in different ways (i.e. using different methods). The panic attack task could be progressed through using an online CBT programme, working through a self-help book, or sessions with a school counsellor. Meetings with teachers and friends could take place with the social worker present, or with Susannah's mother present, and might involve various kinds of preparatory work around what to say to them. Changing Susannah's eating might be something that she and her mother could do together or they might follow a manual or a dietician might be involved. Conversations about methods are not always necessary because the best way of tackling a task may be obvious. Nevertheless, such conversations can be helpful in themselves. Giving consideration to different options around possible change methods and activities increases the likelihood of finding the method that is the best fit for that person at that point in time. By contrast, brilliant, evidence-based suggestions from a counsellor that have worked really well for other clients just may not feel right to a particular client, who will then end up not fully committing to carrying them through (or may quit counselling to avoid being challenged about why they are 'resistant to change'). Another advantage of conversations about methods is that they implicitly convey the message that many valid possibilities exist – even if it turns out that this specific technique does not make a difference to your problem, maybe we can adapt it so that it works better or maybe we need to look at something else. Such an approach can also have the effect of empowering the client by affirming their capacity to know what is right for them and demonstrating that they are in the presence of a helper who takes them seriously.

Work on tasks and review progress

Individuals who have been troubled by issues linked to fearfulness and hopelessness for their whole lives, or for significant parts of their life, need to work hard to be able to shift deeply-ingrained and habitual patterns. Once the necessary step-by-step tasks and appropriate methods have been found, it is a matter of persevering. Regular reviews of progress are helpful, both as a way of checking whether an action plan needs to be readjusted and as a means of verifying whether the results are worth the effort. Within the counselling profession, one of the most important developments in recent years has been the availability of brief self-report measures and open-ended forms that a client can complete on a regular basis and look at with their therapist. Practitioners of embedded counselling, such as nurses, social workers and teachers can play a variety of roles in relation to the ongoing process of life change that a client may be pursuing. As exemplified in most of the brief case vignettes outlined in this chapter, a practitioner of embedded counselling may have a smaller part in this process, rather than being a main protagonist. Many clients make use of multiple sources of emotional and psychological support, even if they are seeing a specialist counsellor or psychotherapist. A teacher or social worker who has known a client over an extended period may be called on at specific moments in a bigger therapeutic journey or may be consulted as someone who is in a position to verify that progress has been achieved. A key implication here is that the helpfulness of an

Box 7.2 Responding to the needs of women who experience fear and stress around childbirth

Pregnancy, giving birth and taking care of a new baby comprise an extended life event that can be highly stressful for women. Slade et al. (2019) analysed available evidence around fear of childbirth and identified themes including fear of not knowing, fear of harm to the baby or to oneself, fear of inability to cope with the pain, fear of not having a voice in decision making and fear of being abandoned and alone. Taken together, these elements added up to an overall sense of feeling terrified. Such strong emotions are found both in women who had previous experience of physical and sexual abuse or absence of emotional support and also women who are culturally and socially disadvantaged. Two contrasting organizational strategies for providing emotional support to women with fear of childbirth have been developed. One approach is for midwives with interest and training in counselling to meet with a woman before the birth to build a relationship, explain what will happen around labour and the birth and to address concerns (Larsson et al. 2019; Wulcan and Nilsson 2019). The other is to give the pregnant woman the option of support from a doula, a trained non-medical helper who will accompany them through all aspects of the pregnancy and post-pregnancy period (McLeish and Redshaw 2019; O'Rourke et al. 2020; Ström et al. 2021). Published studies of midwife counselling have largely focused on support for women identified as being highly anxious, while doula research has predominantly investigated support for women identified as disadvantaged (although in some locations doulas may be accessed by any pregnant women, sometimes on a fee-paying basis). Both approaches are positively assessed by women who have received them. From an organizational perspective, midwife counselling and doula care reflect contrasting strategies for helping an emotionally vulnerable group of service users. The midwife counselling strategy involves providing time and training for existing employees to extend their professional role. The doula strategy involves the creation, from outside the healthcare system, of a new paraprofessional role.

embedded counselling episode should not be assessed in terms of whether a client has fully recovered, but in terms of whether it has made a meaningful contribution at that particular point in time.

Using therapy theories and approaches

One of the central messages of this book is that practitioners of embedded counselling can provide valuable support to troubled clients and service users on the basis of what they already know. However, further training in counselling skills, and learning about therapy theory, have the potential to enhance counselling effectiveness. In relation to helping clients whose problems in living are grounded in anxiety or depression, there are several theoretical approaches that can usefully inform frontline practice. These include:

Psychodynamic, relational and interpersonal approaches. This cluster of theoretical perspectives emphasizes the importance of the ways in which a person acquires an underlying emotional pattern in early childhood – and over later stages of development – that incorporates such features as: the ability to be open (or closed) to their own feelings and emotions and the emotional states of others; capacity to tolerate painful, strong or frightening emotions; and authentic and situationally appropriate expressions of emotion. This pattern or template plays out in relationships in adult life. Therapeutic skills associated with this approach include being able to help the person explore and reflect on their experience and providing a relationship that offers the client a place of safety in which they feel secure enough to express difficult feelings and try out different ways of interacting with another person.

Cognitive-behavioural approaches. Cognitive behavioural therapy (CBT) is based on the principle that behaviour and emotion are triggered and controlled by cognition – how the person appraises, perceives or makes sense of a situation. This approach has proved to be highly effective in relation to anxiety and depression. It draws attention to how these ways of being are maintained through rumination, distorted ways of thinking (e.g. catastrophizing and perfectionism) and critical self-talk and through cyclical processes where behaviour and bodily states are interpreted by the person in ways that serve to intensify and amplify these responses. This perspective has been applied in a widely-used and effective intervention to prevent panic attacks by breaking the cycle (Salkovskis 2007). A further important contribution of CBT for anxiety disorders, depression and other issues, has been the concepts of avoidance and exposure. For example, someone who is anxious will avoid situations that make them afraid (e.g. someone who is claustrophobic avoids using lifts) or a person who is depressed will avoid social contact because they assume that no one will want to talk to them (Peterman et al. 2015). From a CBT perspective, exposure to these situations – following the acquisition of new ways of thinking about them and coping with them – is necessary for the person to finally accept that they are able to handle such scenarios. CBT is also distinctive in its emphasis on teaching the model to clients, so that they can be actively involved in the process of change. To that end, the CBT professional community has produced many self-help manuals for clients, such as *The Anxiety and Worry Workbook* by Clark and Beck (2011). These manuals also provide a straightforward way for practitioners of embedded counselling to learn about CBT and provide worksheets that can be used with clients.

Humanistic approaches. An important and influential tradition within psychotherapy has been approaches that reflect principles of philosophical humanism, such as person-centred therapy, existential therapy and emotion focused therapy (EFT). This way of thinking about therapy emphasizes the value of the therapist being able to offer the client a genuine, empathic and accepting relationship. The assumption is that the experience of such a relationship helps the client to accept feelings and aspects of self that they had previously suppressed or denied. In respect of overcoming anxiety and depression, a humanistic approach argues that it is important to be able to be aware of, accept and appropriately express a wide spectrum of feeling and emotion. Specifically, both depression and anxiety are regarded as fronts or masks, behind which there exist uncomfortable feelings such as anger, loss and sadness, shame and fear of dying. Humanistic practitioners have developed techniques and methods, such as two-chair dialogue and experiential focusing, to facilitate the expression of suppressed emotions and feelings.

More detailed accounts of these ideas can be found in McLeod (2019), along with suggestions for further reading. CBT has been widely adopted by healthcare providers around the world, because it tends to make sense to people who have never had therapy before and is supported by both research and the availability of self-help resources. CBT is also seen as attractive because it is presented as a type of help that will have an effect in a relatively short period of time. However, systematic reviews of research have tended to suggest that all of the established approaches to therapy are broadly equivalent in effectiveness (Cuijpers et al. 2020). In practice, there are important differences between clients in relation to how credible they find different therapy theories. Some clients are open to virtually any ideas about what might be helpful, while others have distinct preferences (Norcross and Cooper 2021). In some situations, for example a client choosing a private practice psychotherapist, the client is able to

Box 7.3 Bravery transfusions

There are many powerful and helpful therapy ideas that exist outside of the mainstream therapy theory and practice. For example, following the tragic and destructive earthquakes that took many lives in Christchurch in 2010, the narrative therapist David Epston was consulted about his advice around how to support young people who had become fearful about participating in everyday activities. His article, titled 'To Christchurch with love', introduced the notion of 'bravery transfusions', through which those with an excess of bravery could share this quality with those who were temporarily lacking in it. What he described relied heavily on a concept (bravery) that was familiar and meaningful in terms of everyday experience, but not an idea that had ever previously been part of a therapy theory or intervention. It also made use of pre-existing relationships of love, affection and trust between young people and older family members.

decide on a therapist whose approach matches their preferences. By contrast, in embedded counselling and other frontline sources of emotional support, it is important for practitioners to be sufficiently flexible to find common ground with any clients who want to work with them. A collaborative approach based in agreeing step-by-step tasks, with different options around how to accomplish these tasks, is intended to maximize the chance of finding such common ground.

Responding at an organizational level

Health, social care and educational organizations typically employ a substantial number of well-qualified and experienced practitioner employees and have the scope to review and re-arrange the work patterns and responsibilities of staff in response to service user need. In relation to responsiveness to client emotional difficulties around fearfulness, anxiety, low mood and depression, there are many ways that staff within an organization or sector can devise forms of support that go beyond the skills and compassion of individual members of staff. Boxes 7.2 and 7.4 offer examples of how healthcare professionals recognized anxiety-oriented issues in some service users – around fear of childbirth and fear of dental treatment – and created formal, evidence-based approaches to ensuring that service users received effective care. The following sections consider some ways that colleagues in an organization can work together, short of developing a formally-recognized package, by developing resources and supporting each other.

Developing resources

In addition to face-to-face conversation, counselling can be augmented through the use of a wide range of learning resources. While it is possible for each practitioner to assemble their own tool-kit of resources, there are advantages to working with colleagues to share ideas and develop new materials. In some instances, technical knowledge and expertise available at an organizational level may be crucial, for instance if it is decided to create dedicated client-facing web pages. In relation to helping clients who are struggling with anxiety and depression, there exist valuable online therapy sites that are only accessible through paid organizational membership, such as Beating the Blues (https://www.beatingtheblues.co.uk) and Togetherall (https://togetherall.com/en-gb/). There are also open access sites such as Kooth (https://www.kooth.com). These packages allow clients to pursue their own learning and healing process in their own time, with the possibility of occasional support from an embedded counselling practitioner.

It can be helpful to build a portfolio of therapists and services in the local area that clients might be referred to or approach under their own initiative. It can be particularly valuable for some clients if the embedded counselling practitioner they are seeing has personal knowledge of a therapist or service that is being recommended and can let them know what to expect. Information about counsellors is available through an online directory maintained on the British Association for Counselling and Psychotherapy (BACP) website and by similar professional bodies in other countries. In the UK, information about local support groups and activities is available through MIND (https://www.mind.org.uk), the leading national mental health charity. There are several national and regional phone lines that support people who are suicidal, children who have been abused and other groups of clients.

In any locality, there are likely to be many potentially therapeutic groups and organizations that are not listed or categorized in directories. These include domestic violence support, sexual violence support, food banks, art projects, dance classes, pop-up initiatives, befriending services, community gardens, yoga centres, men's sheds, community sports, complementary health centres and practitioners, walking and other outdoor pursuits groups, reading groups and many different types of faith and spiritual practice groups. There are also many groups that have been established to support people with specific life experiences and identities, such as carers (and young carers), military veterans, members of ethnic minority communities, trans people and people with other gender identities, people with long-term conditions such as dementia, sight loss, hearing loss, and Parkinson's disease.

Many clients find it helpful to access information about anxiety, depression and related conditions through books, articles, podcasts, TED Talks and similar sources. Local libraries may often provide lists of self-help health titles that are available for loan.

Supporting practitioners whose work involves high levels of emotional intensity

In any kind of counselling work, practitioner access to supervision and consultative support is necessary to ensure that a safe and competent service can be maintained on an ongoing basis (see Chapter 4). This process inevitably needs to take account of the practitioner's emotional response to a client (O'Connor 2020). There can be occasions when the level of emotional intensity arising from meetings with particular clients requires support beyond routine supervision and consultation. The present chapter has largely discussed helping situations in which a client or service user may be experiencing strong and distressing emotions while the listener or embedded counselling practitioner remains relatively calm. However, there are also cases where the practitioner themselves experiences strong emotions and may struggle to retain a professional stance. What can happen in such instances is that the practitioner comes to dread, or even avoid, such contact. There may also be longer term consequences for a practitioner, such as compassion fatigue, trauma reactions, burnout and ensuing sickness absence or change of job. These processes have been particularly well documented in relation to the experiences of child protection/custody social work with families where the parents are angry, hostile and resent any form of professional or legal intrusion into their lives (Albaek et al. 2019, 2020; Ferguson et al. 2020, 2021; Tonning Otterlei and Studsröd 2021). They have also been closely studied in respect of emotionally difficult and harrowing calls handled by nurses employed on telephone consultation helplines (Eriksson et al. 2019, 2020). The study by Ferguson et al. (2020) offers a strikingly detailed and vivid depiction of social work experiences that are at, and often beyond, the limits of what the practitioner can tolerate. What seemed to happen in some of these episodes was that the practitioner was dragged so far out of their comfort zone that their actions and responses served to exacerbate the problem. Many of these social worker–client relationships were never repairable.

Strategies for dealing with such situations, in the moment, included using breathing and other techniques to remain grounded and centred, pausing the conversation to allow reflection time, reminding oneself of one's values and the importance of the work and attempting to pull the interaction back to a pre-planned script or structure (Eriksson et al. 2020; Ferguson et al. 2020; Tonning Otterlei and Studsröd 2021). The single most important factor that made it possible to get the job done, reported by many participants in these studies, was the support and emotional security provided by colleagues. By contrast, lack of collegial solidarity and support made it very hard to continue with the work. A particularly difficult aspect of emotionally challenging meetings with clients was when they took place in the client's home – this was experienced as threatening, sometimes unsafe, and allowing the client the possibility of dominating and controlling the interaction (Ferguson et al. 2020). All of these studies commented that not enough is known about these aspects of human service work and not enough attention is given to the needs and experiences of practitioners exposed to these episodes. Ferguson et al. (2021) suggests that a capacity to function constructively and helpfully in highly conflictual encounters with clients requires practitioners to learn how to offer a 'holding' relationship based on a willingness to get closer to the client's life and concerns, rather than adopting a more distanced approach.

From a psychotherapeutic perspective, the kinds of scenario described by Ferguson et al. (2020) could be seen as arising from interactions with clients who have strong, but usually suppressed, emotions that have their origins in life events where their anger, despair, emotional pain and terror needed to be suppressed. Unlike the majority of clients, who are able to talk about and reflect on how they feel, the only way that these more challenging clients have to express emotion is through actions such as shouting, threatening gestures or throwing things. However, the same patterns of behaviour can equally well be viewed from a socio-political perceptive. People who have been subjected to discriminatory and humiliating treatment on account of poverty, race or other factors have learned to be suspicious of any representative of the state, even teachers, social workers and health professionals who are doing their best to help them.

Box 7.4 Organizational strategies for supporting patients with dental anxiety

Dentistry is a highly technical type of helping activity, that largely consists of a practitioner carrying out procedures on a passive and largely silent patient. However, around 15 per cent of people report significant levels of fear and anxiety around dental treatment, with five per cent at such a level as to make it impossible for them to visit a dentist at all (Hauge et al. 2021). The dental profession has therefore been required to develop ways of supporting such patients. A wide range of low-intensity approaches have been implemented, including music, relaxation and nature imagery (Weisfeld et al. 2021). Although these strategies are evaluated positively by most patients, they are not sufficient in themselves to help the most highly-anxious patients. The two approaches that have been found to be most effective for such individuals are supportive counselling-type consultations, and CBT. In supportive consultations, the dentist spends time with the patient listening empathically to their concerns, explaining what will happen in a treatment session and developing ways for the patient to exert control over the treatment process. This approach seems to be successful because the dentist is able to be more sensitive to subtle cues expressed by the patient and the patient trusts the dentist as a real person who has their best interests at heart (Bernson et al. 2011; Kulich et al. 2000, 2003). The other form of support that works well is CBT training in how to manage fear and panic, delivered either through a single video-assisted session facilitated by a dental assistant (Potter et al. 2016) or in the form of four meetings with the actual dentist (Hauge et al. 2021). These initiatives show how it is possible to enable practitioners with limited previous training in interpersonal skills and psychology to get to a stage of being able to facilitate meaningful behaviour change in service users with extremely high, long-established patterns of anxiety.

Many human service organizations and educational programmes preparing individuals for entry into such occupations routinely provide training around such topics as handling difficult conversations and breaking bad news. While the skills and ideas covered in these courses – and subsequent practical experience – are relevant to the issues outlined in this section, they mainly focus on conversational strategies for making sure that the client or recipient is supported to remain open to information that is hard to hear and to participate in shared decision-making in a meaningful way, even though they may be upset or in a state of crisis (see, for example, Ekberg et al. 2020). By contrast, the studies by Albaek et al. (2019, 2020), Eriksson et al. (2019, 2020) and Fergusson et al. (2020, 2021) refer to a much more visceral, existential and personal engagement in a highly-charged and mutually challenging emotion-laden interaction.

Climate anxiety and grief

The climate crisis and other associated issues such as loss of biodiversity, plastic and chemical pollution and diminished human fertility are becoming more apparent year by year. These changes are increasingly leading to people feeling anxious and depressed about the state of the world and what the future will bring. In terms of issues for which people might seek emotional support from a frontline human services practitioner, at the present time, two main configurations are apparent. First, there are individuals who are troubled by climate change anxiety and grief. Second are those individuals and communities whose lives and emotional well-being have been directly impacted by specific climate and other events and disasters, such as floods, fires, landslides and loss of habitats (see, for example, Middleton et al. 2020). A useful review of current projects around using counselling and psychotherapy to support people experiencing climate anxiety, has been published by Baudon and Jachens (2021). At the present time, it is not clear how best counselling can be implemented in this context. For example, unlike typical everyday situations, such as being anxious about talking in public or having a panic attack in a crowded supermarket, there are many reasons for thinking that anxiety, worry and sadness are appropriate responses to what is happening at a planetary level. Also, for the majority of people – so far – the climate crisis has had a limited effect on them personally. This stands in contrast to more usual anxiety and depression, which undermine a person's capacity to live their life to the full. A further aspect of climate anxiety is that it is experienced more acutely by children and young people, who are less able to initiate contact with helping professionals and counsellors (Hickman 2020; Hickman et al. 2021). As a result, such issues are not coming to the attention of practitioners as much as they might be. Many organizations and agencies in the field of education, health and social care have produced position statements that highlight the climate crisis as a major priority for research and practice. It is therefore likely that practitioners will be increasingly involved in providing emotional support for clients and service users around these concerns.

Conclusions

Anxiety and depression are emotional issues that affect the lives of many people, and are frequently part of the concerns that lead clients and service users to want to talk to a practitioner about personal issues. Anxiety and depression are also areas in which counselling and psychotherapy have tended to record high success rates, with an average of 60 per cent of such clients significantly improving as a result of receiving therapy. To be able to respond effectively to clients with difficulties around anxiety and depression, it is essential to recognize that these constructs are general terms and that clients may describe quite different ways in which these difficulties are manifested in their lives. Similarly, despite the dominant position of CBT as a treatment approach within healthcare systems, there are in fact many ways of supporting and helping clients to move on from lives blighted by fearfulness and low mood. There are also many ways that practitioners of embedded counselling can work alongside inputs from other agencies, services and activities. It is also important for practitioners to be aware that clients are likely to already be familiar with a wide range of everyday coping strategies, which may need to be re-activated or adapted to address the current challenges being experienced by the client. At an organizational level, there are many ways in which groups of practitioners can work collectively to build resources, support each other, and in some cases develop special programmes and services designed to meet the needs of specific client groups.

Learning activities

Exercise 7.1 Your personal emotional profile
How comfortable are you with the expression of emotions? Are there emotions around which you feel relatively comfortable and other emotions that are hard for you to express or hear? What are the implications of your personal emotional profile for your work as a counsellor?

Exercise 7.2 The impact of the organizational context
What is the emotional profile of your workplace? Which emotions are allowed and in what circumstances? Which emotions are suppressed? What happens to people who express taboo emotions in your office or clinic? What are the implications of your organizational emotion profile for you as a practitioner and for the people who use your service?

Exercise 7.3 Being aware of emotions in everyday life
Over the course of a convenient period of time (an hour, a day), keep a note of the emotion and feeling terms that people use in their conversations with you (and you use in your conversations with them). Are there any patterns

that you can identify? For example, do men and women or people from different age, ethnic or social class groups seem to talk in different ways about feelings? What has been the effect on you, and your interactions with others, of specifically listening for emotions?

Exercise 7.4 Responding to anxiety
Within your own workplace, what proportion of your clients express concerns around fearfulness and anxiety or seem to have lives that are restricted by their need to limit their exposure to anxiety-inducing situations? How are such concerns and patterns manifested in their interactions with you? What do you do to help and support such individuals? How much, and in what ways, does your place of employment recognize or prioritize such client issues? Identify at least five practical ways that you, and your organization as a whole, do more to provide emotional support to clients with anxiety problems.

Exercise 7.5 Responding to depression, hopelessness and despair
Within your own workplace, what proportion of your clients express concerns around depression, hopelessness and despair or seem to have lives that are restricted by a depressive attitude to life? How are such concerns and patterns manifested in their interactions with you? What do you do to help and support such individuals? How much, and in what ways, does your place of employment recognize or prioritize such client issues? Identify at least five practical ways that you, and your organization as a whole, do more to provide emotional support to clients with issues of depression, hopelessness and despair.

Exercise 7.6 Coping with highly emotionally intense interactions with clients
Identify one example of an interaction with a client or service user that you experienced – at a personal level – as emotionally troubling, harrowing or even traumatic. How did you deal with your emotions at the time and afterwards? What have you learned, from your reflection on this episode, about how to handle such situations both in terms of working productively with such clients and in respect of how to take care of your own well-being?

Exercise 7.7 Being prepared to respond to climate crisis concerns
What is your own position in relation to the climate crisis and associated issues relating to the destruction of the biosphere by human civilization? What is the position that has been adopted by the organization in which you work? To what extent, and in what ways, are these beliefs, values and attitudes reflected in how you – and other parts of the organization – respond to service users or staff who have concerns around climate change?

CHAPTER 8

Adversity and trauma

Introduction	**156**
Making sense of trauma	**157**
Trauma and PTSD	157
Trauma as betrayal	159
Intergenerational trauma	160
Microaggression	161
Moral injury	162
Precarity	163
Adversity	164
How counselling can help	**166**
Listening	167
Making sense	167
Building a more complete and coherent story of what happened	168
Making use of social support	168
Developing coping skills	170
Brief embedded counselling with a person experiencing extreme trauma and adversity: a case example	171
Responding at an organizational level	**171**
Conclusions	**173**
Learning activities	**173**

Introduction

The previous two chapters have explored how embedded counselling provided by frontline human service practitioners can represent an effective way to support healing and recovery in individuals who are grappling with a crisis in their life, or with issues around anxiety/fearfulness and depression/despair. On the whole – but not always – the people troubled by these conditions tend to be able to draw on a relatively stable and well-functioning sense of who they are. In other words, although they may have difficulties in some areas of their life, they may function effectively in other areas. These personal strengths and capabilities operate as resources that a person can draw from in relation to dealing with episodes of crisis, anxiety or depression.

The present chapter turns to an examination of the experiences of people whose troubles go deeper than anxiety and depression. These are people who have been exposed to trauma – sometimes for long periods of their lives, and possibly even from the moment they were born. Trauma takes many forms and is linked to many sources of social injustice, such as racism, sexism, homophobia, poverty, disability, violence and abuse. As a result, there are many people who have not only been emotionally and psychologically hurt and damaged, but who have also been socially and culturally silenced, marginalized and discriminated against.

A central theme in this chapter is that there are many ways in which embedded counselling can make a useful contribution in relation to helping clients and service users to recover from trauma. Counselling and psychotherapy cannot directly address the material and economic disadvantage associated with trauma and oppressive or restricted life opportunities. On the other hand, initiatives and interventions that focus on material disadvantage do not always have space to explore the kinds of emotional, relationship, interpersonal and identity issues that are caused by adversity. Embedded counselling offers a point of contact between these contrasting forms of help. A teacher who is working with a young person from a family environment characterized by poverty and violence to pass their exams to enter university is in a good position to at least begin a conversation with their student about what it means to them to be moving out of the neighbourhood in which they grew up and into a different social world. A social worker who is supporting a homeless person with addiction issues to find a job and place to stay is similarly in a position to help that individual to come to terms with the huge losses and humiliations they may have undergone in their life up to that point.

In recent years, the concept of trauma-informed care has become increasingly influential within many areas of health, social care, education and the justice system. This movement has grown and expanded to encompass a wide range of perspectives and practices. To be able to use these ideas in embedded counselling, it is necessary to appreciate how they fit together and what each of them has to offer. The first half of the chapter is therefore devoted to explaining how a simple principle – an appreciation of how a traumatic event can affect a person – has unfolded and been implemented. The second half of the chapter focuses on how counselling can help and looks at some of the organizational-level initiatives that have emerged in this field.

Making sense of trauma

Trauma is a concept that has many meanings that have gradually unfolded as an increasing range of trauma-informed practice has evolved. The following sections trace how understanding and knowledge about trauma has developed.

Trauma and PTSD

The concept of trauma refers to a highly stressful, frightening or distressing event. Trauma may be associated with a single incident, such as a sexual assault or car accident. It can also take the form of repeated and prolonged threatening events such as domestic violence, sexual abuse or racial harassment. Complex trauma arises when a person has been subjected to multiple traumatic events.

Historically, the word 'trauma' was used to refer to physical wounds. Hospitals and medical centres often include trauma doctors and nurses, who specialize in dealing with patients who have experienced serious accidents. Although shell-shock in soldiers was well understood, and Freud's psychoanalytic theory was based on the idea that people who had emotional difficulties as adults had been exposed in childhood to emotionally troubling events, the concept of trauma only began to be applied to psychological injuries in the 1970s, largely as a result of studies of Vietnam war veterans. Post-traumatic stress disorder (PTSD) became recognized as a psychiatric disorder in the 1980s. Since that time, various treatment approaches have been developed to address this condition and a substantial research literature has been created, including many neurobiological studies.

It is important to recognize that, even though research and practice on direct bodily trauma (such as physical injury) and around psychological trauma/PTSD have tended to diverge, for many clients and patients the two are closely linked. Interviews conducted by Kellezi et al. (2020) into the experience of patients treated for physical injury trauma found that the emotional sensitivity and listening skills of doctors, nurses and rehab staff made a significant difference to their process of recovery.

Post-traumatic stress disorder occurs when a person has been exposed to a highly traumatic and threatening event. Typical signs of PTSD are intrusive memories of the events, such as flashbacks, alongside attempts to avoid thinking about what had happened. Avoidance can sometimes only be achieved by self-medication through alcohol and drugs. The person suffering PTSD tends to experience a loss of trust in the world, experiences even minor setbacks and stresses as highly threatening, and may become hyper-vigilant. This set of symptoms can lead to sleep loss and fatigue, relationship problems, difficulties at work, depression and suicide. Although the literature on PTSD tends to be dominated by high-profile trauma-inducing events, such as involvement in warfare or being the victim of terrorism or natural disaster, studies have shown that there also exists a substantial amount of 'everyday' traumatic stress. Events such as car accidents, domestic violence, bullying, sexual violence, robbery and childbirth can lead to PTSD reactions. As a result, most human service practitioners will encounter clients and service users with PTSD symptoms on a regular basis.

At the heart of the PTSD response is the need to cognitively process information that is not readily assimilated into the person's previous way of making sense of the world. When we encounter a routine life difficulty or irritation (the car won't start), we can usually make sense of it quite readily (the battery is flat). By contrast, when something traumatic and completely unexpected happens (I was waiting in the queue at the bank and a masked man with a gun rushed in), then it is very hard to make sense of what all this might mean (could I have died? What would have happened to my children? Why me? Could I have done anything differently?). A key principle of counselling for PTSD is to help the client to construct a coherent story or narrative around what happened – to find a place for it within their mental map of social reality. This can be achieved by talking about, remembering and piecing together an account of the event. However, this therapeutic task may be difficult to accomplish – re-living the event or revisiting it in one's memory may be very hard because each strand of memory may be associated with fear and terror.

A further aspect of PTSD relates to the physiological, bodily effects of trauma. Exposure to a traumatic event produces significant, enduring effects on brain chemistry and structure and nervous system functioning. As a result, even if the individual is able to suppress conscious memories of the event, the body 'remembers' (Rothschild 2000). What this means, in terms of everyday experience, is that the person may react to situations through bodily reactions, such as sudden onset of dizziness, nausea or panic, that can be frightening and puzzling.

There exists a huge practice and research literature on PTSD. A good starting point is the website, videos and publications of one of the leading figures in this field, Bessell van der Kolk, in particular his best-selling book *The Body Keeps the Score: Brain, Mind, and Body in the Healing of Trauma* (van der Kolk 2015).

There are many specialist therapies that have been developed to treat PTSD, such as exposure-based CBT and eye movement desensitization and reprocessing (EMDR), that have been shown to be helpful for clients who receive them (Wampold 2019; Watkins et al 2018). However, there are many individuals affected by trauma who do not receive such help, either because these therapies are costly and not available everywhere, or because the trauma symptoms have become overlaid by other difficulties such as addiction, depression, personality disorder or criminality. In addition, these specialist therapies are emotionally very demanding because they generally require the client to recall distressing

Box 8.1 Measuring PTSD

A useful way to get a handle on what psychiatrists and other practitioners mean when they talk about PTSD is to look at how it is defined and measured in the context of research and client assessment. The standard technique for assessing PTSD is the impact of event scale (IES), a 30-item self-report measure originally published in 1979 and revised by Weiss (2007). The questionnaire instructions ask to nominate a specific 'stressful life event' that occurred on a specific day and then use a five-point scale to indicate how much they have been distressed about that event within the last seven days. Examples of items in the scale include 'pictures about it popped into my mind' and 'I tried not to talk about it'. Norms have been produced that suggest a cut-off point for a diagnosis of PTSD. The IES is available for download online. In addition, the CAPS-5, an interview guide for assessing PTSD, has also been developed (Weathers et al. 2018).

events in detail. As a result, there is a high level of drop-out from treatment. What all this means is that practitioners of embedded counselling have important roles in respect of facilitating therapeutic conversations and activities that help their clients to take small steps in relation to undoing the effects of trauma on their lives, and also supporting clients to engage with – and complete – specialist therapies where appropriate.

Trauma as betrayal

A key factor in the psychological and emotional effect of trauma is what Janoff-Bulman (2010) described as 'shattered assumptions' – the person's expectations and beliefs about the world are undermined by the occurrence of something completely out of line with their definition of normality. In many instances, such as being a victim of violence, sexual abuse or humiliation, a crucial part of what has been shattered is the belief that other people are trustworthy, reliable, and essentially good. Birrell and Freyd (2006; Birrell et al. 2017) argued that this kind of experience could be understood as a form of 'betrayal trauma', and that it could have long-term consequences in terms of a general lack of trust in others, reluctance to develop intimacy and a sense that there must be something wrong with oneself for such an event to have taken place at all. These processes can lead to a kind of inner fragmentation and compartmentalization of experience, in which the person can only function in areas such as work and family through being able to fence off the fears and memories associated with their experience of betrayal. In addition to types of traumatic betrayal that are extreme and unlawful, such as rape, sexual abuse, domestic violence and criminal assault, this pattern has been associated with such experiences as workplace bullying (Rodríguez-Muñoz et al. 2010), affairs, theft and vandalism. In their study of the rape experiences of black women and girls, Gómez and Gobin (2020) have shown that racism can have the effect of intensifying betrayal.

The idea that, in addition to psychological and physiological impacts, many forms of trauma also involve interpersonal and relational effects, has important implications for counselling for trauma. Birrell and Freyd (2006) argue that the process of recovery needs to involve ways of repairing emotional bonds and restoring the capacity for connection. It is significant, that alongside well-established and evidence-based psychological therapies for trauma, there also exists an alternative tradition of trauma support in the form of groups and networks, for instance for women who have been subjected to sexual violence or for those who have given military service. An interpersonally-focused approach to therapy can also be conducted on a one-to-one basis. Bleiberg and Markowitz (2019) offer a case example of a black US military veteran who had been exposed to many traumatic experiences during his service in the middle east, including humiliation by white colleagues. Rather than ask this client to talk about what had happened during these incidents, the therapy concentrated on rebuilding relationships, such as with his father, that had been damaged by the way that the consequences of trauma had taken this man into a lonely and isolated place in his life.

Intergenerational trauma

The early phase of research and practice around trauma was grounded in an assumption that this phenomenon necessarily involved a specific, observable event that happened to a particular person. More recently, it has become clear that it also makes sense to think in terms of collective trauma, in which a whole community are affected even if some are more directly involved than others and historical or intergenerational trauma in which individual or collective trauma from members of one generation are passed on to the next generation (and even subsequent generations). Some of the most important research on this topic was carried out in Israel, where it was found that the children of Holocaust survivors mirrored their parents in having difficulties around trust and interpersonal attachment, even in cases where the parents had never talked about their Holocaust experience to their offspring (Bar-On et al. 1998; Danieli 1998). Intergenerational trauma has subsequently been identified in children of war veterans, immigrants, refugees and victims of political oppression such as the cultural revolution in China. Multi-generational trauma effects have been observed – even now – in people whose distant grandparents lived in communities in Africa that were exploited by the slave trade (French 2021) or indigenous First Nations groups in Australia and North America that were almost eradicated by colonial genocide (Bombay et al. 2009; Gone 2013; Marsh et al. 2015). While efforts to address intergenerational trauma have mainly focused on political action (e.g. consciousness-raising and restorative justice) rather than counselling, an appreciation of the nature of intergenerational trauma can contribute to making emotional support more relevant to the needs of clients in certain communities. For example, Carlin et al. (2019) interviewed Aboriginal women in the sparsely-populated Pilbara region of Western Australia about the emotional support that was available to them through their pregnancy. The women in this study reported that health professionals with whom they had been in contact were a key source of support, particularly those who were able to demonstrate a sensitivity to how the effects of intergenerational trauma were manifested in multigenerational histories of alcohol abuse, and to the need to adopt a culturally-appropriate way of talking that displayed kindness, trustworthiness and a capacity for 'having a quiet word'.

Microaggression

The phenomenon of 'microaggression' has been a key area of focus in research and practice that has explored the process of counselling with clients for black and minority ethnic communities and other excluded social groups. Microaggression takes the form of brief, commonplace, everyday verbal and behavioural indignities that convey hostility and contempt toward the recipient. Such responses may be intentional or unintentional, and in some instances may be glossed as humour (Sue et al. 2007). Various types of microaggression have been identified: 'microassault' (offensive language or active discrimination); 'microinsult' (for example, a minority employee is asked, 'How did you get that job?'); and 'microinvalidation' (for example, by telling someone they have overreacted if they comment on having been subjected to negative attitudes) (Sue and Spanierman 2020).

Microassault may be upsetting in the moment or may take a more extreme form, such as intolerable and degrading public humiliation, bullying and loss of status that the person can only manage by withdrawing from a particular situation like leaving their job (Bergner 1987, 1988; Torres and Bergner 2012).

In respect of microinsults and microinvalidations, members of low-status cultural groups (including many women and disabled people) are exposed to excluding and wounding responses on an everyday basis in ways that can occur outside of conscious awareness. The strength of the emotional and psychological impact of such violations draws on both specific personal experience of trauma that has happened to the recipient, and also a more general context of historical or intergenerational trauma that has served as a backdrop to their life as a whole. In effect, small acts of microaggression operate to re-stimulate and reinforce previous hurts. Several carefully-described examples of how this works can be found in an autobiographical account written by R.S. Gandhi (2021), an Indian student studying in the UK. One of the instances recounted by R.S. Gandhi (2021, p.139) refers to an experience when sharing a meal with some friends and mentioning that, traditionally, people in India eat with their fingers, rather than using cutlery. A friend responded, in a jokey way, by saying '...savages'.

There are several ways that an understanding of microaggression is valuable for practitioners of embedded counselling. It is, obviously, important to avoid

> **Box 8.2 The client assesses the counsellor**
>
> The influence of historical trauma, microaggression and experience of traumatic past encounters with human service professionals can play out in early meetings between a client and counsellor. Two studies interviewed black American clients about what it was like for them to participate in a first session with a white counsellor or mental health worker (Earl et al. 2011; Ward 2005). All of the clients in these studies reported that, for them, these meetings were primarily oriented toward assessing the counsellor and scanning the interaction for clues as to whether the counsellor was sufficiently similar in values and beliefs to understand them, whether they were being offered respect and if they could trust and feel safe with this particular practitioner.

making microaggressive statements to a client or service user or to be able to own up to any such episodes and try to repair the client–helper relationship. It is also possible to offer to assist a client to develop and implement strategies for coping with microaggression, such as calling out perpetrators or seeking support from others (Houshmand et al. 2019; Sue and Spanierman 2020). Finally, an awareness of the dynamics of microaggression offers a way of bringing broader social and political perspectives, such as ideas about white fragility and privilege, into the counselling process (DiAngelo 2018).

Moral injury

Gillian was a single parent with three children. Although she had experienced long-term mental health and addiction problems at an earlier stage in her life, she saw herself as now being on a path of recovery. The school attended by her children had noted that on occasion her children had appeared to be hungry and unkempt and had initiated a process through which a social worker had been allocated to support the family. Following accidents in the home that resulted in hospital visits for two of the children, the child protection team decided to review the case, resulting in the children being taken into foster care. Gillian felt ashamed and guilty that she had not been able to take care of her children. She felt violated by the way that teachers and social workers had talked about her during review meetings and she believed that they had lied to her and the children.

Thomas had been an infantry soldier serving in Afghanistan. During a patrol, his platoon returned fire following a Taliban attack on them. Several non-combatant civilians lost their lives in the incident. Thomas had been required to undertake a security sweep of the area while distraught local residents watched on. None of his colleagues were willing to talk about what had happened. As time went on, he felt more and more acute levels of guilt. As platoon leader, he believed that he should have been able to prevent what had happened. He started to doubt his religious faith, which up to that point in his life had been a central aspect of his sense of who he was as a person.

These brief case vignettes represent examples of a type of trauma that has come to be understood as 'moral injury'. Practitioners working with individuals who were assessed as having high levels of PTSD began to recognize that some clients were troubled not by events that threatened them personally or directly, but by incidents that they participated in or observed that transgressed their assumptions and values around right and wrong (Litz et al. 2009). Moral injury is associated with multiple forms of enduring moral distress, including feelings of shame, grief, meaninglessness, remorse, loss of trust, difficulty in forgiving and erosion of religious faith and hope (Koenig and Al Zaben 2021). Moral injury has been observed in military personnel (Litz et al. 2009); healthcare professionals (Mantri et al. 2020), social workers (Haight et al. 2016, 2017a), law enforcement officers (Papazoglou et al. 2020) and members of other occupational groups. It has also been identified in members of the public, such as parents who have had difficulty in looking after their children (Haight et al. 2017b, 2017c), refugees, journalists, teachers, individuals affected by (or involved in) rape, violent crime, abortion and road traffic accidents (Koenig and Al Zaben 2021). A range of therapeutic strategies have been developed to help people who have experienced moral injury (Koenig and Al Zaben 2021). Many of these approaches have involved either integrating spiritual and religious beliefs, and forgiveness principles, into standard therapy approaches or have been delivered by pastors and other faith practitioners who have received training in counselling skills. There is also evidence that many people who experience moral injury are able to recover on the basis of their own self-initiated healing processes (Haight et al. 2017a, 2017b).

The phenomenon of moral injury has important implications for practitioners of embedded counselling. It sensitizes practitioners around being aware of the possibility that some clients and service users may be troubled by trauma that does not fit neatly into a psychological perspective. It also invites attention to the fact that colleagues, and indeed the practitioner themselves, may be suffering from such experiences.

Precarity

The American philosopher Judith Butler has developed the concept of 'precarity' as a means of making sense of how the possibility of trauma is present in the lives of some people, even when it may not have been explicitly triggered. Precariousness is a general and inescapable dimension of being human – at any moment, any of us could receive a diagnosis of a terminal illness or be struck down in the street by a passing car. By contrast, precarity describes the life situation of a specific sub-set of people, for instance those who are employed on zero hours contracts, get by on intermittent employment (e.g. creatives such as musicians, artists and actors), live in refuge hostels or are economically dependent on abusive partners. Precarity appears to be becoming a condition of life for an expanding proportion of the population. It is helpful for practitioners offering emotional support and counselling to individuals who live in a state of precarity to appreciate the emotional implications of this issue. For example, precarity is associated with homelessness and foodbank use – both contexts in which embedded counselling may be available. However, receiving practical and emotional support at that point may help the person to no longer require the services of the foodbank or the homelessness project. But it is probably the case that the person will remain in a state of precarity – they need to be supported to build up a more extensive structure of personal and social resources in order to achieve sufficient security to be able to withstand future stresses or traumas (Hobfoll 2011).

Adversity

The topics discussed in this chapter so far offer an understanding of trauma as a life experience that is multi-faceted, with cognitive, physiological, emotional, interpersonal and moral/ethical dimensions that in turn interact with a range of social, cultural and historical issues. Many frontline practitioners, in health, social care and education, as well as in counselling and psychotherapy, have plentiful first-hand experience of how trauma can have a massively destructive long-term effect on a person's life. However, in order to be able to access resources and funding to support trauma-informed interventions and care, it has been necessary to find ways to collect evidence that will convince politicians, decision-makers and service managers that this is a problem that requires substantial investment. One of the key strategies for building a relevant evidence-base has centred on studies of childhood adversity. The reason why adversity has become an important construct is that collecting data on events that participants would define as explicitly 'traumatic' has the effect of under-estimating the prevalence of trauma. Some informants may be able to recall certain key terrible episodes in their life and disregard others that, by contrast, could be deemed as having been merely stressful or uncomfortable. Others may have suppressed their memories of traumatic events as a coping strategy or be aware of such events but not have enough trust in the researcher to disclose them.

As a means of overcoming at least some of these research challenges, research teams began to develop brief self-report questionnaires that adults could use to retrospectively report adverse experiences to which they had been exposed in childhood. Examples of such scales include the adverse childhood experience (ACE) scale (Felitti et al. 1998) and the childhood trauma questionnaire (Bernstein and Fink 1999). Both of these measures are available online. The ACE asks the participant to indicate whether certain events had happened to them before the age of 18, using items such as 'did a parent or adult in your home ever hit, beat, kick or physically hurt you in any way?' and 'did you live with anyone who was depressed, mentally ill or attempted suicide?'. It is easy to see that these measures are limited in many respects – they depend on accuracy of recall, do not try to estimate the intensity of the event and do not cover all possible adverse events – these, and many other shortcomings, are discussed by Lacey and Minnis (2020). Nevertheless, data from studies using these scales have consistently found that higher childhood adversity/trauma scores are associated with many forms of mental and physical ill-health in adult life, as well as likelihood of spending time in prison. Studies by Schilling et al. (2015, 2016) have found three adversity patterns or clusters in clients who seek counselling or psychotherapy for emotional difficulties. One group has generally low adversity scores, the next scores high on emotional and physical neglect items, while the third group records high levels of physical and sexual abuse. In these studies, therapy was most effective with clients in the first category (low adversity) and least effective in the sexual abuse cluster.

Research into childhood adversity offers only a very broad-brush picture of the links between trauma and problems in living. For example, significant types of trauma, such as being involved in military action, are not captured by childhood measures. It is also undoubtedly true that some people are able to address

Box 8.3 Post-traumatic growth

Although there is no doubt that adverse and traumatic experiences are generally regarded as harmful, with negative psychological effects, they also have the potential to create opportunities for a person to learn and develop in positive directions. The phenomenon of post-traumatic growth has been widely studied. Some of the main characteristics of this process include becoming more aware of one's strengths, seeing new possibilities in life, having a greater sense of purpose, feeling more in control of one's destiny, closer relationships and capacity for intimacy and enhanced appreciation of spiritual experience. These outcomes have been reported in many groups of people who have overcome trauma-related difficulties in their lives, including mental health breakdown (Slade et al. 2019), cancer (Marziliano et al. 2020) and being a nurse in a frontline unit for Covid-19 patients (Chen et al. 2021). From an embedded counselling perspective, they represent therapeutic tasks, or topics to be explored in counselling, that may be relevant for clients as pathways for moving on from the negative effects of trauma. In a study that interviewed individuals who had undergone life-threatening accidents or illness some years previous, Inman and Ogden (2011) found that positive growth was described by participants as arising from a range of factors, including awareness of mortality and realization that life was fragile, the event opening up opportunities to make changes in their life and an overall a sense of comparing themselves differently to others.

childhood trauma without professional help. However, the findings of adverse childhood experience studies have been generally supported by results from other types of research, as well as from clinical practice. Despite their flaws, this body of research has been sufficiently convincing to underpin three highly significant pillars of social and health policy in a range of countries: (i) preventing adverse childhood experience, or minimizing its impact, through such means as anti-poverty measures and helplines and counselling for young people at risk; (ii) redesigning services in such areas as social and health care, addictions and criminal justice to prevent further traumatization of service users or re-activation of their earlier traumas; (iii) the development of specialist counselling and psychotherapy, and embedded counselling, to support clients to address, work through and recover from trauma.

How counselling can help

The use of counselling and psychotherapy to help individuals to recover from PTSD is an area of practice that has generated a wide range of contrasting therapy approaches with efficacy backed up by research evidence. The existence of this evidence base has resulted in two assumptions that are widely-held within the psychotherapy profession. The first assumption is that therapy for PTSD is complex and difficult and requires specialist training. The second is that what makes therapy for PTSD so demanding is that it only works if the client focuses on the trauma memory itself – a process that is likely to be highly upsetting for the client, possibly to the extent of further traumatizing them. However, these conclusions are not in fact supported by critical analysis of the relevant literature. Reviews by Wampold et al. (2010) and Wampold (2019) have shown that there are no differences in overall effectiveness between therapy approaches that require the client to recall the traumatic event(s) and those that do not. They suggest that, in actual practice, all of the ways of supporting clients to come to terms with PTSD and trauma consist of a combination of activities that reflect the needs and preferences of the client at that point in their healing journey. The basic elements of therapy for PTSD and trauma are the same as for any other condition – a safe and trusting relationship with a counsellor who is able to offer a credible rationale for whatever activities are being considered and collaborative agreement around the tasks and goals of therapy. Beyond that, specific tasks and activities that the client may find helpful include: psychoeducation that makes it possible for the person to normalize and make sense of what has happened to them; an opportunity to talk about the trauma and tell their story; building supportive relationships with people who care about them; activating personal strengths and cultural resources; acquiring coping skills for dealing with specific situations and reactions; exposure to trauma-inducing memories and contexts; and learning how to stay safe and stay well. These steps in the direction of recovery from trauma are consistent with what most laypeople believe is helpful (Blackie et al. 2020). A good example of how different helpful activities can be combined in counselling for PTSD can be found in Gersons and Schnyder (2013). Skills and strategies that practitioners of embedded counselling can utilize to facilitate the kinds of therapeutic tasks and processes outlined above are discussed in the following paragraphs.

Listening

Birrell and Freyd (2006) suggest that an intense, sustained commitment to listening is a central element in supporting people around trauma-related issues. There are several reasons why listening is important. The experience of trauma is one in which there may be thoughts, feelings and images that may be hard for the person to put into words, either because they are unclear and jumbled, too painful to talk about or from concern about upsetting the hearer. In instances of trauma caused by another person (e.g. physical or sexual violence from a family member) the person may have been threatened with consequences if they report what happened to anyone else. The person may have tried to describe their trauma to others in the past and not been taken seriously (Mooney 2021; Ungar et al. 2009). The act of listening in itself may be hard to sustain, on account of emotions stirred up in the helper. Birrell and Freyd (2006) argue that essential steps in the direction of healing are for the person to feel as though they are being believed (rather than, for instance, being interrogated in order to determine the accuracy of their account) and for the person to have the experience that they are not alone with their memories and feelings – instead, there is at least the beginning of a shared, mutual understanding. The process of being heard, and having one's story received with acceptance and respect, can take place in a group setting as well as in a one-to-one meeting (see, for example, Lakshmin 2018).

Making sense

Many people are confused and frightened by effects of PTSD, such as being suddenly overcome by fear in a particular situation or unwanted memories. Learning about theory and research into PTSD can help a person to normalize their experience as a standard coping-survival response to an intolerable situation. This kind of theoretical model can also assist a person in terms of recovery from PTSD, for instance in doing their own personal research into trigger situations, so they can anticipate and prepare for them. Information about how to make sense of PTSD can be conveyed during a counselling meeting or a client can be encouraged to read a relevant leaflet or book or access a website and then return for a discussion of what they have learned. Concepts such as intrusion and avoidance can provide a shared language and understanding that can be used in later sessions.

Building a more complete and coherent story of what happened

Usually, a client is able to indicate that something traumatic has happened to them. Typically, they will be able to provide some kind of brief description of what type of event it was and what it involved. In some cases, the person may not be willing to provide any detail at all and may only acknowledge that 'something' happened without going into specifics. From a theoretical perspective, a traumatic experience is hard to assimilate because it is too out-of-the ordinary to fit into the person's pre-existing assumptions about the world. A minimal trauma story would normally indicate an experience that is far from being assimilated. By contrast, someone who has recovered from trauma would be able to recount their experience in as much (or as little) detail as was warranted by the situation. Wigren (1994) has suggested that what happens in counselling around trauma can be understood as comprising a gradual process of 'narrative completion' – as the person's story is re-told, more details are added. Conversely, an effective counsellor is sensitive to gaps in the story and tentatively asks the client if they might wish to fill in these spaces when they feel ready to do so. Some elements of the story may be very hard to put into words, for example because they are associated with overwhelmingly painful emotions or shame and may never be told. The process of filling in the gaps may involve personal research and detective work. For example, a person who knows that they were exposed to traumatic experiences in childhood but is hazy about the details may find it helpful to interview relatives or seek access to their social work file. A potentially valuable way of facilitating the process of gradually building a more complete and coherent trauma story can be to encourage the client to write about their experience on a regular basis. A helpful aspect of writing is that the writer is to some extent emotionally distanced from what is on the page. Also, repeatedly writing about the same event over several days or weeks generally allows a more coherent version to emerge. There are many writing techniques and strategies that have been devised by therapists, such as different instructions, free-writing vs keeping to a structure and use of poetry. Valuable points of entry into the rich tradition of using writing to move on from trauma include Bergqvist and Punzi (2020), Bolton et al. (2004), Gerger et al. (2021), Kerner and Fitzpatrick (2007) and Sloan and Marx (2018).

Making use of social support

The experience of trauma can lead to social isolation – the person may deal with intrusive images in ways (e.g. alcohol and drug use) that are baffling and threatening to others in their life and push them away; the person may become hyper-vigilant and suspicious of others; or they may find that others are unwilling or unable to tolerate their stories of what has happened. In addition, a person

Box 8.4 Trauma counselling in prisons

A high proportion of those serving prison sentences have a history of trauma. In particular, many women in prison have been subjected to neglect and physical and sexual abuse in childhood, and further traumatization through rape, enforced sex work, homelessness and loss through addiction-induced death in adult life. Women in prison may also have undergone additional trauma through loss of custody of their children. Increasing awareness of these factors has led criminal justice and prison services to develop procedures for limiting the extent of re-traumatization associated with imprisonment and also providing trauma therapy in prison settings. Important initiatives within this movement have been the Healing Trauma for Women and Exploring Trauma for Men programmes developed by Dr Stephanie Covington (Covington 2003, 2015; Covington and Rodriguez 2016). This approach is gender-sensitive, reflecting different patterns of trauma experienced by men and women and is usually delivered by trained peer facilitators (long-term prisoners) in six small two-hour group sessions. Topics covered in sessions include awareness of relationships and understanding trauma, alongside practical and experiential learning tasks drawn from cognitive behavioural therapy (CBT), mindfulness meditation techniques, expressive arts, body-oriented grounding exercises and yoga. These groups have been found to be effective in reducing PTSD and other symptoms such as depression and anger in participants. Notably, those helped most by these trauma groups are participants who have recorded the highest rates of adverse childhood experiences (Messina and Schepps 2021). Further insights into the relevance and effectiveness of such programmes can be found in Miller and Najavits (2012) and Najavits (2019).

who has been through serious trauma may conclude that they are irretrievably damaged and that other people are better off without them. Re-establishing relationships, connection and trust and re-building social capital are key tasks in facilitating recovery from trauma. Most categories of traumatic event, such sexual abuse, domestic violence and military service, have generated group-based approaches to accessing social support, such as peer self-help groups, networks and websites and various types of therapy group. Embedded counselling can involve supporting a client to establish or re-engage with other people and helping them to access appropriate organized groups. The process of learning to trust and talk to a counsellor can be an important step in the direction of relating more openly to people in everyday life contexts.

> **Box 8.5 Counselling for people who are homeless**
>
> Homelessness is a condition that is closely connected to the experience of precarity and trauma. Many people who are homeless have a history of adverse childhood experience, or a more recent trauma such as loss of job or refugee status, that has triggered loss of a personal place to stay. By itself, being homeless opens a person to multiple trauma, such as insults and violence. People who are homeless have a sense of being marginalized, dehumanized and excluded, which can make them very wary of any type of professional help (Magwood et al. 2019). It can be hard to integrate formal counselling into homelessness services, partly because of client suspiciousness but also because of lack of suitable meeting spaces (Chaturvedi 2016; Cormack 2009). However, counselling and psychotherapy providers who have been able to overcome these barriers have reported positive outcomes with some clients (Cockersell 2011; Conolly 2018). Embedded counselling offered by practitioners who work closely with homeless people, such as social workers or homeless shelter staff, has been described by people who have eventually moved into more stable lives as having been extremely useful to them (Eyrich-Garg 2008; Thompson et al. 2004). In a study that interviewed homeless people about their experience of this kind of support, Walsh et al. (2010) found that it was important to have been able to spend informal time with the helper before moving into more serious conversation. It was also vital to find an appropriate place to talk – sometimes this might be in an office, but for other clients it might need to be outside in a social space. A key element was the capacity of the helper to be genuine, trustworthy and down-to-earth, to respect the client as a person of worth and to be willing to listen.

Developing coping skills

There are many separate stressful and distressing aspects of PTSD, such as flashbacks, exhaustion associated with vigilance and inability to sleep, waves of anxiety and wariness and uncertainty in relationships. One of the ways in which embedded counselling can be helpful is to support a person to cope with these specific life difficulties. For example, part of the service offered by a centre for women who had been subjected to traumatic sexual violence was participation in yoga sessions that were run solely for centre members (Steven and McLeod 2019). One of the most useful outcomes of these classes was learning a yoga breathing technique that could be applied in everyday situations as a means of alleviating fearfulness and anxiety. Other activities provided by the centre helped women to acquire other valuable coping skills, such as how to be more assertive in relationships, how to develop a healthy lifestyle that produced a sense of positive well-being, and how to counteract harshly self-critical internal dialogues.

Brief embedded counselling with a person experiencing extreme trauma and adversity: a case example

Our colleague Emily-May Barlow wrote the following account of her voluntary work with a refugee charity supporting individuals and families trying to gain sanctuary in the UK.

This incident happened during a visit to Dunkirk, during my time with Care-4Calais. The gentleman had arrived at the Dunkirk site alone, only an hour earlier. He had no tent and limited belongings. Unfortunately, we were not able to provide the items he needed for shelter, warmth and something to eat.

The man sat on the rail tracks, crying. I approached and asked if I could sit with him. He spoke good English and told me he had tried to kill himself the day before. When I asked why, he told me, 'I am so tired' and 'This world has been very cruel to me'.

His journey travelling from Kurdistan to France had taken years. During this time, his father had died and he had lost contact with his sister and mother (he could not reach them using known contact details and he did not know what had happened). He had no friends or other family.

He recounted the turbulent events in Kurdistan, which determined his decision to leave, in addition to his very difficult journey. He missed Kurdistan terribly and described feeling disconnected from any sense of personal or cultural identity. This seemed to be furthering his feelings of being alone.

Whilst I am a mental health nurse, facilitating a suicide intervention in these circumstances is beyond my scope of practice. How do you assess and safety plan on a refugee site? How do you provide appropriate support and treatment when undocumented people are literally thrown out of French hospitals, despite them needing essential medical interventions?

Most people who are suicidal don't want to die, rather they just cannot see a way to carry on living in the circumstances they find themselves in. I couldn't imagine being able to live in this man's circumstances either.

I listened to this man's story and tried to hold the hope; he was young, he was resilient and he was certainly motivated to find a better existence. His strength is certain, but he was exhausted.

The man cried and thanked me. He told me that being noticed, being asked questions and being listened to had reminded him that 'there is lots of good in this world'. The conversation had taken only 20 minutes. I am forever astounded by the power of connection and its ability to hold a little hope for those who are sitting in the dark.

Responding at an organizational level

As with other areas of embedded counselling explored in this book, there are many organizational strategies that can be deployed to facilitate emotional support for people struggling with issues of adverse childhood experience and trauma. Various organizations and agencies build on the efforts of individual practitioners by such means as making relevant information available to clients, developing access pathways to specialist services and support groups, employment of dormer clients and the use of interpreters and cultural brokers. However, this area of practice differs from other fields of embedded counselling in also being able to call on a philosophical and policy stance that has been adopted in a wide range of agencies – trauma-informed care. The key ideas behind trauma-informed care/practice are that a high proportion of clients and service users in all frontline services have a history of trauma and that it is important to take that fact into account in relation to all aspects of service provision. For example, trauma-informed care involves being able to understand how many of the difficulties experienced by clients are a result of trauma and adversity and making sure that interventions do not re-traumatize clients or exacerbate their problems. This requires a relationship-oriented approach that highlights the necessity of safety, trust, collaboration, choice and empowerment. The aim is that any service that is being delivered (e.g. education, housing, criminal justice, healthcare, social work) has the effect of promoting recovery and post-traumatic growth. These principles have been articulated in different ways in each practice sector (see, for example, Levenson 2017; Oral et al. 2016). The actual implementation of trauma-informed care is not straightforward because it can require a substantial shift in attitude and may call for additional resources and training at a time when budgets are already under pressure. Examples of how trauma-informed care has been integrated into routine practice include Levenson (2020) and Wilson et al. (2015). Goodman et al. (2016) have developed a useful tool to assist auditing the effectiveness of delivery of trauma-informed care. It is important to recognize that the principle of trauma-informed care has been criticized by some social policy researchers and theorists because it can take resources away from more tangible forms of help such as housing and income support and can run the risk of medicalizing service users (e.g. encouraging them to enter therapy) at the expense of long-established systems of mutual support and solidarity that exist within society (Smith et al. 2021).

Conclusions

Trauma represents a particular type of difficult situation. It occurs without warning, so that the person has little or no opportunity to prepare for it. It is, at least for a period of time, an overwhelming and all-encompassing experience. It threatens the person's sense of who they are and their assumptions about how the world works in a manner that may create an internal separation or split between the ongoing world of everyday experience and an inner world populated by disturbing images and memories. It may also threaten the person's life or appear to be capable of doing this. Quite often, trauma has a moral meaning – what has happened is not something that a good person would do. In addition to all of this, we live in a somewhat fragmented society in which other people may not notice that something awful has happened to someone or may not care. Also – compared to indigenous and traditional cultures – there are few healing rituals available through which other members of the community can draw close and help one to come to terms with what has happened. As a result of all these factors, many people suffer trauma in silence and it hits hard. An appreciation of the reality of trauma, and a commitment to trauma-informed care, are vital aspects of the movement toward humanizing health and social care. Practitioners of embedded counselling can make a crucial contribution in this area. Specialist trauma therapies or interventions for clients whose long-standing trauma has led to complex difficulties are technically and emotionally demanding for any therapist and require dedicated training and supervision. But at the same time, there are many aspects of the healing process that can be facilitated on a step-by-step basis by practitioners who are willing to listen and are able to assist a client to engage with other forms of support that are available in the community.

Learning activities

The following activities may be explored individually and/or with a group of learning partners.

Exercise 8.1 Reflecting on your own trauma
What is your own personal experience of trauma and adverse childhood experience? What helped you to come to terms with, and recover from, these events in your life? What was unhelpful? In what ways can you use your personal learning and experience in these areas to inform your capacity to respond to clients and service users who need support to deal with their own adversity and trauma issues?

Exercise 8.2 Reflecting on the trauma of others
How have you observed others (friends, family members, clients) dealing with their own experiences of trauma adverse and childhood experience? What seemed to be helpful and unhelpful for them?

Exercise 8.3 How your organization approaches trauma
To what extent, and in what ways, has the organization in which you work adopted a trauma-informed approach? What do they do well in relation to these principles? In what ways could their approach be improved?

CHAPTER 9

Transitions

Introduction	**176**
Examples of episodes of embedded counselling around transition issues	**176**
Making sense of transition	**178**
Theoretical perspectives	180
Stages of transition models	*180*
Psychodynamic life-course theory	*181*
The narrative disruption model of transition	*183*
An ecological perspective on transitions	*184*
Methods for working with clients around negotiating a life transition	**186**
Talking	186
Developing a shared understanding	186
Normalizing	187
Mapping	187
Writing	188
Exploring cultural meaning	189
Rituals	189
Organizational perspectives on transition counselling	**190**
Conclusions	**192**
Learning activities	**192**

Introduction

Individuals may have periods in their life when relatively little change takes place, and then other periods that are characterized by fairly dramatic shifts from one status or way of living to another, when their personal world is significantly disrupted in a major way. The idea of 'transition' is a valuable concept in counselling, because it provides a way of thinking about personal change events that may have implications for many aspects of a person's life. Significant and enduring emotional difficulties can often be associated with life transition such as leaving home, becoming a parent, losing a job, loss of mobility or sight and many other types of personally impactful change episodes that can occur over the course of a life. Practitioners of embedded counselling are often employed within organizations that exist to facilitate life transitions and as a result may encounter clients who are troubled or stuck in some way around their capacity to negotiate a transition. For example, facilitating transition is an integral aspect of education at all levels (Ecclestone et al. 2010). The present chapter discusses the process and meaning of transition and the ways that frontline practitioners in health, education and social care can support clients and service users in a process of successful resolution of such life episodes.

This chapter explores some possible ways to work with clients in order to enable them to negotiate different types of life transition. The chapter considers ways of making sense of the transition process and methods of facilitating production conversation and action around transition issues.

Examples of episodes of embedded counselling around transition issues

The following examples illustrate some of the counselling goals, tasks and methods that can be associated with working together around life transitions:

> Margaret and her three children had lived on a Caribbean island that was largely destroyed by a volcanic eruption. Evacuated by the Navy, they ended up in Britain being taken care of by a Church group who provided housing and other support for refugees. Although Margaret and her children spoke English, they had great difficulty in understanding the accents of the people in the neighbourhood within which they had been located and in turn, being understood by their neighbours. The country seemed dark, damp and unwelcoming. Over the space of two years, a small team of support workers helped Margaret and her children to reconstruct their lives, using a combination of assistance in practical issues around work, health and education alongside a willingness to take time to listen and talk.

Judith is several weeks into the first year of senior school. She enjoyed junior school, where she knew everyone and had a good relationship with her class teacher. However, the transition to senior school has been very difficult. She feels as though she has been separated from her friends, is unable to make new friends and has not come to terms with the demands of the timetable and homework. The teacher responsible for support and guidance notices Judith's isolation and distress and asks if she would be willing to meet during the lunch hour. When invited to talk, Judith bursts into tears and describes a long list of problems. With Judith's permission, the teacher makes a list of these problems and suggests that they might look at how they can deal with them one at a time. Over the next three weeks, they come up with a set of coping strategies that Judith can employ and keep monitoring how they can be applied within the different difficult situations that Judith encounters during her school day. By the Christmas break, Judith has settled in and at their final lunchtime meeting, her teacher brings in a special cake to celebrate her achievements.

Agnes and Simon are going through a process of applying to adopt a child. The social worker carrying out their assessment tells them that they have the potential to be excellent parents – they have a strong relationship, they are financially secure and have good support from their own families. She adds, 'But over the meetings I have had with the two of you, the same question arises in my mind – are you *ready* to make this huge change in your lives? You seem to really enjoy the life you have. I get a sense that you both feel you are going to lose all of that if a child moves into the spare bedroom upstairs. Is this something we could talk about?'

Andy works in a shelter for homeless young people. The main part of his job consists of making sure that food and bedding is available and that his clients have access to healthcare. When he can, he tries to listen to their stories and help them to make sense of their lives. When interviewed by a journalist about his work, he says that 'the largest group we get here are kids from families where their mum and dad have been alcoholics or drug users, or have been abusive to them in some other way. They get to a stage when they just can't take it any more so they move out. It's just like any of us – there comes a point where you have to leave home and try to make it on your own. But for them, there's no support, no preparation, no fall-back, nothing. So they crash.'

These brief examples show how transition issues can emerge as a central focus in embedded counselling work. Judith's teacher used her own adaptation of CBT methods, culminating in the use of a ritual (eating together), to mark the completion of the change in personal status that had taken place. With Margaret and her family, a team of support workers developed relationships that were supportive and resourceful. With Agnes and Simon, a social worker skilfully used supportive challenge to invite further exploration of a contradiction in her clients' feelings and attitudes.

Making sense of transition

Life transitions can be unexpected and unplanned or relatively predictable. A study that powerfully captures the qualities of a shocking and unexpected transition is Lowes et al. (2005) on the experience of parents whose child has just received a diagnosis of diabetes. Studies that explore the ways that even predicted transition can leave the person with a sense of being unprepared include Velsor-Friedrich and Hogan (2021) on the experience of leaving home to attend college for young people with asthma, and Bordia et al. (2020) on the experience of retirement. The importance of research – and practice-based learning – into specific transition processes is that they highlight the specific social, cultural and personal factors that are in play. Although there exist some very valuable general models of transition (discussed below), in a counselling role it is essential to be sensitive to what makes this individual (or group of people) unique.

Examples of sudden transitions are:

- losing a job
- winning the lottery
- becoming ill
- divorce
- the loss of a loved one
- termination of pregnancy
- moving to another area or country.

In addition, there are predictable or 'normative' changes, built into the life-course, that inevitably affect all (or most) of us, such as:

- leaving home
- becoming a parent
- retirement from work.

An understanding of the process of transition is valuable for anyone in a counselling role, because it is at such moments of transition that a person may feel the need to talk to someone (e.g. a counsellor or helper) outside of their immediate situation, who can help them to gain some perspective on what is happening.

Box 9.1 Leaving military service

The transition from military service to civilian life is one of the most closely-studied topics within the transition literature (Jones et al. 2019; Mobbs and Bonanno 2018). There also exist many examples of programmes and initiatives designed to support individuals through this phase of their lives (Iversen et al. 2005; Stevenson 2020; Weir et al. 2019). Distinctive and challenging aspects of military–civilian transition are the shift from the all-encompassing structure of service life to the open-ended opportunities afforded by everyday society, the possibility that military service may have left the veteran with physical injuries and disabilities, PTSD or alcohol dependency, the extent to which the family of the service-person are involved, and the necessity of competing in a competitive job market. What is clear in the literature on the transition experiences of military veterans is that there are a wide range of therapeutic tasks that may be relevant and equally many therapeutic methods and activities that may be used to accomplish these tasks. For most military veterans, the process of receiving support typically involves supportive interactions with practitioners in many fields, including healthcare and career guidance, alongside whatever help is available from military sources, charities and self-help groups. Information that can be used to develop embedded counselling practice about the types of issue that veterans might want to talk about, and activities that make a difference, can be found in Ahern et al. (2015), Greer (2017), Mobbs and Bonanno, 2018) and Westwood et al. (2010) and in a series of papers published in a special military transitions issue 166 (2020) of the journal *New Directions for Adult and Continuing Education*.

Negotiating a difficult life transition represents an important and frequently-occurring counselling task – it is therefore necessary for any practitioner who offers emotional support to others to have a conceptual framework for making sense of the transition process and skills for supporting clients through it.

There are many specialist counselling agencies that offer help to people undergoing specific transitions, such as marital separation and divorce or bereavement. It is valuable for frontline human services practitioners to be aware of the agencies and resources that might be relevant to their clients relatively. However, relatively few people make use of such established support systems (compared to the overall number of potentially eligible individuals). There are also many transitions that do not fall readily into the terms of reference of these agencies. For these reasons, many people experiencing transition look for counselling and emotional support from whatever professional source is available to them, such as a nurse, doctor or other worker.

Theoretical perspectives

One of the most useful things that a counsellor can do for clients who are experiencing transition issues is to suggest to them that it might be helpful to understand that what is happening can be understood as involving a life transition of some kind. Usually, clients are caught up in coping with immediate pressures and difficulties and do not necessarily think about their stress in terms of a bigger picture. The invitation to consider day-to-day difficulties in terms of a transition from one stage of life to the next immediately allows the client to adopt a broader perspective. There are several theoretical frameworks that have been developed by psychologists and other social scientists that can be offered to clients as a means of making sense of the transition through which they are passing. Four of these frameworks are described below: stages of transition models; psychodynamic life-course theory; narrative disruption theory; and the ecological perspective.

Stages of transition models

There are several influential models of transition that can be used to inform a counselling process (Bridges 2004; Hopson and Adams 1976; Hopson 1989; Sugarman 2003, 2016). These models provide frameworks for making sense of the experience of the person seeking help. All of these models suggest that a person in transition goes through a series of stages of readjustment such as:

1 Loss – previous relationships, habits and way of life are no longer available or no longer relevant or functional.
2 Shock – exhibited either as excitement ('this is great') or numbness ('it's not really happening').
3 Provisional adjustment – the 'honeymoon period', 'it's all wonderful, so many new possibilities'.
4 Gradual loss of confidence. Increase in depression and self-doubt ('I can't cope', 'I will never get through this').
5 Crisis point – despair and hopelessness – sometimes experienced as a liminal or in-between phase.
6 Reconstruction/rebuilding a new life – *either* accepting the new situation and reconstructing self/identity (leading to a higher level of confidence/ competence than at the start), *or* quitting and giving up.

When using a transition model (or any model of stages of development) it is essential to be flexible – in any individual case the progression from one stage to another may occur quickly, or take a long time, and the individual may 'skip' stages or repeat them.

The implications of this kind of transition model for the work of the counsellor are that it has the potential to:

- draw attention to the fact that transition involves ups and downs – it is not a smooth process
- identifying different types of therapeutic task that may help a person through a transition, such as:
  - acknowledging what has been lost
  - letting go of previous attitudes, relationships and behaviours
  - acquiring new knowledge and ways of interaction (e.g. learning new skills, making new friends)
  - cognitive restructuring (learning to see yourself in a different light).

For any counsellor working with a particular group of people seeking help, it is important to become attuned to the specific ways that the transition cycle plays out in the lives of that set of people and that context. For instance, in bereavement it may take many months or even years before a person is ready to reflect on the implications of their loss, whereas in students beginning studies in another country the pressure to readjust and to deal with the experience of transition is immediate.

Psychodynamic life-course theory

Transition models focus on the specific time frame before, during and after a transition episode. By contrast, psychodynamic theories consider how specific transitions occur in the context of a person's entire life-course, from birth to death, and make it possible to see how each transition both evokes unresolved issues from previous life-shifts and has implications for subsequent ones.

The psychodynamic approach to counselling and psychology has evolved from the psychoanalytic ideas of Sigmund Freud (see McLeod 2019 for a detailed account of this important therapy tradition). One of the cornerstones of psychodynamic thinking is the assumption that someone's personality or sense of identity evolves and develops over the course of their life. From a psychodynamic perspective, therefore, it is always useful to think about the problems being presented by a client in *developmental* terms – what are the developmental processes that have occurred in the past that have resulted in the person possessing certain strengths and problems and what is the developmental challenge that the person is facing right now? The psychodynamic model of stages in the life-course that was devised by Erik Erikson is widely used by counsellors and other practitioners as a means of making sense of transition issues (see Table 9.1) (Knight 2017; Sugarman 2004). Further explanation of the content of the Erikson model is available in Sugarman (2003, 2016) and innumerable introductory and developmental psychology textbooks and websites.

There are several aspects of the Erikson model that can be applied to counselling and discussed with clients. In using these ideas with clients, it is of course essential to use language that makes sense to the client. For example, the concept of 'autonomy' may come across to some people as abstract and academic – 'being

Table 9.1 Erikson's model of psycho-social stages

Psycho-social issue/stage of development	Age
Trust-mistrust	Birth to 18 months
Autonomy-shame	18 months to 3 years
Initiative-guilt	3–5 years
Industry-inferiority	5–12 years
Identity-role confusion	12–18 years
Intimacy-isolation	18–35 years
Generativity-self-absorption	35–60 years
Integrity-despair	60 years to death

able to stand up for yourself' could be an alternative and more acceptable way of talking about this idea. One of the ways in which the model can be used in counselling is that it suggests that people need to work out different kinds of personal and emotional issues at different points in their life. For example, teenage years are often characterized by a struggle to define 'who am I?', reflected in rebellion against parental values and trying out different roles and lifestyles. However, the model suggests that there is a shift in early adulthood to a new question, 'how can I form a close and loving relationship?' and then later in adulthood to 'how can I be a parent and offer something to the next generation?' The stages identified by Erikson therefore allow clients to get some kind of handle on the broad emotional and interpersonal agenda that they are facing at any particular point in their lives. This can be particularly relevant at the point of entering or leaving a new stage.

A further aspect of Erikson's model is that it suggests that the success that the person has had in negotiating previous stages will have an influence on how well-prepared he or she is in respect of handling the next stage that they enter. For example, a person who has learned to trust other people, and to have a balanced sense of their own autonomy as a human being, is in a good position to develop intimacy in a close relationship. By contrast, someone who has never been able to trust will possibly find it quite hard to manage intimacy in a relationship. In counselling, this perspective allows the person to begin to make links between the current issues around which they are struggling and the kind of love and support (or lack of these qualities) that was available to them at earlier times in their life.

Erikson's theory is in fact very hopeful and optimistic about these matters. He argued that each developmental stage allows the person to revisit, and relearn interpersonal skills that were not fully developed in the past. So, for instance, a person who experienced inconsistent or negligent parenting in the early years of their life may have an underlying distrust of other people and the world in general, but then finds new opportunities to learn about trust at school, in peer relationships in adolescence, in partner relationships in young adulthood and so on.

The final facet of this model that is relevant for counselling is that it suggests that most of the time we are not consciously aware that these processes are occurring. If we do become aware of these issues, we are able to do something about them – we become able to learn and to change. One of the counselling skills that is highly relevant here is that of 'meaning-making' – the counsellor is able to offer the client, in a collaborative and open way, the possibility that some of Erikson's ideas (or the ideas of similar theorists) might help them to be aware of what is happening for them and to make sense of what they are experiencing.

The narrative disruption model of transition
From a narrative perspective, we create and maintain our personal identity and are known to other people through the stories that we tell about ourselves. Underpinning the day-to-day stories of what we do, there is a basic life story, an overall life-narrative or script that sums up who we are. For example, maybe people live their lives in accordance with a storyline that is along the lines of 'I will work hard, look after my family and children and make a contribution to society, then I will be able to enjoy the fruits of my labours in my later years'. When a person experiences a serious illness, this life story is shattered – it cannot be told, it no longer fits the reality of life on an everyday level. For example, a person who is crippled by multiple sclerosis or coronary heart disease may not be able to work and may find that instead of caring for others, they has become an object of care. This kind of narrative disruption has been studied by many health psychologists and sociologists (Frank 1995, 1998, 2000; Williams 1984), who argue that many of the emotional and relationship problems experienced by people who are suffering from chronic health conditions can be understood as arising from the challenge of reshaping and realigning their life story. One of the most influential models of this process has been developed by the American sociologist Arthur Frank (1995), who argues that a health crisis triggers a period of narrative 'chaos' for the individual – they no longer know how to talk about who they are and other people in their life are similarly constrained. For many people, there is a strong pull to develop a 'restitution' narrative – 'things are bad, but I will do everything possible to get back to the way I was before I got ill'. Other people develop a 'quest' narrative – 'I have to learn to move on in my life and find meaning and connection with people in different ways'. An appreciation of the significance of these contrasting ways of talking about a transition is potentially valuable for counsellors, for example in reflecting back to the person the alternative ways of making sense of their situation and the implications of these stories for them as individuals as well as for the other people in their lives.

In a valuable paper, Donnelly (2021) explores the way that being in a state of only having a chaos narrative – being unable to describe a life that possesses a sense of purpose, agency or direction – is characteristic of the experience of many people with disabilities. As a consequence, because there is considerable societal pressure to tell life stories that have happy or redemptive endings, these individuals have great difficulty in being heard. From a philosophical perspective,

Reader (2007) describes this state as 'patiency' – a term that she devised as a way of talking about the opposite of agency. Both chaos narratives and patiency represent conditions in which embedded counselling may be particularly helpful for a person. One of the key tasks of the counsellor is to listen for what is hard to say and to assist the person to find the words to say it.

Although research into narrative aspects of transition has mainly focused on the experiences of people undergoing health crises, it seems clear that these ideas are also highly relevant for those whose transitions are in other areas of their life, such as employment, marital status, housing, being subject to natural disasters or being a victim of crime.

An ecological perspective on transitions

A recurring image throughout this book is that of a person as existing within a social and cultural *ecological* system – engaged in making a space, niche or home for himself or herself within the social and cultural world within which he or she lives. The global culture within which we, all of us, live our lives is immensely complicated and presents us with multiple possibilities and choices. In the distant past, human society was organized around relatively small, highly structured groups, such as clans or tribes, that lived close to nature. In the absence of a written language, knowledge and information were conveyed in the form of songs and stories. Many of the characteristics of that earlier way of life still remain with us, for example in the importance that most people place on loyalty and in the power of narrative. But the development of written language, mechanized transport, an economic system based on money and capital and the information technology revolution, have contributed to the existence of a culture of cities. In a city, many separate and different cultural worlds can co-exist within the same geographical area.

Building a 'personal niche' involves at least three types of interlocking activity (Willi 1999). First, there is the task of connecting to other people by maintaining a network of personal relationships. These relationships usually include some mix of family and kinship ties, intimate or partner relationships, friendships, work colleagues and casual acquaintances. Second, a person lives within a set of stories that he or she tells about himself or herself, and which are told about him or her. These stories reflect, and draw upon, the stock of stories that are available within a culture, for example in myths, novels and movies. Third, a personal niche comprises objects, spaces and territories that have meaning for a person, for example the musical instrument that they play, the food they eat, their bedroom, their garden, a view from the top of a particular hill. A highly significant object and space, always, is the physical body of the person and how they create a home for their self in their body and express their identity through their body.

A sense of well-being, or satisfaction with life, depends on the extent to which the personal niche reflects a sufficient degree of coherence or integration between the story that a person lives within and the relationships and objects through which their story is played out. For example, if someone has constructed their personal world around a story of being 'happily married' and their partner wants to leaves them, then they have a problem. If someone has created a world around 'being a student' and has constructed a niche that is based on access to a university campus and involvement in student activities, then undergoes a transition to 'being a civil servant', a new personal niche may need to be created.

An ecological perspective provides a useful set of ideas for counsellors working with people undergoing life transitions. The task of negotiating a transition can be viewed as involving building a new niche. This encompasses deciding on what relationships, places and activities need to be in the niche and how to identify and engage with these elements. It requires deciding on which parts of the old niche can be retained and which need to be left behind. This way of thinking highlights the purposefulness, resourcefulness and creativity of the client.

Box 9.2 Transition support by nurses in an infertility clinic

Important insights into how embedded counselling can be used to facilitate transition can be gleaned from research into the experience of women undergoing treatment in a fertility clinic to enable them to have a child (Allan 2001, 2007). This research used in-depth interviews and participant observation to capture what went on during an extended and highly stressful (and often unsuccessful) transition process. What emerged from this study was that many of women were in an extended liminal period, somewhere along an uncertain journey to becoming a parent. They had few other outlets for expressing their hopes, fears and disappointments and looked to nurses for emotional support. However, it could be hard for the nurses and medical staff to engage with what their patients were feeling, due to lack of training, time and organizational recognition for this element of their role. Allan (2001: 53) described how the nurses conveyed 'emotional awareness' to their patients through 'hovering' and 'focused support'. Hovering occurred when the nurse might be listening or focusing on a doctor–patient consultation while carrying out another activity and might intervene in a way that was helpful to the patient. Focused support took the form of a brief supportive connection such as a touch, an explanation, a joke or acting on the patient's behalf as an advocate to question a doctor's order. Even these fairly minimal forms of connection and empathic acknowledgement of the emotional pain being felt by women receiving infertility treatment was enough to create some sense of the clinic as a supportive environment. Similar themes and needs emerged from research by Cunningham (2014). Studies such as these have contributed to the development of policy and practice that places more emphasis on the importance of emotional support for women undergoing fertility treatment (Shreffler et al. 2017).

Methods for working with clients around negotiating a life transition

There are no evidence-based therapy protocols that have been developed for working with people around negotiating their way through life transitions. Usually, working on transitions issues breaks down into a set of tasks, specific to each client, that can be pursued using counselling skills such as listening, helping the person to talk, making sense of their situation, developing ideas about what they can do and putting these ideas into action. Some suggestions around working with clients around transition-related tasks are outlined below.

Talking

Usually, there is a lot to talk in relation to an experience of transition about where the person has come from in their life, where they are heading to, where they are now or what is aiding or inhibiting them in their journey. Often, what is talked about in counselling sits in some kind of contrast to the kinds of conversations that the client is having with other people. It may be that the client uses counselling to rehearse and try out things that they want to say to other people in their life. Or there may be issues that they do not ever want to discuss with their friends or family, but need a space where they can look at these matters on their own. For example, Gillian had left her marriage because of her husband's violence. During the time that she and her children spent in a women's shelter, she found that one of the support workers was easy to talk to and always seemed to be on the same wavelength. Gillian spent hours talking to her. She needed to take stock of her life in order to be able to come to terms with what had happened and begin to get a sense of what she needed to do next. She wanted to be clear about what she would, and would not, tell her mother and sister and her mother-in-law. She was also trying to make sense of her own part in the breakdown of the marriage – a topic that she very much saw as private. In respect of any of these topics, Gillian was not expecting her support worker to provide her with new insights or action plans. After years of keeping these things secret, she just wanted to get them out in the open so she could look at them.

Developing a shared understanding

When working with a client around life transition issues, it is crucial to develop a shared understanding of what the client actually wants, and needs, to do at that point. For some clients, it may be enough merely to acknowledge that a transition is taking place. Others may want to work on specific tasks, such as letting go and saying goodbye to aspects of a past life or making plans for how to handle challenges associated with a new role or identity. It can also be helpful to identify tasks that may not be a priority at that moment but may become necessary or relevant at some point in the future. For example, for some clients, it may be useful to hear the suggestion of creating a ritual or action that marks their entry into a new status, even though they will only be ready to carry it out many years hence.

A recurring metaphor within the research and practice literature on the process of supporting people in relation to life transitions is the image of being a 'navigator' or guide – someone who has sufficient understanding of the routes and pathways that are available, to be in a position to assist the person to find their way to wherever it is they want to get to. Particularly evocative and powerful renderings of this perspective can be found in a study by Boddy et al. (2020) of the experiences of young adults who have been in care and two studies of supportive social work with unaccompanied asylum-seeking young people by Devenney (2020) and Nelson et al. (2017). Developing a shared understanding may involve finding a metaphor or image – such as a guide, a journey, navigating or pathfinding – that serves as a shorthand way of referring to what a counsellor and client are trying to achieve together.

Normalizing

It is not unusual for a client to feel confused around the multiple concerns and challenges that they may be confronting during a transition process. A sense of having 'lost one's bearings' may be particularly intense in the liminal phase of transition, when the person has left a previous important identity, role or place behind, but has not yet arrived at the next one. The skill of 'normalizing' involves using transition theory to help the client to make sense of what is happening in their life. It is essential to avoid any suggestion that stages or themes that are highlighted in transition models represent any kind of fixed, inevitable or 'right' way of thinking about a transition. What tends to be helpful is to present ideas in a spirit of offering a perspective that may or may not be helpful.

Mapping

In the spirit of seeing a transition as a process that is akin to being on a journey and finding a route that will lead to a desired end-point, it can be valuable to introduce activities that use 'mapping'. Compared to verbal communication and talk, a visual representation, such as a map or a diagram, has the advantage that multiple items of information can be considered all at once. In many spheres of life, visual mapping and diagramming are used to find patterns and choice points in complex data – clients may already be familiar with such ideas and have their own ideas about how to use them. One such activity that can be used in counselling is constructing a timeline – a graph made by the client, usually with time (years or months) along a horizontal axis drawn across the centre of the page and well-being or sense of security or some other valued state plotted on the horizontal axis, with positive times indicated above the horizontal axis and negative times below it. The person might also annotate the graph with images or phrases that function as labels for specific events (for example, 'when my mother died', 'when I met George'). A timeline is a useful means for enabling a client to reflect on processes in their life that have occurred over a period of time. Typically, a timeline is drawn during a counselling session and then forms the basis for a discussion between the counsellor and client. The client may add elements to the graph during the course of the conversation to record memories or understandings that have emerged. It is important that the client retains ownership and control over the timeline, rather than the counsellor writing on it. Toward the end of the discussion, in some circumstances it can be useful for the counsellor to invite the client to think about the future – 'ideally, what would you like to happen next? Fill in the graph for the next 12 months or so…'.

A 'choice map' is another form of visual representation that can be used in counselling around a transition issue. A valuable means of reframing stressful life transitions is to view them as creating opportunities to make new choices around the direction of one's life. The choice map technique developed by Lewchanin and Zubrod (2001) represents a powerful visual tool for clients to plot the choices they have made at previous transition points in their life and thus to be able to view their current choice-point in the context of fulfilling or self-denying decisions that they have made in the past.

A further visual method is to use photographs and other artefacts to represent key points in a transition and to stimulate reflection and meaning-making around the significance of that moment (or period of time) for the client. For example, some people build up large collections of photographs of family events. It can be useful to invite the client to bring in a selection of pictures that reflect stages or themes in their life. A photograph functions as an external object with meaning that can be discussed by the client and counsellor together. Photographs are emotionally evocative and close examination of each picture will typically allow nuances in relationships and emotional states to emerge. A further means of using photographs is to invite the client to take pictures of their current personal niche or life space, and if relevant a recent past niche, as a way of opening up discussion and reflection around what is important in the person's life and also what might be missing. This technique is sometimes described as 'photovoice' (Jarldorn, 2018). Examples of different ways that photographs and photography can be used in transition counselling include Berman (1993), Feingold et al. (2021), Keating (2021), Loewenthal (2013, 2015) and Streng et al. (2004).

Writing

An autobiography is the equivalent of a narrative version of a timeline, a written – rather than visual – representation stretching over the whole of a person's life. Clearly, writing an autobiography is time-consuming and the client would need to be willing to devote time to this activity outside of counselling sessions. The counsellor also needs to be willing to spend time reading the client's autobiography.

This kind of writing is quite demanding and it can be valuable to offer the client some guidelines, such as those developed by McAdams (1993), which include ideas such as starting off by identifying the different 'chapters' in one's life and giving each chapter a title. Another useful strategy for constructing an autobiography is to think about the key 'scenes' in one's life (as if writing a movie script). The value of an autobiography is that it allows all kinds of transition shifts over the course of a life to be identified and also allows the writer plenty of opportunity for reflection on the meaning of past events. Once completed, an autobiography becomes a document that can be shared with others and an accomplishment that represents a source of pride and satisfaction for the writer.

Exploring cultural meaning

There is a sense in which all major world cultures are organized around beliefs and rituals to mark the significance of normative life-course transitions such as birth, marriage and death. Particular subcultures may also develop rituals around transition events such as leaving school, graduating from university, leaving home, coming out as gay, moving into a new neighbourhood, divorce, retiring from paid employment and so on. There are several ways in which the cultural meaning of transition may be relevant for counselling. It may be that the person is troubled by a transition because they have somehow missed out on a valued cultural ritual ('I left that firm after 20 years of hard work and nobody seemed to care'). It may be that there are support groups, internet communities or self-help books available for people undergoing particular transitions (cultural resources). It may also be that the person is troubled by cultural meanings or messages around their transition. These meanings may not even be fully in awareness, but all the same are shaping the person's attitudes and feelings. For instance, in some middle-class communities, young people take a 'gap year' between school and university. An individual who did not follow that path might be haunted by a sense that he or she is therefore 'boring' or 'unadventurous'. In counselling, the use of the word 'should' can be a clue to this kind of issue – 'I *should* have taken more opportunity to travel when I was younger'.

Rituals

A ritual is an event that brings people together to share a meaningful and memorable experience that embodies certain core values and beliefs about the world. World cultures have developed innumerable rituals or *rites de passages* to facilitate transition from one status to another – for example single to married, life to death. In contemporary society, rituals that are based in organized religion may be highly relevant to some clients but meaningless for others. However, it is possible to devise personal or family rituals that serve the same function and which may even have a special meaning for participants by dint of being personalized and unique. A party is a form of transition ritual that is widely used – for example,

> **Box 9.3 Meeting a person in a state of liminality**
>
> The liminal phase of transition is one in which the person can be viewed as existing in a state of being rather than doing. From an emotional support point of view, it is not so much a matter of working on future-oriented tasks, but being willing to be with the client in whatever way makes sense to them. Andrew et al. (2021) investigated the experience of people with dementia in relation to the support provided by befrienders who visited them in their home on a regular basis. What was helpful was that the befriender was a presence in the person's life, and in particular was able to respond to unmet needs in the form of types of relationship that were not available from other people in their life. In responding in this manner, the helper exhibited an appreciation that their client was in a state of living *in* loss (Kelly 2008) or what Sjöberg et al. (2018) have characterized as 'existential loneliness'. In a study of the kind of support provided by hospice support workers, Vanderstichelen et al. (2020) found that, among other functions, these helpers were able not only to engage with the liminality of their clients, but convey messages about what the client might need, that busy doctors and nurses might not have the time to tune into. In a study that involved interviews with support workers themselves, Simpson et al. (2018) reported that these helpers saw themselves as occupying a marginal or liminal role within their place of work. Their informants believed that, while it could be uncomfortable to lack the professional recognition and status afforded to their colleagues who were mainstream health professionals, their own position had the advantage of allowing them to get closer to the concerns and needs of patients.

a family leaving a neighbourhood might hold a leaving party, someone who has been divorced might hold a party to mark their freedom. Other rituals are more idiosyncratic, such as setting fire to lecture notes on completion of a degree or burying one's favourite running shoes at the top of a hill when illness makes it impossible to continue to run marathons. Classic sources by Imber-Black and Roberts (1992) and Wyrostok (1995) continue to provide accessible and sensible introductions to the use of rituals in counselling. Lakshmin et al. (2018) describe the use of a public testimony ritual in immigrant survivors of intimate partner violence who are in a process of transition to a new life.

Organizational perspectives on transition counselling

Transition counselling is similar to other areas of embedded counselling, in the types of organizational support, supervision, training and resource development that are required to support effective helping. However, there are also important ways in which transition counselling has a unique type of relationship with the organizational settings in which it is provided. As mentioned at the start of this chapter, many human service organizations, such as schools, social work agencies and some branches of health care, owe their existence to a societal need to take care of people around transition points in their lives. What this means is that transition counselling is more closely aligned with organizational goals than – for instance – counselling for anxiety, depression or trauma. In addition, there are many specialist counselling services that have a specific focus on life transition issues, such as student counselling, bereavement counselling and career counselling. As a result, there exists a valuable body of knowledge, research, training and experience that embedded practitioners can draw on. A further distinctive aspect of embedded counselling around transition issues is that it opens up possibilities around different forms of preventive work – if it is going to be hard for many new students at a university or new mothers in a health centre to negotiate the transition they are facing, it makes sense to offer them information and support ahead of the event, to prepare them for what they are facing and to maximize the chances that they will seek help from trained practitioners at an early stage if they need it.

Conclusions

The concept of transition, and the notion that an important aspect of counselling can involve assisting people to make sense of life transitions, represent powerful ideas within counselling theory and practice. The concept of transition bypasses medical or psychiatric definitions of troubles and instead positions the difficulties that the person is experiencing firmly within a socio-cultural perspective. In addition, the concept of transition invites access to a rich array of cultural resources, practices and traditions. The concept of transition also carries a message of hope – yes, the person is deeply troubled and in pieces, but this is a necessary and inevitable step towards a different role or life stage. Transition-informed counselling is a vast topic – the present chapter can provide only a broad introduction to the ideas and approaches that are available within the research and practice literature around this topic. Useful sources of further information include Anderson et al. (2021), Bridges (2004) and Sugarman (2016).

Learning activities

The following activities may be explored individually, and/or with a group of learning partners.

Exercise 9.1 Reflecting on your own experience of transition
Choose a recent significant experience of transition in your own life. In thinking about how that process unfolded, can you identify stages that you passed through, in terms of your feelings, attitudes to what was happening and your behaviour? What helped you to get through this shift in your life? What was hindering on unhelpful? Finally – what can you take from your own personal experience of transition that can inform the way that you work with clients around similar issues?

Exercise 9.2 Reflecting on your own experience of liminality
An important theme in the present chapter has been the importance of liminality – the experience of being between an identity, role or way of being that has been lost or is in the process of being left behind, and another (or next) state that represents one's future. An appreciation of liminality, and capacity to empathically engage with the client's experience of this quality, is crucial for any counsellor working with clients around transition issues. In addition, many people report that being in a state of liminality offers unique and valuable insight into the human condition. Reflect on your own personal experience of liminality – this could be something that occupied a brief period of time or that might have continued for days or months. What was this like for you? How did you relate to other people during this stage? What was helpful or unhelpful for you, in respect of how other people interacted

with you or tried to be supportive? What can you take from your own personal experience of liminality that can inform the way that you work with clients? It can be particularly useful to meet with learning partners to share your reflections around liminality – this is a topic where hearing someone else's story can stimulate the emergence of further aspects of one's own story.

Exercise 9.3 Your own skills in working with transition
Based on your personal life experience, and also your counselling training and reading, what ideas and methods do you feel comfortable and competent in using with clients around transition issues? Are there particular transition events that are frequently reported by the clients in the organization in which you work? What are the cultural resources that are available within the organization, or in the broader community, to support people undergoing such transitions? Taking these questions as a whole, what is the counselling menu that you feel able to offer clients in relation to the task of negotiating life transitions?

Exercise 9.4 How your organization responds to transition issues
Are there specific transition issues and difficulties that are reported on a regular basis by clients who make use of the services offered by the organization in which you work? What does the organization currently do, in terms of acknowledging such issues and providing appropriate emotional support and counselling? How effective is what is currently offered and what kind of evidence is available in relation to this question? How might your organization improve its response to clients in transition? How could it learn from other organizations within the same sector, or from innovative practices in other sectors?

CHAPTER 10
Bereavement and loss

Introduction	194
Challenges around working with loss	195
A task-oriented approach to bereavement counselling	197
Making sense of the experience of loss and grief	199
Stages of coming to terms with grief	199
The use of attachment theory in bereavement counselling	200
Worden's bereavement tasks model	202
Assimilation of problematic experiences	202
The dual process model of coping with bereavement	203
A narrative perspective on bereavement	204
Methods for working with bereavement issues	206
The organizational context of bereavement work	209
Conclusions	212
Learning activities	212

Introduction

Loss is an inevitable part of life. It is intrinsic to being human that we form relationships and bonds with other people and that over the course of our lifetime many of these individuals will move on or die. Issues around coming to terms with loss are present in most counselling work, even when they do not represent the primary presenting problem of the client or service user. The present chapter explores some of the ways in which a collaborative pluralistic approach to embedded counselling can be used in working with clients around grief and loss. Although the chapter focuses largely on the challenge of working with people who have been bereaved, it also includes discussion of how the basic principles of bereavement counselling can be applied in counselling for other loss experiences such as being a refugee or being made unemployed.

Bereavement potentially has an impact on the whole of a person's life, from their innermost feelings and beliefs through to where they live and how much money they have to spend. A task-oriented approach to counselling tasks provides a flexible framework that allows practitioners to take account of how different people deal with their grief in different ways. This chapter therefore discusses a range of models and methods that can be used to help people with bereavement issues.

The process of coming to terms with a bereavement can take a considerable amount of time. It is unlikely that any one practitioner will be involved with a client all the way through from the stage of anticipating a death to the point where they are able to look back on their loss in a reflective manner. It makes sense to think in terms of a 'loss journey' (Machin 2013) – different practitioners (doctors, nurses, funeral directors, social workers, police, housing managers and others) interact with the person at different points in the journey and provide support around specific tasks at each stage. It is certain, therefore, that practitioners working in all human service agencies will come across grieving clients on a regular basis. As a result, this chapter also looks at ways that organizations can embed bereavement support within the routine service delivery.

Challenges around working with loss

Bereavement and loss represent profound areas of human experience. The loss of someone close can lead to a state of mourning, missing and searching, withdrawal from everyday activity and relationships, imagining the here-and-now presence of the person who has died, and experience of a wide range of emotions including sadness, despair, longing, loneliness, anger, relief and pervasive general emotional pain, as well as questions about one's identity and what life will be like in future. The death of someone close is also a reminder of our own mortality and a trigger for remembering other losses that one has undergone in the past. It brings into sharp relief the quality and consistency of support available from others and one's own capacity to accept and be nourished by that support. The conditions under which the death occurred may lead to a quest for explanation and understanding.

The complexity of bereavement is also reflected in the ways in which the meaning of a loss is shaped by who died and the circumstances in which they passed on: ageing, illness, accidents, suicide, murder, addictions, in the course of military action. It is possible to be deeply affected by the loss of a pet, farm animal or service animal. Some people may be excluded from the circle of mourning: former life partners, lovers, gay and lesbian companions.

Any of these aspects of the experience of loss can trigger a response in those who are trying to help a bereaved person. Practitioners offering support or counselling may find themselves remembering or re-experiencing painful losses in their own life.

The multi-faceted effects of bereavement are manifested in different areas of a person's life, in ways that lead to more frequent interactions with healthcare workers and practitioners of other caring and human service professions. In a study carried out by Becker et al. (2021) recently-bereaved individuals in Japan were invited to complete a survey questionnaire distributed by funeral directors. Around 10% of the sample reported significant difficulties around health issues, financial problems and difficulties in functioning at work. Analysis of government-collected health data sets in Scotland found similar patterns, as well as showing that those who had been bereaved had a lower life expectancy than comparable non-bereaved individuals (Stephen et al. 2015; Tseng et al. 2018). The literature reviews in these studies, as well as in Ennis and Majid (2021), consistently show that evidence collected in many other countries report that people who have been bereaved are more likely to suffer health problems, along with social disadvantage. From a counselling perspective, such studies can be interpreted as suggesting that, for some people, the emotional impact of loss of a loved one may be expressed at a bodily level as an experience of physical pain or vulnerability to becoming ill. In addition, the stress of loss of income or struggling to maintain work productivity and attendance may exacerbate emotional problems.

Because death is a universal aspect of life, throughout human history all cultures have developed rituals that allow communities to honour the dead and support those who have lost family members. How a culture responds to death is a reflection of its core beliefs and values. A large number of ethnographic studies have been conducted on grief rituals in different cultures (Silverman, Baroiller and Hemer 2021). Recent contributions to the anthropology of grief include the account by Otaegui (2021) of the grief songs of the Ayoreo people in Paraguay and the analysis by Silverman (2021) of American Jewish mourning rituals. In contrast, in most European, North American and other westernized countries, these traditional rituals have been lost and the prevailing response to death has become largely medicalized and secularized, with limited grief rituals and minimal ongoing recognition of loss. As a result, the task of supporting those who have become bereaved has to a significant extent been appropriated by professional grief specialists, such as counsellors. This trend is a source of regret for many people. A notable critic on how death is handled in western societies is Stephen Jenkinson, a social worker who directed a palliative care service in Canada for many years (Jenkinson 2015; see also videos of his lectures at https://orphanwisdom.com). Along with other critics, Jenkinson (2015) has argued that, by losing touch with traditional collective rituals, western death practices produce people who are unable to incorporate an understanding of death into their sense of who they are. This, in turn, reinforces destructive consumerism, various mental health problems and a pervasive sense of disconnection between people.

The persistence, in some cultures, of death rituals that bring communities together, along with the relative absence of such rituals and practices in western societies, has two major implications for bereavement counsellors and practitioners of embedded counselling working with bereaved clients. First, a psychological approach that focuses on cognitive and emotional functioning is never going to be sufficient. The narrative model of bereavement counselling, described in a later section of the present chapter, seeks to address this issue by encouraging clients to find ways to talk about their loss with family members and other people who have known the deceased. The second implication is that western-style counselling is generally not helpful for a person who has a living connection to meaningful culturally-based grief rituals (Mayland et al. 2021) unless their counsellor is able to accommodate these traditional beliefs and practices into their work together (see, for example, Marsh et al. 2015; Schreiber 1995).

An important theme in contemporary theory and practice of bereavement counselling has been a movement toward trying to accommodate traditional ideas. An important example of this approach has been a recognition that having experiences of the here-and-now presence of a deceased person are not signs of a mental disorder but instead represent normal and healthy manifestations of the ongoing significance of that individual (Hayes and Steffen 2017; Steffen and Coyle 2017). Another example is increased emphasis in counselling around helping the person to find ways to keep alive their memories of, and emotional bond with, the person who has died (Klass and Steffen 2017) rather than assuming that a 'healthy' or well-adjusted response requires moving on and leaving behind those feelings.

A task-oriented approach to bereavement counselling

The following example shows how it is possible for health and social care practitioners to use collaborative counselling skills to help a person to come to terms with a massively difficult and tragic experience of loss.

Judith is a midwife in a community maternity unit, with a particular interest in the emotional needs of parents of stillborn children. She completed a certificate course in counselling skills and was encouraged by the manager of the unit to develop counselling provision specifically for grieving parents. A designated counselling room was created in the unit where she could meet with parents and she was allocated half a day each week to visit clients in their homes. One of the patients with whom she worked with over a 12-month period was Sheena, an unmarried young woman of 21 whose son died in the neonatal intensive care room shortly after he was born. Judith's involvement with Sheena incorporated a range of counselling tasks:

Talking though an issue in order to understand things better. There were many occasions where Sheena just needed to talk, to 'get this stuff out of my head'. At the beginning, Sheena talked a lot to her partner, mother and friends, but felt as though she needed to protect them from some of the pain she was experiencing and saw Judith as a safe place to say anything she needed to say. As time went on, other people became less willing to talk about the baby, so Judith became an even more important outlet.

Making sense of an event or experience that is puzzling and problematic. There were several situations where Sheena was shocked and scared about her own reactions to events: she thought that she saw her baby in the hospital and in prams in supermarkets; she became very angry with one of the doctors; and she had powerful dreams. These were embarrassing things for Sheena to discuss with anyone other than Judith, who was able to help her to understand her experiences in terms of processes of grief.

Problem-solving, planning and decision-making. Judith helped Sheena to make plans for a commemoration event for her son and to create a box with objects and photographs from her time in the maternity unit. She also helped Sheena to make contact with a support group for parents of stillborn babies.

Changing behaviour. Sheena became quite isolated after the bereavement and did not want to socialize with other people. She realized that this pattern was unhelpful for her and talked with Judith about strategies for re-entering social life.

Dealing with difficult feelings and emotions. For several months, Sheena described herself as living in a world of emotional pain. Talking with Judith helped her to disentangle the strands of the pain into a sense of loss and a powerful rage. Judith introduced some ways of channelling these emotions, using artwork and two-chair work, that provided opportunities for Sheena to 'give in to her tears'.

Finding, analysing and acting on information. Soon after the death of her son, Sheena was desperate to understand what had happened. Judith supported her in arranging a meeting with the consultant to get an explanation of how and why her baby had died. Part of the preparation for this meeting involved deciding on which questions to ask and how to remain rational.

Undoing self-criticism and enhancing self-care. A major theme in Sheena's thinking after the event was that she must be to blame for what had happened. This psychological self-criticism spilled over into lack of self-care around diet. Judith offered support and challenge around these issues during counselling conversations.

Negotiating a life transition. The bereavement was experienced by Sheena as a major turning point in her life. Toward the end of their contact with each other, Judith invited Sheena to spend one of their meetings reflecting on what she had learned from her loss and how she wanted her life to be different moving into the future.

Dealing with difficult or painful relationships. Sheena had always had a troubled relationship with her mother. Through the time of the bereavement, her mother made a great effort to be supportive, but Sheena found it hard to accept her help. At the same time, Sheena's partner became more and more emotionally withdrawn and eventually they separated. These issues were explored in counselling, with the result that Sheena became able to differentiate between 'mum then' and 'mum now', allowing her mother to be closer to her and talk openly to her mother about what the loss of her baby had meant to her.

Accessing other sources of help. Judith's involvement with Sheena comprised several meetings in the weeks immediately after the loss of her child, then monthly face-to-face or online sessions, and then finally more intensive contact in the run-up to the anniversary of the death and participation in the commemoration event. They then had one final session to explore sources of ongoing support, including the possibility of further contact if a crisis occurred, but also information about bereavement counselling and general counselling services available in the city where Sheena lived.

This case was unusual in the sense that one practitioner-counsellor was able to accompany her client all the way through her grief journey. It illustrates the pervasive quality of the impact of loss and the value of adopting a counselling framework that regards all aspects of the client's experience as potential tasks that might be need to be tackled. For Judith as a practitioner of embedded counselling, the idea of a counselling 'menu' consisting of a range of tasks, provided an invaluable means of separating out the different strands of Sheena's life that needed to be repaired. On most of the times they met, Sheena was 'all over the place', struggling to cope with the messy interconnectedness of various issues. In response, Judith offered a reliable presence that was empathic and supportive but also business-like – 'what I am picking up from you is that these three things are really bothering you today – X and Y and Z. Does that seem right to you, or have I missed something? OK, what order will we take them in? Let's see if we can make some progress on each of them, one at a time, in the time we have available.'

In different circumstances, for example if Sheena had been seen in a maternity unit that did not have a midwife-counsellor, each of the tasks described above might have been facilitated by a range of other practitioners and helpers, such as a doula, her GP or practice nurse, a priest or other religious adviser, a social worker, members of a peer support group or an eating disorders therapist.

Making sense of the experience of loss and grief

As with any problem that a client brings to counselling, it is helpful for a client experiencing a bereavement to be able to get some kind of handle on what they are feeling, in terms of a coherent and convincing explanatory framework. The following sections describe some theoretical frameworks that have been widely used by bereavement counsellors: stages of grief model, psychodynamic attachment theory, Worden's tasks model, the assimilation of problematic experiences model, the dual process model, and narrative theory.

Stages of coming to terms with grief

Many bereavement counselling textbooks and training programmes are organized around the idea that the person experiencing loss needs to pass through a transition that comprises a series of stages. Examples of stage theories are the model developed by Elisabeth Kubler-Ross suggesting that both dying people and those who are bereaved go through five stages of grieving: denial, anger, bargaining, depression, and, finally, acceptance (Kubler-Ross and Kessel 2005), and the four-stage model of bereavement formulated by Colin Murray Parkes (2006): shock and numbness; yearning and searching; disorganization and despair; and reorganization and recovery. These models have been highly influential, because they provide readily accessible ideas about how coming to terms with loss is a process that takes time, while at the same time sensitizing helpers, carers and those who have been bereaved to the kind of responses and themes that might be expected. However, almost from the moment that these models were developed in the 1970s, they were criticized by researchers and practitioners who question the notion of fixed stages. In a classic and widely-cited paper, Wortman and Silver (1989) reviewed the research literature on loss and grief and came to the conclusion that there are no fixed and predictable patterns of coping with loss. Instead, there are major differences between people in terms of how severely they are affected, how long the grieving process takes, whether they go through stages of anger and depression and so on. Wortman and Silver (1989) urge caution on the part of those working in the field of bereavement, against allowing themselves to be caught up in prevailing 'myths' around the grieving process. These conclusions were reinforced in a subsequent detailed review by Stroebe, Schut and Boerner (2017), who concluded their analysis by making a heartfelt plea for those involved in supporting the bereaved to consign stage models to the pages of history and make use of other ways of thinking about grief.

The use of attachment theory in bereavement counselling

The psychoanalytic psychotherapist and researcher John Bowlby made a contribution to counselling and psychotherapy theory and practice that had an immense impact over the last 50 years. Bowlby highlighted the significance of 'attachment' bonds in human relationships. The basic idea behind Bowlby's work is the notion that the survival of babies and infants is contingent on their capacity to form a secure attachment with a caregiver or caregivers. Babies are not able to look after themselves, so need to have someone else who will feed them, keep them warm and dry and provide stimulation and social contact. This aspect of life is so important for human beings that attachment mechanisms are biologically 'wired-in' to the human nervous system. Bowlby was able to show that the availability of an emotional 'secure base' in early childhood was associated with an ability to enjoy successful intimate relationships, friendships and work collaboration in later life. By contrast, when the mother or other caregivers behaved in a way that was inconsistent or neglectful, the person was likely to develop a pattern of 'insecure attachment' that persisted through the rest of their life. In an extensive programme of research, attachment researchers have been able to identify three distinct patterns of insecure attachment:

- preoccupied/ambivalent – the person has received inconsistent patterns of care in childhood, which has left them wishing to be close to others, but feeling powerless to do anything to make this happen, angry when other people let them down, and not easily comforted.
- dismissive – in childhood, the person's physical needs were taken care of, but there was little emotional closeness – as an adult they act as though they do not need to be close to anyone else.
- fearful – the child was exposed to active neglect or abuse, and as a result wants to be close to others but experiences high levels of fear and anxiety when this happens.

These ideas have several implications for bereavement counselling. Attachment patterns are exhibited in the way that an individual copes with loss. On the whole, a person who has a secure attachment style is likely to be able to use anyone else who is available to them (friends, family, professionals) to work through their grief in a generally straightforward and balanced manner. Their own sense of who they are as a person is unlikely to be threatened by their loss and they are able to form new attachments as appropriate.

By contrast, people who have emerged from childhood with different types of insecure attachment patterns may find it harder to deal with bereavement. For example, a person with an ambivalent attachment style may blame others as a means of deflecting attention from their own vulnerability. A dismissive attachment pattern is associated with appearing to be unaffected by a loss, until feelings are triggered by a later event, while a fearful attachment is expressed through turmoil – a chaotic response to the loss that shifts unpredictably between emotional states. These attachment styles are reflected not only in the way that the person exhibits grief and loss in their everyday life, but also in the way that he or she relates to counsellors and other professional practitioners around the issue of their bereavement.

In addition, the counsellor's own attachment style may shape their way of responding to a bereaved client. For example, a practitioner with an insecure attachment style may minimize the significance of a client's loss because they find it too emotionally threatening to put themselves in a position in which their own unresolved losses might be triggered. On the other hand, a counsellor who has more of what Bowlby described as an emotional and interpersonal 'secure base' is in a better position to accompany a troubled client into what may be an overwhelmingly bleak phase of their life.

In the context of bereavement counselling, the value of an attachment perspective is that it makes sense of how and why the impact of loss reaches beyond the present situation, by evoking fears and memories around troubled and broken relationships and experiences of betrayal in the past. It also suggests that one of the best ways to heal these wounds is by establishing a secure and trusting relationship with a therapist and then learning how to apply this capacity to build satisfactory and meaningful everyday relationships (Kosminsky 2017). A bereavement counselling textbook that is grounded in an attachment perspective and illustrates how these ideas can be used to make sense of many aspects of the bereavement process is Lendrum and Syme (2004).

Worden's bereavement tasks model

Many widely-used bereavement counselling texts have been replaced by the idea that dealing with bereavement confronts the person with a set of tasks that may differ in salience for each individual and which may be carried out in no particular order. An influential model of bereavement was formulated by William Worden (2018), who identified four key tasks of mourning:

1. To accept the reality of the loss
2. To work through the pain of grief
3. To adjust to an environment in which the deceased is missing
4. To emotionally relocate the deceased and move on with life.

Worden (2018) and Worden and Winokuer (2011) argue that the notion of stages or phases of grief implies a certain level of passivity on the part of the grieving person – there is nothing much that they can do, other than wait for the effect of time and life experience to heal their loss. By contrast, his task model opens up an agenda for the client and counsellor to work together on making a difference. The Worden model is consistent with the task model and counsellor's menu outlined in the present book. However, the Worden tasks are broader in scope than the task list introduced in Chapter 3: the latter specify micro-steps that can be taken within specific counselling meetings, whereas the Worden tasks model is more relevant for exploring with the client the work that they may need to do in broader or more general terms. It is important to note that Worden's (2018) book covers a lot more than just the tasks of a mourning model. In it, he discusses the nature of grief in great detail and the ways in which different psychological and social factors can have an influence on the grieving process. The book also incorporates several vivid case vignettes.

Assimilation of problematic experiences

The assimilation of problematic experiences model was developed by Bill Stiles and colleagues to explain the change process that occurs when a person is faced with a need to come to terms with a difficult or troubling event or situation. This model has been widely used in the field of counselling and psychotherapy in relation to a wide range of troubling life experiences, including bereavement, loss and cultural change (e.g. being an immigrant or refugee) and is supported by a substantial body of research (Stiles 2001, 2011). The assimilation model suggests that different life experiences are expressed as parts of the self, or 'voices', that exist within an internal dialogue of a person, such as debates within their own head about what to do and how to be, as well as in the way they talk, where different voices have contrasting voice qualities such as harsh or soft, interrupt each other, etc. (Honos-Webb and Stiles 1998; Osatuke et al. 2005). From an assimilation perspective, the psychological and emotional functioning of a person can be viewed as operating like a community of voices that can agree or disagree. Problematic experiences such as a bereavement or becoming a refugee disrupt the ongoing process of dialogue and meaning-making that occurs within the person. An important aspect of this process is the emergence of silenced or warded-off voices or areas of experience and the struggle to allow these threads of meaning to be heard in the face of established voices. For example, someone who has suffered a bereavement may experience fleeting images and memories of the deceased, which are suppressed by a stronger, dominant voice that tells them to be strong, move on and forget. In a situation in which the person has space to be aware of silenced voices (e.g. counselling, in a support group or through interaction with a sensitive and empathic priest, nurse or other practitioner), what happens is that gradually a conversation or dialogue between voices is able to unfold and meaning bridges between different voices can begin to be built.

An analysis of the application of the assimilation model in bereavement is available in Wilson (2011) and studies of how it can be used to makes sense of the experience of loss in immigrants and refugees have been carried out by Henry (2012; see also Henry et al. 2005, 2009, 2017). The value of the assimilation model, in the context of counselling for bereavement and loss, is that it describes a process of change without making any assumptions about the content of what happens at each stage (i.e. whether the person might be expected to have entered the Kubler-Ross stages of anger, denial, etc.). Instead, it is a general framework developed within the field of psychotherapy that can helpfully sensitize the counsellor to subtle aspects of what is happening for the client, such as beginning to be aware of a warded-off area of experience or engaging in dialogue between different ways of responding to loss or grief.

The dual process model of coping with bereavement

A widely-applied perspective on the experience of coping with loss has been developed by Margaret Stroebe and Henk Schut (2005), who identify two broad types of psychological activity that are involved in grieving: loss-oriented and restoration-oriented. Loss-oriented tasks include dealing with the intrusion of feelings of loss and despair and letting go of ties with the deceased person. Restoration tasks include doing new things and developing new relationships. Clearly, in any individual case, the balance between these tasks will be unique. One of the ways in which this model is relevant for counselling is that Stroebe and Schut (1999) suggest that the person 'oscillates' between these two orientations.

For example, a period of time devoted to restoration-oriented activities may be helpful for a person, but will inevitably expose them to many reminders and emotional triggers ('it was great to go to the theatre today with my new friends, but it was also painful that X could not be there'). Similarly, a period of time immersed in feelings and memories will inevitably lead to a sense of wanting to do something different. The dual process model implies that the kinds of tasks identified by Worden (2018) occur in a dynamic back-and-forward manner. For example, while it may be necessary to experience and work through the pain of grief, it is also helpful to take time off from this task and turn instead for a while to the task of developing new roles, identities, and relationships. The concept of oscillation is valuable from a counselling perspective, because it takes away any sense of failure at lack of progress in relation to any specific theme or task. It suggests, instead, that maybe it is just time to work on something else. It also dissolves any tension between maintaining emotional bonds or relinquishing them – a dual process stance suggests that both are important. A final helpful aspect of the dual process model is that it offers a way of making sense of gender differences in the grieving process. On the whole, women tend to be more familiar and comfortable with the emotional and relational focus of loss-oriented tasks and try to tackle their grief in this way. By contrast, men may have spent their lives engaging in the kind of cognitive and action-focused ways of coping that are characteristic of the restorative element of grief work and are likely to apply these skills to the tasks of recovering from loss. The decision to seek counselling is triggered, at least in part, by the failure of the client's strategies for dealing with their grief. It is possible, therefore, that offering strategies that are different from the person's previously favoured approach might be more effective than merely supporting them to do more of the same. This is what was found in a study by Schut et al. (1997) – widows benefitted more from counselling that was problem-focused, while widowers did better when their therapist initiated an emotion-focused way of working. Of course, gender differences are complex and client preferences for therapy interventions reflect a wide variety of influences. Nevertheless, the dual process model of coping with bereavement offers a useful framework for at least opening up a conversation with clients about what they think might be helpful (and what the counsellor thinks might be helpful) and why.

A narrative perspective on bereavement

A narrative approach to grief and loss emphasizes the idea that well-being and meaningful engagement in social life is based on being able to develop a rich and coherent life story or biography, which is connected in myriad ways to the stories and biographies of others, whether alive or dead. From a narrative perspective, therefore, the process of coming to terms with bereavement involves finding an enduring place for the story of the deceased person in the ongoing lives and stories of those who knew them. This idea is summarized very well in a classic paper by the British sociologist and loss theorist Tony Walter (1999), who suggests that, following a bereavement or loss, the person will generally have a desire to talk about the deceased and to talk with others who knew them and work together to construct a story that places the dead within their lives, a story that he characterizes as 'capable of enduring through time'. Walter (2017) argues that many people living in modern industrial societies have a great deal to learn in respect of mourning from the attitudes and practices of people in traditional societies, where the dead are 'placed within life' in many ways on an everyday basis.

There are many strategies for using counselling to accomplish this kind of narrative continuity of the deceased. One example can be found in the 'saying hello' method devised by one of the leading figures in narrative therapy, Michael White (1998). In one case study, White (1998) described a way of working that centred on a process of incorporating the deceased person into the life of a surviving spouse (Mary) who was still deeply affected by the loss of her husband, Ron, five years after his death. White asked questions that invited Mary to 'say hello' to Ron, such as:

- if you were seeing yourself through Ron's eyes right now, what would you be noticing about yourself that you would appreciate?
- what do you know about yourself that you are awakened to when you bring about the enjoyable things that Ron knew about you?
- how could you let others know that you have reclaimed some of the discoveries about yourself that were clearly visible to Ron?

This kind of conversation, which is informed by a narrative therapy approach, positions the deceased person not as a fixed set of memories that exist in the mind of the grieving person, but as an active participant in the life not only of the survivor but also the lives of other people as well.

An alternative version of a narrative approach to grief counselling, informed by constructivist philosophy and principles, can be found in the writings of the American psychotherapist Robert Neimeyer and his colleagues (Neimeyer 2001; Neimeyer, Klass and Dennis, 2014; www.robertneimeyerphd.com). A detailed and powerful account of how Neimeyer works in practice is available in the 'treatment approaches' section of Neimeyer (2019). Central to this process is the effort to help the client to tell their story, in order to be able to make meaning out of a loss that has shattered their world. Being able to tell the story enables the person to connect or reconnect with other people – possibly initially with their counsellor or members of a support group and subsequently with other people in their life. A narrative approach emphasizes the therapeutic value of talking as a way of both retaining the bond with the deceased by keeping their memory alive, and beginning to forge new and different relationships. This type of meaning-making can be facilitated through writing, participation in theatre and many other activities (Hedtke and Winslade 2016; Smigelsky and Neimeyer 2018).

The various theoretical perspectives on the grieving process that have been discussed in this section should not be viewed as mutually exclusive. It is probably

> **Box 10.1 Bereavement as a result of suicide**
>
> A situation in which someone finds himself or herself bereaved due to the suicide of a friend, family member or close work colleague represents a particularly challenging area of counselling. The usual process of grief is overlaid with complex layers of confusion, shock, guilt, shame, betrayal and anger and questions about whether vital clues were missed and opportunities to save the person were lost (Shields et al. 2017). For the survivor, there can also be a sense of stigma – what happened is difficult to talk about with other people (Goulah-Pabst 2021) with the result that the topic is avoided (Nam 2016) – factors that undermine the usual process of coming to terms with a loss by using social support. Articles by John R. Jordan (Jordan 2015; Jordan and McGann 2017) provide a useful overview of counselling tasks that may be relevant in work with clients who have experienced loss through suicide. Books that function as valuable self-help and psychoeducational resources (for both practitioners and clients) in relation to bereavement by suicide include: *Silent Grief: Living in the Wake of Suicide* (Lukas and Seiden 2007); *A Special Scar: The Experiences of People Bereaved by Suicide* (Wertheimer 2001); *Dying To Be Free: A Healing Guide for Families After a Suicide* (Cobain and Larch 2018).

not helpful to be guided by stage models such as those developed by Kubler-Ross and Parkes, because research studies have been unable to confirm that they correspond to the real-life experiences of those who have been bereaved. Grief and loss are complex phenomena and different people make sense of it in different ways or at different points in their grief journey. The theories outlined above (with the exception of stage models) can be regarded as offering resources for understanding. Other theoretical perspectives on grief are discussed in Small (2001) and Stroebe and Schut (2001). The writings of Sasha Bates (2021a,b) provide many powerful examples of how different ideas about loss, and therapeutic activities, can be helpful for different people at different times over the course of their loss journey.

Methods for working with bereavement issues

The case of Sheena, introduced earlier in this chapter, illustrates the all-encompassing nature of bereavement, and the way that counselling may involve many different types of counselling task and many different counselling methods. In principle, all of the methods described in previous chapters may be potentially relevant when working with a client around issues of bereavement and loss. As with any issue, the single most helpful method is probably providing a safe space within which the person is able to talk openly about their feelings and memories.

In a study by Klasen et al. (2017), individuals who had received bereavement counselling were interviewed about what they had found helpful in the therapy they had received. This paper is worth reading as a whole, in terms of the vividness and clarity with which clients' voices and experiences are presented. A key theme within its findings was the experience of a high level of affirmation from the counsellor, in terms of their capacity to accept whatever the person was thinking and feeling at that moment. Other helpful aspects included a collaborative approach ('let's work together to see what we can achieve'), use of creative techniques, gentle probing, psychological education about grief and being encouraged to engage in meaningful outside activities (e.g. walking). Counselling was described as hard work that required the person to be honest and as a learning experience. A study by Steffen, Timotijevic and Coyle (2020) into the experiences of family members affected by sudden cardiac death of a child or sibling, provides insight into how these helpful processes can be facilitated through membership of a support group. In these, and other studies, there is a strong emphasis on offering a flexible and responsive approach to counselling, rather than seeking to implement a standardized model.

Exploratory and empathic dialogue represents the foundation of all bereavement counselling. An edited book by Neimeyer (2012) comprises an invaluable source of information on techniques used in counselling for grief and loss, including examples of methods that are widely used by bereavement practitioners such as:

Using metaphor. People who are struggling with loss may have sense that what is happening for them is chaotic and out of control and also that it lacks meaning. Within the person's way of talking, however, he or she may be using metaphors that can be further developed to create hope and meaning. It may also be useful for the counsellor to offer such metaphors. The kinds of metaphors that can be particularly useful in bereavement counselling include the idea that life is a 'journey' and that the loss is a stage in that journey, and that as beings in nature we all participate in a 'cycle' of death and renewal similar to growing things such as plants. In some situations, it can be useful to convey a metaphor in the form of a 'healing story' (Burns 2005, 2007).

Creative arts methods. The use of creative art media such as drawing and painting, sculpting, music, and photography, can play a key role in many aspects of the bereavement counselling process. For example, in a counselling session, the emotional reality of the client's feelings for the lost person may be more readily expressed if the client brings in a photograph of the person, or a piece of music that is associated with the person. Creating a drawing, painting, montage or sculpture may allow the person an outlet for feelings and also a way of representing and organizing different strands of thought and feeling. Creating a piece of art, such as a picture, can also assist reflection and meaning-making by functioning as an external object that the client and counsellor can discuss together. Such objects also serve as markers of progress – 'I remember the emotional state that led me to make that picture and I realize that I don't feel like that now'. Further information, and examples, around the use of creative methods in grief counselling can be found in Renzenbrink (2021) and Thompson and Neimeyer (2014).

Dealing with unfinished business. For someone who has been bereaved, there can be unresolved issues (unfinished business) with the one who has died, such as things they would have wanted to say to them, or feelings that were never expressed during their life. The counselling technique of two-chair work, in which the client imagines that the other person is sitting facing them in an empty chair and talks to them, has been used to tackle this task (Holland et al. 2020; Neimeyer 2019; Payne et al. 2002).

Cultural resources. There are many cultural resources that people can use as sources of meaning and guides to action when dealing with loss. These resources include: novels; poems; music; movies and drama; self-help books and websites; and support networks and groups for people experiencing different types of loss. In addition to these bereavement-specific cultural resources, there are innumerable generic cultural resources, ranging from tending a garden through to joining an evening class, that may be experienced as healing by particular individuals. Poetry is experienced by many as a potentially helpful cultural resource in relation to giving expression to painful emotions of loss. Margaret Strobe (2018) has written about poems that have been important to her in her work as a bereavement therapist and Robert Neimeyer has published many of his own poems (see www.robertneimeyerphd.com).

Box 10.2 A meaningful death

The writings and teachings of Stephen Jenkinson (2015) have contributed to a growing awareness of the ways in which what he describes as the 'managed' or medicalized dying process has the effect of keeping the experience of death at a distance. This makes it hard for surviving family members, and communities, to assimilate the reality and inevitability of death into their own lives and relationships. It also limits the power and scope of collective ritual experience around the death of a member of a community, which represents a cornerstone of the sense of belonging that can be found in indigenous cultures. Although the loss of someone close is always painful, it can be argued that the way such events are handled in contemporary society leads to negative long-term emotional and interpersonal effects. In recent years, there have been attempts to provide an alternative non-medicalized approach to dying through the use of end-of life doulas (or death doulas) who accompany the person through their death, with the aim of making the experience as meaningful as possible for all concerned (Gaspard et al. 2021; Krawczyk and Rush 2020; Rawlings et al. 2020).

Spirituality. For many people, spiritual practices and religious observance represent important ways in which they make sense of bereavement and loss and make healing connection with other people. In working with clients who are experiencing bereavement, it is always useful to invite them to talk about their religious and spiritual involvement and the ways in which they are able to draw on these areas in coping with their loss.

Cultural sensitivity. The meaning of death, and the rituals that are associated with it, vary significantly across different cultures. When counselling a client around bereavement issues, it is helpful to ask about any cultural beliefs and expectations that might be relevant to the way they are feeling.

The organizational context of bereavement work

There are a number of specialist bereavement counselling services that have been established, such as CRUSE in the UK, which tend to focus on the needs of people with more severe grief reactions, and usually work with clients some time after the bereavement, rather than in the immediate aftermath of the loss. There are also counselling services and social workers trained in counselling approaches within most hospices. Alongside these sources, the majority of bereaved people who seek help and support from beyond their family network also tend to turn for emotional support to a wide range of practitioners including clergy, other members of faith communities, healthcare professions, funeral directors, teachers and social workers.

The evidence from research seems to suggest that while formal bereavement counselling is effective in many cases (Schut and Stroebe 2005; Stroebe, Schut and Stroebe 2005), there are many clients who enter counselling but do not seem to be at the right point to make best use of it – it is those people with complicated and severe grief reactions that are helped most by formal, regular scheduled therapy. Formal counselling services that have been organized on an 'outreach' basis, where all people in a community who have been bereaved are routinely invited to receive counselling, do not appear to be particularly helpful (Schut and Stroebe 2005). The key factors here are that the person has not made a deliberate decision to seek help, may not be motivated or ready to take advantage of counselling, may not need it or may even be disturbed by the offer of help. These findings make intuitive sense – in the time immediately following a death, a person is to a large extent in a state of shock and not ready to talk. Also, there are many cultural resources available to people to help them cope with their grief (Hockey, Katz and Small 2001; Walter 1999). Religious rituals and teachings are immensely valuable for many people during their experience of loss. There are also many novels and movies that sensitively present healing images of the meanings of death. Professional nurses, doctors, teachers and others who may be the first line of support for people who have been bereaved, and are sensitive enough to respond to moments when the person wishes to talk, have a particularly important role to play. It is essential for those offering embedded counselling to be aware of situations where the person is undergoing complicated grief, where the loss has perhaps triggered other underlying issues, and to be prepared to make a referral to a specialist service.

Within large organizations in fields such as education, healthcare and social services, responding to the needs of clients and service users who are coping with death and bereavement is a recurring issue. Typically, such organizations tend to provide training for practitioners in how to support clients who have experienced loss and how to develop links with representatives of faith communities and counselling services. Large organizations may also develop policies around staff absence around family or colleague bereavement, methods for conveying accurate information to members of the organization (for example, when a child has died, everyone in the school needs to be told) and remembrance services or other similar events. It is usually helpful if there is one person who has responsibility for co-ordinating these functions. At an organizational level, a death can have a 'ripple' effect. For instance, in a busy hospital, patients will die every day, but the unexpected death of a well-known member of staff may have an impact on dozens of patients and colleagues. The way that an organization responds to loss is likely to remain in the memory of staff and service users – it represents a key symbolic and practical indicator of the caring ethos of the organization as a whole.

Emotional support for women and couples who have lost a baby during pregnancy, or soon after birth, represents an area that has been associated with a wide range of organizational initiatives, including counselling training for midwives, provision of counselling rooms, liaison with faith groups and other community resources, follow-up meetings and creation of places where the loss can be recorded, such as memorial areas or trees. Another significant area of research and practice around organizational response to bereavement has occurred within schools (Abraham-Steele and Edmonds 2021; Costelloe et al 2020; Holland 2016; Lytje 2013). The challenge within the school environment is to find ways of making constructive use of a social institution that is a hugely important resource in the lives of students and their families without disrupting teaching and learning. Bereavement support in a school is a complex process that needs to take account of the different possible contributions that can be made by practitioners, such as teachers, learning support workers, administrators, clergy and school counsellors, in relation to a range of types of loss that can encompass the private experience of a young person who has lost a family member, through to the collective grief experienced across a whole school community when a group of friends have died together in a road traffic accident. School-based initiatives may also encompass the dimension of suicide prevention (McConnellogue and Storey 2017).

Other organizational contexts in which there have been significant developments around strategic approaches to emotional support for people who have been bereaved include services for people with learning difficulties (Read 2007;

Read and Elliott 2007), the criminal justice system (Read et al. 2018) and social work (Mowll 2017).

Some organizations have developed strategies and procedures for appropriately acknowledging the loss by suicide of a member of a community and supporting survivors (e.g. the friends and family of the person who has committed suicide) to deal with their response to what has happened. This area of work has been described as suicide 'postvention'. For example, Gulliver et al. (2016) describe procedures that have evolved in fire and rescue services and Veilleux et al. (2016) within counselling, psychotherapy and mental health training programmes and clinics. Jordan and McGann (2017) discuss the general principles that inform such guidelines and how they are implemented in practice.

Beyond the level of the kind of response that is possible for local organizations, there are also bereavement counselling services that are organized on a regional or national level to respond to the needs of people at times of natural disasters, pandemics, accidents, war, terrorist attacks, and multiple shooting incidents. This can also be accompanied by collective remembrance, in the form of memorials, art work, events such as religious services and special days.

Conclusions

In many ways, the issues associated with bereavement counselling function as a microcosm for the field of counselling as a whole. Coping with bereavement and loss is a universal human experience. Bereavement is not primarily a 'mental health' issue (although it may become one), but instead represents a life event that potentially can challenge all aspects of a person's being and relationships. Counselling can be valuable in coming to terms with bereavement, but so can many other types of activity – the question of the place of counselling alongside other cultural resources arises as a central question in respect of how bereavement support is organized and delivered. Bereavement is an experience that inevitably impacts on the work roles of practitioners in all areas of human service provision and raises questions around the level of training and preparedness that is provided for those working in such roles.

The main message of this chapter is that there exists a rich literature around the topic of bereavement counselling, and many ideas about how to make sense of grief and loss and how to facilitate a process of personal healing. The multi-faceted nature of reactions to loss, and the fact that bereaved individuals may seek emotional support from different sources at different stages in the grief journey, underscores the value of adopting a flexible approach to embedded counselling that focuses on collaboration around specific tasks that are most salient for the person at particular moments.

Learning activities

The following activities may be explored individually and/or with a group of learning partners.

Exercise 10.1 Your personal experience of loss

Construct a loss timeline. Use this line to illustrate the losses you have experienced in your life and how these events have been associated with high and low points across the course of your life as a whole. Once you have created your loss timeline, reflect on the extent to which you have been able to come to terms with various losses or whether there are some grieving processes that are still ongoing for you. Finally, give some further consideration to the ways in which your experience of loss has left you with knowledge and sensitivity that you can use in your work with grieving clients or areas of vulnerability that might make you resistant to opening yourself up to the grief of another person. It can be very helpful to carry out this learning activity in the context of a supportive group.

Exercise 10.2 Mourning in different cultures
Write a description of the mourning rituals that are associated with your own cultural group – for example, how funerals are conducted and what happens at home and within families to commemorate losses. Interview at least two other people from different cultural backgrounds around how these issues are dealt with in their cultures. If you are a member of a learning group that includes representatives from different cultures, you may be able to carry out this activity in your group. The aim of this learning exercise is to develop awareness of the diversity of ways in which grief can be understood and managed.

Exercise 10.3. How bereavement is handled in your organization
What happens in the organization in which you are employed when someone dies? Are there different responses in relation to whether the person was a colleague or client or depending on the cause of death? In what ways might these policies and procedures be improved in light of what you have learned in the present chapter and your further reading on this topic?

CHAPTER 11

Making changes

Introduction	**214**
Deciding	**215**
Shared decision-making	215
Decision-making skills and strategies	217
From ambivalence to action: making decisions that stick	219
The stages of change model	220
Motivational interviewing	221
Changing	**224**
Facilitating change: skills and strategies	224
Structured approaches	226
Cognitive behavioural therapy (CBT)	226
Problem-solving	228
Recovery-oriented approaches	231
Skills for supporting recovery	231
Activating client strengths and resources	233
Organizational strategies	**237**
Conclusions	**238**
Learning activities	**238**

Introduction

Earlier chapters in this book primarily focused on how to support clients to deal with difficult situations that they experienced as having befallen them: crisis, anxiety states, depression, trauma, transition and loss. The present chapter, by contrast, explores skills and strategies in helping clients to accomplish self-initiated change tasks and maintain progress and momentum in relation to self-managed recovery processes. A key dimension of embedded counselling consists of supporting clients in lifestyle changes around addiction, diet, exercise, recovery from mental health breakdown and the after-effects of trauma. Practitioners may be the primary point of contact for a client engaged in making such changes in their life – for instance a practice nurse guiding a client through a weight-loss or smoking cessation programme or a guidance teacher in a school helping a young person to attend classes. Alternatively, a client may seek support from a practitioner at a point when a lifestyle or behaviour change process has become problematic in some way. For example, a patient may consult their GP on their intention to suspend their healthy lifestyle plan because of worries about whether a particular fitness class is appropriate in the light of their heart condition.

This chapter looks at how to draw on the extensive body of theory, skills and research in counselling/psychotherapy around understanding and facilitating behaviour change and helping a client to move on in their life. The first part of the chapter examines strategies for how to facilitate clients to make decisions around whether to initiate change and the direction that change should take. The emphasis then turns to consideration of options around how to work with clients to follow through on change projects that they have set in motion.

Further coverage of topics addressed in the present chapter can be found in McLeod and McLeod (2022) and McLeod (2019).

Deciding

Helping professionals are often viewed as authoritative and trusted figures to be consulted around potential life decisions (e.g. moving an elderly relative into care or choice of career/study pathway). The following sections consider a range of perspectives, skills and strategies that may be relevant to the task of supporting a client or service user to make a decision about a course of action that involves a significant degree of life change.

Shared decision-making

The concept of shared decision-making refers to a process in which a practitioner and client meet together to arrive at a joint decision around the best course of action in relation to a problem or difficulty in the client's life. Principles and models of shared decision-making, and associated resources and training programmes, were originally developed in the field of medicine and health care. However, these ideas and practices are increasingly influential across all human service professions. An important implication of the widespread recognition of the value of shared decision-making is that many practitioners of embedded counselling are likely to already be familiar with this perspective. There is also considerable organizational and governmental support for shared decision-making – such policies are viewed as essential means of promoting active client participation and choice. As a result, being able to present embedded counselling as a way of enhancing the effectiveness of shared decision-making may be an effective strategy for securing organizational resources.

The process of shared decision-making is generally viewed as following a series of steps: establishing that a decision needs to be made, explaining why the client's views are important, making sure that the client has access to information about the options that are available, allowing the client time to reflect on options and ask questions and then meeting to finally arrive at a shared decision (Cleary et al. 2018; Elwyn et al. 2017; Gibson et al. 2020; Mulley et al. 2012; Stiggelbout et al. 2015). Although this set of steps may seem on the face of it to comprise a rational and straightforward course of action, in practice it can be problematic to implement. Some clients do not want to be involved in decision-making, but instead just want the practitioner to take care of things. There are substantial differences in power and knowledge between the client and practitioner. Some practitioners find it hard to set aside their hard-won (and real) professional expertise. Practitioners may be under time pressure. In some circumstances it is difficult to describe what a course of treatment may involve in terms that are readily understandable to a client. It is important to emphasize that, despite these challenges, there is considerable evidence that shared decision-making – when done well – can enhance both client satisfaction and treatment outcomes.

The use of shared decision-making in healthcare settings is mainly focused on agreeing on a course of treatment that is then implemented. For example, a person with a mental health problem may go to see their GP and end up agreeing to take antidepressant medication for six months (rather than seeing a psychologist or using an online self-help package) and then return for a review. By comparison, in embedded counselling (or any type of counselling and psychotherapy) shared decision-making is more integral to the entire helping process. For example, each counselling session or episode may start with a brief decision-making conversation about what topics or tasks are going to be explored within that meeting or counselling may involve exploring the client's ability or readiness to make a decision. The model of embedded counselling introduced in Chapter 3 is built around an assumption that effective client-counsellor collaboration requires dipping in and out of shared decision-making mode throughout the entire counselling process.

An example of where clients appreciate ongoing embedded counselling and emotional support in addition to formal shared decision-making was highlighted in a study of women's experiences of pregnancy termination in Norway (Aamlid et al. 2021). Following a shared decision-making process that included detailed information, women could opt to take abortion medication at home. Follow-up interviews found that some women felt insecure and frightened when the medication started to take effect because it was only then that they realized that they had not fully understood the information that had been provided. They also missed not having a health professional actually physically beside them to offer support, or would have wanted their practitioner to pro-actively call them to make sure they were alright. The Aamlid et al. (2021) study explored the experiences of women who were generally well-informed and clear about what they wanted. Other studies of the decision process in pregnancy termination have identified the complexity of this process when the client is ambivalent or is less well-informed (Kjelsvik et al. 2018, 2019; Nguyen et al. 2010; Ueno et al. 2020). Research into the experiences of women survivors of intimate partner violence illustrate a similar pattern of multi-layered, complex decision-making around such questions as whether to stay in a relationship or when to leave sheltered safe accommodation (Fisher and Stylianou 2019; Herrero-Arias et al. 2021; Liang et al. 2005; Storer et al. 2021). What these studies – and research on other types of life decision – show is that there exist many decision-making situations where there are many factors that need to be taken into account, including personal emotions and cultural values. In these scenarios, although clients and practitioners may follow a process that approximates to classical models of shared decision-making, in reality the person seeking help is likely to consult several different practitioners at different points, including accessing support to adjust their plan in the light of unforeseen circumstances. Valuable insights into what shared decision-making can feel like from a client perspective can be found in Fox (2021), written by a mental health service user on the basis of a 30-year involvement in receiving services.

Decision-making skills and strategies

There are many techniques that have been developed by counsellors, psychotherapists, psychologists, management consultants and others to facilitate and support processes of problem-solving, planning and decision-making. The single most useful method that can be employed in relation to decision-making is the use of empathic dialogue. It can be enormously helpful to listen and reflect back in such a way that makes it possible for a person to look at a choice from all angles and explore how they feel about all the options in a situation where the listener has no preconceived ideas about which course of action is right or wrong. However, it can also be that sometimes the person circles endlessly around a problem or decision without arriving at any conclusions. It is therefore valuable to be able to offer clients some kind of structure through which they can organize the activity of decision-making. An initial period of exploratory discussion can be useful, even if the counsellor feels sure that sooner or later some structuring devices will need to be introduced. There are many common-sense cultural resources that can be used to structure conversations around decision-making and problem solving. Some people find it helpful to construct some kind of 'balance sheet' – a piece of paper where the factors for and against each choice are listed and may then be weighted in terms of which is the most important. A slightly more elaborate version of a balance sheet is a 'force-field analysis', where the forces pressing in different directions can be mapped on a piece of paper. This technique can be helpful in identifying the sources of different forces ('it's my mother who want me to follow option A, while it's my boyfriend who is pressing me to take option B'). In some situations, for example when a person is thinking about a career choice, a SWOT (strengths, weaknesses, opportunities and threats) analysis may be valuable. An important part of the value of any of these mapping techniques is that they slow down the decision-making process, thus allowing more time for reflection. They also allow the person to generate a comprehensive analysis of the factors involved. Written maps 'externalize' the task, enabling the person and counsellor to work side-by-side to come up with ideas and move them around on the page.

Another useful strategy in relation to decision-making is to introduce the concept of 'implications'. Using a brainstorming approach ('let's just imagine – without censoring any ideas that come up – what might happen if you decided to...') or a mapping technique, the person can be encouraged to look beyond the immediate consequences of a decision and consider the long-term consequences. Alternatively, it may be that some imagined catastrophic long-term consequences ('if I quit this job I'll never find another one') can be seen as being not too awful once they are openly discussed with a counsellor. A further widely-used strategy is to *prioritize* aspects of the issue – for example, how satisfactory is each of the possible solutions that have been generated in respect of a problem?

In recent years, there has emerged a valuable body of research that has sought to explore what actually happens in shared decision-making between health professionals and patients. A particularly influential set of studies was conducted by Toerien et al. (2018) on transcripts of consultations between neurologists and patients. What this research showed quite clearly was that, compared to simply making a recommendation, situations in which the clinician listed options were much more effective in terms of opening up a genuinely shared agreement on how to move forward. Irvine et al. (2021) looked at similar processes in telephone assessment sessions for patients referred to an NHS psychological therapy service. In this study, the call handlers were most likely to make a simple recommendation. If the patient objected to what had been suggested, the call handler would offer another option. Relatively rarely did they offer a list of options from which the patient could choose. These observations are consistent with findings from other research into the same service, which found a high proportion of clients not attending their first scheduled counselling session following the initial assessment call. Duncan et al. (2020) interviewed patients on their experience of shared decision-making in early sessions of psychotherapy for depression. Participants reported that they had found it useful to be invited to talk about their preferences, even if it could sometimes be daunting. A study by Toerien (2021) specifically explored what happened in a subset of neurology consults in which the patient exercised their right to refuse treatment. In almost all of these cases,

Box 11.1 Using supportive challenging to facilitate problem-solving

During the process of working through a decision-making or problem-solving task, one of the responses that the person may well appreciate from the counsellor is a certain degree of *supportive challenging*. Most people, when faced with a decision, will recognize the value of a "critical friend" or "devil's advocate" role. Of course, the primary task of the counsellor is to maintain a supportive and collaborative relationship, so it is important to make sure that challenging does not become adversarial in ways that might undermine or threaten that relationship. The most effective challenging is based on a capacity to gently point out possible inconsistencies or contradictions in what the person has said ('from what you are saying now, the key factor seems to be X ... but it seemed to me that from what you were saying a few minutes ago, the key factor was Y – I'm not sure how these factors fit together for you'). Another type of facilitative challenging can involve pointing out when the person might be avoiding some aspect of the decision ('you have written down all these 'for' and 'against' statements on the balance sheet – I'm aware that we have discussed all of them apart from these statements in the corner that you wrote in a red pen').

the physician–patient dialogue did not turn into a duel. Instead, doctors tended to continue a collaborative discussion that respected the patient's decision. This is an important study because it indicates that in situations in which there is a lot at stake, and the physician is under pressure to maintain their duty of care to the patient, they are willing to prioritize patient preferences. A study by Lian et al. (2021) also focused on a subset of consultations – in this instance, where the patient was highly involved in the decision-making process. What they observed was that patient involvement mainly consisted of rejection of options put forward by the doctor, with relatively few examples of patients presenting their own suggestions. Also, toward the end of these discussions, the majority of these assertive patients tended to accede to the views of the doctor. A particularly interesting aspect of this paper is that it includes some quite long transcripts of doctor–patient dialogue that illustrate the authenticity and compassion with which these processes were facilitated. Taken as a whole, these studies reflect a growing appreciation on the part of healthcare practitioners of the importance of shared decision-making and how to put it into action.

From ambivalence to action: making decisions that stick

We are all familiar, in our own lives as well as through observation of other people, with the reality that some decisions are hard to make – there may be too many factors to take into account, there may be too much at stake, or the person may get lost in a fruitless search for certainty and a perfect plan of action. A significant proportion of conversations between practitioners and clients consist of explorations of 'what if' that never turn into tangible action. A capacity to understand what is happening at such moments, and an ability to move things on, represents crucial aspects of embedded counselling competence. These issues are explored in relation to the widely used 'stages of change' model developed by James Prochaska and Carlo DiClemente (see Krebs et al. 2019), and the 'motivational' interviewing approach by William R. Miller and Stephen Rollnick (2012).

The stages of change model

The stages of change perspective has been widely used in a range of health and social care settings as a way of making sense of how practitioners may need to tailor their support to take account of the point that the client occupies on their change trajectory. The key idea in the stages of change model is that there exists an 'action' stage, when a client is committed to making a significant change in their life and working hard at relevant tasks. However, many clients who are seeking help from health and social care practitioners lack a basic 'readiness' to change – even though other people may be telling them that they need to stop smoking or eat less, or they have an intellectual understanding of the importance of making such changes, they are unable (or not yet ready) to engage in action. In addition, even after a client has been successful in changing their lifestyle or behaviour, they may relapse. The stages of change created by Prochaska and DiClemente suggests that the change process as a whole can be viewed as comprising six discrete stages:

1. *Pre-contemplation.* The person has no immediate intention to make changes in relation to problematic or dysfunctional patterns of behaviour. They may be vaguely aware that there is a problem, but are generally able to ward it off and not think about it.
2. *Contemplation.* At this stage, the person has decided to change their behaviour – not to change now, but at some point in the future, for example at some point in the next six months.
3. *Preparation.* The person has started to take some tentative steps in the direction of behaviour change. For example, they may have collected information about support services that are available and read articles about their condition.
4. *Action.* The person has made meaningful progress in relation to changing their problematic behaviour and consolidating new patterns of behaviour.
5. *Maintenance.* Preventing relapse, or coping with episodes of relapse when they occur.
6. *Termination.* The person has reached a point where they no longer need to devote attention to their earlier problematic behaviour.

The stages of change model shows that quite different practitioner skills and strategies are necessary at different stages of the change process. For example, at the pre-contemplation phase it may be useful to supply information but a waste of time to initiate actual change activities. A review of recent evidence around the stages of change model can be found in Krebs et al. (2019). An article that illustrates the change model in a particularly vivid manner is Kruzan and Whitlock (2019). These researchers interviewed people who had problems around non-accidental self-injury (e.g. cutting oneself) at different points along the change pathway and categorized what they said into four overarching domains: relational, behavioural, self-knowledge and barriers. For example, participants who had not given any serious consideration to addressing their self-injuring (pre-contemplative) described this pattern as 'an old friend' whose return they were 'always pleased to see'. By contrast, those in the action phase described how they were alert to environmental triggers that had led in the past to cutting episodes and spent considerable time analysing situations in which they had been tempted to harm themselves.

An aspect of the stages of change cycle that has received particular attention from practitioners has been the shift from contemplation/preparation to action, because taking this step is crucial for clients in relation to moving away from a self-destructive lifestyle. It is also a difficult step to take, because it requires giving up important sources of enjoyment and connection with others. The technique of 'motivational interviewing' was designed for the purpose of supporting clients to navigate their way through the ambivalence and resistance associated with this phase.

Motivational interviewing

Motivational interviewing is an approach to facilitating decision-making that emerged in the 1980s (Miller and Rollnick 2012). The main area of application for motivational interviewing has been in the area of addictions, in working with people with drug and alcohol problems around making a decision or commitment to change their behaviour. However, the principles of motivational interviewing can be employed in any situation in which a person is struggling to make a major life decision around behaviour change.

The theoretical roots of motivational interviewing are in a synthesis of the client-centered/person-centred approach to therapy developed by Carl Rogers and ideas from cognitive behavioural therapy (CBT). A central element of motivational interviewing is the capacity of the helper to empathically engage with, and affirm, the point of view of the client (Moyers and Miller 2013). However, in classic client-centred therapy, the counsellor adopts a rigorously non-directive stance, in the sense of a willingness following the client's track in respect of whatever topic the client wishes to explore. By contrast, in motivational interviewing the counsellor negotiates with the client that they will specifically work together to focus on a decision that the client needs to make. This kind of attention to a specific goal is characteristic of CBT.

In practice, motivational interviewing relies on four basic principles:

1 *Empathy* – the counsellor seeks to view the issue from the frame of reference of the client
2 *Developing discrepancy* – the counsellor explores with the client tensions between how the client wants their life to be (the ideal) and their current behaviour (the actual)
3 *Acceptance* or 'rolling with resistance' – the counsellor does not try to pressure the client to make a decision, but instead accepts that a reluctance to change is natural, and invites exploration of this resistance
4 *Client autonomy* – the counsellor respects the client as someone who has the capacity to arrive at whatever is the right decision for themselves in the present circumstances.

When these principles are implemented, a counselling space is constructed in which the client feels that they are in a relationship in which it is possible to talk honestly about all aspects of a decision, and as a result are able to eventually make a genuine commitment to a new course of action that is grounded in a comprehensive exploration of all possible aspects of the issue.

An example of motivational interviewing in action:

Eleanor is a young woman who is a single parent with a two-year-old son. She has had involvement with social workers for many years around a range of issues. Her current dilemma is whether to place her son (Stephen) in a nursery so she can restart her own career. Her mother strongly believes that Eleanor should make use of the nursery place that is on offer and will not listen to any other point of view. On the other hand, Eleanor's neighbour strongly believes that children can be emotionally damaged by nursery education. As part of the process of making a decision on this issue, Eleanor decides to speak to her social worker.

Eleanor: I'm really desperate. I need to decide by next week whether or not to take the place at the nursery and I don't know what to do.
Social worker: It's such a big decision for you to make. I get the sense that you're feeling under a lot of pressure and that this stress isn't helping you to get to the point that you are comfortable about what is best (*an empathic response that reflects an appreciation of the client's situation, and is not trying to persuade her what to do*).
Eleanor: Absolutely – I feel completely at the end of my rope.
Social worker: From what you have said to me before about this, my understanding is that ideally you think that it would be good for Stephen to mix more with other children and good for you to meet people in a work situation and have more money, but that you are not sure whether he is ready for nursery yet (*acknowledging*

	discrepancy). Is that the way it seems to you, or are there other aspects of the situation that are important too? *(acknowledging the client as the 'expert'– reinforcing client autonomy)*.
Eleanor:	Yes, those are the main things.
Social worker:	That suggests that there are other aspects of it too…? *(affirming client autonomy)*.
Eleanor:	Yes, maybe. I just don't know if I could cope with him being upset. You know, like leaving him there if he was crying or having a tantrum.
Social worker:	Because that would upset you…and maybe also make you worried that he was being traumatized? *(empathy)*
Eleanor:	Exactly.
Social worker:	Can I say how it seems to me? *(personal feedback)* I'm wondering whether there are two parts to this. At one level, you know that nursery is the right thing for you and for Stephen. But at another level, it's scary to think about what will be involved practically around things like 'can I cope with him being upset'? *(reframing)*
Eleanor:	You're right: deep down I *do* know what I want *(example of 'commitment talk')*.

One of the advantages of motivational interviewing is that it has generated a great deal of support materials and activities, in the form of books, websites and training courses. There is substantial research evidence that motivational interviewing is effective with a range of different client groups. Motivational interviewing is a good example of a counselling protocol that consists of a set of basic counselling skills that have been packaged together in a particular way in order to enable a particular type of therapeutic task to be completed. When using motivational interviewing, it is essential to keep two things in mind. The first is that motivational interviewing strikes a subtle balance between facilitation and persuasion. In some of the motivational interviewing literature, it can come across as though the role of counsellor is to lead the client in the direction of what is self-evidently the 'right' answer (e.g. losing weight, stopping drinking, etc.) because that option corresponds to prevailing societal values. However, the power of motivational interviewing is based on counsellor openness to whatever is right for the client at that point in their life and genuine acceptance of the client's right to choose. The case of Eleanor illustrates this point – it could have been a good decision for her to stay at home with her child and it could equally have been a good decision for her to use the nursery place that was on offer. Her social worker favouring one choice rather than the other would probably have resulted in a continuation of the decisional impasse. The second critical aspect of motivational interviewing is that, strictly speaking, it is a method for making a commitment around a decision and not an all-purpose counselling approach. For example, Eleanor might have arrived at a point where she made a definite decision to send her son to nursery but still might need some further support from her social worker around dealing with her strong emotions around 'abandoning' him, or being assertive with the nursery staff around how she wanted them to respond to her son.

Useful analyses of skills involved in motivational interviewing are available in Lundahl et al. (2019: Table 4) and Westra and Aviram (2013). Workbooks for developing motivational interview skills have been published by Matulich (2017) and Wood (2020). There are also many training programmes and online training materials that are available.

Changing

Once a person has arrived at a point of making a commitment to changing an aspect of their life, the focus then turns to how to achieve that goal and then how to maintain what has been gained. Behaviour or lifestyle change is often hard to accomplish. There are some situations in which change is relatively easy. For instance, in recent years there has been a general consensus that using single-use plastic bags to collect shopping from a supermarket is not a good idea or that smoking in public places is anti-social. Similarly, in the time of Covid-19, most people readily adopted the practice of mask-wearing. In these examples of behaviour change, there was a widely-accepted rationale, social pressure to conform (and approval for doing so) and little to be lost by changing one's habitual pattern of behaviour. By contrast, self-destructive involvement in over-eating, self-starving, gambling or consumption of alcohol, drugs, cigarettes or pornography are patterns of behaviour that are generally locked into and reinforced by long-established relationships, sources of pleasure and satisfaction and sense of identity. They may also be linked to neurological and bodily systems. For example, anyone who has tried to give up sugar or coffee will almost certainly experience cravings and withdrawal symptoms. The following sections consider some strategies for supporting a person to overcome these challenges.

Facilitating change: skills and strategies

The model of embedded counselling outlined in Chapter 3 provides a general framework for facilitating change. The basic assumption is that the most effective way to proceed is to work together. The client and helper collaborate to identify what the client wants to achieve, break down these goals into step-by-step tasks, find effective ways to accomplish these tasks (activities, methods) and review progress on a regular basis. For all this to come together, the client needs to trust the helper, who in turn needs to be empathic, affirming, genuine and responsive. It is important that the underlying shared understanding that this process is built on – agreement over goals and tasks – is talked about explicitly rather than assumed. In some situations it may be useful to take some time to develop an action plan (sometimes described by therapists as a case formulation, case conceptualization or contract). It can be helpful to write this down, as a set of action points or in a diagram, so that both parties can check that they are working towards the same ends. It can also be useful to be able to review the plan on a regular basis and make adjustments. For some clients, the idea of working together for a specific purpose may be made more tangible by giving it a name, such as calling it a project, a mission, a journey or recovery process, 'building a new me' or some other phrase that personalizes the work and allows the client to have ownership of it.

An example of how a practitioner of embedded counselling may support a client through a difficult change process can be found in a study carried out in a GP practice in the UK by Dibb et al. (2019), on the experiences of patients in relation to the support offered by healthcare staff (doctors and nurses) in respect of their goal of losing weight. The majority of the research participants had disorders, such as diabetes, cardiac issues, or knee and back problems, that made weight loss a major priority for them. The patients talked about lack of support from some practitioners, in the form of being judged, criticized and 'made to feel like a criminal', and by practitioners who avoided talking frankly about the implications of obesity. At the same time, participants reported that they had received excellent support from other staff. They particularly highlighted being provided with information, charting and reviewing progress, suggestions and help around change activities (e.g. free gym or weight loss group membership), and a sense that the practitioner was on their side and genuinely interested in their well-being. In addition, they believed that practice staff had functioned as catalysts for change through communicating with them in an honest and direct way. The findings of this study demonstrate that these frontline practitioners, who had little training in behaviour change techniques, nevertheless possessed skills and strategies that were sufficient to make a positive difference to their patients. However, there needed to exist a sufficient shared understanding of what would be helpful (or not) at a specific moment – frank talk might be perceived as judgemental at one point in the change journey, but immensely valuable at another point.

The picture of the significance of emotional support during attempts to lose weight, presented by Dibb et al. (2019), is reinforced by the findings of interviews carried out on similar patients (and practitioners working with them) in Canada by Rand et al. (2017). In the latter study, clients reported that they consistently felt criticized and judged by practitioners and the emotional meaning of their eating was rarely or never taken into consideration. Most of those who took part in this study (both patients and practitioners) believed that these factors significantly reduced the effectiveness of the weight-loss treatment that was provided.

A theme that is apparent in both the Dibb et al. (2019) and Rand et al. (2017) studies is the importance of the helper adopting a non-judgemental stance. This was particularly important for clients, given the degree to which they felt criticized and shamed in everyday situations.

A study by Carey et al. (2007) invited clients who had received therapy (for a wide range of problems) from psychologists to describe, in retrospect, what it was that helped them to change. Most of them said that they had reached a stage of being ready to change – they had been desperate or had reached rock bottom and realized that they had to face up to issues that they had previously been avoiding. They viewed the change process that had occurred for them as comprising a combination of incremental shifts, alongside occasional, highly memorable moments (similar to the powerfully direct conversations mentioned by the patients interviewed by Dibb et al. 2019). They also emphasized that it had been helpful to have the opportunity to talk without being judged.

Similar themes were identified in a study by Gianakis and Carey (2011) into the experiences of individuals who had undergone change in relation to personal problems in the absence of any professional support at all. A significant common ground across these studies – and many other investigations of how people experience change – is that clients generally have a good basic understanding of what needs to happen to enable them to shift their lives on to a different track, and practitioners generally possess skills and strategies that can be helpful in respect of these endeavours.

The following sections explore additional skills and perspectives that can enable practitioners to consolidate, build on and expand their existing knowledge and capabilities.

Structured approaches

There can be significant benefits gained from using a structured approach to behaviour change, which involves constructing some kind of plan of action that is then followed through. Cognitive behavioural therapy (CBT) is a therapy model that operates in this way and has been found to be useful and effective in respect of many areas of behaviour and lifestyle change. It is also a way of working that intuitively makes sense to many clients. Problem-solving therapy is a variant of CBT that focuses on addressing specific barriers to change.

Cognitive behavioural therapy (CBT)

CBT consists of an extensive family of therapy models and techniques that have a shared purpose around facilitating cognitive and behavioural change. This approach is supported by a massive number of books, articles, training programmes and therapeutic resources (workbooks, online packages, forms). The breadth and scope of CBT is explored in McLeod (2019) and many other therapy textbooks. There are many examples of health and social care practitioners being trained to apply CBT skills in their work with clients (see, for example, Roberts et al. 2021).

As with any form of counselling, the effective use of CBT requires a client–practitioner relationship characterized by empathy, acceptance and trust. The underlying assumption in CBT is that problems result from learning ways of responding to the world that may have been functional at the time (e.g. as a means of coping with a stressful situation), but are currently undermining the person's capacity to live a productive and satisfying life. The aim of CBT, therefore, is to create opportunities for the person to learn new ways of thinking and acting. This guiding assumption has important implications for the client–helper relationship. The helper or practitioner mainly adopts a teacher/coach role in relation to the client. The client is also positioned as an active learner – the hope is that, as soon as possible, the client will begin to be able to implement CBT techniques and ideas on their own initiative.

The starting point for most types of CBT intervention is to initiate a conversation with the client about what is troubling them and what they want to achieve. As far as possible, the client's concerns and goals are described in terms of specific, concrete actions and thought processes, rather than in more general terms. This information is then brought together into an action plan that takes account of how the problem developed, how it is maintained, the goals of counselling, ideas about how to achieve these goals and any barriers that may need to be overcome. Typically, a counsellor implementing a CBT approach will use some kind of visual diagram to represent and explain how the different parts of the plan fit together. There is a strong emphasis in CBT on adopting a collaborative approach in which the client makes suggestions and asks questions. Within the CBT literature, this kind of planning phase is usually referred to as a case conceptualization or case formulation (see Box 11.2). Its purpose is to enable the client to understand what they need to do, and why, in order to bring about changes in their life that are important for them. A plan or formulation can help the client to feel hope and may also be reassuring and anxiety-reducing by showing that their problems are manageable.

In most embedded counselling contexts, it is unlikely that there would be enough time to produce a detailed case formulation. Nevertheless, it can be useful for embedded counselling practitioners to be sufficiently knowledgeable about the formulation process to be able to adapt this procedure to fit their own particular circumstances. For example, a task that can often be relevant for a client is 'making sense of what might help' or even 'having some sort of notion of what it is I need to do to get out of this mess'. Behind the concept of a case formulation is a basic human accomplishment of being able to agree a plan.

An array of change activities may be used in CBT, depending on what is required in any particular case. These can be illustrated by considering the support given by a homelessness project manager to a client who has previously lived rough and is now committed to eliminating alcohol from his life and re-establishing his relationships with his parents and extended family. The practitioner received some training in CBT and is comfortable about integrating these skills into the routine practical support that represents the core of his job. He is able to have fairly regular informal discussions with this client and they have arrived at a shared understanding and action plan around what the client might do to move forward in his life. On this occasion, the client wants to talk about how to handle a visit home for a family gathering at which everyone else will be drinking. He is concerned about how he will deal with pressure to consume alcohol. The conversation includes the following CBT techniques:

- discussion and agreement of the client's goal – what he wants to happen. The client describes a good outcome as being able to stay for the whole family event, talk to at least three family members who are particularly important to him and appropriately decline any offers of alcohol.
- challenging irrational thoughts. The counsellor notices that the client is 'catastrophizing' – using an extreme and exaggerated way of talking such as 'my dad would be *devastated* if I turned down a drink', 'I am *terrified* about seeing my gran after all the pain I caused her'. They discuss how these ways of talking and thinking have the effect of amplifying his level of anxiety and fear and practise different ways of talking and thinking such as 'my dad *may be disappointed*'.
- they identify strategies for handling the situation, such as phoning his mother and cousin before the event and asking for their support and how he might respond if pressured to drink. They practise how to deal with these situations, with the counsellor taking the role of various family members.
- they discuss and practise grounding, breathing and relaxation techniques that the client might use to be more calm during stressful moments at the family get-together.
- they agree to meet again on the day following the event to review what happened.

These activities make use of the CBT techniques of cognitive restructuring (identifying thought processes that distort reality and trigger emotions and practising different ways of thinking) and social skills training in the behavioural experiment (trying out new emotion regulation skills and communication skills in a challenging real-life situation). All this is carried out in a way that is consistent with an agreed plan or formulation. If the client has a positive experience at the family event, he will be empowered to go further and try out these skills in other situations. By contrast, if the client had found it hard to enact some of these strategies, they can look at what further practice might be necessary or how the strategies might need to be adjusted.

Problem-solving
Clients who commit themselves to behaviour or lifestyle change and recovery typically encounter situations in which they feel stuck and uncertain about how to proceed, and as result feel that they may have no option other than suspending or abandoning their change project. Such scenarios can be highly upsetting and lead to requests for support from health, social care or other practitioners. In these scenarios, a useful strategy can be to work together with the client to address the specific problems that represent barriers to change.

Box 11.2 Case formulation

A typical CBT case formulation takes account of:

- current issues/presenting problems/stated goals
- underlying causes/vulnerability (why does the person have these problems?)
- mechanisms/actions/processes through which these difficulties are maintained (why haven't they disappeared by now? Why hasn't the person been able to deal with these problems already?) How do these mechanisms connect the underlying and the current problems?
- why now? What has precipitated the need for help now?
- how can the problem be tackled in counselling? (treatment plan)
- what are the obstacles to therapy?
- what are the client's strengths?

An interesting and informative brief introduction to this type of case formulation is available in Kuyken et al. (2008). The use of case formulation as a means of developing an agreed action plan and shared understanding was pioneered in CBT and there is considerable evidence that clients value this activity (Kahlon et al. 2014; Redhead et al. 2015). More recently, a wide range of other approaches to formulation have evolved (Johnstone and Dallos 2014). Information about our own approach to formulation, which is highly collaborative and uses a timeline diagram, is available in McLeod and McLeod (2016, 2020).

Problem-solving therapy is an approach that has been developed by Arthur and Christine Nezu and Thomas D'Zurilla in the United States, Dennis Gath in the UK, and others. The basic assumption in this approach is that poor problem-solving skills will result in demoralization, lack of hope, anxiety and depression. Counselling therefore has two parallel goals: to help the person to resolve specific current problems and to develop skills and confidence around their general problem-solving ability.

The problem-solving process developed within this approach consists of seven steps:

1. Clarify and define the problem
2. Set a realistic goal
3. Generate multiple solutions
4. Evaluate and compare solutions
5. Select a feasible solution

6 Implement the solution

7 Evaluate the outcome.

In advance of working through these stages of problem-solving, the counsellor explains the model to the client and makes sure that he or she understands the rationale for the approach being taken. Throughout the counselling, this understanding is reinforced through regular reviews of progress and the use of handouts and worksheets. If the client has more than one problem, it is important to decide on which problem to address first and complete the sequence in relation to that issue before moving on to the next. The counselling process also includes identifying rewards that the client can claim on successful completion of each problem-solving task.

The literature on problem-solving therapy represents a valuable resource for practitioners of embedded counselling because it encompasses extensive discussion of theory and research and a wealth of practical examples of problem-solving

---

Box 11.3 Learning from people who have experienced transformational change

Almost all of the counselling and psychotherapy literature on how to facilitate behavioural and lifestyle change is focused on theories and practical strategies that counsellors use during the process of working with clients. However, there exists an alternative behaviour change literature, based on the retrospective accounts of people who have been successful in making major, transformational changes in their lives in areas such as smoking, overcoming obesity or recovering from addiction. On the whole, the people interviewed in these studies do not report, to any great extent, that the change they experienced resulted from being in therapy. By contrast, such changes more often seem to be triggered by a life crisis or a moment of epiphany (Ogden and Hills 2008; Kottler 2018; Miller 2004; Naor and Mayseless 2020; Russo-Netzer and Davidov 2020) that results in a fundamental shift in self-identity (Epiphaniou and Ogden 2010), which needs to be continually worked on to avoid slipping back into the old self (Natvik et al. 2018). An important implication of these studies is that it is important to be realistic about what can be achieved through embedded counselling – or, indeed, any type of counselling or psychotherapy. Counselling can help people to make incremental gains and improvements and can support people to remain well following a significant personal shift. But the kind of transformation that takes a person to a point in their life where they have irrevocably left a self-destructive pattern of behaviour behind seems to depend on a coming-together of various factors and inputs from many different people that are hard to manufacture or control.

in relation to a wide range of client issues (Nezu et al. 2013, 2019, 2021). Examples of integration of problem-solving therapy into routine healthcare delivered by frontline practitioners can be found in Gee and Agras (2014) and Pierce (2012).

The healthy conversation skills model is similar in many respects to problem-solving therapy, but has been specifically designed to be used by health and social care workers in the context of relatively brief interactions with clients. This approach is based on practitioners learning to use particular ways of talking with clients that encourage them to find their own solutions to emotional or interpersonal problems that are blocking their efforts to accomplish lifestyle change and then identify and implement steps towards resolving these difficulties (Black et al. 2014; Hollis et al. 2021; Lawrence et al. 2016).

Recovery-oriented approaches

Structured action-plan strategies for facilitating behaviour change can be highly effective in many situations. However, they also have some drawbacks. Laying out a set of goals and procedures in advance opens up the possibility of failure. For example, a client engaging in CBT-type homework tasks may find that they are not able to do what was agreed with their practitioner and as a result may lose motivation or even drop out of counselling. Also, some people see their change process in more holistic terms, as something that involves all aspects of their life rather than necessarily following a linear trajectory within a specific life domain such as eating or exercise. Finally, structured approaches tend to assume that one therapist or practitioner works with one client, whereas in reality it is more often the case that a person pursuing a change project makes use of several sources of support at the same time.

Skills for supporting recovery
The recovery perspective or movement has emerged in the last 30 years as an alternative to the general assumption in mainstream counselling, psychotherapy and clinical psychology that the best way to facilitate behaviour change is through therapy delivered by an expert specialist practitioner and that the best way to establish whether change has occurred is to measure the level of change in the client's symptoms. A recovery perspective, by contrast, is based in the idea that people with problems in living are actively involved in pursuing their own healing through any means possible, drawing on a wide range of activities and supportive relationships (Davidson et al. 2021; Slade and Longden 2015). The success of such efforts needs to be evaluated not in terms of symptom change, but in respect of how effective the person has been in building a life for themselves in a specific community. The meaning of recovery is vividly captured in a study by Wilson and Giddings (2010) that documents the multiple sources of learning and healing used by women recovering from severe depression. Within such a matrix, practitioners of embedded counselling have the potential to make

meaningful contributions to a client's recovery at different steps in their process of recovering.

Because the concept of recovery refers to a form of change that is flexible, fluid and idiosyncratic, it is not possible – as in CBT or other therapy approaches – to identify explicit skills that are used by practitioners. Nevertheless, in a review of research into recovery, Klevan et al. (2021) were able to highlight several forms of practitioner ways of working that were consistently viewed by clients as helpful. These included:

- being helped on one's own terms, with respect for one's preferences, personal knowledge and life experience
- timely helping – sufficient practitioner responsiveness and sensitivity to be aware of what was needed at a particular moment
- putting words to feelings
- being open to involving family members in therapy
- co-creating therapeutic activities, rather than following a pre-determined treatment manual
- openness in the possibilities associated with many different activities
- belief and hope in the client's capacity to learn and grow
- helping for different needs – willingness to provide practical assistance and 'battle' with 'bureaucracy' on the client's behalf
- supporting the client to develop their own strengths
- support to develop an identity and sense of self that was not defined in negative terms such as being an alcoholic, binge eater or addict
- willingness on the part of the practitioner to engage in interprofessional working, rather than allowing the client to be lost in a maze of systems and services.

A study that condenses these various attributes down into a brief statement of what clients and family members are looking for has been produced by Soggiu et al. (2020).

A key element of recovery-oriented practice is collaboration and co-production – the capacity of the client and practitioner to work together. A network of practitioners in Norway, who had been committed to collaborative recovery support with clients for many years, conducted several research studies on these initiatives and then synthesized what they had learned into a model of collaborative practice (Ness et al. 2014; Sundet et al. 2020). What emerged from this programme was the idea that effective collaboration could be best understood as a process of 'walking along together' in which each participant spoke in turn, as a means of building up a shared understanding of where they were heading toward and how best to get there. Important sub-elements of this process included 'seizing the moment' and 'putting difference to work'. There was a lot of evidence across the body of research carried out by this team that, alongside a general ongoing to-and-fro of supportive dialogue, there were also moments when something new and different seemed to happen. For example, either the client or the practitioner might say something that was particularly honest and direct or represented a new way of seeing a problem. At that specific point in time, the significance of what had been said and done might be far from clear, but these moments often turned out to be crucial in terms of moving the work forward. The theme of 'putting difference to work' referred to the importance of capitalizing on the fact that the client and practitioner would inevitably have different ideas and feelings about things and that these differences represented opportunities for developing new insights. A further aspect of putting difference to work was the significance of occasions when the client said 'no'. Given the greater knowledge and professional experience of the practitioner, a common pattern in all counselling is for the therapist to make a suggestion about how to tackle an issue and the client to agree. The client saying 'no' opens a space for collaboration, based on discussion of what lies behind their refusal.

Activating client strengths and resources
A recovery perspective on change implies that each individual possesses their own knowledge and experience that can be used to help them to achieve their change objectives, as well as a capacity to access a range of relevant activities, groups and relationships both within their immediate social circle and more

> **Box 11.4 Political, social and cultural dimensions of behaviour change**
>
> It is clear that many behaviour and lifestyle change issues, for example around food (binge eating or starving) or addiction to smoking, alcohol, prescription drugs, street drugs, shopping, gambling and pornography, reflect areas of life in which certain products and activities are being promoted in the interest of those who are making a profit. In all of these areas, the level of profit is such that those concerned are able to influence the way that their products are represented in the media (e.g. images of thinness in women, association between alcohol and sport). In addition, the existence of such conditions is culturally and historically specific, with a tendency to follow degree of industrialization and adherence to western values. In response to social, political and cultural factors, some therapists have sought to develop solidarity in clients affected by particular issues and active political resistance, as in the anti-anorexia movement supported by the narrative therapy community (Maisel et al. 2004). In their research on collaborative, recovery-oriented practice, Ness et al. (2014) found that, given the opportunity, many clients actively chose to talk about political aspects of their problems.

widely within the community. Compared to therapies and treatments delivered by specialist mental health professionals, attention to the client's strengths and resources represents a significant shift in the counselling process. Recovery-oriented practice requires the counsellor or embedded practitioner to develop skills and strategies around how to ensure that potentially useful resources are not only identified, but also put to work. There exists a growing therapy literature that discusses how this approach can be implemented in practice with clients (Bohart and Tallman 1996; Fluckiger et al. 2010; Murphy and Sparks 2018, Scheel et al. 2013; Smith 2006). This way of thinking about the helping process has also been highlighted in social work (Saleebey 2000, 2012) and in the extensive literature on how individuals engage in self-care in relation to a variety of health conditions (Narasimhan et al. 2019).

It can be useful to make a distinction between personal strengths and cultural resources. In this context, a strength refers to a personal quality or accomplishment that the person can identify by reflecting on their life story. By contrast, a cultural resource refers to an aspect of the social world inhabited by the client that may have the potential to help them to overcome a personal problem. Strengths and resources are often interconnected. For instance, 'It was when I was part of the rock-climbing group (a cultural resource) that I realized how brave I can be (a personal strength).' The value of discussing these concepts separately is that sometimes they occupy different spaces: 'I get strength from my memory of how I was able to stand up against a boy who bullied me when I was at school' (personal strength); 'I know that attending a book club can be a good way to meet people' (cultural resource). The 'standing up against a bully' memory, as a source of strength, can be understood in terms of what Mearns and Cooper (2018) describe as an 'existential touchstone', a personal experience that sits at the heart of a person's sense of who they are. By contrast, book club membership is more likely to be 'out there' – a possibility that exists in the community.

The main skills in terms of working with a client's strengths and resources are to assume that such attributes and assets exist for a person, to be curious, to ask about them, to use one's imagination and to initiate conversations around how to use strengths and resources to facilitate change.

Given that a person is only likely to consult a professional helper when they have a problem and are suffering, there is an understandable tendency for practitioners to predominantly adopt a problem-oriented stance that focuses on difficulties, deficits and adversity. A major theme in the writings of strengths-oriented practitioners such as Bohart and Tallman (1996), Murphy and Sparks (2018) and Saleebey (2000) is the importance of being open to client capabilities.

It can be instructive to listen closely for evidence of strengths and resources. A useful concept from narrative therapy is the notion of the 'absent but implicit' (Carey et al. 2009; Chiu 2020; White 2007; Young 2020). When a person is talking about a problem, it is as though two stories are being told. The explicit story is a tale of difficulties and problems. However, in the background there is an implicit story about the personal qualities that enable the person to get through such difficulties or to ask for help. This skill involves using one's imagination to begin to build a sense of what these qualities might have been and invite the client to join in – 'that time you met your biological mother for the first time was so painful for you...but I'm wondering what it says about you, that you had the courage to make it happen in the first place and even to be here with me trying to figure out how to make it a more real and meaningful relationship...for both of you.'

Evidence of strengths and resources can also be generated through curiosity about the person's everyday life, for example asking them to tell you the kinds of activities that they engage in and who is around for them in their life. It is then possible to explore what the person gets from each of these activities and relationships, whether there may be more or different things that they could get and how a more productive use of the resource could be accomplished. On the whole, it is more helpful to focus on the cultural resources that the person has used at some point in their own life that could be revisited and used in a better way, rather than making suggestions about new activities that the person has never tried before (Marley 2011). For example, there is a lot of evidence that exercise classes and reading self-care books can be helpful for people struggling with mental health and behaviour change problems. As a consequence, well-meaning practitioners may advise or prescribe such activities to their clients and patients. However, attending an exercise class in a gym may be a daunting prospect if you have never done this before in your life and are currently depressed or overweight.

The key to productive use of client strengths and resources is to be willing to work together with the client to develop a shared understanding of how the personal quality or activity might function in relation to behaviour change tasks. Moving on from a destructive gambling habit is an example of a type of behaviour change where activating personal strengths and resources can play a crucial role (Nixon et al. 2005, 2013). Molly had developed a gambling addiction in her 60s. Following a streak of losing bets, she ran out of money for food and rent and turned to her church for help. Her minister arranged for her to receive food parcels and talked her though how to handle her rent arrears and other debts. They then had a long conversation about how the gambling habit had developed and what it meant to Molly. It emerged that Molly had been subjected to sustained physical and emotional abuse in childhood, that had left with a sense of worthlessness and 'kind of numb feeling inside'". A leisure bingo player throughout her life, after her children moved to another country, then her husband died, she had started to feel that her life was no longer worth living. Casino gambling provided a refuge and escape and sense of excitement. When Molly came to the end of her story, her minister responded that, from his perspective, she seemed to have become isolated and lonely and desperate and that gambling was the only thing at that moment that gave her any sense of purpose and pleasure. She agreed. They then talked about whether it might be helpful to find other ways of achieving these ends. He asked if there had ever been anywhere else, at any point in her life, where she had experienced any of the good feelings that the casino was able to give her or any activity that she could imagine now that might have that effect. She found these questions hard to answer, but eventually started to talk about her life immediately after leaving college, when she had been a teacher of young children – 'I have always been someone who had the capacity to help other people fulfil themselves.'. She also talked about two holidays in north Africa – 'somehow I really connected with people there. It was the first time I had felt truly alive.'

Molly's minister asked if she might be willing to consider some possibilities for making changes in her life that might allow her to move on from her gambling addiction. They discussed the possibility of seeing a counsellor attached to the church community, to look at the painful early experiences that seemed to continue to undermine her sense of herself as a worthwhile person. They looked at the possibility of going together to meet with the organizers of a residential refugee support centre, to see if there was some work she might do with the children there that might bringing some joy and excitement into her life. Molly had also mentioned how guilt she felt about gambling and how at the end of the day it all came down to putting money in the pockets of rich casino owners. They talked about seminars and groups held in the church that might help Molly to see gambling, and her life as a whole, from a broader faith perspective.

The example of Molly illustrates a few of the wide range of possibilities associated with a helping process that draws on client strengths and resources. What is clear from this case is that identifying strengths and resources is only the first step – a lot of further work needed to be done to establish these new activities and relationships as replacements for previous, unhealthy and self-undermining patterns. However, there are important change processes that are activated from the beginnings of such a process. As with Molly, a client can begin to feel some hope, on the basis that alternatives do exist – even if the particular activities that have been identified do not entirely work out, there are more possibilities out there somewhere. A further valuable change process is based on the principle of 'self-efficacy' (believing that you have the capacity to do something) – conversations

> ### Box. 11.5 Using apps
>
> In relation to behaviour change, a client may be very clear about what they are going to do, and why they are going to it, in the context of a conversation with a practitioner. However, faced by the stress, complexity and competing demands of everyday life, it may be hard to turn these good intentions into action on a consistent basis. One strategy that has proved to be helpful in this respect is the use of apps that a person can access through their smartphone or smartwatch. Some of these tools are openly available and widely used, such as step counting apps. Other apps have been devised for specific client groups, such as the one developed by Pagoto et al. (2018) to remind clients aiming to lose weight of problem-solving strategies that have been agreed with their counsellor.

about strengths and resources are grounded in, and build on, the knowledge and life experience of the client.

Organizational strategies

Facilitating behaviour and lifestyle change requires all of the forms of organizational support discussed in previous chapters, such as availability of consultation and supervision. In addition, there are some other ways in which this kind of work can be enhanced through specific organizational initiatives. The process of shared decision-making involves providing information about choices. In many settings this can be carried out on an organization-wide basis, for instance using the client-facing area of its website. This information can also include some kind of rationale for clients about why shared decision-making is valuable and what it involves. Having this kind of decision-aid information all in one place (and in different languages and formats) is empowering for clients and can also save time in counselling sessions. A further way that organizations can maximize the effectiveness of behaviour-change counselling carried out by its staff is to review training needs and invest in relevant training. Important decision-making and behaviour change approaches discussed in the present chapter, such as motivational interviewing, CBT, problem-solving therapy, healthy conversations, narrative therapy and recovery methods, are associated with accessible and affordable brief training programmes for non-specialist practitioners. There are many other training programmes and workshops that provide training in similar approaches not mentioned in this chapter.

A central theme of the present chapter is that, most of the time, behaviour change projects are essentially driven forward by the energy, commitments and ideas of clients and members of their family, with further support being provided by practitioners when required. However, this does not always work out. There are some clients, for example those whose difficulties are rooted in sustained exposure to multiple sources of adversity, who need a more intensive form of help. As a result, there exist many treatment programmes and residential centres that have been established to serve clients with complex, long-term difficulties in areas such as addiction and personality disorder. It is valuable if practitioners in health and social care and criminal justice know about the availability of such services in their region, know about how to refer clients, how to cover costs and how to support clients on completion of such programmes.

Another organizational dimension of this area of work, highlighted in Klevan et al. (2021) and many other commentators, is the importance of maintaining effective interprofessional co-operation. From a client perspective, it is all too easy for momentum that they have built up around making difficult changes in their life to be lost if they are shunted onto waiting lists for months on end, or if interventions advice and services from different agencies are contradictory or do not fit together (e.g. appointments in different places on the same day).

Conclusions

Change is a broad topic – the ideas and examples discussed in the present chapter are relevant to issues addressed in other chapters. One key message from this chapter is that there are many ways of helpfully facilitating change. Both structured and focused approaches and more holistic approaches, such as a recovery perspective, can be helpful. What is important is to find what works for each client. Individuals differ a great deal in terms of barriers to change such as experiences of adversity and abuse that have undermined their self-confidence and access to material and cultural resources that can support change. A further key message is that successful change typically requires inputs and involvement from a range of people – frontline practitioners in human service roles have a key role as catalysts and enablers at critical moments in the change journey. A final crucial point that needs to be made is that not all clients want to change, or need, to change. On the whole, people consult a counsellor or psychologist because they want to change something in their lives. As a result, the question of how to facilitate change dominates the therapy literature. By contrast, a significant proportion of service users in health and social care, or who come into contact with the police (e.g. victims of crime), are people whose main intention is to find a way of living with a situation such as poverty, disability or ageing that at a fundamental level is not amenable to change. Morally and ethically, it is essential to respect the need of such individuals to live with a condition or situation rather than change it (or change themselves). Change is an important aspect of counselling, but so is acceptance, understanding and compassion.

Learning activities

The following activities may be explored individually and/or with a group of learning partners.

Exercise 11.1 Your personal experience of deciding to change your behaviour
Reflect on an occasion when you decided that you needed to change some aspect of your lifestyle or behaviour (e.g. around eating, exercise, spending habits, etc.). What was the process that you went through in making this decision? Were there distinct stages in the process? Who or what helped you to arrive at a decision? What was unhelpful? What ideas can you take from this personal experience that you can apply in helping your clients to make decisions?

Exercise 11.2 Reviewing your repertoire of methods for facilitating client problem-solving and decision-making tasks

Divide a piece of paper into two columns. In one column, make a list of methods or strategies that you already possess that you can draw on when a client identifies a decision-making task. In the other column, make a list of decision-making methods or strategies that you have read about in this chapter, or in other sources, that you would like to learn more about.

Exercise 11.3 Your experience of behaviour change

Reflect on an episode in your life when you accomplished meaningful change in relation to a significant aspect of your lifestyle or behaviour. What was helpful for you? What was unhelpful? What ideas can you take from this personal experience that you can apply in helping your clients to make changes in their lifestyle and behaviour?

Exercise 11.4. Cultural resources in your own life

Consider the list of cultural resources below. These are activities that have the potential to contribute to your sense of personal identity, give meaning to life, give pleasure, provide opportunities to connect with others and can help you to tackle problems in your life.

Reading books	Holidays and travel
Movies, plays	Work/employment
Visual arts	Gardening
Music	Pets and animals
Complementary therapies	Physical activity
(acupuncture, herbal remedies, etc)	Sex
Sport	Education
Spirituality	Crafts
Nature	Religion
Politics	Pilgrimage
Voluntary work	Writing
Walking	The internet
Hobbies	History
Self-help groups	Philosophy
Interior design	Dance
Family and friends	Eating and food

Make a personalized list of the cultural resources that are most relevant to you. Be as specific as possible. For example, rather than 'nature', you might write 'walking along St Andrews beach with my dog', etc.

What is the 'horizon' of your cultural resources? What are the resources that you would like to develop, or make available to yourself, in future? Add these to your list.

What are some of the resources that you have had in the past, for example resources from your childhood or adolescence, that you no longer use? Add these to your list.

For each of the items on your list (or as many of them as you can consider in the time available), briefly note down what it is that is made possible for you through your engagement with this resource, and what possibilities (which may not always be actualized) are opened up for you through engaging with the resource (or possibly even just thinking about it).

For each of the items on your list (or as many of them as you can consider in the time available), briefly note down when, and how often, you use that resource. How satisfied are you with the frequency with which you use each resource?

If you have had the experience of being a client in therapy (or received embedded counselling from a healthcare practitioner, teacher, etc.) indicate which of these resources were ever mentioned, or discussed, and how helpful (or otherwise) that was for you.

In your current practice, reflect on how often your clients mention such resources and the interest that you show in these areas of life when they are mentioned.

Think about one client with whom you are working on behaviour/lifestyle change issues: what are the cultural resources available to this person? To what extent, and in what ways, have you been able to help this person to access these resources to achieve preferred changes in their life? What else might you have done to activate these strengths and resources?

References

Aamlid, I. B., Dahl, B. and Sommerseth, E. (2021). Women's experiences with information before medication abortion at home, support during the process and follow-up procedures – A qualitative study. *Sexual & Reproductive Healthcare*, *27*, 100582.

Abraham-Steele, M. and Edmonds, C. (2021). A thematic analysis of teachers' perspectives on supporting victims of childhood bereavement in British primary schools. *Review of Education*, *9*(3), e3297.

Adams, D. F. (2017). The embedded counseling model: An application to dental students. *Journal of Dental Education*, *81*(1), 29–35.

Adams, K., Cimino, J. E. W. Arnold, R. M. and Anderson, W. G. (2012). Why should I talk about emotion? Communication patterns associated with physician discussion of patient expressions of negative emotion in hospital admission encounters. *Patient Education and Counseling*, *89*, 44–50.

Ahern, J., Worthen, M., Masters, J., Lippman, S. A., Ozer, E. J. and Moos, R. (2015). The challenges of Afghanistan and Iraq veterans' transition from military to civilian life and approaches to reconnection. *PloS One*, *10*(7), e0128599.

Albaek, A. U., Binder, P. E. and Milde, A. M. (2019). Entering an emotional minefield: professionals' experiences with facilitators to address abuse in child interviews. *BMC Health Services Research*, *19*(1), 1–12.

Albaek, A. U., Binder, P. E. and Milde, A. M. (2020). Plunging into a dark sea of emotions: Professionals' emotional experiences addressing child abuse in interviews with children. *Qualitative Health Research*, *30*(8), 1212–1224.

Allan, H. (2001). A 'good enough' nurse: Supporting patients in a fertility unit. *Nursing Inquiry*, *8*, 51–60.

Allan, H. (2007). Experiences of infertility: Liminality and the role of the fertility clinic. *Nursing Inquiry*, *14*, 132–139.

Anderson, M., Goodman, J. and Schlossberg, N.K. (2021). *Counseling Adults in Transition*. 5th edn. New York: Springer.

Anderson, S. and Brownlie, J. (2011) Build it and they will come? Understanding public views of 'emotions talk' and the talking therapies. *British Journal of Guidance and Counselling*, *39*, 53–66.

Anderson, S., Brownlie, J. and Given, L. (2009) Therapy culture? Attitudes toward emotional support in Britain. In A. Park, J. Curtice, K. Thomson, M. Phillips and E. Clery (eds.) *British Social Attitudes: The 25th Report*. London: Sage.

Andreoli, A., Burnand, Y., Cochennec, M. F., Ohlendorf, P., Frambati, L., Gaudry-Maire, D. ... and Frances, A. (2016). Disappointed love and suicide: a randomized controlled trial of 'abandonment psychotherapy' among borderline patients. *Journal of Personality Disorders*, *30*(2), 271–287.

Andreoli, A., Burnand, Y., Frambati, L., Manning, D. and Frances, A. (2021). Abandonment psychotherapy and psychosocial functioning among suicidal patients with borderline personality disorder: A 3-year naturalistic follow-up. *Journal of Personality Disorders*, *35* (1), 73–83.

Anjum, R. L., Copeland, S. and Rocca, E. (2020). *Rethinking causality, complexity and evidence for the unique patient: a causehealth resource for healthcare professionals and the clinical encounter*. Cham, Switzerland: Springer Nature.

Andrew, J., Wilkinson, H. and Prior, S. (2021). 'Guid times wi the bad times': The meanings and experiences of befriending for people living alone with dementia. *Dementia*, *21*(1), 21–40.

Arborelius, E. and Österberg, E. (1995). How do GPs discuss subjects other than illness?: Formulating and evaluating a theoretical model to explain successful and less successful approaches to discussing psychosocial issues. *Patient Education and Counseling*, *25*(3), 257–268.

Atkins, D. C. and Christensen, A. (2001). Is professional training worth the bother? A review of the impact of psychotherapy training on client outcome. *Australian Psychologist, 36*(2), 122–130.

Attanasio, L. B., DaCosta, M., Kleppel, R., Govantes, T., Sankey, H. Z. and Goff, S. L. (2021). Community perspectives on the creation of a hospital-based Doula program. *Health Equity, 5*(1), 545–553.

Axelsen, M. (2009). The power of leisure: 'I was an anorexic; I'm now a healthy triathlete'. *Leisure Sciences, 31*(4), 330–346.

Axline, V. M. and Rogers, C. R. (1945). A teacher–therapist deals with a handicapped child. *Journal of Abnormal and Social Psychology, 40*, 119–142.

Back, A. L. and Arnold, R. M. (2013). 'Isn't there anything more you can do?': When empathic statements work, and when they don't. *Journal of Palliative Medicine, 16*(11), 1429–1432.

Back, A. L., and Arnold, R. M. (2014). 'Yes it's sad, but what should I do?': moving from empathy to action in discussing goals of care. *Journal of Palliative Medicine, 17*(2), 141–144.

Banchard, M. and Farber, B.A. (2020). 'It is never okay to talk about suicide': Patients' reasons for concealing suicidal ideation in psychotherapy. *Psychotherapy Research, 30*(1), 124–136.

Bank, M. and Nissen, M. (2018). Beyond spaces of counselling. *Qualitative Social Work, 17*(4), 509–536.

Banks, S. (2016). Everyday ethics in professional life: Social work as ethics work. *Ethics and Social Welfare, 10*(1), 35–52.

Banks, S. (2020). *Ethics and values in social work*. London: Bloomsbury Publishing.

Banks, S., Cai, T., De Jonge, E., Shears, J., Shum, M., Sobočan, A. M., ... and Weinberg, M. (2020). Practising ethically during COVID-19: Social work challenges and responses. *International Social Work, 63*(5), 569–583.

Bar-On, D., Eland, J., Kleber, R. J., Krell, R., Moore, Y., Sagi, A., Soriano, E., Suedfeld, P., van der Velden, P. G. and van IJzendoorn, M. H. (1998). Multigenerational perspectives on coping with the Holocaust experience: An attachment perspective for understanding the developmental sequelae of trauma across generations. *International Journal of Behavioral Development, 22*, 315–338.

Barker, C. and Pistrang, N. (2002) Psychotherapy and social support: Integrating research on psychological helping. *Clinical Psychology Review, 22*, 361–79.

Bates, S. (2021a). *Languages of Loss: A psychotherapist's journey through grief*. London: Yellow Kite.

Bates, S. (2021b). *A Grief Companion: Practical support and a guiding hand through the darkness of loss*. London: Yellow Kite.

Baudon, P. and Jachens, L. (2021). A scoping review of interventions for the treatment of eco-anxiety. *International Journal of Environmental Research and Public Health, 18*(18), 9636.

Bauman, Z. (2004) *Wasted Lives: Modernity and its Outcasts*. Cambridge: Polity.

Becker, C. B., Taniyama, Y., Kondo-Arita, M., Sasaki, N., Yamada, S., and Yamamoto, K. (2021). Unexplored costs of bereavement grief in Japan: Patterns of increased use of medical, pharmaceutical, and financial services. *OMEGA-Journal of Death and Dying, 83*(1), 142–156.

Bedi, R.P., Davis, M.D. and Williams, M. (2005) Critical incidents in the formation of the therapeutic alliance from the client's perspective. *Psychotherapy: Theory, Research, Practice, Training, 42*, 311–323.

Beks, T. A., Cairns, S. L., Smygwaty, S., Miranda Osorio, O. A., and Hill, S. J. (2018). Counsellor-in-residence: Evaluation of a residence-based initiative to promote student mental health. *Canadian Journal of Higher Education/Revue canadienne d'enseignement supérieur, 48*(2), 55–73.

Bellier, A., Chaffanjon, P., Krupat, E., Francois, P. and Labarère, J. (2020). Cross-cultural adaptation of the 4-Habits Coding Scheme into French to assess physician communication skills. *PloS One, 15*(4), e0230672.

Berglund, M., Westin, L., Svanström, R. and Sundler, A. (2012). Suffering caused by care –Patients' experiences from hospital settings. *International Journal of Qualitative studies on Health and Well-being, 7*(1), 18688.

Bergner, R. M. (1987). Undoing degradation. *Psychotherapy, 24*(1), 25–30.

Bergner, R. M. (1988). Status dynamic psychotherapy with depressed individuals. *Psychotherapy, 25*(2), 266–272.

Bergqvist, P. and Punzi, E. (2020). 'Living poets society'–a qualitative study of how Swedish psychologists incorporate reading and writing in clinical work. *Journal of Poetry Therapy, 33*(3), 152–163.

Bergström, T., Seikkula, J., Holma, J., Mäki, P., Köngäs-Saviaro, P. and Alakare, B. (2019). How do people talk decades later about their crisis that we call psychosis? A qualitative study of the personal meaning-making process. *Psychosis, 11*(2), 105–115.

Berman, L. (1993) *Beyond the Smile: The Therapeutic Use of the Photograph.* London: Routledge.

Bernson, J. M., Hallberg, L. R. M., Elfström, M. L. and Hakeberg, M. (2011). 'Making dental care possible – a mutual affair'. A grounded theory relating to adult patients with dental fear and regular dental treatment. *European Journal of Oral Sciences, 119*(5), 373–380.

Bernstein, D. and Fink, L. (1999). *Childhood Trauma Questionnaire (CTQ).* San Antonio: Psychological Corporation.

Bhola, P. and Chaturvedi, S. K. (2017). Through a glass, darkly: Ethics of mental health practitioner–patient relationships in traditional societies. *International Journal of Culture and Mental Health, 10*(3), 285–297.

Birrell, P. J. and Bruns, C. M. (2016). Ethics and relationship: From risk management to relational engagement. *Journal of Counseling & Development, 94*(4), 391–397.

Birrell, P.J., Bernstein, R.E. and Freyd, J.J. (2017). With the fierce and loving embrace of another soul: Finding connection and meaning after the profound disconnection of betrayal trauma. In E.M. Altmaier (ed.), *Reconstructing Meaning after Trauma: Theory, Research and Practice.* (pp 29–43). London: Academic Press.

Birrell, P. J. and Freyd, J. J. (2006). Betrayal trauma: Relational models of harm and healing. *Journal of Trauma Practice, 5*(1), 49–63.

Black, C., Lawrence, W., Cradock, S., Ntani, G., Tinati, T., Jarman, M., ... and Baird, J. (2014). Healthy conversation skills: increasing competence and confidence in front-line staff. *Public Health Nutrition, 17*(3), 700–707.

Blackie, L. E., Colgan, J. E., McDonald, S. and McLean, K. C. (2020). A qualitative investigation into the cultural master narrative for overcoming trauma and adversity in the United Kingdom. *Qualitative Psychology.* Advance online publication. https://doi.org/10.1037/qup0000163

Blanchard, M. and Farber, B. A. (2020). 'It is never okay to talk about suicide': Patients' reasons for concealing suicidal ideation in psychotherapy. *Psychotherapy Research, 30*(1), 124–136.

Blease, C. R., Walker, J., Torous, J. and O'Neill, S. (2020). Sharing clinical notes in psychotherapy: A new tool to strengthen patient autonomy. *Frontiers in Psychiatry, 11*, 1095.

Blease, C., Kelley, J. M. and Trachsel, M. (2018). Informed consent in psychotherapy: Implications of evidence-based practice. *Journal of Contemporary Psychotherapy, 48*(2), 69–78.

Bleiberg, K. L. and Markowitz, J. C. (2019). Interpersonal psychotherapy for PTSD: Treating trauma without exposure. *Journal of Psychotherapy Integration, 29*(1), 15–22.

Boddy, J., Bakketeig, E. and Østergaard, J. (2020). Navigating precarious times? The experience of young adults who have been in care in Norway, Denmark and England. *Journal of Youth Studies, 23*(3), 291–306.

Bόe, T.D., Larsen, I.B. and Topor, A. (2019). Nothing matters: The significance of the unidentifiable, the superficial and nonsense. *International Journal of Qualitative Studies on Health and Well-being, 14*(1), 1684780.

Bohart, A. and Tallman, K. (1996) The active client: Therapy as self–help, *Journal of Humanistic Psychology, 36*(3), 7–30.

Bolton, G., Howlett, S., Lago, C. and Wright, J.K. (eds.) (2004). *Writing Cures: An Introductory Handbook of Writing in Counselling and Psychotherapy.* London: Brunner-Routledge.

Bombay, A., Matheson, K. and Anisman, H. (2009). Intergenerational trauma: Convergence of multiple processes among First Nations peoples in Canada. *Journal of Aboriginal Health/ Journal de la santé autochtone, 5*(3), 6–47.

Booth, A., Scantlebury, A., Hughes-Morley, A., Mitchell, N., Wright, K., Scott, W., and McDaid, C. (2017). Mental health training programmes for non-mental health trained professionals coming into contact with people with mental ill health: A systematic review of effectiveness. *BMC Psychiatry, 17*(1), 1–24.

Booysen, P. and Staniforth, B. (2017). Counselling in social work: A legitimate role? *Aotearoa New Zealand Social Work, 29*(1), 16–27.

Bordia, P., Read, S. and Bordia, S. (2020). Retiring: Role identity processes in retirement transition. *Journal of Organizational Behavior, 41*(5), 445–460.

Branch, W.T and Malik, T.K. (1993) Using 'windows of opportunities' in brief interviews to understand patients' concerns. *Journal of the American Medical Association, 269*, 1667–8.

Branson, D. C. (2019). Vicarious trauma, themes in research, and terminology: A review of literature. *Traumatology, 25*(1), 2–10.

Bridges, W. and Bridges, S. (2019). *Transitions: Making sense of life's changes*. New York: Hachette Books.

Brock, R. L., O'Hara, M. W. and Segre, L. S. (2017). Depression treatment by non-mental-health providers: Incremental evidence for the effectiveness of Listening Visits. *American Journal of Community Psychology, 59*(1-2), 172–183.

Broström, S., Johansson, B. A., Verhey, R. and Landgren, K. (2021). 'Seeing a brighter future'. Experiences of adolescents with common mental disorders receiving the problem-solving therapy 'Youth Friendship Bench' in Zimbabwe. *Issues in Mental Health Nursing 42*(11), 1–11.

Brown, J. S., Evans-Lacko, S., Aschan, L., Henderson, M. J., Hatch, S. L. and Hotopf, M. (2014). Seeking informal and formal help for mental health problems in the community: A secondary analysis from a psychiatric morbidity survey in South London. *BMC Psychiatry, 14*(1), 1–15.

Brownlie, J. (2014). *Ordinary Relationships. A Sociological Study of Emotions, Reflexivity and Culture*. Palgrave MacMillan.

Brüggemann, A. J. and Swahnberg, K. (2013). What contributes to abuse in health care? A grounded theory of female patients' stories. *International Journal of Nursing Studies, 50*(3), 404–412.

Buchhold, B., Lutze, S., Arnold, A., Julich, A., Daeschlein, G. and Wendler, M. (2018). Psychosocial distress and desire for support among skin cancer patients – impact of treatment setting. *Journal der Deutschen Dermatologischen Gesellschaft, 16*, 861–871.

Burns, G.W. (2005). *101 Healing stories for kids and teens: using metaphors in therapy*. New York: Wiley.

Burns, G.W. (ed)(2007). *Healing with stories: your casebook collection for using therapeutic metaphors*. New York: Wiley.

Bylund, C.L. and Makoul, G. (2005). Examining empathy in medical encounters: an observational study using the empathic communication coding system. *Health Communication, 18*(2) 123–140.

Bylund, C.L. and Makoul, G. (2002). Empathic communication and gender in the physician–patient encounter. *Patient Education and Counseling, 48*, 207–216.

Cait, C. A., Skop, M., Booton, J., Stalker, C. A., Horton, S. and Riemer, M. (2017). Practice-based qualitative research: Participant experiences of walk-in counselling and traditional counselling. *Qualitative Social Work, 16*(5), 612–630.

Cannistrà, F., Piccirilli, F., Paolo D'Alia, P., Giannetti, A., Piva, L., Gobbato, F.... and Pietrabissa, G. (2020). Examining the incidence and clients' experiences of single session therapy in Italy: A feasibility study. *Australian and New Zealand Journal of Family Therapy, 41*(3), 271–282.

Carey, M., Walther, S. and Russell, S. (2009). The absent but implicit: A map to support therapeutic enquiry. *Family Process, 48*, 319–331.

Carey, T. A., Carey, M., Stalker, K., Mullan, R. J., Murray, L. K. and Spratt, M. B. (2007). Psychological change from the inside looking out: A qualitative investigation. *Counselling and Psychotherapy Research, 7*(3), 178–187.

Carlin, E., Atkinson, D. and Marley, J. V. (2019). 'Having a quiet word': Yarning with Aboriginal women in the Pilbara region of Western Australia about mental health and mental health screening during the perinatal period. *International journal of environmental research and public health, 16*(21), 4253.

Carney, D. M., Castonguay, L. G., Janis, R. A., Scofield, B. E., Hayes, J. A. and Locke, B. D. (2021). Center effects: Counseling center variables as predictors of psychotherapy outcomes. *The Counseling Psychologist, 49*(7), 1013–1037.

Carrell, S.E. (2001) *The Therapist's Toolbox*. Thousand Oaks, CA: Sage.

Carroll, M. (2014). *Effective Supervision for the Helping Professions*. 2nd edn. London: Sage.

Chaturvedi, S. (2016). Accessing psychological therapies: Homeless young people's views on barriers and facilitators. *Counselling and Psychotherapy Research*, 16(1), 54–63.

Chen, R., Sun, C., Chen, J. J., Jen, H. J., Kang, X. L., Kao, C. C. and Chou, K. R. (2021). A large-scale survey on trauma, burnout, and post-traumatic growth among nurses during the COVID-19 pandemic. *International Journal of Mental Health Nursing*, 30(1), 102–116.

Chibanda, D., Mesu, P., Kajawu, L., Cowan, F., Araya, R. and Abas, M. A. (2011). Problem-solving therapy for depression and common mental disorders in Zimbabwe: Piloting a task-shifting primary mental health care intervention in a population with a high prevalence of people living with HIV. *BMC public health*, 11(1), 1–10.

Chiu, T. C. (2020). Stories and knowledge of responding to hard times: A narrative approach to collective healing in Kong Kong. *International Journal of Narrative Therapy and Community Work*, (3), 32–42.

Choi, G. Y., An, S., Cho, H. and Koh, E. (2021). Understanding the complexity of domestic violence service delivery through the lived experiences of domestic violence advocates. *International Social Work*, 00208728211041673.

Chowdhury, R., Winder, B., Blagden, N. and Mulla, F. (2021). 'I thought in order to get to God I had to win their approval': A qualitative analysis of the experiences of Muslim victims abused by religious authority figures. *Journal of Sexual Aggression*, 1–22. https://doi.org/10.1080/13552600.2021.1943023

Clark, D. M. (2018). Realizing the mass public benefit of evidence-based psychological therapies: The IAPT program. *Annual Review of Clinical Psychology*, 14, 159–183.

Clark, D.A. and Beck, A.T. (2011). *The Anxiety and Worry Workbook: The Cognitive Behavioral Solution*. New York: Guilford Press.

Cleary, M., Raeburn, T., West, S., Escott, P. and Lopez, V. (2018). Two approaches, one goal: How mental health registered nurses' perceive their role and the role of peer support workers in facilitating consumer decision-making. *International Journal of Mental Health Nursing*, 27(4), 1212–1218.

Cobain, B. and Larch, J. (2018). *Dying to be Free: A Healing Guide for Families After a Suicide*. Center City, Minn.: Hazelden Publishing.

Cockersell, P. (2011). Homelessness and mental health: adding clinical mental health interventions to existing social ones can greatly enhance positive outcomes. *Journal of Public Mental Health*, 10(2), 88–98.

Conolly, J. M. P. (2018). Pre-treatment therapy: a central London counselling service's enhanced response to complex needs homelessness. In J. Levy and R. Johnson (eds.). *Cross-Cultural Dialogues on Homelessness: From Pretreatment Strategies to Psychologically Informed Environments*, (pp. 49–69). Ann Arbor, MI: Loving Healing Press.

Cooke, J., Ivey, G., Godfrey, C., Grady, J., Dean, S., Beaufoy, J. and Tonge, B. (2020). Patient-reported reasons for discontinuing psychotherapy in a low-cost psychoanalytic community clinic. *Counselling and Psychotherapy Research*, 21(3), 697–709.

Cooper, M. (2019). *Integrating counselling and psychotherapy: Directionality, synergy, and social justice*. London: Sage.

Cooper, M. and McLeod, J. (2010) *Pluralistic counselling and psychotherapy*. London: Sage.

Coren, S. and Farber, B. A. (2019). A qualitative investigation of the nature of 'informal supervision' among therapists in training. *Psychotherapy Research*, 29(5), 679–690.

Corey, G., Corey, M. and Callanan, P. (2021) *Issues and Ethics in the Helping Professions*, 10th edn. Pacific Grove, CA: Brooks/Cole.

Cormack, J. (2009). Counselling marginalised young people: A qualitative analysis of young homeless people's views of counselling. *Counselling and Psychotherapy Research*, 9(2), 71–77.

Costelloe, A., Mintz, J. and Lee, F. (2020). Bereavement support provision in primary schools: An exploratory study. *Educational Psychology in Practice*, 36(3), 281–296.

Coveney, C. M., Pollock, K., Armstrong, S. and Moore, J. (2012). Callers' experiences of contacting a national suicide prevention helpline. *Crisis, 33*, 313–324.

Covington, S. (2003). *Beyond trauma: A healing journey for women* (rev. 2016). Center City, Minn.: Hazelden Publishing.

Covington, S. (2015). *Beyond violence: A prevention program for criminal justice-involved women participant workbook*. New York: John Wiley & Sons.

Covington, S. S., and Rodriguez, R. (2016). *Exploring trauma: A brief intervention for men*. Center City, Minn.: Hazelden Publishing.

Cowen, E.L. (1982) Help is where you find it: four informal helping groups. *American Psychologist, 37*, 385–395.

Cowen, E.L., Gesten, E.L., Boike, M., Norton, P., Wilson, A.B. and DeStefano, M.A. (1979) Hairdressers as caregivers: A descriptive profile of interpersonal help-giving involvements. *American Journal of Community Psychology, 7*, 633–648.

Crandall, R. and Allen, R. (1981) The organisational context of helping relationships. In T. A. Wills (ed.) *Basic Processes in Helping Relationships*. New York: Academic Press.

Cuijpers, P., Karyotaki, E., de Wit, L. and Ebert, D. D. (2020). The effects of fifteen evidence-supported therapies for adult depression: a meta-analytic review. *Psychotherapy Research, 30*(3), 279–293.

Cunningham, N. (2014). Lost in transition: Women experiencing infertility. *Human Fertility, 17*(3), 154–158.

Daly-Lynn, J., Daly, C. and Rhys, C. (2016). The elephant in the room: Dealing with an unprosecuted criminal disclosure in a therapeutic setting. *Journal of Forensic Psychology, 1*(4), 1–8.

Danieli, Y. (ed.). (1998). *International handbook of multigenerational legacies of trauma*. New York: Plenum Press.

Davidson, L., Rowe, M., DiLeo, P., Bellamy, C., and Delphin-Rittmon, M. (2021). Recovery-oriented systems of care: A perspective on the past, present, and future. *Alcohol Research: Current Reviews, 41*(1).

Day, P., Lawson, J., Mantri, S., Jain, A., Rabago, D., and Lennon, R. (2021). Physician moral injury in the context of moral, ethical and legal codes. *Journal of Medical Ethics*. http://dx.doi.org/10.1136/medethics-2021-107225

Dean, M. and Street Jr, R. L. (2014). A 3-stage model of patient-centered communication for addressing cancer patients' emotional distress. *Patient Education and Counseling, 94*(2), 143–148.

Dell, N. A., Long, C. and Mancini, M. A. (2021). Models of mental health recovery: An overview of systematic reviews and qualitative meta-syntheses. *Psychiatric Rehabilitation Journal, 44*(3), 238–253.

Denneny, D., Frijdal, A., Bianchi-Berthouze, N., Greenwood, J., McLoughlin, R., Petersen, K.... and Williams, A. C. D. C. (2020). The application of psychologically informed practice: Observations of experienced physiotherapists working with people with chronic pain. *Physiotherapy, 106*, 163–173.

Denovan, A. and Macaskill, A. (2017). Building resilience to stress through leisure activities: A qualitative analysis. *Annals of Leisure Research, 20*(4), 446–466.

Depow, G. J., Francis, Z. and Inzlicht, M. (2021). The experience of empathy in everyday life. *Psychological Science, 32*(8), 1198–1213.

Derksen, F. A. W. M., Hartman, T. O., Lagro-Janssen, A. L. M. and Kramer, A. W. M. (2021). Clinical empathy in GP-training: Experiences and needs among Dutch GP-trainees. 'Empathy as an element of personal growth'. *Patient Education and Counseling, 104*(12), 3016–3022.

Devenney, K. (2020). Social work with unaccompanied asylum-seeking young people: Reframing social care professionals as 'co-navigators'. *The British Journal of Social Work, 50*(3), 926–943.

Dewar, B. and MacBride, T. (2017). Developing Caring Conversations in care homes: An appreciative inquiry. *Health and Social Care in the Community, 25*(4), 1375–1386.

Diamond, D. J. and Diamond, M. O. (2017). Parenthood after reproductive loss: How psychotherapy can help with postpartum adjustment and parent–infant attachment. *Psychotherapy, 54*(4), 373–379.

DiAngelo, R. (2018). *White fragility: Why it's so hard for white people to talk about racism*. Boston, MA: Beacon Press.

Dibb, B., Hardiman, A. and Rose, J. W. (2019). Obese patients' views of the practitioners' role in initiating and managing weight loss. *Journal of Obesity and Medical Complications*, *1*(1), 1–5.

Dieser, R. B., Christenson, J. and Davis-Gage, D. (2015). Integrating flow theory and the serious leisure perspective into mental health counseling. *Counselling Psychology Quarterly*, *28*(1), 97–111.

Dimitropoulos, G., Cullen, E., Cullen, O., Pawluk, C., McLuckie, A., Patten, S.... and Arnold, P. D. (2021). 'Teachers often see the red flags first': perceptions of school staff regarding their roles in supporting students with mental health concerns. *School Mental Health*, 1–14. https://doi.org/10.1007/s12310-021-09475-1

Donnelly, C. (2021). Claiming chaos narrative, emerging from silence. *Disability & Society.*, https://doi.org/10.1080/09687599.2021.1983420

Draper, B., Snowdon, J. and Wyder, M. (2008). A pilot study of the suicide victim's last contact with a health professional. *Crisis*, *29*(2), 96–101.

Dryden, W. (2019). *Single-session therapy (SST): 100 key points and techniques*. New York: Routledge.

Dryden, W. (2020a). *Single-Session Therapy and Its Future: What SST Leaders Think*. New York: Routledge.

Dryden, W. (2020b). Single-Session One-At-A-Time Therapy: a personal approach. *Australian and New Zealand Journal of Family Therapy*, *41*(3), 283–301.

Dryden, W. (2020c). Single-session one-at-a-time therapy: a personal approach. *Australian and New Zealand Journal of Family Therapy*, *41*(3), 283–301.

Duffey, T. and Haberstroh, S. (eds.)(2020). *Introduction to Crisis and Trauma Counseling*, Alexandria, VA: American Counseling Association.

Earl, T. R., Alegría, M., Mendieta, F., and Linhart, Y. D. (2011). 'Just be straight with me': An exploration of Black patient experiences in initial mental health encounters. *American Journal of Orthopsychiatry*, *81*(4), 519–525.

Easton, S. and van Laar, D. (1995) Experiences of lecturers helping distressed students in higher education. *British Journal of Guidance and Counselling*, *23*, 173–178.

Ecclestone, K., Biesta, G., and Hughes, M. (eds.). (2010). *Transitions and learning through the lifecourse*. London: Routledge.

Eide, H., Frankel, R., Haaversen, C, Vaupel, K., Graugard, P. and Finset, A. (2004) Listening for feelings: identifying and coding empathic and potential empathic opportunities in medical dialogues. *Patient Education and Counseling*, *54*, 291–7.

Ekberg, S., Parry, R., Land, V., Ekberg, K., Pino, M. and Antaki, C. (2020). Communicating with patients and families about difficult matters: A rapid review in the context of the COVID-19 pandemic. medRxiv.

Ellis-Hill, C., Pound, C. and Galvin, K. (2021). Making the invisible more visible: Reflections on practice-based humanising lifeworld-led research–existential opportunities for supporting dignity, compassion and wellbeing. *Scandinavian Journal of Caring Sciences*. https://doi.org/10.1111/scs.13013

Ellis, T. E. (2004). Collaboration and a self-help orientation in therapy with suicidal clients. *Journal of Contemporary Psychotherapy*, *34*(1), 41–57.

Elton, M. (2021). *Talking it Better: From insight to change in the therapy room*. Monmouth: PCCS Books.

Elwyn, G., Durand, M. A., Song, J., Aarts, J., Barr, P. J., Berger, Z., ... and Van der Weijden, T. (2017). A three-talk model for shared decision making: Multistage consultation process. *British Medical Journal*, *359*. https://doi.org/10.1136/bmj.j4891

Engebretson, J. (2000) Caring presence: A case study. *International Journal for Human Caring*, *4*, 211–223.

Engebretson, J. C., Peterson, N. E., and Frenkel, M. (2014). Exceptional patients: narratives of connections. *Palliative and Supportive Care*, *12*(5), 269–276.

Ennis, J. and Majid, U. (2021). 'Death from a broken heart: A systematic review of the relationship between spousal bereavement and physical and physiological health outcomes. *Death Studies*, *45*(7), 538–551,

Epiphaniou, E., and Ogden, J. (2010). Successful weight loss maintenance and a shift in identity: From restriction to a new liberated self. *Journal of Health Psychology, 15*(6), 887–896.

Epston, D. (2014). To Christchurch with love: family, neighbourhood and community responses to earthquake-related trauma. *Australian and New Zealand Journal of Family Therapy, 35*(3), 341–352.

Eriksson, I., Ek, K., Jansson, S., Sjöström, U., and Larsson, M. (2019). To feel emotional concern: A qualitative interview study to explore telephone nurses' experiences of difficult calls. *Nursing Open, 6*(3), 842–848.

Eriksson, I., Wilhsson, M., Blom, T., Broo Wahlström, C., and Larsson, M. (2020). Telephone nurses' strategies for managing difficult calls: A qualitative content analysis. *Nursing Open, 7*(6), 1671–1679.

Eyles, C., Leydon, G. M., and Brien, S. B. (2012). Forming connections in the homeopathic consultation. *Patient Education and Counseling, 89*(3), 501–506.

Eyrich-Garg, K.M. (2008) Strategies for engaging adolescent girls at an emergency shelter in a therapeutic relationship: Recommendations from the girls themselves. *Journal of Social Work Practice, 22,* 375–388.

Falkenström, F., Grant, J., and Holmqvist, R. (2018). Review of organizational effects on the outcome of mental health treatments. *Psychotherapy Research, 28*(1), 76–90.

Feingold, J. H., Kaye-Kauderer, H., Mendiolaza, M., Dubinsky, M. C., Keefer, L., and Gorbenko, K. (2021). Empowered transitions: Understanding the experience of transitioning from pediatric to adult care among adolescents with inflammatory bowel disease and their parents using photovoice. *Journal of Psychosomatic Research, 143,* 110400.

Feinstein, R. E. (2021). Crisis intervention psychotherapy in the age of COVID-19. *Journal of Psychiatric Practice, 27*(3), 152.

Felitti, V., Anda, R.F., Nordenberg, D., Williamson, D.F., Spitz, A.M., Edwards, V.and Marks, J.S. (1998). Relationship of childhood abuse and household dysfunction to many of the leading causes of death in adults. *American Journal of Preventive Medicine, 14,* 245–258.

Ferguson, H., Disney, T., Warwick, L., Leigh, J., Cooner, T. S., and Beddoe, L. (2021). Hostile relationships in social work practice: anxiety, hate and conflict in long-term work with involuntary service users. *Journal of Social Work Practice, 35*(1), 19–37.

Ferguson, H., Warwick, L., Disney, T., Leigh, J., Cooner, T. S., and Beddoe, L. (2022). Relationship-based practice and the creation of therapeutic change in long-term work: Social work as a holding relationship. *Social Work Education, 41*(2), 209-227.

Feuer, B. S. (2021). First responder peer support: An evidence-informed approach. *Journal of Police and Criminal Psychology, 36,* 365–371.

Finset, A. (2012). 'I am worried, Doctor!' Emotions in the doctor–patient relationship. *Patient Education and Counseling, 88*(3), 359–363.

Fisher, E. M., and Stylianou, A. M. (2019). To stay or to leave: Factors influencing victims' decisions to stay or leave a domestic violence emergency shelter. *Journal of interpersonal violence, 34*(4), 785–811.

Flückiger, C., Wampold, B. E., Delgadillo, J., Rubel, J., Vîslă, A., and Lutz, W. (2020). Is there an evidence-based number of sessions in outpatient psychotherapy? A comparison of naturalistic conditions across countries. *Psychotherapy and Psychosomatics, 89*(5), 333–335.

Fluckiger, C., Wüsten, G., Zinbarg, R. and Wampold, B. (2010). *Resource Activation: Using Clients' Own Strengths in Psychotherapy and Counseling.* Oxford: Hogrefe and Huber.

Fogarty, S., Smith, C. A., Touyz, S., Madden, S., Buckett, G., and Hay, P. (2013). Patients with anorexia nervosa receiving acupuncture or acupressure; their view of the therapeutic encounter. *Complementary Therapies in Medicine, 21*(6), 675–681.

Forslund, T., Kosidou, K., Wicks, S., and Dalman, C. (2020). Trends in psychiatric diagnoses, medications and psychological therapies in a large Swedish region: a population-based study. *BMC psychiatry, 20*(1), 1–9.

Fox, J. (2021). Shared Decision-Making: An autoethnography about service user perspectives in making choices about mental health care and treatment. *Frontiers in Psychiatry, 12,* 284.

Frank, A (1995). *The Wounded Storyteller: Body, Illness, and ethics*. Chicago: The University of Chicago Press.

Frank, A. (1998). Just listening: narrative and deep illness. *Families, Systems and Health, 16*, 197–212.

Frank, A. (2000). Illness and autobiographical work: Dialogue as narrative destabilization. *Qualitative Sociology, 23*, 135–156.

French, H.W. (2021). *Born in Blackness: Africa, Africans, and the Making of the Modern World, 1471 to the Second World War*. New York: Liveright Publishing.

Freshwater, D. (2005). *Counselling Skills for Nurses, Midwives and Health Visitors*. London: Open University Press.

Fricker, M. (2007). *Epistemic Injustice: Power and the Ethics of Knowing*. Oxford: Oxford University Press.

Gabbay, J. and le May, E. (2010). *Practice-based evidence for health care: Clinical mindlines*. London: Routledge.

Gabriel, L. and Casemore, R. (2009). *Relational Ethics in Practice: Narratives from Counselling and Psychotherapy*. London: Routledge.

Galvin, K. T., Pound, C., Cowdell, F., Ellis-Hill, C., Sloan, C., Brooks, S., and Ersser, S. J. (2020). A lifeworld theory-led action research process for humanizing services: improving 'what matters' to older people to enhance humanly sensitive care. *International Journal of Qualitative Studies on Health and Well-being, 15*(1), 1817275.

Galvin, K., and Todres, L. (2013). *Caring and well-being: A lifeworld approach*. London: Routledge.

Gandhi, R. S. (2021). Being brown: An autoethnographic exploration of internalised colonisation. *Psychodynamic Practice, 27*(2), 127–143.

Gaspard, G., Gadsby, C., and Mallmes, J. (2021). Indigenous end-of-life doula course: Bringing the culture home. *International Journal of Indigenous Health, 16*(2), 151–165.

Gee, L., and Agras, W. S. (2014). A randomized pilot study of a brief outpatient problem-solving intervention to promote healthy eating and activity habits in adolescents. *Clinical Pediatrics, 53*(3), 293–296.

Geller, J.D., Norcross, J.C. and Orlinsky, D.E. (2005) *The Psychotherapist's own Psychotherapy: Patient and Clinician Perspectives*. New York: Oxford University Press.

Gerger, H., Werner, C. P., Gaab, J., and Cuijpers, P. (2021). Comparative efficacy and acceptability of expressive writing treatments compared with psychotherapy, other writing treatments, and waiting list control for adult trauma survivors: a systematic review and network meta-analysis. *Psychological Medicine*, 1–13. https://doi.org/10.1017/S0033291721000143

Gersons, B. P., and Carlier, I. V. (1992). Post-traumatic stress disorder: The history of a recent concept. *British Journal of Psychiatry, 161*(6), 742–748.

Gersons, B. P., and Schnyder, U. (2013). Learning from traumatic experiences with brief eclectic psychotherapy for PTSD. *European Journal of Psychotraumatology, 4*(1), 21369.

Gianakis, M., and Carey, T. A. (2011). An interview study investigating experiences of psychological change without psychotherapy. *Psychology and Psychotherapy: Theory, Research and Practice, 84*(4), 442–457.

Gibson, A., Cooper, M., Rae, J., and Hayes, J. (2020). Clients' experiences of shared decision making in an integrative psychotherapy for depression. *Journal of Evaluation in Clinical Practice, 26*(2), 559–568.

Gidugu, V., Rogers, E. S., Gordon, C., Elwy, A. R., and Drainoni, M. L. (2021). Client, family, and clinician experiences of Open Dialogue-based services. *Psychological Services, 18*(2), 154–163.

Gilliland, A. L. (2011). After praise and encouragement: Emotional support strategies used by birth doulas in the USA and Canada. *Midwifery, 27*(4), 525–531.

Giroldi, E., Timmerman, A., Veldhuijzen, W., Muris, J., van der Vleuten, C., and van der Weijden, T. (2020). How doctors recognise that their patients are worried: A qualitative study of patient cues. *Patient Education and Counseling, 103*(1), 220–225.

Golia, G. M., and McGovern, A. R. (2015). If you save me, I'll save you: The power of peer supervision in clinical training and professional development. *British Journal of Social Work, 45*(2), 634–650.

Gómez, J. M., and Gobin, R. L. (2020). Black women and girls & #MeToo: Rape, cultural betrayal, & healing. *Sex Roles, 82*(1), 1–12.

Gone, J. P. (2013). Redressing First Nations historical trauma: Theorizing mechanisms for indigenous culture as mental health treatment. *Transcultural Psychiatry, 50*(5), 683–706.

Goodman, L. A., and Smyth, K. F. (2011). A call for a social network-oriented approach to services for survivors of intimate partner violence. *Psychology of Violence, 1*(2), 79–92.

Goodman, L. A., Banyard, V., Woulfe, J., Ash, S., and Mattern, G. (2016). Bringing a network-oriented approach to domestic violence services: A focus group exploration of promising practices. *Violence against women, 22*(1), 64–89.

Goodman, L. A., Fauci, J. E., Sullivan, C. M., DiGiovanni, C. D., and Wilson, J. M. (2016). Domestic violence survivors' empowerment and mental health: Exploring the role of the alliance with advocates. *American Journal of Orthopsychiatry, 86*(3), 286–296.

Goodman, L. A., Sullivan, C. M., Serrata, J., Perilla, J., Wilson, J. M., Fauci, J. E., andDiGiovanni, C. D. (2016). Development and validation of the Trauma Informed Practice Scales. *Journal of Community Psychology, 44*, 747–764.

Goulah-Pabst, D. M. (2021). Suicide loss survivors: Navigating social stigma and threats to social bonds. *OMEGA Journal of Death and Dying*, 00302228211026513.

Greer, T. W. (2017). Career development for women veterans: Facilitating successful transitions from military service to civilian employment. *Advances in Developing Human Resources, 19*(1), 54–65.

Greer, T.W. (2020). Adult learning and development goals for female veterans' career transitions amid cultural adaptation and identity formation. *New Directions for Adult and Continuing Education, 20* (166), 151–162.

Grubb, A. R., Brown, S. J., Hall, P., and Bowen, E. (2021). 'The more you do, the more comfortable you feel': The police hostage and crisis negotiator journey. *Journal of Police and Criminal Psychology*, 1–17.

Gruber, K. J., Cupito, S. H., and Dobson, C. F. (2013). Impact of doulas on healthy birth outcomes. *The Journal of Perinatal Education, 22*(1), 49–58.

Gulliver, S. B., Pennington, M. L., Leto, F., Cammarata, C., Ostiguy, W., Zavodny, C., ...and Kimbrel, N. A. (2016). In the wake of suicide: Developing guidelines for suicide postvention in fire service. *Death Studies, 40*(2), 121–128.

Gupta, A. (2017). Learning from others: an autoethnographic exploration of children and families social work, poverty and the capability approach. *Qualitative Social Work, 16*(4), 449–464.

Haight, W., Sugrue, E., Calhoun, M. and Black, J. (2016). A scoping study of moral injury: identifying directions for social work research. *Children and Youth Services Review, 70*, 190–200.

Haight, W., Sugrue, E. P. and Calhoun, M. (2017a). Moral injury among Child Protection Professionals: Implications for the ethical treatment and retention of workers. *Children and Youth Services Review, 82*, 27–41.

Haight, W., Sugrue, E., Calhoun, M. and Black, J. (2017b). 'Basically, I look at it like combat': Reflections on moral injury by parents involved with child protection services. *Children and Youth Services Review, 82*, 477–489.

Haight, W., Sugrue, E., Calhoun, M. and Black, J. (2017c). Everyday coping with moral injury: The perspectives of professionals and parents involved with child protection services. *Children and Youth Services Review, 82*, 108–121.

Hall, A., McKenna, B., Dearie, V., Maguire, T., Charleston, R. and Furness, T. (2016). Educating emergency department nurses about trauma informed care for people presenting with mental health crisis: A pilot study. *BMC Nursing, 15*(1), 21.

Halpern, J. (2001). *From detached concern to empathy: Humanizing medical practice*. Oxford: Oxford University Press.

Halpern, J. (2014). From idealized clinical empathy to empathic communication in medical care. *Medicine, Health Care and Philosophy 17* (2): 301–311.

Hänninen, V. and Valkonen, J. (2019). Losing and regaining grip: depression and everyday life. *Sage Open, 9*(1), 2158244018822371.

Hannon, M.D., Mohabir, R.K., Cleveland, R.E. and Hunt, B. (2019). School counselors, multiple student deaths, and grief: a narrative inquiry. *Journal of Counseling and Development*, *97*(1), 43–52.

Hanser, C. H. (2020). A space between: Social work through the lens of a mobile tiny house encounter space. *Qualitative Social Work*, *19*(3), 380–405.

Harrison, M. G. (2019). Relationship in context: Processes in school-based counselling in Hong Kong. *Counselling and Psychotherapy Research*, *19*(4), 474–483.

Hart, N. (1996). The role of tutor in a college of higher education – a comparison of skills used by personal tutors and by student counsellors when working with students in distress. *British Journal of Guidance and Counselling*, *24*, 83–96.

Harvey, G., and Tapp, D. M. (2020). Exploring the meaning of critical incident stress experienced by intensive care unit nurses. *Nursing Inquiry*, *27*(4), e12365.

Hauge, M. S., Stora, B., Vassend, O., Hoffart, A., and Willumsen, T. (2021). Dentist-administered cognitive behavioural therapy versus four habits/midazolam: An RCT study of dental anxiety treatment in primary dental care. *European Journal of Oral Sciences*, e12794.

Hawkins, P. and McMahon, A. (2020) *Supervision in the Helping Professions*. 5th edn. London: Open University Press.

Hayes, J. and Steffen, E. M. (2017). Working with welcome and unwelcome presence in grief. In D. Klass and E.M. Steffen (eds). *Continuing bonds in bereavement. New directions for research and practice*. (pp. 163–175). New York: Routledge.

Hedtke, L. and Winslade, J. (2016). *The crafting of grief: Constructing aesthetic responses to loss*. New York: Routledge.

Henderson, P., and Johnson, M. H. (2002). Assisting medical students to conduct empathic conversations with patients from a sexual medicine clinic. *Sexually Transmitted Infections*, *78*(4), 246–249.

Henretty, J. R. and Levitt, H. M. (2010). The role of therapist self-disclosure in psychotherapy: A qualitative review. *Clinical Psychology Review*, *30*(1), 63–77.

Henry, H. M. (2012). African refugees in Egypt: Trauma, loss, and cultural adjustment. *Death Studies*, *36*(7), 583–604.

Henry, H. M., Stiles, W. B. and Biran, M. W. (2005). Loss and mourning in immigration: Using the assimilation model to assess continuing bonds with native culture. *Counselling Psychology Quarterly*, *18*(2), 109–119.

Henry, H. M., Stiles, W. B. and Biran, M. W. (2017). Continuing bonds with native culture. In D. Klass and E.M. Steffen (eds). *Continuing bonds in bereavement. New directions for research and practice*. New York: Routledge.

Henry, H. M., Stiles, W. B., Biran, M. W., Mosher, J. K., Brinegar, M. G. and Banerjee, P. (2009). Immigrants' continuing bonds with their native culture: Assimilation analysis of three interviews. *Transcultural Psychiatry*, *46*(2), 257–284.

Herrero-Arias, R., Truong, A. N., Ortiz-Barreda, G. and Briones-Vozmediano, E. (2021). Keeping silent or running away. The voices of Vietnamese women survivors of Intimate Partner Violence. *Global Health Action*, *14*(1), 1863128.

Hickman, C. (2020). We need to (find a way to) talk about… Eco-anxiety. *Journal of Social Work Practice*, *34*(4), 411–424.

Hickman, C., Marks, E., Pihkala, P., Clayton, S., Lewandowski, R. E., Mayall, E. E. … and van Susteren, L. (2021). Climate anxiety in children and young people and their beliefs about government responses to climate change: A global survey. *The Lancet Planetary Health*, *5*(12), e863–e873.

Hobfoll, S. E. (2011). Conservation of resources theory: Its implication for stress, health, and resilience. In S. Folkman (ed.), *The Oxford handbook of stress, health, and coping* (pp. 127–147). Oxford: Oxford University Press.

Hockey, J. Katz and N. Small (eds.) *Grief, mourning and death ritual*. Maidenhead: Open University Press.

Hoffberg, A. S., Stearns-Yoder, K. A., and Brenner, L. A. (2020). The effectiveness of crisis line services: a systematic review. *Frontiers in Public Health*, *7*, 399.

Holland, J. (2016). *Responding to Loss and Bereavement in Schools: A Training Resource to Assess, Evaluate and Improve the School Response*. Philadelphia, PA: Jessica Kingsley Publishers.

Holland, J. M., Klingspon, K. L., Lichtenthal, W. G., and Neimeyer, R. A. (2020). The Unfinished Business in Bereavement Scale (UBBS): Development and psychometric evaluation. *Death Studies*, 44(2), 65–77.

Hollis, J. L., Kocanda, L., et al. (2021). The impact of Healthy Conversation Skills training on health professionals' barriers to having behaviour change conversations: a pre-post survey using the Theoretical Domains Framework. *BMC Health Services Research*, 21(1), 1–13.

Holmes, G., Clacy, A., Hermens, D. F. and Lagopoulos, J. (2021). Evaluating the longitudinal efficacy of SafeTALK suicide prevention gatekeeper training in a general community sample. *Suicide and Life-Threatening Behavior*, 51(5), 844–853.

Holt-Lunstad, J. (2021a). The major health implications of social connection. *Current Directions in Psychological Science*, 30(3), 251–259.

Holt-Lunstad, J. (2021b). Loneliness and Social Isolation as Risk Factors: The Power of Social Connection in Prevention. *American Journal of Lifestyle Medicine*, 15598276211009454.

Holt-Lunstad, J., Robles, T. F. and Sbarra, D. A. (2017). Advancing social connection as a public health priority in the United States. *American Psychologist*, 72(6), 517–530.

Honos-Webb, L. and Stiles, W.B. (1998). Reformulation of assimilation analysis in terms of voices. *Psychotherapy*, 35, 23–33.

Hopper, E. K., Bassuk, E. L., and Olivet, J. (2010). Shelter from the storm: Trauma-informed care in homelessness services settings. *The Open Health Services and Policy Journal*, 3(2), 80–100.

Hopson, B. (1989) Life transitions and crises. In N. Niven (ed.) *Health Psychology*. Edinburgh: Churchill Livingstone.

Hopson, B. and Adams, J. (1976) Towards an understanding: defining some boundaries of transition dynamics. In Adams, J., Hayes, J. and Hopson, B. (eds.) *Transition: Understanding and Managing Personal Change*. London: Martin Robertson.

Horspool, K., Drabble, S. J. and O'Cathain, A. (2016). Implementing street triage: A qualitative study of collaboration between police and mental health services. *BMC Psychiatry*, 16(1), 1–11.

Houshmand, S., Spanierman, L. B. and De Stefano, J. (2019). 'I have strong medicine, you see': Strategic responses to racial microaggressions. *Journal of Counseling Psychology*, 66(6), 651–664.

Hoyt, M.F. Young, J. and Rycroft, P. (2021). *Single Session Thinking and Practice in Global, Cultural, and Familial Contexts. Expanding Applications*. New York: Routledge.

Hunter, M. and Struve, J. (1998). *The Ethical Use of Touch in Psychotherapy*. Thousand Oaks, CA: Sage.

Imber-Black, E. and Roberts, J. (1992). *Rituals for our Times: Celebrating Healing and Changing our Lives and Relationships*. New York: HarperCollins.

Inman, C. and Ogden, J. (2011). Facing mortality: Exploring the mechanisms of positive growth and the process of recalibration. *Psychology, Health & Medicine*, 16(3), 366–374.

Irvine, A., Drew, P., Bower, P., Ardern, K., Armitage, C. J., Barkham, M., ... and Bee, P. (2021). 'So just to go through the options...': Patient choice in the telephone delivery of the NHS Improving Access to Psychological Therapy service. *Sociology of Health & Illness*, 43(1), 3–19.

Iversen, A., Dyson, C., Smith, N., Greenberg, N., Walwyn, R., Unwin, C., ... and Wessely, S. (2005). 'Goodbye and good luck': The mental health needs and treatment experiences of British ex-service personnel. *British Journal of Psychiatry*, 186(6), 480–486.

Jaffe, J. (2017). Reproductive trauma: Psychotherapy for pregnancy loss and infertility clients from a reproductive story perspective. *Psychotherapy*, 54(4), 380–385.

James, R.K. and Gilliland, B.E. (2020). *Crisis Intervention Strategies*. 8th edn. Belmont, CA: Wadsworth.

Jangland, E., Gunningberg, L. and Carlsson, M. (2009) Patients' and relatives' complaints about encounters and communication in health care: Evidence for quality improvement. *Patient Education and Counseling*, 75, 199–204.

Janoff-Bulman, R. (2010). *Shattered assumptions: Toward a new psychology of trauma*. New York: Simon and Schuster.

Jansen, J., van Weert, J.C.M., de Groot, J., van Dulmen, S., Heeren, J. and Bensing, J.M. (2010) Emotional and informational patient cues: The impact of nurses' responses on recall. *Patient Education and Counseling, 79*, 218–24.

Jarldorn, M. (2018). *Photovoice handbook for social workers: Method, practicalities and possibilities for social change.* New York: Springer.

Jenkins, P. (2017). *Professional Practice in Counselling and Psychotherapy: Ethics and the Law.* London: Sage.

Jenkinson, S. (2015). *Die wise: A manifesto for sanity and soul.* Berkeley, CA: North Atlantic Books.

Jennings, L., Sovereign, A, Bottorff, N., Mussell, M.P. and Vye, C. (2005). Nine ethical values of master therapists. *Journal of Mental Health Counseling, 27,* 32–47.

Jevne, R.F. (1987). Creating stillpoints: beyond a rational approach to counselling cancer patients. *Journal of Psychosocial Oncology, 5,* 1–15.

Jevne, R.F. Nekolaichuk, C.L. and Williamson, F.H.A. (1998) A model for counselling cancer patients. *Canadian Journal of Counselling, 32,* 213–29.

Jobes, D.A. (2016). *Managing suicidal risk: a collaborative approach.* 2nd edn. New York: Guilford.

Johnson, B. (2008). Teacher-student relationships which promote resilience at school: A micro-level analysis of students' views. *British Journal of Guidance and Counselling, 36,* 385–398.

Johnson, W. B., Barnett, J. E., Elman, N. S., Forrest, L., & Kaslow, N. J. (2012). The competent community: Toward a vital reformulation of professional ethics. American Psychologist, 67(7), 557–569.

Johnson, W. B., Barnett, J. E., Elman, N. S., Forrest, L. and Kaslow, N. J. (2012). The competent community: Toward a vital reformulation of professional ethics. *American Psychologist, 67*(7), 557–569.

Johnstone, L. and Dallos, R. (eds.)(2014) *Formulation in Psychology and Psychotherapy: Making sense of people's problems.* 2nd edn. London: Routledge.

Jones, E., Bhui, K. and Engelbrecht, A. (2019). The return of the traumatized army veteran: A qualitative study of UK ex-servicemen in the aftermath of war, 1945 to 2000. *International Review of Psychiatry, 31*(1), 14–24.

Jordan, J. R. (2015). Grief after suicide: The evolution of suicide postvention. In J. M. Stillion and T. Attig (eds.), *Death, dying, and bereavement: Contemporary perspectives, institutions, and practices* (pp. 349–362). New York, NY: Springer.

Jordan, J. R. and McGann, V. (2017). Clinical work with suicide loss survivors: Implications of the US postvention guidelines. *Death Studies, 41*(10), 659–672.

Jordan, J.V. (2000). The role of mutual empathy in relational/cultural therapy. *Journal of Clinical Psychology, 56,* 1005–1016.

Jordan, J.V. (ed.) (2008). *The power of connection: Recent developments in relational–cultural theory.* New York: Haworth Press.

Jorm, A. F. and Ross, A. M. (2018). Guidelines for the public on how to provide mental health first aid: Narrative review. *BJPsych Open, 4*(6), 427–440.

Jorm, A. F., Medway, J., Christensen, H., Korten, A. E., Jacomb, P. A. and Rodgers, B. (2000). Public beliefs about the helpfulness of interventions for depression: Effects on actions taken when experiencing anxiety and depression symptoms. *Australian & New Zealand Journal of Psychiatry, 34*(4), 619–626.

Jorm, A. F., Ross, A. M. and Colucci, E. (2018). Cross-cultural generalizability of suicide first aid actions: An analysis of agreement across expert consensus studies from a range of countries and cultures. *BMC Psychiatry, 18*(1), 1–8.

Kahlon, S., Neal, A. and Patterson, T. G. (2014). Experiences of cognitive behavioural therapy formulation in clients with depression. *The Cognitive Behaviour Therapist, 7,* e8 DOI: https://doi.org/10.1017/S1754470X14000075

Kanel, K. (2014). *A guide to crisis intervention.* Stamford, CT: Cengage Learning.

Keating, F. (2021). Black men's conversations about mental health through photos. *Qualitative Social Work, 20*(3), 755–772.

Kehoe, L. E., Hassen, S. C. and Sandage, S. J. (2016). Relational ecologies of psychotherapy: The influence of administrative attachment on therapeutic alliance. *Psychodynamic Practice, 22*(1), 6–21.

Kellezi, B., Earthy, S., Sleney, J., Beckett, K., Barnes, J., Christie, N., ... and Kendrick, D. (2020). What can trauma patients' experiences and perspectives tell us about the perceived quality of trauma care? A qualitative study set within the UK National Health Service. *Injury*, 51(5), 1231–1237.

Kelly, A. (2008). Living loss: an exploration of the internal space of liminality. *Mortality*, 13(4), 335–350.

Kelly, M., Svrcek, C., King, N., Scherpbier, A. and Dornan, T. (2020). Embodying empathy: A phenomenological study of physician touch, *Medical Education*, 54(5): 400–7.

Kelly, M.A., Nixon, L., McClurg, C., Scherpbier, A., King, N. and Dornan, T. (2018) Experience of touch in health care: A meta-ethnography across the health care professions, *Qualitative Health Research*, 28(2): 200–12.

Kenny, D. T. (2004). Constructions of chronic pain in doctor–patient relationships: bridging the communication chasm. *Patient Education and Counseling*, 52(3), 297–305.

Kentish-Barnes, N., Cohen-Solal, Z., Souppart, V., Galon, M., Champigneulle, B., Thirion, M., ... and Azoulay, E. (2017). 'It was the only thing I could hold onto, but…': Receiving a letter of condolence after loss of a loved one in the ICU: A qualitative study of bereaved relatives' experience. *Critical Care Medicine*, 45(12), 1965–1971.

Kerner, E. A. and Fitzpatrick, M. R. (2007). Integrating writing into psychotherapy practice: A matrix of change processes and structural dimensions. *Psychotherapy*, 44(3), 333–346.

Kidwell, M. C. and Kerig, P. K. (2021). To trust is to survive: Toward a developmental model of moral injury. *Journal of Child & Adolescent Trauma*, 1–17.

Kinnier, R. T., Hofsess, C., Pongratz, R. and Lambert, C. (2009). Attributions and affirmations for overcoming anxiety and depression. *Psychology and Psychotherapy: Theory, Research and Practice*, 82(2), 153–169.

Knight, Z. G. (2017). A proposed model of psychodynamic psychotherapy linked to Erik Erikson's eight stages of psychosocial development. *Clinical Psychology and Psychotherapy*, 24(5), 1047–1058.

Kjelsvik, M., Sekse, R. J. T., Moi, A. L., Aasen, E. M., Nortvedt, P. and Gjengedal, E. (2019). Beyond autonomy and care: Experiences of ambivalent abortion seekers. *Nursing Ethics*, 26(7–8), 2135–2146.

Kjelsvik, M., Tveit Sekse, R. J., Moi, A. L., Aasen, E. M. and Gjengedal, E. (2018). Walking on a tightrope – Caring for ambivalent women considering abortions in the first trimester. *Journal of Clinical Nursing*, 27(21–22), 4192–4202.

Klasen, M., Bhar, S. S., Ugalde, A. and Hall, C. (2017). Clients' perspectives on outcomes and mechanisms of bereavement counselling: A qualitative study. *Australian Psychologist*, 52(5), 363–371.

Klass, D. and Steffen, E. M. (eds.). (2017). *Continuing bonds in bereavement: New directions for research and practice*. New York: Routledge.

Klevan, T., Sommer, M., Borg, M., Karlsson, B., Sundet, R. and Kim, H. S. (2021). Part III: Recovery-oriented practices in community mental health and substance abuse services: A meta-synthesis. *International Journal of Environmental Research and Public Health*, 18(24), 13180.

Koenig, H. G. and Al Zaben, F. (2021). Moral injury: An increasingly recognized and widespread syndrome. *Journal of Religion and Health*, 60(5), 2989–3011.

Kohrt, B. A., Jordans, M. J., et al. (2015). Therapist competence in global mental health: Development of the Enhancing Assessment of Common Therapeutic factors (ENACT) rating scale. *Behaviour Research and Therapy*, 69, 11–21.

Kola, L., Kohrt, B. A., et al. (2021). COVID-19 mental health impact and responses in low-income and middle-income countries: reimagining global mental health. *The Lancet Psychiatry*, 8(6), 535–550.

Kosminsky, P. S. (2017). Working with continuing bonds from an attachment theoretical perspective. In D. Klass and E.M. Steffen (eds). *Continuing bonds in bereavement. New directions for theory and practice*. (pp. 112–128). New York: Routledge.

Kottler, J. A. (2018). *Change: What really leads to lasting personal transformation*. Oxford: Oxford University Press.

Krawczyk, M. and Rush, M. (2020). Describing the end-of-life doula role and practices of care: Perspectives from four countries. *Palliative Care and Social Practice*, 14, 2632352420973226.

Krebs, P., Norcross, J.C., Nicholson, J.M. and Prochaska, J.O. (2019) Stages of change. In J.C. Norcross and B.E. Wampold (eds.) *Psychotherapy Relationships that Work, Vol. 2: Evidence-Based Therapist Responsiveness*. 3rd edn. New York: Oxford University Press (pp. 296–328).

Kristoffersen, A. E., Broderstad, A. R., Musial, F. and Stub, T. (2019). Prevalence, and health-and sociodemographic associations for visits to traditional and complementary medical providers in the seventh survey of the Tromsö study. *BMC Complementary and Alternative Medicine*, *19*(1), 1–11.

Krupat, E., Frankel, R., Stein, T. and Irish, J. (2006). The Four Habits Coding Scheme: validation of an instrument to assess clinicians' communication behavior. *Patient Education and Counseling*, *62*(1), 38–45.

Kruzan, K. P. and Whitlock, J. (2019). Processes of change and nonsuicidal self-injury: A qualitative interview study with individuals at various stages of change. *Global Qualitative Nursing Research*, *6*, 2333393619852935.

Kubler-Ross, E. and Kessler, D. (2005). *On grief and grieving: Finding the meaning of grief through the five stages of loss*. New York: Scribner.

Kulich, K. R., Berggren, U. and Hallberg, L. R. M. (2000). Model of the dentist-patient consultation in a clinic specializing in the treatment of dental phobic patients: A qualitative study. *Acta Odontologica Scandinavica*, *58*(2), 63–71.

Kulich, K. R., Berggren, U. and Hallberg, L. R. M. (2003). A qualitative analysis of patient-centered dentistry in consultations with dental phobic patients. *Journal of Health Communication*, *8*(2), 171–187.

Kuyken, W., Padesky, C. A. and Dudley, R. (2008). The science and practice of case conceptualization. *Behavioural and Cognitive Psychotherapy*, *36*, 757–768.

Lacey, R. E. and Minnis, H. (2020). Practitioner review: twenty years of research with adverse childhood experience scores–advantages, disadvantages and applications to practice. *Journal of Child Psychology and Psychiatry*, *61*(2), 116–130.

Lahad, M. (2000). *Creative Supervision: the Use of Expressive Arts Methods in Supervision and Self-supervision*. London: Jessica Kingsley.

Lakshmin, P., Slootsky, V., Polatin, P. B. and Griffith, J. L. (2018). Testimonial psychotherapy in immigrant survivors of intimate partner violence: A case series. *Transcultural Psychiatry*, *55*(5), 585–600.

Langaard, K. and Toverud, R. (2009). 'Caring involvement': A core concept in youth counselling in school health services. *International Journal of Qualitative Studies on Health and Well-being*, *4*(4), 220–227.

Langaard, K. and Toverud, R. (2010). Youth counselling in school health services: The practice of 'intentional attentiveness'. *Vård i Norden*, *30*(4), 32–36.

Langås-Larsen, A., Salamonsen, A., Kristoffersen, A. E. and Stub, T. (2018). 'The prayer circles in the air': A qualitative study about traditional healer profiles and practice in Northern Norway. *International journal of circumpolar health*, *77*(1), 1476638.

Lange, K. W. (2021). Task sharing in psychotherapy as a viable global mental health approach in resource-poor countries and also in high-resource settings. *Global Health Journal*, *5*(3), 120–127.

Larance, L.Y. and Porter, M.L. (2004). Observations from practice: Support group membership as a process of social capital formation among female survivors of domestic violence. *Journal of Interpersonal Violence*, *19*, 676–690.

Larson E.B. and Yao. X. (2005) Clinical empathy as emotional labor in the patient–physician relationship. *Journal of the American Medical Association*, 293, 1100–6.

Larsson, B., Hildingsson, I., Ternström, E., Rubertsson, C. and Karlström, A. (2019). Women's experience of midwife-led counselling and its influence on childbirth fear: A qualitative study. *Women and Birth*, *32*(1), e88–e94.

Laurenzi, C. A., Skeen, S., Rabie, S., Coetzee, B. J., Notholi, V., Bishop, J., ... and Tomlinson, M. (2021). Balancing roles and blurring boundaries: Community health workers' experiences of navigating the crossroads between personal and professional life in rural South Africa. *Health & Social Care in the Community, 29*(5), 1249–1259.

Lawrence, W. et al. (2016). 'Making every contact count': evaluation of the impact of an intervention to train health and social care practitioners in skills to support health behaviour change. *Journal of Health Psychology, 21*(2), 138–151.

Levine, B. E. (2007). *Surviving America's depression epidemic. How to find morale, energy, and community in a world gone crazy.* White River Junction, VT: Chelsea Green Publishing.

Lewis, S. D., Henriksen Jr, R. C. and Watts, R. E. (2015). Intimate partner violence: The recovery experience. *Women & Therapy, 38(3-4),* 377–394.

Lave, J. and Wenger, E. (1991). *Situated learning: Legitimate peripheral participation.* Cambridge University Press.

Lawton, B. and Feltham, C. (eds.) (2000). *Taking Supervision Forward: Enquiries and Trends in Counselling and Psychotherapy.* London: Sage.

Leavey, G., Loewenthal, K. and King, M. (2007). Challenges to sanctuary: The clergy as a resource for mental health care in the community. *Social Science and Medicine, 65*(3), 548–559.

Lendrum, S. and Syme, G. (2004). *Gift of tears: A Practical Approach to Loss and Bereavement in Counselling and Psychotherapy.* 2nd edn. London: Brunner-Routledge.

Levenson, J. (2017). Trauma-informed social work practice. *Social Work, 62,* 105–113.

Levenson, J. (2020). Translating trauma-informed principles into social work practice. *Social Work, 65*(3), 288–298.

Lewchanin, S. and Zubrod, L.A. (2001). Choices in life: A clinical tool for facilitating midlife review. *Journal of Adult Development, 8,* 193–196.

Lian, O. S., Nettleton, S., Grange, H. and Dowrick, C. (2021). 'I'm not the doctor; I'm just the patient': Patient agency and shared decision-making in naturally occurring primary care consultations. *Patient Education and Counseling.* https://doi.org/10.1016/j.pec.2021.10.031

Liang, B., Goodman, L., Tummala-Narra, P. and Weintraub, S. (2005). A theoretical framework for understanding help-seeking processes among survivors of intimate partner violence. *American Journal of Community Psychology, 36,* 71–84.

Linden, S. and Grut, J. (2002) *The Healing Fields: Working with Psychotherapy and Nature to Rebuild Shattered Lives.* London: Frances Lincoln.

Lindgren, B.-M., Sture, A. and Graneheim, U.H. (2010) Held to ransom: Parents of self-harming adults describe their lived experience of professional care and caregivers. *International Journal on Qualitative Studies of Health and Well-being, 5,* 1–10.

Litz, B. T., Stein, N., Delaney, E., Lebowitz, L., Nash, W. P., Silva, C. and Maguen, S. (2009). Moral injury and moral repair in war Veterans: A preliminary model and intervention strategy. *Clinical Psychology Review, 29*(8), 695–706.

Loewenthal, D. (2013). *Phototherapy and Therapeutic Photography in a Digital Age.* London: Routledge.

Loewenthal, D. (2015). The therapeutic use of photographs in the United Kingdom criminal justice system. *European Journal of Psychotherapy and Counselling, 17,* 39–56.

Love, H. A. and Morgan, P. C. (2021). You can tell me anything: Disclosure of suicidal thoughts and behaviors in psychotherapy. *Psychotherapy, 58*(4), 533–543.

Lowes, L., Gregory, J. W. and Lyne, P. (2005). Newly diagnosed childhood diabetes: A psychosocial transition for parents? *Journal of Advanced Nursing, 50*(3), 253–261.

Lu, S., Li, W., Oldenburg, B., Wang, Y., Jorm, A. F., He, Y. and Reavley, N. J. (2020). Cultural adaptation of the mental health first aid guidelines for depression used in English-speaking countries for China: A Delphi expert consensus study. *BMC Psychiatry, 20*(1), 1–12.

Lukas, C. and Seiden, H.M. (2007). *Silent Grief: Living in the Wake of Suicide.* 2nd edn. London: Jessica Kingsley.

Lundahl, B., Droubay, B. A., Burke, B., Butters, R. P., Nelford, K., Hardy, C., ... and Bowles, M. (2019). Motivational interviewing adherence tools: A scoping review investigating content validity. *Patient Education and Counseling, 102*(12), 2145–2155.

Lynch, K., Baker, J., Lyons, M., Feeley, M., Hanlon, N., Walsh, J. and Cantillon, S. (2009). *Affective equality: Love, care and injustice*. London: Palgrave Macmillan.

Lynch, K., Kalaitzake, M. and Crean, M. (2021). Care and affective relations: Social justice and sociology. *The Sociological Review, 69*(1), 53–71.

Lytje, M. (2013). Handling bereavement in Danish schools–A system at a crossroad? *Bereavement Care, 32*(3), 131–139.

Machin, L. (2013). *Working with loss and grief: a theoretical and practical approach*. London: Sage.

Magwood, O., Leki, V. Y., Kpade, V., Saad, A., Alkhateeb, Q., Gebremeskel, A., ... and Pottie, K. (2019). Common trust and personal safety issues: A systematic review on the acceptability of health and social interventions for persons with lived experience of homelessness. *PloS One, 14*(12), e0226306.

Maisel, R., Epston, D. and Borden, A. (2004). *Biting the hand that starves you: Inspiring resistance to anorexia/bulimia*. New York: Norton.

Mancini, M. A. (2019). Strategic storytelling: An exploration of the professional practices of mental health peer providers. *Qualitative Health Research, 29*(9), 1266–1276.

Manthei, R. (2021). How common is brief counselling in New Zealand? *New Zealand Journal of Counselling, 41*(1), 5–20.

Mantri, S., Lawson, J. M., Wang, Z. and Koenig, H. G. (2020). Identifying moral injury in healthcare professionals: The moral injury symptom scale-HP. *Journal of Religion and Health, 59*(5), 2323–2340.

Markin, R. D. and Zilcha-Mano, S. (2018). Cultural processes in psychotherapy for perinatal loss: Breaking the cultural taboo against perinatal grief. *Psychotherapy, 55*(1), 20–26.

Marley, E. (2011). Self-help strategies to reduce emotional distress: What do people do and why? A qualitative study. *Counselling and Psychotherapy Research, 11*(4), 317–324.

Marsh, T. N., Coholic, D., Cote-Meek, S. and Najavits, L. M. (2015). Blending Aboriginal and Western healing methods to treat intergenerational trauma with substance use disorder in Aboriginal peoples who live in Northeastern Ontario, Canada. *Harm Reduction Journal, 12*(1), 1–12.

Marson, S. M. and McKinney Jr, R. E. (eds.). (2019). *The Routledge Handbook of Social Work Ethics and Values*. London: Routledge.

Marziliano, A., Tuman, M. and Moyer, A. (2020). The relationship between post-traumatic stress and post-traumatic growth in cancer patients and survivors: A systematic review and meta-analysis. *Psycho-Oncology, 29*(4), 604–616.

Maslach, C. (2000). *The Truth About Burnout: How Organizations Cause Personal Stress and What to Do About It*. San Franciso: Jossey-Bass.

Mascayano, F., Toso-Salman, J., et al. (2016). 'What matters most': Stigma towards severe mental disorders in Chile, a theory-driven, qualitative approach. *Revista de la Facultad de Ciencias Médicas, 72*(4), 250–260.

Matulich, B. (2017). *How to Do Motivational Interviewing: A Guidebook*. 2nd edn.

Mayland, C. R., Powell, R. A., Clarke, G., Ebenso, B. E. and Allsop, M. J. (2021). Bereavement care for ethnic minority communities: A systematic review of access to, models of, outcomes from, and satisfaction with, service provision. *PLoS One, 16*(6), e0252188.

Mazzer, K., O'Riordan, M., Woodward, A. and Rickwood, D. (2020). A systematic review of user expectations and outcomes of crisis support services. *Crisis: The Journal of Crisis Intervention and Suicide Prevention, 42*(6), 465-473.

McAdams, D.P. (1993) *The Stories We Live By: Personal Myths and the Making of the Self*. New York: William Murrow.

McConnellogue, S. and Storey, L. (2017). System constraints on efficacious teacher behaviours in school-based suicide prevention initiatives; a qualitative study of teacher views and experiences. *Emotional and Behavioural Difficulties, 22*(2), 174–183.

McLeish, J. and Redshaw, M. (2019). "Being the best person that they can be and the best mum": a qualitative study of community volunteer doula support for disadvantaged mothers before and after birth in England. *BMC Pregnancy and Childbirth, 19*(1), 1–11.

McLellan, J. (1991). Formal and informal counselling help: students' experiences. *British Journal of Guidance and Counselling, 19*, 149–158.

McLeod, J. and McLeod, J. (2015). Research on embedded counselling: An emerging topic of potential importance for the future of counselling psychology. *Counselling Psychology Quarterly, 28*(1), 27–43.

McLeod, J. (2016). Helping clients feel happier and combat depression. In Cooper, M. & Dryden, W. (eds) *The Handbook of Pluralistic Counselling and Psychotherapy*, London: Sage.

McLeod, J. and McLeod, J. (2016) Assessment and formulation in pluralistic counselling and psychotherapy. In Cooper, M. and Dryden, W. (eds.) *The Handbook of Pluralistic Counselling and Psychotherapy*. London: Sage.

McLeod, J. (2018). *Pluralistic therapy: distinctive features*. London: Routledge.

McLeod, J. (2019). *An Introduction to Counselling and Psychotherapy: Theory, Research and Practice*. 6th edn. London: Open University Press.

McLeod, J. and McLeod, J. (2020). The pluralistic approach. In N. Moller, A. Vossler, D.W. Jones and D. Kaposi (eds.) *Understanding mental health and counselling*. London: Sage. (pp. 341–368).

McLeod, J., and McLeod, J. (2022). *Counselling Skills: Theory, Research and Practice*. 3rd edition. London: Open University Press.

McNeill, B. W. and Worthen, V. (1989). The parallel process in psychotherapy supervision. *Professional Psychology: Research and Practice, 20*, 329–333.

McVeigh, M. J. and Heward-Belle, S. (2020). Necessary and good: A literature review exploring ethical issues for online counselling with children and young people who have experienced maltreatment. *Children Australia, 45*(4), 266–278.

Mearns, D. and Cooper, M. (2018). *Working at relational depth in counseling & psychotherapy*. 2nd edn. London: Sage.

Menzies Lyth, I. (1988). *Containing Anxiety in Institutions: Selected Essays*. London: Free Association.

Menzies Lyth, I. (1989). *The Dynamics of the Social: Selected Essays*. London: Free Association.

Menzies, I. (1959). A case-study in the functioning of social systems as a defence against anxiety: A report on a study of the nursing service of a general hospital. *Human Relations, 13*, 95–121.

Menzies, R. E., Sharpe, L. and Dar-Nimrod, I. (2019). The relationship between death anxiety and severity of mental illnesses. *British Journal of Clinical Psychology, 58*(4), 452–467.

Messina, N. P. and Schepps, M. (2021). Opening the proverbial 'can of worms' on trauma-specific treatment in prison: The association of adverse childhood experiences to treatment outcomes. *Clinical Psychology & Psychotherapy, 28*(5), 1210-1221.

Middleton, A., Gunn, J., Bassilios, B. and Pirkis, J. (2016). The experiences of frequent users of crisis helplines: A qualitative interview study. *Patient Education and Counseling, 99*(11), 1901–1906.

Middleton, J., Cunsolo, A., Jones-Bitton, A., Shiwak, I., Wood, M., Pollock, N., ... and Harper, S. L. (2020). 'We're people of the snow': Weather, climate change, and Inuit mental wellness. *Social Science & Medicine*, 113137.

Milani, A. and Leschied, A. (2020). Muslim women's service utilization for intimate partner violence: Front line service providers' perceptions of what constitutes a culturally informed response. *Health Care for Women International*, 1–21.

Miller, N. A. and Najavits, L. M. (2012). Creating trauma-informed correctional care: A balance of goals and environment. *European Journal of Psychotraumatology, 3*(1), 17246.

Miller, W. R. (2004). The phenomenon of quantum change. *Journal of Clinical Psychology, 60*(5), 453–460.

Miller, W.R. & Rollnick, S. (2012). *Motivational Interviewing: Preparing People for Change*. 3rd edn. New York: Guilford Press.

Milne, D., McAnaney, A., Pollinger, B., Bateman, K. and Fewster, E. (2004). Analysis of the forms, functions and facilitation of social support in one English county: A way for professionals to improve the quality of health care. *International Journal of Health Care Quality Assurance, 17*, 294–301.

Milne, D.L. (1999). *Social therapy: A guide to social support interventions for mental health practitioners*. Chichester: Wiley.

Milne, D.L. and Mullin, M. (1987). Is a problem shared a problem shaved? An evaluation of hairdressers and social support. *British Journal of Clinical Psychology, 26*, 69–70.

Mitchell, J. T. and Everly, G. S. (2006). Critical incident stress management in terrorist events and disasters. In L.A. Schien (eds). *Psychological effects of catastrophic disasters* (pp. 425–480). New York: Routledge.

Mjelve, L.H., Ulleberg, I. and Vonheim, K. (2020). 'What do I share?' Personal and private experiences in educational psychological counselling. *Scandinavian Journal of Educational Research, 64*(2), 181–194.

Mobbs, M. C. and Bonanno, G. A. (2018). Beyond war and PTSD: The crucial role of transition stress in the lives of military veterans. *Clinical Psychology Review, 59*, 137–144.

Moleski, S.M. and Kiselica, M.S. (2005) Dual relationships: a continuum ranging from the destructive to the therapeutic. *Journal of Counseling and Development, 83*, 3–11.

Mooney, J. (2021). How adults tell: a study of adults' experiences of disclosure to child protection social work services. *Child Abuse Review, 30*(3), 193-209.

Morley, G., Ives, J. and Bradbury-Jones, C. (2019a). Moral distress and austerity: An avoidable ethical challenge in healthcare. *Health Care Analysis, 27*(3), 185–201.

Morley, G., Ives, J., Bradbury-Jones, C. and Irvine, F. (2019b). What is 'moral distress'? A narrative synthesis of the literature. *Nursing Ethics, 26*(3), 646–662.

Morley, G., Field, R., Horsburgh, C. C., & Burchill, C. (2021). Interventions to mitigate moral distress: A systematic review of the literature. *International Journal of Nursing Studies, 121*, 103984.

Morris, S. E. and Block, S. D. (2015). Adding value to palliative care services: the development of an institutional bereavement program. *Journal of Palliative Medicine, 18*(11), 915–922.

Morris, S. E., Moment, A. and Thomas, J. D. (2020). Caring for bereaved family members during the COVID-19 pandemic: before and after the death of a patient. *Journal of Pain and Symptom Management, 60*(2), e70–e74.

Moult, A., Kingstone, T. and Chew-Graham, C. A. (2020). How do older adults understand and manage distress? A qualitative study. *BMC Family Practice, 21*(1). https://doi.org/10.1186/s12875-020-01152-7.

Moulton, L. (2016). *The naked consultation: A practical guide to primary care consultation skills.* 2nd edn. London: Routledge.

Mowll, J. (2017). Supporting family members to view the body after a violent or sudden death: A role for social work. *Journal of Social Work in End-of-life & Palliative Care, 13*(2–3), 94–112.

Moyers, T. B. and Miller, W. R. (2013). Is low therapist empathy toxic? *Psychology of Addictive Behaviors, 27*(3), 878–884.

Mulley, A., Trimble, C. and Elwyn, G. (2012). *Patients' preferences matter. Stop the silent misdiagnosis.* London: King's Fund.

Murphy, J.J. and Sparks, J.A. (2018). *Strengths-based therapy: distinctive features*. Abingdon: Routledge.

Myer, R. A., Whisenhunt, J. L. and James, R. K. (2021). *Crisis intervention ethics casebook*. New York: Wiley.

Myer, R., Lewis, J. and James, R. (2013). The introduction of a task model for crisis intervention. *Journal of Mental Health Counseling, 35*(2), 95–107.

Najavits, L. M. (2019). *Finding your best self: Recovery from addiction, trauma, or both.* 2nd edn. New York: Guilford Press.

Najavits, L. M., Weiss, R. D. and Shaw, S. R. (1997). The link between substance abuse and post-traumatic stress disorder in women: A research review. *American Journal on Addictions, 6*(4), 273–283.

Nam, I. (2016). Suicide bereavement and complicated grief: Experiential avoidance as a mediating mechanism. *Journal of Loss and Trauma, 21*(4), 325–334.

Naor, L. and Mayseless, O. (2020). How personal transformation occurs following a single peak experience in nature: A phenomenological account. *Journal of Humanistic Psychology, 60*(6), 865–888.

Narasimhan, M., Allotey, P. and Hardon, A. (2019). Self care interventions to advance health and wellbeing: a conceptual framework to inform normative guidance. *British Medical Journal, 365*.

Natvik, E., Råheim, M., Andersen, J. R. and Moltu, C. (2018). Living a successful weight loss after severe obesity. *International Journal of Qualitative Studies on Health and Well-being*, *13*(1), 1487762.

Neander, K. and Skott, C. (2008). Bridging the gap–The co-creation of a therapeutic process: Reflections by parents and professionals on their shared experiences of early childhood interventions. *Qualitative Social Work*, *7*(3), 289–309.

Neander, K. and Skott, C. (2006). Important meetings with important persons: Narratives from families facing adversity and their key figures. *Qualitative Social Work*, *5*(3), 295–311.

Neimeyer, R.A., Harris, D.L., Winokuer, H.R. and Thornton, G.F. (eds.)(2011). *Grief and bereavement in contemporary society: Bridging research and practice*. New York: Routledge.

Neimeyer, R. A. (2019). Meaning reconstruction in bereavement: Development of a research program. *Death Studies*, *43*(2), 79–91.

Neimeyer, R. A. (ed.) (2001). *Meaning reconstruction and the experience of loss*. Washington, DC: American Psychological Association.

Neimeyer, R. A. (ed.). (2012). *Techniques of grief therapy: Creative practices for counseling the bereaved*. London: Routledge.

Neimeyer, R., Klass, D. and Dennis, M. (2014). A social constructionist account of grief: Loss and the narration of meaning. *Death Studies*, *38*(8), 485–498.

Nelson, D., Price, E. and Zubrzycki, J. (2017). Critical social work with unaccompanied asylum-seeking young people: Restoring hope, agency and meaning for the client and worker. *International Social Work*, *60*(3), 601–613.

Ness, O., Borg, M., Semb, R. and Karlsson, B. (2014). 'Walking alongside': Collaborative practices in mental health and substance use care. *International Journal of Mental Health Systems*, *8*(1), 1–8.

Nezu, A. M. and Nezu, C. M. (2021). *Emotion-centered problem-solving therapy*. Washington, DC: American Psychological Association.

Nezu, A. M., Nezu, C. M. and D'Zurilla, T. (2013). *Problem-solving therapy: A treatment manual*. New York: Springer.

Nezu, A. M., Nezu, C. M. and Gerber, H. R. (2019). (Emotion-centered) problem-solving therapy: An update. *Australian Psychologist*, *54*(5), 361–371.

Nguyen, H. K. H., Martin, P., Chinh, N. Q. and Cong, D. D. (2010). Guiding change: Provider voices in youth pre-abortion counselling in urban Vietnam. *Culture, Health & Sexuality*, *12*(S1), S55–S71.

Nicholas, A., Pirkis, J. and Reavley, N. (2020). What responses do people at risk of suicide find most helpful and unhelpful from professionals and non-professionals? *Journal of Mental Health*, 1–10. https://doi.org/10.1080/09638237.2020.1818701

Nixon, G., Evans, K., Grant Kalischuk, R., Solowoniuk, J., McCallum, K. and Hagen, B. (2013). Female gambling, trauma, and the not good enough self: An interpretative phenomenological analysis. *International Journal of Mental Health and Addiction*, *11*(2), 214–231.

Nixon, G., Solowiniuk, J., Hagen, B. and Williams, R. J. (2005). 'Double trouble': The lived experience of problem and pathological gambling in later life. *Journal of Gambling Issues*, 14. https://hdl.handle.net/10133/374

Norcross, J. C. and Cooper, M. (2021). *Personalizing psychotherapy: Assessing and accommodating patient preferences*. Washington, DC: American Psychological Association.

Nyatsanza, M., Schneider, M., Davies, T. and Lund, C. (2016). Filling the treatment gap: Developing a task sharing counselling intervention for perinatal depression in Khayelitsha, South Africa. *BMC Psychiatry*, *16*(1), 1–12.

O'Brien, L. (2018). Engaging with and shaping nature: A nature-based intervention for those with mental health and behavioural problems at the Weston Birt arboretum in England. *International Journal of Environmental Research and Public Health*, *15*(10), 2214.

O'Connor, L. (2020). How social workers understand and use their emotions in practice: A thematic synthesis literature review. *Qualitative Social Work*, *19*(4), 645–662.

O'Kane, S. and Millar, R. (2002). A qualitative study of pastoral counselling of Catholic priests in Northern Ireland. *British Journal of Guidance & Counselling, 30*, 189–206.

O'Rourke, K. M., Yelland, J., Newton, M. and Shafiei, T. (2020). An Australian doula program for socially disadvantaged women: Developing realist evaluation theories. *Women and Birth, 33*(5), e438–e446.

Obholzer, A. and Roberts, V. Z. (eds.) (1994). *The Unconscious at Work: Individual and Organizational Stress in the Human Services*. London: Routledge.

Ogbe, E., Jbour, A., Rahbari, L., Unnithan, M. and Degomme, O. (2021). The potential role of network-oriented interventions for survivors of sexual and gender-based violence among asylum seekers in Belgium. *BMC Public Health, 21*(1), 1–15.

Ogden, J. and Hills, L. (2008). Understanding sustained behavior change: the role of life crises and the process of reinvention. *Health, 12*(4), 419–437.

Oldenburg, R. (1999). *The Great Good Place: Cafés, coffee shops, bookstores, bars, hair salons, and other hangouts in the heart of the community*. New York: Marlowe.

Oldenburg, R. and Brissett, D. (1982). The third place. *Qualitative Sociology, 5*(4), 265–284.

Olfson, M. and Marcus, S. C. (2010). National trends in outpatient psychotherapy. *American Journal of Psychiatry, 167*(12), 1456–1463.

Ong, B. and Buus, N. (2021). What does it mean to work 'dialogically' in Open Dialogue and Family Therapy? A narrative review. *Australian and New Zealand Journal of Family Therapy, 42*(3), 246-260.

Oral, R. et al. (2016). Adverse childhood experiences and trauma informed care: the future of health care. *Pediatric Research, 79*(1), 227–233.

Ort, D. (2020). Opening up while locked down: Client disclosure in correctional settings. *Journal of Clinical Psychology, 76*(2), 308–321.

Osatuke, K., Humphreys, C. L., Glick, M. J., Graff-Reed, R. L., McKenzie Mack, L. and Stiles, W. B. (2005). Vocal manifestations of internal multiplicity: Mary's voices. *Psychology and Psychotherapy: Research and Practice, 78*, 21–44.

Otaegui, A. (2021). 'In those times she was strong'. Singing the grief among the Ayoreo from the Paraguayan Chaco. *Death Studies, 45*(1), 9–18.

Ouansafi, I., Chibanda, D., Munetsi, E. and Simms, V. (2021). Impact of Friendship Bench problem-solving therapy on adherence to ART in young people living with HIV in Zimbabwe: A qualitative study. *PloS One, 16*(4), e0250074.

Page, I. S., Sparti, C., Santomauro, D. and Harris, M. G. (2021). Service demand for psychological interventions among Australian adults: a population perspective. *BMC Health Services Research, 21*(1), 1–10.

Page, S. and Wosket, V. (2014). *Supervising the counsellor: A cyclical model*. 3rd edn. London: Routledge.

Pagoto, S., Tulu, B., Agu, E., Waring, M. E., Oleski, J. L. and Jake-Schoffman, D. E. (2018). Using the habit app for weight loss problem solving: development and feasibility study. *JMIR mHealth and uHealth, 6*(6), e9801.

Papazoglou, K., Blumberg, D. M., Chiongbian, V. B., Tuttle, B. M., Kamkar, K., Chopko, B., ... and Koskelainen, M. (2020). The role of moral injury in PTSD among law enforcement officers: a brief report. *Frontiers in Psychology, 11*, 310.

Parker, G., Tavella, G. and Eyers, K. (2021). *Burnout: A guide to identifying burnout and pathways to recovery*. London: Allen and Unwin.

Parkes, C. M. (2006). *Love and loss: The roots of grief and its complications*. London: Routledge.

Parks, M., Priest, H., Dodd, P., Forrester-Jones, R., Bowman, T., Larkin, P. J., ... and Guerin, S. (2014). *Supporting people with intellectual disabilities experiencing loss and bereavement: Theory and compassionate practice*. London: Jessica Kingsley Publishers.

Parr, H. (2007). Mental health, nature work, and social inclusion. *Environment and Planning D: Society and Space, 25*(3), 537–561.

Parry, P. (2012). *How to Stay Sane*. London: School of Life.

Paterson, C., Evans, M., Bertschinger, R., Chapman, R., Norton, R. and Robinson, J. (2012). Communication about self-care in traditional acupuncture consultations: The co-construction of individualised support and advice. *Patient Education and Counseling, 89*(3), 467–475.

Payne, S., Jarrett, N., Wiles, R. and Field, D. (2002). Counselling strategies for bereaved people offered in primary care. *Counselling Psychology Quarterly, 15*(2), 161–177.

Pecanac, K. E., LeSage, E. and Stephens, E. (2021). How hospitalized older adults share concerns during daily rounds. *Patient Education and Counseling, 104*(7), 1652–1658.

Pedersen, G. A., Lakshmin, P. et al. (2020). Common factors in psychological treatments delivered by non-specialists in low-and middle-income countries: Manual review of competencies. *Journal of Behavioral and Cognitive Therapy, 30*(3), 165–186.

Peterman, J. S., Read, K. L., Wei, C. and Kendall, P. C. (2015). The art of exposure: Putting science into practice. *Cognitive and Behavioral Practice, 22*(3), 379–392.

Perry, P. (2019). *The book you wish your parents had read (and your children will be glad that you did)*. London: Penguin.

Perry, P. (2020). *Couch fiction: A graphic tale of psychotherapy*. London: Penguin.

Pierce, D. (2012). Problem solving therapy: Use and effectiveness in general practice. *Australian Family Physician, 41*(9), 676–679.

Potter, C. M., Jensen, D., Kinner, D. G., Tellez, M., Ismail, A. and Heimberg, R. G. (2016). Single-session computerized cognitive behavioral therapy for dental anxiety: A case series. *Clinical Case Studies, 15*(1), 3–17.

Poulsen, C. D., Wilson, P., Graungaard, A. H. and Overbeck, G. (2020). Dealing with parental concerns: A study of GPs' practice. *Patient Education and Counseling, 103*(12), 2430–2436.

Pound, C. and Jensen, L. R. (2018). Humanising communication between nursing staff and patients with aphasia: potential contributions of the Humanisation Values Framework. *Aphasiology, 32*(10), 1225–1249.

Pratt-Eriksson, D., Bergbom, I. and Lyckhage, E. D. (2014). Don't ask don't tell: Battered Women living in Sweden encounter with healthcare personnel and their experience of the care given. *International Journal of Qualitative Studies on Health and Well-being, 9*(1), 23166.

Priebe, S., Omer, S., Giacco, D. and Slade, M. (2014). Resource-oriented therapeutic models in psychiatry: Conceptual review. *The British Journal of Psychiatry, 204*(4), 256–261.

Puntis, S., Perfect, D., Kirubarajan, A., Bolton, S., Davies, F., Hayes, A., ... and Molodynski, A. (2018). A systematic review of co-responder models of police mental health 'street' triage. *BMC Psychiatry, 18*(1), 1–11.

Puntis, S., Perfect, D., Kirubarajan, A., Bolton, S., Davies, F., Hayes, A., ... and Molodynski, A. (2018). A systematic review of co-responder models of police mental health 'street' triage. *BMC Psychiatry, 18*(1), 1–11.

Putman, N. and Martindale, B. (eds).(2021).*Open Dialogue for Psychosis. Organising Mental Health Services to Prioritise Dialogue, Relationship and Meaning*. Lodnon: Routledge.

Qian, M., Gao, J., Yao, P. and Rodriguez, M. A. (2009). Professional ethical issues and the development of professional ethical standards in counseling and clinical psychology in China. *Ethics & Behavior, 19*(4), 290–309.

Quirk, M., Mazor, K., Haley, H., Philbin, M., Fischer, M., Sullivan, K. and Hatem, D. (2008) How patients perceive a doctor's caring attitude. *Patient Education and Counseling, 72*, 359–366.

Raine, S. and Kent, S. A. (2019). The grooming of children for sexual abuse in religious settings: Unique characteristics and select case studies. *Aggression and violent behavior, 48*, 180–189.

Raja, S., Hoersch, M., Rajagopalan, C. F. and Chang, P. (2014). Treating patients with traumatic life experiences: providing trauma-informed care. *The Journal of the American Dental Association, 145*(3), 238–245.

Rakel, D., Barrett, B., Zhang, Z., Hoeft, T., Chewning, B., Marchand, L. and Scheder, J. (2011). Perception of empathy in the therapeutic encounter: effects on the common cold. *Patient Education and Counseling, 85*(3), 390–397.

Rand, K., Vallis, M., Aston, M., Price, S., Piccinini-Vallis, H., Rehman, L. and Kirk, S. F. (2017). 'It is not the diet; it is the mental part we need help with.' A multilevel analysis of psychological, emotional, and social well-being in obesity. *International Journal of Qualitative Studies on Health and Well-being*, *12*(1), 1306421.

Rawlings, D., Litster, C., Miller-Lewis, L., Tieman, J. and Swetenham, K. (2020). The voices of death doulas about their role in end-of-life care. *Health & Social Care in the Community*, *28*(1), 12–21.

Read, S. (2007). *Bereavement counselling for people with learning disabilites. A manual to develop practice*. London: Quay Books.

Read, S. and Elliott, D. (2007). Exploring a continuum of support for bereaved people with intellectual disabilities: A strategic approach. *Journal of Intellectual Disabilities*, *11*(2), 167–181.

Read, S., Santatzoglou, S. and Wrigley, A. (eds.). (2018). *Loss, dying and bereavement in the criminal justice system*. New York: Routledge.

Reader, S. (2007). The other side of agency. *Philosophy*, *82*(4), 579–604.

Redhead, S., Johnstone, L. and Nightingale, J. (2015). Clients' experiences of formulation in cognitive behaviour therapy. *Psychology and Psychotherapy: Theory, Research and Practice*, *88*, 453–467.

Reeves, A. and Bond, T. (2021). *Standards and ethics for counselling in action*, 5th edn. London: Sage.

Reeves, A., Bowl, R., Wheeler, S. and Guthrie, E. (2004). The hardest words: Exploring the dialogue of suicide in the counselling process. A discourse analysis. *Counselling and Psychotherapy Research*, *4*(1), 62–71.

Regehr, C., Bogo, M., LeBlanc, V. R., Baird, S., Paterson, J. and Birze, A. (2016). Suicide risk assessment: Clinicians' confidence in their professional judgment. *Journal of Loss and Trauma*, *21*(1), 30–46.

Rennie, D.L. (1998). *Person–centred Counselling: An Experiential Approach*. London: Sage.

Renzenbrink, I. (2021). *An Expressive Arts Approach to Healing Loss and Grief: Working Across the Spectrum of Loss with Individuals and Communities*. London: Jessica Kingsley Publishers.

Reynaert, D., Dijkstra, P., Knevel, J., Hartman, J., Tirions, M., Geraghty, C., ... and van den Hoven, R. (2019). Human rights at the heart of the social work curriculum. *Social Work Education*, *38*(1), 21–33.

Richardson, K., Berman, D. and Galyean, E. (2020). Check-in groups: A novel structured Crisis Intervention Model. *Crisis, Stress, and Human Resilience: An International Journal*, *2*(3), 96–111.

Roberts, A. R. and Ottens, A. J. (2005). The seven-stage crisis intervention model: A road map to goal attainment, problem solving, and crisis resolution. *Brief Treatment and Crisis Intervention*, *5*(4), 329.

Roberts, L., White, D., David, L., Vadher, B. and Stoner, N. (2021). The development and testing of a novel Cognitive Behavioural Therapy (CBT)-based intervention to support medicines-related consultations for healthcare professionals. *International Journal of Pharmacy Practice*, *29*(Supplement 1), i2–i3.

Rodgers, M., Thomas, E. W. S., Dalton, J. E., Harden, M. and Eastwood, A. J. (2019). Police-related triage interventions for mental health-related incidents: A rapid evidence synthesis. *Health Services and Delivery Research*.

Rodgers, S. and Hassan, S. (2021). Therapeutic Crisis Intervention in Schools (TCI-S): An international exploration of a therapeutic framework to reduce critical incidents and improve teacher and student emotional competence in schools. *Journal of Psychologists and Counsellors in Schools*, 1–8.

Rodríguez-Muñoz, A., Moreno-Jiménez, B., Sanz Vergel, A. I. and Garrosa Hernández, E. (2010). Post-traumatic symptoms among victims of workplace bullying: Exploring gender differences and shattered assumptions. *Journal of Applied Social Psychology*, *40*(10), 2616–2635.

Rosen, C. S., Greene, C. J., Young, H. E. and Norris, F. H. (2010). Tailoring disaster mental health services to diverse needs: an analysis of 36 crisis counseling projects. *Health & social Work*, *35*(3), 211–220.

Ross, A. (2003) *Counselling Skills for Church and Faith Community Workers*. London: Open University Press.
Rothschild B (2000). *The body remembers: The psychophysiology of trauma and trauma treatment*. New York: W.W. Norton and Company.
Rothschild, B. (2006). *Help for the helper: The psychophysiology of compassion fatigue and vicarious trauma*. New York: W.W. Norton.
Royce, T. (2005). The negotiator and the bomber: Analyzing the critical role of active listening in crisis negotiations. *Negotiation Journal*, *21*(1), 5–27.
Rushton, C. H., Thomas, T. A., Antonsdottir, I. M., Nelson, K. E., Boyce, D., Vioral, A., ... and Hanson, G. C. (2022). Moral injury and moral resilience in health care workers during COVID-19 pandemic. *Journal of Palliative Medicine*, *25*(5), 712-719.
Russo-Netzer, P. and Davidov, J. (2020). Transformative life experience as a glimpse into potentiality. *Journal of Humanistic Psychology*, 0022167820937487.
Sabatello, M., Burke, T. B., McDonald, K. E. and Appelbaum, P. S. (2020). Disability, ethics, and health care in the COVID-19 pandemic. *American Journal of Public Health*, *110*(10), 1523–1527.
Saleebey, D. (2000). Power in the people: Strengths and hope. *Advances in Social Work*, *1*(2), 127–136.
Saleebey, D. (2012). *The strengths perspective in social work practice*. 6th edn. New York: Pearson.
Salkovskis, P. M. (2007). Cognitive-behavioural treatment for panic. *Psychiatry*, *6*(5), 193–197.
Sandage, S. J., Moon, S. H., Rupert, D., Paine, D. R., Ruffing, E. G., Kehoe, L. E., ... and Hassen, S. C. (2017). Relational dynamics between psychotherapy clients and clinic administrative staff: A pilot study. *Psychodynamic Practice*, *23*(3), 249–268.
Scantlebury, A., Parker, A., Booth, A., McDaid, C. and Mitchell, N. (2018). Implementing mental health training programmes for non-mental health trained professionals: A qualitative synthesis. *PloS One*, *13*(6), e0199746.
Scheel, M.J., Davis, C.K. and Henderson, J.D. (2013). Therapist use of client strengths: A qualitative study of positive processes, *The Counseling Psychologist*, *41*(3): 392–427.
Schein, E.H. (2004). *Organizational Culture and Leadership*. 3rd edn. San Franciso, CA: Jossey-Bass.
Schilling, C., Weidner, K., Brähler, E., Glaesmer, H., Häuser, W. and Pöhlmann, K. (2016). Patterns of childhood abuse and neglect in a representative German population sample. *PloS one*, *11*(7), e0159510.
Schilling, C., Weidner, K., Schellong, J., Joraschky, P. and Pöhlmann, K. (2015). Patterns of childhood abuse and neglect as predictors of treatment outcome in inpatient psychotherapy: A typological approach. *Psychopathology*, *48*(2), 91–100.
Schreiber, S. (1995). Migration, traumatic bereavement and transcultural aspects of psychological healing: loss and grief of a refugee woman from Begamer County in Ethiopia. *British Journal of Medical Psychology*, *68*, 135–142.
Schreier, B. A., Anderson, C. L., Galligan, P. K., Greenbaum, B., Corkery, J., Schnelle, T., ... and Kivlighan III, D. M. (2021). Embedded therapists: Who do they serve? How are they funded? And where are they housed? A foundational survey of emerging models. *Journal of College Student Psychotherapy*, 1–11. https://doi.org/10.1080/87568225.2021.1913686
Schut, H.A., and Stroebe, M. S. (2005). Interventions to enhance adaptation to bereavement. *Journal of Palliative Medicine*, *8*(supplement 1), s-140.
Schut, H. A., Stroebe, M. S., van den Bout, J. and De Keijser, J. (1997). Intervention for the bereaved: Gender differences in the efficacy of two counselling programmes. *British Journal of Clinical Psychology*, *36*(1), 63–72.
Seden, J. (2005). *Counselling skills in social work practice*. 2nd edn. Maidenhead: Open University Press.
Seema, R. (2020). The counselling self-efficacy scale for teachers: Action research. *Educational Action Research*, 1–15.
Sennett, R. (1998). *The corrosion of character: The personal consequences of work in the new capitalism*. New York: WW Norton & Company.

Segre, L. S., Stasik, S. M.' O'Hara, M. W. and Arndt, S. (2010). Listening visits: An evaluation of the effectiveness and acceptability of a home-based depression treatment. *Psychotherapy Research*, *20*(6), 712–721.

Seikkula, J. and Olson, M. E. (2003). The open dialogue approach to acute psychosis: Its poetics and micropolitics. *Family Process*, *42*(3), 403–418.

Seikkula, J. and Trimble, D. (2005). Healing elements of therapeutic conversation: Dialogue as an embodiment of love. *Family process*, *44*(4), 461–475.

Shahmalak, U., Blakemore, A., Waheed, M. W. and Waheed, W. (2019). The experiences of lay health workers trained in task-shifting psychological interventions: a qualitative systematic review. *International Journal of Mental Health Systems*, *13*(1), 1–15.

Shakespeare, J., Blake, F. and Garcia, J. (2006). How do women with postnatal depression experience listening visits in primary care? A qualitative interview study. *Journal of Reproductive and Infant Psychology*, *24*(02), 149–162.

Shdaimah, C. S. and McGarry, B. (2018). Social workers' use of moral entrepreneurship to enact professional ethics in the field: Case studies from the social justice profession. *British Journal of Social Work*, *48*(1), 21–36.

Shields, C., Kavanagh, M. and Russo, K. (2017). A qualitative systematic review of the bereavement process following suicide. *OMEGA*, *74*(4), 426–454.

Shreffler, K. M. (2017). Contextual understanding of lower fertility among US women in professional occupations. *Journal of Family Issues*, *38*(2), 204–224.

Sikveland, R.O., Kevoe-Feldman, H. and Stokoe. K. (2022). *Crisis talk negotiating with individuals in crisis*. London: Routledge.

Silverman, G.S. (2021). Saying kaddish: Meaning-making and continuing bonds in American Jewish mourning ritual. *Death Studies*, *45*(1), 19–28.

Silverman, G.S., Baroiller, A. and Hemer, S.R. (2021). Culture and grief: Ethnographic perspectives on ritual, relationships and remembering. *Death Studies*, *45*(1), 1–8.

Simpson, A., Oster, C. and Muir-Cochrane, E. (2018). Liminality in the occupational identity of mental health peer support workers: A qualitative study. *International Journal of Mental Health Nursing*, *27*(2), 662–671.

Singer, J. B., Erbacher, T. A. and Rosen, P. (2019). School-based suicide prevention: A framework for evidence-based practice. *School Mental Health*, *11*(1), 54–71.

Singer, S., Götze, H., Möbius, C., Witzigmann, H., Kortmann, R.-D., Lehmann, A. et al. (2009). Quality of care and emotional support from the inpatient cancer patint's perspective. *Langenbecks Archives of Surgery*, *394*, 723–731.

Sinha, A., Bhola, P., Raguram, A. and Chandra, P. S. (2017). 'Power positions are embedded in our minds': Focus group discussions on psychotherapy ethics in India. *International Journal of Culture and Mental Health*, *10*(2), 217–227.

Sjöberg, M., Beck, I., Rasmussen, B. H. and Edberg, A. K. (2018). Being disconnected from life: Meanings of existential loneliness as narrated by frail older people. *Aging & Mental Health*, *22*(10), 1357–1364.

Skatvedt, A. (2017). The importance of 'empty gestures' in recovery: Being human together. *Symbolic Interaction*, *40*(3), 396–413.

Skatvedt, A. and Schou, K. C. (2008). The beautiful in the commonplace. *European Journal of Cultural Studies*, *11*(1), 83–100.

Skatvedt, A. and Schou, K. C. (2010). The potential of the commonplace: A sociological study of emotions, identity and therapeutic change. *Scandinavian Journal of Public Health*, *38*(5), 81–87.

Skovholt, T.S. and Trotter-Mathison, M. (2016). *The resilient practitioner: Burnout and compassion fatigue prevention and self-care strategies for the helping professions*. New York: Routledge.

Slade, M. and Longden, E. (2015). Empirical evidence about recovery and mental health. *BMC Psychiatry*, *15*(1), 1–14.

Slade, M., Rennick-Egglestone, S., Blackie, L., Llewellyn-Beardsley, J., Franklin, D., Hui, A., ... and Deakin, E. (2019). Post-traumatic growth in mental health recovery: Qualitative study of narratives. *BMJ Open*, *9*(6), e029342.

Slade, P., Balling, K., Sheen, K. and Houghton, G. (2019). Establishing a valid construct of fear of childbirth: Findings from in-depth interviews with women and midwives. *BMC Pregnancy and Childbirth, 19*(1), 1–12.

Sloan, D. M. and Marx, B. P. (2018). Maximizing outcomes associated with expressive writing. *Clinical Psychology: Science and Practice, 25*(1), e12231. https://doi.org/10.1111/cpsp.12231

Small, N. (2001). Theories of grief: a critical review. In J. Hockey, J. Katz and N. Small (eds.) *Grief, mourning and death ritual*. Maidenhead: Open University Press.

Smigelsky, M. A. and Neimeyer, R. A. (2018). Performative retelling: Healing community stories of loss through playback theatre. *Death Studies, 42*(1), 26–34.

Smith, E.J. (2006) The strength-based counseling model, *The Counseling Psychologist, 34*(1), 13–79.

Smith, L., Hill, N. and Kokanovic, R. (2015). Experiences of depression, the role of social support and its impact on health outcomes. *Journal of Mental Health, 24*(6), 342–346.

Smith, M., Monteux, S. and Cameron, C. (2021). Trauma: An ideology in search of evidence and its implications for the social in social welfare. *Scottish Affairs, 30*(4), 472–492.

Smith, T. S. (2021). Therapeutic taskscapes and craft geography: Cultivating well-being and atmospheres of recovery in the workshop. *Social & Cultural Geography, 22*(2), 151–169.

Snaman, J. M., Kaye, E. C., Torres, C., Gibson, D. V. and Baker, J. N. (2016). Helping parents live with the hole in their heart: The role of health care providers and institutions in the bereaved parents' grief journeys. *Cancer, 122*(17), 2757–2765.

Snyder, J.A. (1971). The use of gatekeepers in crisis management. *Bulletin of Suicidology, 8*, 39–44.

Soggiu, A. S. L., Klevan, T., Davidson, L. and Karlsson, B. (2020). A sort of friend: narratives from young people and parents about collaboration with a mental health outreach team. *Social Work in Mental Health, 18*(4), 383–397.

Stein, D. M. and Lambert, M. J. (1984). On the relationship between therapist experience and psychotherapy outcome. *Clinical Psychology Review, 4*(2), 127–142.

Steffen, E. M., Timotijevic, L. and Coyle, A. (2020). A qualitative analysis of psychosocial needs and support impacts in families affected by young sudden cardiac death: The role of community and peer support. *European Journal of Cardiovascular Nursing, 19*(8), 681–690.

Steffen, E. and Coyle, A. (2017). 'I thought they should know... that daddy is not completely gone.' A case study of sense-of-presence experiences in bereavement and family meaning-making. *OMEGA-Journal of Death and Dying, 74*(4), 363–385.

Stein, T. Frankel, R.M. and Krupat, E. (2005). Enhancing clinician communication skills in a large healthcare organization: a longtitudinal case study. *Patient Education and Counseling, 58*, 4–12.

Stein, T., Krupat, E. and Frankel, R.M. (2010). *Talking with patients. Using the Four Habits Model*. San Franciso, CA: Kaiser Permanente.

Stephen, A. I., Macduff, C., Petrie, D. J., Tseng, F.-M., Schut, H., Skář, S., Corden, A., Birrell, J., Wang, S., Newsom, C. and Wilson, S. (2015). The economic cost of bereavement in Scotland. *Death Studies, 39*(1–5), 151–157.

Stevens, K. and McLeod, J. (2019). Yoga as an adjunct to trauma-focused counselling for survivors of sexual violence: a qualitative study. *British Journal of Guidance & Counselling, 47*(6), 682–697.

Stevenson, B. J. (2020). Psychotherapy for veterans navigating the military-to-civilian transition: A case study. *Journal of Clinical Psychology, 76*(5), 896–904.

Stiggelbout , A.M., Pieterse, A.H. and De Haes, J.C. (2015). Shared decision making: Concepts, evidence, and practice. *Patient Education and Counseling, 98*, 1172–1179.

Stiles, W. B. (2001). Assimilation of problematic experiences. *Psychotherapy, 38*, 462–465.

Stiles, W. B. (2011). Coming to terms. *Psychotherapy Research, 21*, 367–384.

Stiver, I.P., Rosen, W., Surrey, J. and Miller, J.B. (2008). Creative moments in Relational-Cultural therapy. *Women & Therapy, 31*(2–4), 7–29.

Stoll, J., Müller, J. A. and Trachsel, M. (2020). Ethical issues in online psychotherapy: A narrative review. *Frontiers in Psychiatry, 10*, 993.

Stoll, M. and McLeod, J. (2020). Guidance teachers' and support staff's experience of working with pupils with mental health difficulties in two secondary schools: an IPA study. *British Journal of Guidance & Counselling*, 48(6), 815–825.

Storer, H. L., Rodriguez, M. and Franklin, R. (2021). 'Leaving was a process, not an event': The lived experience of dating and domestic violence in 140 characters. *Journal of interpersonal violence*, 36(11–12), NP6553–NP6580.

Streng, J. M., Rhodes, S., Ayala, G., Eng, E., Arceo, R. and Phipps, S. (2004). Realidad Latina: Latino adolescents, their school, and a university use photovoice to examine and address the influence of immigration. *Journal of Interprofessional Care*, 18(4), 403–415.

Stroebe, M. (2018). The poetry of grief: beyond scientific portrayal. *OMEGA-Journal of Death and Dying*, 78(1), 67–96.

Stroebe, M. S. and Schut, H. (2001). Models of coping with bereavement: A review. In M. S. Stroebe, R. O. Hansson, W. Stroebe and H. Schut (eds.), *Handbook of bereavement research: Consequences, coping, and care* (pp. 375–403). Washington, DC: American Psychological Association.

Stroebe, M., Schut, H. and Boerner, K. (2017). Cautioning health-care professionals: Bereaved persons are misguided through the stages of grief. *OMEGA-Journal of Death and Dying*, 74(4), 455–473.

Stroebe, M.S. and Schut, H.W. (1999). The dual process model of coping with bereavement: Rationale and description. *Death Studies*, 23, 197–224.

Stroebe, W., Schut, H. and Stroebe, M. (2005). Grief work, disclosure and counselling: Do they help the bereaved? *Clinical Psychology Review*, 25, 395–414.

Ström, I., Söderman, A. and Johansson, M. (2021). Experiences of working as a cultural doula in Sweden: An interview study. *European Journal of Midwifery*, 5. https://doi.org/10.18332%2Fejm%2F137365

Stylianou, A. M., Counselman-Carpenter, E. and Redcay, A. (2021). 'My sister is the one that made me stay above water': How social supports are maintained and strained when survivors of intimate partner violence reside in emergency shelter programs. *Journal of Interpersonal Violence*, 36(13–14), 6005–6028.

Sucala, M., Cuijpers, P., Muench, F., Cardoş, R., Soflau, R., Dobrean, A., ... and David, D. (2017). Anxiety: There is an app for that. A systematic review of anxiety apps. *Depression and Anxiety*, 34(6), 518–525.

Sue, D. W. et al. (2007). Racial microaggressions in everyday life: implications for clinical practice. *American Psychologist*, 62(4), 271–286.

Sue, D. W. and Spanierman, L. (2020). *Microaggressions in everyday life*. Hoboken, NJ: John John Wiley & Sons.

Sue, D. W., Calle, C. Z., Mendez, N., Alsaidi, S. and Glaeser, E. (2021). *Microintervention Strategies: What You Can Do to Disarm and Dismantle Individual and Systemic Racism and Bias*. Hoboken, NJ: John Wiley and Sons.

Sugarman, L (2004). *Counselling and the Life Course*. London: Sage.

Sugarman, L. (2016). Designing your life map. In B. Douglas, R. Woolfe, S. Strawbridge, E. Kasket and V. Galbraith (eds). *Handbook of Counselling Psychology*. 4th edn. London: Sage.

Sullivan, C. M. (2018). Understanding how domestic violence support services promote survivor well-being: A conceptual model. *Journal of Family Violence*, 33(2), 123–131.

Sundet, R., Kim, H. S., Karlsson, B. E., Borg, M., Sælòr, K. T. and Ness, O. (2020). A heuristic model for collaborative practice–Part 1: a meta-synthesis of empirical findings on collaborative strategies in community mental health and substance abuse practice. *International Journal of Mental Health Systems*, 14(1), 1–16.

Talmon, S. (1990). *Single session therapy: Maximising the effect of the first (and often only) therapeutic encounter*. San Franciso: Jossey-Bass.

Tandon, S. D., Johnson, J., et al. (2021). Comparing the effectiveness of home visiting paraprofessionals and mental health professionals delivering a postpartum depression preventive intervention: A cluster-randomized non-inferiority clinical trial. *Archives of Women's Mental Health*, 24(4), 629–640.

Tavella, G. and Parker, G. (2020). A qualitative re-examination of the key features of burnout. *The Journal of Nervous and Mental Disease*, 208(6), 452–458.

Taylor, A. K., Gregory, A., Feder, G. and Williamson, E. (2019). 'We're all wounded healers': A qualitative study to explore the well-being and needs of helpline workers supporting survivors of domestic violence and abuse. *Health & Social Care in the Community*, 27(4), 856–862.

Taylor, C. (1989). *Sources of the self: The Making of modern identity*. Cambridge, MA: Harvard University Press.

Tew, J. (2013). Recovery capital: What enables a sustainable recovery from mental health difficulties? *European Journal of Social Work*, 16(3), 360–374.

Thompson, B. E. and Neimeyer, R. A. (eds.) (2014). *Grief and the expressive arts: Practices for creating meaning*. New York: Routledge.

Thompson, S. J., Pollio, D. E., Eyrich, K., Bradbury, E. and North, C. S. (2004). Successfully exiting homelessness: Experiences of formerly homeless mentally ill individuals. *Evaluation and Program Planning*, 27(4), 423–431.

Tinati, T., Lawrence, W., Ntani, G., Black, C., Cradock, S., Jarman, M., ... and Barker, M. (2012). Implementation of new Healthy Conversation Skills to support lifestyle changes–what helps and what hinders? Experiences of Sure Start Children's Centre staff. *Health & Social Care in the Community*, 20(4), 430–437.

Tischler, V., Edwards, V. and Vostanis, P. (2009). Working therapeutically with mothers who experience the trauma of homelessness: An opportunity for growth. *Counselling and Psychotherapy Research*, 9(1), 42–46.

Todres, L., Galvin, K.T. and Holloway, I. (2009). The humanization of healthcare: A value framework for qualitative research. *International Journal of Qualitative Studies on Health and Well-being*, 4, 68–77.

Toerien, M. (2021). When do patients exercise their right to refuse treatment? A conversation analytic study of decision-making trajectories in UK neurology outpatient consultations. *Social Science & Medicine*, 290, 114278.

Toerien, M., Reuber, M., Shaw, R. and Duncan, R. (2018). Generating the perception of choice: the remarkable malleability of option-listing. *Sociology of Health and Illness*, 40(7), 1250–1267.

Tonning Otterlei, M. and Studsrød, I. (2022). Breaking bad news: Child welfare workers' informing parents of care order proceedings. *Child and Family Social Work*, 27(2), 121-131.

Topor, A., Bøe, T. D. and Larsen, I. B. (2018). Small things, micro-affirmations and helpful professionals everyday recovery-orientated practices according to persons with mental health problems. *Community Mental Health Journal*, 54(8), 1212–1220.

Topor, A., Borg, M., Mezzina, R., Sells, D., Marin, I. and Davidson, L. (2006). Others: The role of family, friends, and professionals in the recovery process. *Archives of Andrology*, 9(1), 17–37.

Topor, A., von Greiff, N. and Skogens, L. (2021). Micro-affirmations and recovery for persons with mental health and alcohol and drug problems: User and professional experience-based practice and knowledge. *International Journal of Mental Health and Addiction*, 19, 374–385.

Torres, W. J. and Bergner, R. M. (2012). Severe public humiliation: Its nature, consequences, and clinical treatment. *Psychotherapy*, 49(4), 492–501.

Trachsel, M. (2019). How to strengthen patients' meaning response by an ethical informed consent in psychotherapy. *Frontiers in Psychology*, 10, 1747.

Trygged, S. (2012). Embedded counselling in advisory work with clients in debt. *Journal of Social Work Practice*, 26(2), 245–258.

Tsai, M., Callaghan, G. M. and Kohlenberg, R. J. (2013) The use of awareness, courage, therapeutic love, and behavioral interpretation in Functional Analytic Psychotherapy. *Psychotherapy*, 50, 366–370.

Tsai, M., Kohlenberg, R., Kanter, J., Holman, G., and Plummer Loudon, M. (2012) *Functional analytic therapy: Distinctive features*. London: Routledge.

Tsai, M., Yard, S. and Kohlenberg, R. J. (2014) Functional analytic psychotherapy: A behavioral relational approach to treatment. *Psychotherapy*, 51, 364–371.

Tseng, F.-M., Petrie, D., Wang, S., Macduff, C. and Stephen, A. I. (2018). The impact of spousal bereavement on hospitalisations: Evidence from the Scottish longitudinal study. *Health Economics*, 27(2), e120–e138.

Tummala-Narra, P. (2015). Cultural competence as a core emphasis of psychoanalytic psychotherapy. *Psychoanalytic Psychology*, 32(2), 275–287.

Turner, K. M., Chew-Graham, C., Folkes, L. and Sharp, D. (2010). Women's experiences of health visitor delivered listening visits as a treatment for postnatal depression: A qualitative study. *Patient Education and Counseling*, 78(2), 234–239.

Twigg, S. (2020). Clinical event debriefing: a review of approaches and objectives. *Current Opinion in Pediatrics*, 32(3), 337–342.

Ueno, Y., Kako, M., Ohira, M. and Okamura, H. (2020). Shared decision-making for women facing an unplanned pregnancy: A qualitative study. *Nursing and Health Sciences*, 22(4), 1186–1196.

Ungar, M., Barter, K., McConnell, S.M., Tutty, L.M. and Fairholm, J. (2009). Patterns of abuse disclosure among youth. *Qualitative Social Work*, 8, 341–356.

Van der Kolk, B. (2015). *The Body Keeps the Score: Brain, Mind, and Body in the Healing of Trauma*. London: Penguin.

Van Deurzen, E. (2021). *Rising from Existential Crisis: Life beyond calamity*. Monmouth: PCCS Books.

Vanderstichelen, S., Cohen, J., Van Wesemael, Y., Deliens, L. and Chambaere, K. (2020). The liminal space palliative care volunteers occupy and their roles within it: A qualitative study. *BMJ Supportive and Palliative Care*, 10(3), e28–e28.

Veilleux, J. C. and Bilsky, S. A. (2016). After a client death: Suicide postvention recommendations for training programs and clinics. *Training and Education in Professional Psychology*, 10(4), 214.

Velsor-Friedrich, B. and Hogan, N. S. (2021). Being unprepared: A grounded theory of the transition of asthma self-care in college students. *Journal of Pediatric Nursing*, 61, 305–311.

Verhey, I. J., Ryan, G. K., Scherer, N. and Magidson, J. F. (2020). Implementation outcomes of cognitive behavioural therapy delivered by non-specialists for common mental disorders and substance-use disorders in low-and middle-income countries: A systematic review. *International Journal of Mental Health Systems*, 14, 1–14.

Walfish, S., Barnett, J. E., Marlyere, K. and Zielke, R. (2010). 'Doc, there's something I have to tell you': Patient disclosure to their psychotherapist of unprosecuted murder and other violence. *Ethics & Behavior*, 20(5), 311–323.

Wallén, A., Eberhard, S. and Landgren, K. (2021). The experiences of counsellors offering problem-solving therapy for common mental health issues at the youth friendship bench in Zimbabwe. *Issues in Mental Health Nursing*, 1–18.

Walsh, C. A., Rutherford, G. E., Sarafincian, K. N. and Sellmer, S. E. (2010). Making meaning together: an exploratory study of therapeutic conversation between helping professionals and homeless shelter residents. *Qualitative Report*, 15(4), 932–947.

Walter, T. (2017). How continuing bonds have been framed across millennia. In D. Klass and E.M. Steffen (eds). *Continuing bonds in bereavement. New directions for research and practice*. New York: Routledge.

Walter, T. (1999). A new model of grief: bereavement and biography. *Mortality*, 1, 7-25.

Wampold, B. E. (2019). A smorgasbord of PTSD treatments: What does this say about integration? *Journal of Psychotherapy Integration*, 29(1), 65–71.

Wampold, B. E., Imel, Z. E., Laska, K. M., Benish, S., Miller, S. D., Flückiger, C., ... Budge, S. (2010). Determining what works in the treatment of PTSD. *Clinical Psychology Review*, 30, 923–933.

Ward, E. C. (2005). Keeping it real: A grounded theory study of African American clients engaging in counseling at a community mental health agency. *Journal of Counseling Psychology*, 52(4), 471–481.

Warrender, D., Bain, H., Murray, I. and Kennedy, C. (2021). Perspectives of crisis intervention for people diagnosed with 'borderline personality disorder': An integrative review. *Journal of Psychiatric and Mental Health Nursing*, 28(2), 208–236.

Wasil, A., Venturo-Conerly, K., Shingleton, R. and Weisz, J. (2019). The motivating role of recovery self-disclosures from therapists and peers in eating disorder recovery: Perspectives of recovered women. *Psychotherapy*, 56(2), 170–180.

Watkins, L. E., Sprang, K. R. and Rothbaum, B. O. (2018). Treating PTSD: A review of evidence-based psychotherapy interventions. *Frontiers in Behavioral Neuroscience*, 12, 258.

Watson, T., Hodgson, D., Watts, L. and Waters, R. (2021). Historiography of empathy: Contributions to social work research and practice. *Qualitative Social Work*. https://doi.org/10.1177%2F14733250211033012

Weaks, D. O. T., Wilkinson, H. and McLeod, J.. (2015). Daring to tell: the importance of telling others about a diagnosis of dementia. *Ageing & Society*, 35(4), 765–784.

Weaks, D., McLeod, J. and Wilkinson, H (2006). Dementia. *Therapy Today*, 17, 12–15.

Wearn, A., Clouder, L., Barradell, S. and Neve, H. (2019). A qualitative research synthesis exploring professional touch in healthcare practice using the threshold concept framework. *Advances in Health Sciences Education*, 25(3), 731–54.

Weathers, F. W., Bovin, M. J., Lee, D. J., Sloan, D. M., Schnurr, P. P., Kaloupek, D. G., ... and Marx, B. P. (2018). The clinician-administered PTSD scale for DSM-5 (CAPS-5): Development and initial psychometric evaluation in military veterans. *Psychological Assessment*, 30, 383–395.

Weinberg, M. and Banks, S. (2019). Practising ethically in unethical times: Everyday resistance in social work. *Ethics and Social Welfare*, 13(4), 361–376.

Weir, B., Cunningham, M., Abraham, L. and Allanson-Oddy, C. (2019). Military veteran engagement with mental health and well-being services: A qualitative study of the role of the peer support worker. *Journal of Mental Health*, 28(6), 647–653.

Weisfeld, C. C., Turner, J. A., Bowen, J. I., Eissa, R., Roelk, B., Ko, A., ... and Benfield, E. (2021). Dealing with anxious patients: an integrative review of the literature on nonpharmaceutical interventions to reduce anxiety in patients undergoing medical or dental procedures. *The Journal of Alternative and Complementary Medicine*, 27(9), 727-737.

Weiss, D.S. (2007). The Impact of Event Scale-Revised. In J.P. Wilson and T.M. Keane (eds.) *Assessing psychological trauma and PTSD: a practitioner's handbook*. 2nd edn. New York: Guilford Press. (pp. 168–189).

Wenzel, A. (2017). Cognitive behavioral therapy for pregnancy loss. *Psychotherapy*, 54(4), 400–405.

Werner, A. and Malterud, K. (2016). Encounters with service professionals experienced by children from families with alcohol problems: a qualitative interview study. *Scandinavian Journal of Public Health*, 44(7), 663–670.

Wertheimer, A. (2001). *A Special Scar: The Experiences of People Bereaved by Suicide*. New York: Routledge.

Westra, H.A. and Aviram, A. (2013). Core skills in motivational interviewing. *Psychotherapy*, 50(3), 273–278.

Westwood, M. J., McLean, H., Cave, D., Borgen, W. and Slakov, P. (2010). Coming home: A group-based approach for assisting military veterans in transition. *The Journal for Specialists in Group Work*, 35(1), 44–68.

Whitaker, R., and Cosgrove, L. (2015). *Psychiatry under the influence: Institutional corruption, social injury, and prescriptions for reform*. New York: Springer.

White, C. and Hales, J. (eds.) (1997) *The personal is the professional: Therapists reflect on their families, lives and work*. Adelaide: Dulwich Centre Publications.

White, M. (1998). Saying hullo again. The incorporation of the lost relationship in the resolution of grief. In C. White and D. Denborough (eds.) *Introducing narrative therapy: A collection of practice-based writings*. Adelaide: Dulwich Centre Publications.

White, M. (2007). *Maps of narrative practice*. New York, NY: W.W. Norton.

Wigrem, J. (1994). Narrative completion in the treatment of trauma. *Psychotherapy*, 31, 415–523.

Willi, J. (1999) *Ecological Psychotherapy: Developing by Shaping the Personal Niche*. Seattle, WA: Hogrefe and Huber.

Williams, G. (1984). The genesis of chronic illness: narrative re-construction. *Sociology of Health & Illness*, 6(2), 175–200.

Wilson, J. (2011). The assimilation of problematic experiences sequence: An approach to evidence-based practice in bereavement counseling. *Journal of Social Work in End-of-life & Palliative Care, 7*(4), 350–362.

Wilson, J. M., Fauci, J. E. and Goodman, L. A. (2015). Bringing trauma-informed practice to domestic violence programs: A qualitative analysis of current approaches. *American journal of Orthopsychiatry, 85*(6), 586.

Wilson, J. and Giddings, L. (2010). Counselling women whose lives have been seriously disrupted by depression. *New Zealand Journal of Counselling, 30*, 23–39.

Winiarski, D. A., Rufa, A. K. and Karnik, N. S. (2019). Using layperson-delivered cognitive-behavioral therapy to address mental health disparities. *Psychiatric Annals, 49*(8), 353–357.

Wolderslund, M., Kofoed, P. E. and Ammentorp, J. (2021). The effectiveness of a person-centred communication skills training programme for the health care professionals of a large hospital in Denmark. *Patient Education and Counseling, 104*(6), 1423–1430.

Wood, A. (2020). *The motivational interviewing workbook: Exercises to decide what you want and how to get there.* Emeryville, CA: Rockridge Press.

Wood, J. D., Watson, A. C. and Fulambarker, A. J. (2017). The 'gray zone' of police work during mental health encounters: findings from an observational study in Chicago. *Police Quarterly, 20*(1), 81–105.

Wood, L., Clark, D., Heffron, L. C. and Schrag, R. V. (2020). Voluntary, survivor-centered advocacy in domestic violence agencies. *Advances in Social Work, 20*(1), 1–21.

Worden, J. W. (2018). *Grief counseling and grief therapy. A handbook for the mental health practitioner.* 5th edn. New York: Springer Publishing.

Worden, J. W. and Winokuer, H. R. (2011). A task-based approach for counseling the bereaved. In R. A. Neimeyer, D. L. Harris, H. R. Winokuer and G. F. Thornton (eds.), *Grief and bereavement in contemporary society: Bridging research and practice* (pp. 57–67). New York: Routledge/Taylor & Francis Group.

Wortman, C.B. and Silver, R.C. (1989). The myths of coping with loss. *Journal of Consulting and Clinical Psychology, 57*, 349–57.

Wosket, V. (2006) *Egan's Skilled Helper model.* London: Routledge.

Wulcan, A. C. and Nilsson, C. (2019). Midwives' counselling of women at specialised fear of childbirth clinics: A qualitative study. *Sexual & Reproductive Healthcare, 19*, 24–30.

Wyrostok, N. (1995). The ritual as a psychotherapeutic intervention. *Psychotherapy, 32*(3), 397–404.

Yalom, I.D. (2017). *Becoming myself: a psychiatrist's memoir.* London: Piatkus.

Yalom, I.D. (2002). *The gift of therapy: Reflections on being a therapist.* London: Piatkus.

Yalom, I.D. (1989). *Love's Executioner and Other Tales of Psychotherapy.* Harmondsworth: Penguin.

Yalom, I.D. (2005). *The Schopenhauer Cure.* New York: HarperCollins.

Yang, L. H., Chen, F. P., et al. (2014). 'What matters most': A cultural mechanism moderating structural vulnerability and moral experience of mental illness stigma. *Social Science & Medicine, 103*, 84–93.

Young, H. (2017). Overcoming barriers to grief: supporting bereaved people with profound intellectual and multiple disabilities. *International Journal of Developmental Disabilities, 63*(3), 131–137.

Young, H. and Garrard, B. (2016). Bereavement and loss: Developing a memory box to support a young woman with profound learning disabilities. *British Journal of Learning Disabilities, 44*(1), 78–84.

Young, J. and Dryden, W. (2019). Single-session therapy – past and future: An interview. *British Journal of Guidance & Counselling, 47*(5), 645–654.

Young, K. (2020). Multi-story listening: Using narrative practices at walk-in clinics. *Journal of Systemic Therapies, 39*(3), 34–45.

Zur, O. (2021). *Dual relationships, multiple relationships and boundaries in psychotherapy, counseling and mental health.* Retrieved 01/13/2022 from http://www.zurinstitute.com/dualrelationships.html.

Zust, B. L., Housley, J. and Klatke, A. (2017). Evangelical Christian pastors' lived experience of counseling victims/survivors of domestic violence. *Pastoral Psychology, 66*(5), 675–687.

Index

Page numbers with 't' are tables.

Aamlid, I. B. 216–17
abandonment therapy 126
Adams, K. 11
adverse childhood experience (ACE) scale 164–5
adversity 164–6
alert, being on 64
anxiety 153
   and depression 137–9
   emotion tasks in counselling 131–3
   meaning of 134–5
   skills and strategies for 139–48
apps 236
Arnold, R. M. 11
assimilation of problematic experiences model 202–3
attachment theory, and bereavement counselling 200–2
autobiography 188–9
autonomy 71
   and confidentiality 76
   and consent 74

Back, A. L. 11
balance sheets, and decision-making 217–18
Banks, S. 71–2
Barlow, Emily-May 171
Bauman, Zygmunt 4
behaviour changing *see* making changes
beneficence 71
bereavement 152, 194–5, 212
   methods for working 206–9
   task-oriented approach 197–9
   theoretical frameworks 199–206
   working with 195–7
betrayal, and trauma 159–60
Birrell, P. J. 159, 160, 167
Boerner, K. 200
boundaries 96–7
Bowlby, John 200, 201
Branch, W. T. 10

bravery transfusions 147
burnout 107–9
Butler, Judith 163

Carey, T. A. 226
caring 28, 85
caring conversations model 9
case formulation 225, 227, 229
catastrophizing 134, 137, 146, 228
catharsis 132
changes *see* making changes
checking out 42, 60, 61–2, 97, 122
Chibanda, Dixon 13
childbirth fears 145
childhood adversity 164–6
choice maps 188
climate anxiety 152
codes of ethics 68, 71
cognitive behavioural therapy (CBT) 135, 146, 147–8, 221, 226–8, 229
cognitive restructuring 181, 228
collaboration 35, 40, 42
   with the client 58–62, 232–3
   and crisis intervention 124
collective responsibility 80
collective trauma 160–1
collectivist ways of living 34
colonialism 34
communities of practice 111–13
compassion fatigue 108
competence
   and community resources 93
   limits of 76–7
complicated grief 210
confidentiality 75–6, 85, 90, 107, 123
connections, and therapy 25–9
consent *see* informed consent
consultation 100–6
continuing professional development 103
contracts, counselling 97
conversation, and counselling space 96–9
coping skills development 170

273

counselling, defined 22–3
counselling menus 44–6, 199
craftsmanship 113
creative arts, and bereavement counselling 207–8
criminal behaviour 82
crisis 117–19, 129
   culturally sensitive practice 127
   intervention models 119–22
   organizational strategies 122–7
   supervision and support 127–8
crisis intervention team (CIT) approach 124
cultural resources 5–6, 208, 209
culture
   and anxiety and depression 137
   and bereavement 196–7, 205, 209
   and crisis 127
   differences in 80
   exploring cultural meaning 189
   organizational 93–6
   transitions 184–5, 189–90
cure, defined 33
curiosity 140
cyclical model of supervision 103–6

decision-making 35, 58–62, 120, 215–17
   skills/strategies 217–19
dementia
   and liminality 190
   task model 54–5
dental anxiety 151
depression 153
   and anxiety 137–9
   emotion tasks in counselling 131–3
   meaning of 136–7
   skills and strategies for 139–48
Dibb, B. 225
DiClemente, Carlo 220–1
difference-making activities 30
directionality 33
diversity and fragmentation of therapy theory 21
domestic violence 43, 121, 124
Donnelly, C. 183
doulas
   birth 12, 145, 199
   death 208
dual process model of coping with bereavement 203–4

dual relationships 78–80
Duncan, R. 218
duty of care 71, 80, 127, 219
D'Zurilla, Thomas 229–31

ecological perspective on transitions 184–5
either/or assumptions 77
embedded counselling (defined) 14–16
emotional honesty 28
emotional support 2–3, 17
   frontline practitioners 7–13
   sources 4–7
emotions 131
   and organizational culture 95
   skills and strategies 139–48
   tasks in counselling 131–3
   see also anxiety; depression
empathic dialogue 217
Epston, David 147
Erikson, Erik 181–2, 182t
ethical practice 72–84
   confidentiality 75–6, 85
   and cultural differences 80
   dual relationships 78–80
   informed consent 73–4
   limits of competence 76–7
   risk/self-harm 81–2
   using touch 83–4
ethics 67–8, 85
   core principles 70–2
   ethical practice 72–84
   examples of dilemmas 69–70, 85
ethics work 71–2

family/friends, and crisis intervention 124–6
fear *see* anxiety
Ferguson, H. 150
first aid, mental health 127
force-field analysis 218
four habits model 100
Frank, Arthur 183
Frank, Jerome, *Persuasion and Healing* 22
Frankel, R. M. 99–100
Freyd, J. J. 159, 160, 167
friendship benches 13

gambling addiction 235–6
Gandhi, R. S. 161

garden settings 98
Gath, Dennis 229
gender
  and bereavement 204
  and caring 85
  and trauma counselling in prisons 169
generalized anxiety disorder (GAD) 135
Gianakis, M. 226
Gilliland, B. E. 120
goals 48–52, 62–5
Goodman, L. A. 121
grief *see* bereavement
growth, post-traumatic 165
guides/navigators 187

Hanser, C. H. 13
Hawkins, P. 102, 103
healing stories 207
healthy conversation skills model 231
Heidegger, M. 28
helplines 122–3
holding relationship 150
homelessness, and trauma counselling 170
hope, and transitions 192
humanistic approaches 146–7
humanizing care 8–9
Hunter, M. 83–4

implications approach to decision-making 218
individualism 36
infertility clinic, and transitions 185
informed consent 73–4, 76
intergenerational trauma 160–1
interpersonal approaches 146
interpersonal process recall (IPR) 110
interpersonal skills 13
Irvine, A. 218

James, R. K. 120
Janoff-Bulman, R. 108, 159
Jenkinson, Stephen 196, 208
Jevne, R. F. 99
justice 71, 73, 85

Kaiser Permanente approach 99–100
kind, being 140–1
Klasen, M. 207
Klevan, T. 232, 237
Krupat, E. 99–100

Kruzan, K. P. 221
Kubler-Ross, Elisabeth 200, 203, 206

language, and shared decision-making 60, 62
Lewchanin, S. 188
Lian, O. S. 219
liminality 190
line management 101
listening 26–7, 44, 140
  checking out 42, 60, 61–2, 97, 122
  to wants of the client 141–2
  and trauma counselling 167
listening visits 12
loneliness 6

McMahon, A. 102, 103
making changes 214–15, 238
  changing 224–37
  deciding to change 215–24
  organizational strategies for 237
making sense, and trauma counselling 167
mapping, and transition 187–8
Maslach, Christina 107–8
meaning-making 25, 183, 203, 205, 207
meaningful death 208
menus, counselling 44–6, 199
Menzies Lyth, Isabel 95
metacommunication 61–2
metaphor, and bereavement counselling 207
methods 55–8, 62–5, 106–7
microaggression 161–2
military-civilian transition 179
Miller, William R. 221–4
model of embedded counselling 40–3
  being ready 40–1
  facilitating a counselling episode 41–2
  and making changes 224–6
  using organizational resources 42–3
moral injury/distress 72, 162–3
moral responsibility 82
motivational interviewing approach 221–4
multiculturalism 21
Myer, R. 120

narrative approach, and bereavement 204–6
narrative completion 168

narrative disruption model of transition 183–4
navigators/guides 187
negative emotion 11
Neimeyer, Robert 205, 207
Nezu, Arthur and Christine 229–31
niches, personal 184–5
normalizing, and transition 187
Norway, and shared decision making 216–17

Oldenburg, Ramon 5
online counselling/therapy 84, 148
open dialogue therapy 124–6
organizations
   anxiety/depression strategies 148–53
   context 90–100, 113
   crisis strategies 122–7
   and trauma 171–2
oscillation, and bereavement 203–4
over-reach/confidence 34, 36

Page,, S. 103–6
parallel process 95–6, 102
Parkes, Colin Murray 200
patiency 184
personal therapy 109
personality disorder 126
photographs, and transition 188
physical contact 83–4
post-traumatic growth 165
post-traumatic stress disorder (PTSD) 157–9
   counselling 166–71
precarity 163–4
prisons, trauma counselling in 169
problem-solving therapy 228–31
problems in living 3–4, 48–52
Prochaska, J. O. 220–1
psychodynamic approaches 146
psychodynamic life-course theory 181–3, 182t
psychosis 125–6
psychotherapy, defined 22–3

qualifications *see* training

racism 34, 160
Rand, K. 225
Reader, S. 184

recovery, defined 33
recovery-oriented approaches for change 231–7
referral networks 91
reflection, on practice 103
relational approaches 146
relationships 71
   dual 78–80
   holding 150
relevance 31–2
research 35–6, 111
resourcefulness 113
resources
   clients' 233–7
   community 93
   therapy 106–7, 148–9
risk 81–2
rituals
   and bereavement 196, 209
   and transition 189–90
Rogers, Carl 221
Rollnick, Stephen 221–4
rules 96–7
rupture 64

safety, and therapy 24, 27
schools, and bereavement support 210
Schut, H. 200, 203, 204
secondary traumatization 108
self-care 107–9, 234
self-disclosure, counsellor 57
self-efficacy 236–7
self-harm/suicide 81–2, 119, 126, 171
   bereavement as result of 206, 211
   see also crisis
self-healing, and anxiety and depression 138
self-practice 110
Sennett, Richard 3–4
sessions, number of 32
shared decision-making 35, 58–62, 120, 215–19, 237
shared understanding, and transition 186–7
shattered assumptions 108, 159
Silver, R. C. 200
single-session therapy 32, 122–3
situated counselling 12–13
skills/strategies 44–62, 65
   counselling menus 44–6

methods 53–8
  shared decision-making 58–62
  tasks 52–3
  wants of the clients 47–52
social connection 6
social justice 71
social support 3, 4–5
  and trauma counselling 168–70
sources, of emotional support 4–7
space 90, 96–9
spirituality, and bereavement counselling 209
stages of change model 220–1
Stein, T. 99–100
Stiles, Bill 202–3
stillpoints 99
strengths, clients' 233–7
Stroebe, M. 200, 203
Struve, J. 83–4
suicide *see* self-harm/suicide
supervision 91, 100–1
  crisis intervention 128–9
  process of 102–3
support 91, 100–6
  finding 1–3
  network 92–3
  for practitioners 149–51
supportive challenging 219

talking
  and therapy 23–5
  and transition 186
talking through 52
task sharing/shifting 11–12
tasks 52–3, 62–5
  and bereavement 197–9, 202, 203–4
  emotion (anxiety/depression) 131–3, 142–5
temporary impairment 77
therapy 23–33, 37
  affirming and caring connections 25–9
  developing new skills/perspectives 30–1
  enabling the person to see how current difficulties fit into their life 31–2
  and making a space to talk it through 23–5
  personal 109
  potentially unhelpful aspects 34–6

supporting the person to move forward 33
theories and approaches for anxiety/depression 145–8
working together to activate strengths/resources 29–30
therapy theory 20–2
'third places' 5
time 90, 97–8
timelines 187–8
Todres, L. 8
Toerien, M. 218
touch, use of 83–4
training 109–11
transformational change 230
transition models 180–1
transitions 176–9, 192
  methods to help 186–90
  organizational counselling 190–1
  theoretical perspectives 180–5, 182t
transparency 76, 82
trauma 156–7, 173
  and counselling 166–71
  organizational response 171–2
  understanding and knowledge 157–66
traumatization, secondary 108
trust, and therapy 27–8
two-chair work 147, 208

unfinished business, and bereavement counselling 208

Walfish, S. 82
Walter, Tony 204–5
Wampold, B. E. 166
wants, of the client 47–52, 141–2
White, Michael 205
Whitlock, J. 221
windows of opportunity 9–11
Winokuer, H. R. 202
Worden, William 202, 204
Wortman, C. B. 200
Wosket, V. 103–6
writing, and transition 188–9

yoga 170

Zubrod, L. A. 188